Establishing Zion

The Mormon Church in the American West,
1847–1869

Establishing Zion

The Mormon Church in the American West, 1847–1869

Eugene E. Campbell

Signature Books
Salt Lake City
1988

Cover and book design by Smith & Clarkson.

Cover illustration by Rob Magiera.

All photographs are reproduced courtesy of The Utah State Historical Society Library;
Special Collections, Marriott Library, University of Utah; and Photo Archives, Church of
Jesus Christ of Latter-day Saints.

Library of Congress Cataloging-in-Publication Data

Campbell, Eugene E., 1915–1986
    Establishing Zion: the Mormon church in the American West,
1847–69 / Eugene E. Campbell.
        p.   cm.
    Bibliography: p.
    Includes Index.
    ISBN 0–941214–62–1
    1. Mormon Church—Great Basin—History—20th century. 2. Church
of Jesus Christ of Latter-Day Saints—Great Basin—History—19th
century. 3. Great Basin—Church history.   I. Title.
BX8611.C28 1988
289.3 '79—dc19

Table of Contents

Publisher's Foreword

Eugene E. Campbell was born to Edward and Betsy Ann Bowen Campbell on 26 April 1915 in Tooele, Utah, a small farming community west of Salt Lake City. Following bachelor's and master's studies at the University of Utah, he married Beth Larsen in 1939. Together they raised five children. World War II interrupted his doctoral work at the University of Souther California, while he served as a chaplain for the Church of Jesus Christ of Latter-day Saints in Germany. After the war, he completed his Ph.D. studies, taught LDS seminary and Institute of Religion classes, and joined the history faculty of Brigham Young University in 1956, where he remained until his retirement in 1980.

As a historian and teacher, Dr. Campbell's influence was significant and far-reaching. Besides the thousands of undergraduates he taught at BYU, he directed nearly ninety graduate students through their master's and doctoral programs. In addition, he authored or co-authored several books, including *The United States: An Interpretive History*, *Fort Bridger: Island in the Wilderness*, *Fort Supply: Brigham Young's Green River Experiment*, and *The Life and Thought of Hugh B. Brown*. He was an associate editor of *Utah's History* and a consulting editor for *Utah: A Guide to the State*.

Dr. Campbell also wrote more than a dozen scholarly articles, which were published in a variety of journals. Two of his essays received special recognition from the history community. "Brigham Young's Outer Cordon: A Reappraisal," published in 1973 in the

Utah Historical Quarterly, won both the Mormon History Association Best Article Award for that year and the Utah State Historical Society's Dale L. Morgan Award for the best scholarly article published in the *Quarterly*. Three years later, Dr. Campbell became the first person to win the Morgan award twice, this time for an essay he co-authored with his son Bruce, "Divorce Among Mormon Polygamists: Extent and Explanations." Others of Dr. Campbell's accomplishments include co-founding the Mormon History Association, acting as president of the Mormon History Association, serving as a consultant to the National Endowment of the Humanities, and winning the Utah State Historical Society's most distinguished honor, being named Historical Society Fellow.

At the time of his death in April 1986, Dr. Campbell was at work on what he believed would be his most important contribution to Mormon and western studies, a history of the first twenty years of the Mormon church in the American West. Commissioned in late 1972, Dr. Campbell's history was to have been part of the Mormon church's much anticipated sesquicentennial sixteen-volume series, "A History of the Latter-day Saints," to be issued under the direction of the LDS Church Historian. By early 1981, however, the multivolume history project had been terminated and the various authors allowed to seek publication of their respective manuscripts on their own.

Signature Books first contacted Dr. Campbell about the possibility of publishing his history in 1981. At the time, he voiced an interest in pursuing publication with Signature Books, a desire he reiterated in 1985, less than nine months before his death. Following Dr. Campbell's passing, his family, represented by his daughter Mary Ann Payne, was approached. The Campbell family expressed their commitment to publication and agreed to make available Dr. Campbell's manuscript for review and editing. Final arrangements—including the signing of a contract—were made in June 1987.

Upon receipt of the manuscript, it became apparent that Dr. Campbell had completed research on his history in 1981-82 and had virtually finished writing by 1984-85. The manuscript necessitated only the normal amount of content and copy editing required of any other manuscript being prepared for publication. Dr. Campbell already had established the order of the contents and written drafts for every chapter—some even existed in more than one version. In editing the various drafts for publication, preference was given to the most recent version. The only unresolved question was the issue of documentary references. Dr. Campbell had provided endnotes for some, but not all, of the chapters. For consistency's sake, bibliographic references, where they existed, were incorporated into the body of the chapter text rather than appear as footnote, endnote, or parenthetical citations. Full source citations can be found in the bibliography. Readers wishing to consult the original manuscript will find it located in the Eugene E. Campbell papers at the archives and manuscripts division of Special Collections, Harold B. Lee Library, Brigham Young University.

Dr. Campbell was aided at various times during his research by colleagues and students, notably Fred Gowans, James Jacobs, Paul Peterson, and David Whittaker, as well as by the staffs of the LDS church historical department, the BYU library, the University of Utah library, and the Utah State Historical Society. Leonard J. Arrington, Fred Gowans, Brigham Madsen, D. Michael Quinn, and David Whittaker kindly agreed to read the edited manuscript for content. As historians of considerable expertise, their cooperation was especially important. Also essential was Gene's family, especially his wife, Beth, who supported him throughout the ten years he devoted to the project. At Signature Books, Lavina Fielding Anderson, Ian G. Barber, Gary J. Bergera, Connie Disney, Deborah Hirth, Richard Ouellette, Ronald Priddis, Susan Staker, and Richard S. Van Wagoner were responsible, at various stages, for editing, verifying the references, or production.

Of his early history of the Mormons in the American West, Dr. Campbell once wrote, "There is something about pioneer stories that catches the attention of young and old alike. Probably more books and articles have been written about these years than any other comparable period in church history. Sensing this, I find myself looking for new approaches to or revised versions of these oft-related events. And yet I know that major change is sometimes resented and even viewed as destructive of faith to some.

"So this is the challenge I face: How do I bring a fresh, new approach to a subject that has been heard many times before by church members without upsetting their faith or—better yet—while strengthening their faith? Let me suggest one rule that I learned over twenty years ago while I was an LDS institute director in Logan, Utah. One of my colleagues suggested a number of rules he had developed during his years as a teacher. But the one I remember best, and which I have tried to incorporate into the following history, is this: 'I will never knowingly teach my students something they will have to "unlearn" later on.'"

Introduction

When the Mormons began colonizing the Rocky Mountains during the mid-nineteenth century, more than mere geography had changed for them. In the Great Basin, they were no longer outcasts but "pioneers." Although the term initially referred to members of the 1847 advance company, Mormons who made the journey later the same year also came to be known as the "Pioneers of '47." And by the 1870s, virtually everyone who had "gathered to Zion" before the completion of the transcontinental railroad could lay claim to the title "pioneer." It became a symbol of Mormonism, embracing such qualities as courage, dedication to the cause, physical endurance, resoluteness, ingenuity, and faith. Even those who ridiculed Mormon beliefs admired the Saints' pioneering accomplishments. This "pioneer heritage" has become a source of pride and unity in Mormon culture.

THE NAME PIONEER

Some historians have suggested that the Mormons' pioneer experience in the American West made possible the survival and future expansion of their Church of Jesus Christ of Latter-day Saints. In a desert environment demanding ingenuity, and with little outside "interference" during the first generation, the Mormons established their church on a solid foundation from which they could successfully meet later problems ranging from the federal polygamy persecutions of the 1880s to the civil rights and identification crises of the 1960s. *LEFT ALONE FOR GENERATION — STEEL ER*

Nineteenth-century developments in America, and to a lesser degree in Europe, provide important contemporary context for the

Mormon experience in the Great Basin. The Saints' migration from
Nauvoo, Illinois, to the Rocky Mountains began early in 1846, the
"Year of Decision," according to Bernard DeVoto. The Oregon controversy with Britain would be settled later that year, but difficulties
with Mexico would soon lead to war. The subsequent enlistment of
a battalion of more than 500 Latter-day Saint men, known as the
Mormon Battalion, as part of the United States Army would force
the pioneers to halt temporarily on the banks of the Missouri River.
Large-scale migrations to Oregon and California also marked the
year, and before its close the tragic Donner-Reed party would become
marooned in the Sierra snows after blazing a route through the
Wasatch Mountains into the Salt Lake Valley which the Mormons
would follow the next year.

In April 1847, when Mormon leader Brigham Young's pioneer
contingent left Winter Quarters (near present-day Omaha, Nebraska)
for the Great Basin, the U.S. war with Mexico was still undecided. In
fact, federal troops began advancing into the interior of Mexico on
the same day the Mormons left Winter Quarters. However, troops
did not enter Mexico City until 14 September 1847, almost two
months after the Mormons arrived in the Great Salt Lake Valley. California was subdued by early 1847, and members of the Mormon
Battalion served as occupation troops; but ownership of Upper California, including the Rocky Mountain Great Basin, would not be
decided until after the Mormons began to settle there.

The California discovery of gold in January 1848 would lead to
important changes in the Far West, the nation, and the world. Ironically, the discovery ended Mormon dreams of isolation and indirectly
dimmed hopes of political autonomy. The gold rush of 1849 brought
such a sizable population to California that the region's application
for statehood could hardly be denied. This led to the Compromise of
1850, which gave statehood to California and made Utah a territory,
subject to federally appointed officials. The resulting conflict between
Mormon leaders and federal officials postponed Utah statehood for
forty-five years and ultimately threatened the existence of the Latter-
day Saint church.

The popular sovereignty formula proposed as a solution to slavery in the territories kept the Mormons in the national spotlight.
When the Republican party linked the Mormon practice of polygamy with slavery in 1856 as "twin relics of barbarism," prejudice
against the Mormons increased, making it easy for disgruntled federal officials to convince national leaders that the Saints were disloyal citizens in rebellion against federal authority. The resulting

2

"invasion" of the territory by the U.S. Army in 1857 and ensuing Mormon resistance created a confrontation that could have ended Mormon civilization in the Great Basin. Fortunately, the difficulty was settled peacefully.

National involvement in the Civil War would give the Latter-day Saints a few years of respite, but after the war, a Congress bent on reconstructing the South also found time to try to "reconstruct" the Mormons. Although the Wade, Ashley, Cragin, and Cullom bills, designed to "Americanize" the Mormons, would fail to pass both the House and Senate, they were warnings of things to come.

The transcontinental railroad, delayed by the Civil War, was completed with the help of the Mormons. And with the driving of the golden spike at Promontory Summit, Utah, on 10 May 1869, the early pioneering period of the Mormons came to an end. RAILROAD

Throughout these twenty years, thousands of Mormon converts poured into the territory. Many came from the British Isles, Scandinavia, and other parts of Europe. These were only a fraction of the millions of emigrants who left Europe as a result of the overpopulation and social dislocation following industrial growth and political upheavals. But the Mormon emigrants wanted not only to better themselves economically and socially but also to build their Kingdom of God in preparation for the second coming and millennial reign of Jesus Christ. By 1869, nearly 100,000 Mormons had colonized the Great Basin and contiguous areas, establishing about 250 towns. But their leader, Brigham Young, had only a few years to live, and their existence as a legal institution was being threatened. Only time would tell whether the foundations of the kingdom they had helped to establish could withstand federal opposition while nurturing the changes necessary for survival and growth.

When the pioneers first began plowing the soil of the Great Salt Lake Valley in mid-1847, they were in Mexican territory which might or might not eventually belong to the United States. Still, Mormon leaders spoke confidently of becoming part of the Union. Apparently they made no contact with Mexican officials about colonizing the region, although they knew enough of Mexican policies to realize that they would be expected to become Roman Catholics. They were primarily concerned with finding a place of refuge and isolation for their followers and were confident that they could deal with the question of national allegiance later.

The story of Mormonism's two-fold struggle—the colonization of the Great Basin and surrounding areas as a place of refuge and the confrontation with desert, Indians, and federal officials as the

3

Saints tried to establish their Kingdom of God within the geographical and political structures of the United States—forms the subject of this book. Details about immigration, Mormon missionary endeavors in various parts of the world, and social and cultural developments during this period are discussed only in passing.

What follows is an interpretation of a major movement in the history of the American West. It is a story which, I believe, needs to be understood both by Latter-day Saints, who may recognize reasons for their heritage of persecution, and by non-Mormons, who may not understand the pride Mormons feel in their pioneer heritage and the possessiveness they sometimes exhibit for the Great Basin area. If nothing else, such an understanding can lead to tolerance—a necessary first step toward a fuller appreciation of the Mormon community which is today made up of so many diverse elements.

1.
Colonizing
the Base

According to contemporary accounts, it was a relatively happy group of Mormons that began colonizing the Great Salt Lake Valley during the closing days of July 1847. They had earlier received enough information to anticipate what the area might be like, but nothing could have prepared them for the scene they encountered upon emerging from the mountain canyons. Perhaps the initial reaction was best expressed by Apostle Orson Pratt, who, with Erastus Snow, was the first of the pioneer company to enter the valley. Writing in his diary for 21 July, Pratt reported, "[We] ascended this hill, from the top of which [was] a broad open valley, . . . We could not refrain from a shout of joy which almost involuntarily escaped from our lips the moment this grand and lovely scenery was within our view." The next day, William Clayton followed the trail the ill-fated Donner-Reed party had blazed the previous October, observing that the valley appeared fertile. He objected only to the lack of timber.

The Saints' president and prophet, Brigham Young, had been ill for several days and did not see the valley until 23 July. His manuscript history recounts: "We ascended and crossed over Big Mountain, when on its summit I directed Elder [Wilford] Woodruff, who kindly tendered me the use of his carriage, to turn the same half way round, so I could have a view of a portion of Salt Lake Valley. The Spirit of the Lord rested upon me and hovered over the valley, and I felt that there the Saints would find protection and safety.

5

We descended and encamped at the foot of the Little Mountain."[1]

[Apostle Woodruff] penned a more detailed account the following day, when Young and he came in full view of the valley:

> We gazed with wonder and admiration upon the vast rich, fertile valley which lay for about 25 miles in length and 16 miles in width, clothed with the heaviest garb of green vegetation in the midst of which lay a large lake of salt water . . . Our hearts were surely made glad . . . to gaze upon a valley of such vast extent and entirely surrounded with a perfect chain of everlasting hills and mountains covered with eternal snows . . . presenting at one view the grandest and most sublime scenery probably that could be obtained on the globe.

But the most memorable reaction was Thomas Bullock's simple outburst, "I could not help shouting 'hurra, hurra, hurra, here's my home at last'—the sky is very clear, the air is delightful, and all together looks glorious."

True, there were some negative expressions. According to Daniel Tyler's history of the Mormon Battalion, Samuel Brannan complained that "the Saints could not possibly subsist in the Great Salt Lake Valley, as, according to the testimony of the mountaineers, it froze every month of the year, and the ground was too dry to sprout seeds without irrigation, and irrigated with the cold mountain streams the seeds planted would be chilled and prevented from growing; but if they did grow they would be sickly and fail to mature." Lorenzo Dow Young, Brigham Young's brother, remembered that except for two or three cottonwoods along the streams no other trees were in sight. Lorenzo's wife Harriet lamented, "Weak and weary as I am, I would rather go a thousand miles further than to remain in such a forsaken place as this." Her daughter added that she "was heartbroken because there were no trees to be seen" and that the other women of the party also "felt a sense of desolation and loneliness—in the new country to which they had come."

---

[1] In his *Comprehensive History of the Church*, B. H. Roberts, an early twentieth-century Mormon historian, notes that Wilford Woodruff reported a similar incident occurring at the mouth of Emigration Canyon on 24 July. Woodruff's account is important because it apparently is the source for the famous "This is the place" statement, attributed to Brigham Young. According to his biographer Matthias Cowley, Woodruff wrote in his journal on 24 July 1869, "Twenty-two years ago . . . I drove the team which brought President Brigham Young into this city. He lay upon a bed sick in my carriage. As soon as his eyes rested upon this beautiful yet desert scene of the valley before us he said, 'This is the place; for the Lord has shown it to me in a vision.'" Unfortunately, Woodruff does not include such an event in his journal for either 24 July 1869 or 24 July 1847, and no contemporary account has yet been found that records Young saying, "This is the place" on 24 July 1847.

6

NEG. FIRST IMPRESSIONS

But the general response was enthusiastic, and as they began testing the soil, scanning the towering mountains to the south and east of their new home, the majority was no doubt anxious to begin colonizing the new land.

Since "pioneer" refers to "one who prepares the way for others" or to "the first explorers, settlers or colonists of a country," the real pioneering did not begin until 23 July 1847 when the main portion of Brigham Young's company passed through the Wasatch Mountains and chose a spot on City Creek for a settlement. For the Mormon trek from Missouri to Fort Bridger had been made on well-established trails with maps and almost daily contacts with people going to or returning from the West. The trail from Fort Bridger to the Salt Lake Valley was not as well marked, but companies of California-bound emigrants had traversed the route as far as the Weber River during the summer of 1846. One of these, the Donner-Reed party, had actually pioneered the trail the Mormons followed into the Salt Lake Valley. There were still obstacles to remove and better roads to build, but the route had already been pioneered.

Nor were the Mormons the first explorers of the region. Various Indian tribes had lived in the area for centuries and knew virtually every valley, stream, canyon, and mountain. The Spanish missionary-explorers Dominguez and Escalante and their party had entered the region in 1776 near present-day Vernal, Utah, making their way into Utah Valley and south to the Colorado River by way of present-day Nephi, Milford, Beaver, and Hurricane. During the first decades of the nineteenth century, Spanish and Mexican traders had established the Spanish Trail from Santa Fe to Los Angeles by way of Moab, Green River, and the canyon passes through the Wasatch Mountains, and on to Beaver, Mountain Meadows, and Santa Clara Creek.

It is not known if the Spanish and the Mexicans also explored the Great Salt Lake, but some mountain men had. Jim Bridger explored the Bear River to the shores of the salty lake in the fall of 1824, and possibly Etienne Provost and others saw the great body of water earlier that summer. Jedediah Smith, returning from California to his Bear Lake rendezvous in 1827, said that when he saw the Great Salt Lake he knew he had survived the desert and was back in familiar country. Benjamin de Bonneville, whose name was later given to the large prehistoric lake of which the Great Salt Lake was only a remnant, did not visit the region, but some of his party, under Joseph Walker, explored the lake in 1835.

It remained for another explorer, John C. Fremont, to leave the most accurate observations of Salt Lake Valley and the Great Salt

Lake. In 1843, Fremont entered the valley from the north and, from his camp near present-day Ogden, explored the lake, tested the water, and made scientific observations of the altitude, soils, and climate which were included in his maps and official reports. Leaving the Salt Lake Valley, he went to Oregon, and then to California, where he spent the winter. He returned to the East in 1844 by way of southern Utah, Utah Valley, and the Uinta region. Mormon leaders carefully studied Fremont's maps and reports, published by Congress.

Other than Indians, the only residents of the Great Salt Lake area in early 1847 were Miles Goodyear, his Indian wife, and his partner, a Captain Wells, who had established a trading post near the juncture of the Ogden and Weber Rivers in 1846. The pioneers met Goodyear near Fort Bridger and obtained valuable information from him concerning the best route into the region, as well as his assurances that crops could grow there. They then hurried to the valley to begin colonizing the region.

[margin note: GOODYEAR WEBER AREA TRADING POST]

The Mormons realized that the planting season was late and were anxious to begin. Plowing began on 23 July after Orson Pratt led his advance company to the banks of City Creek and dedicated the spot for the new settlement. En route from Emigration Canyon, the pioneers discovered several types of grass. In his diary, Thomas Bullock reported "wheat grass growing 6 or 7 feet high and some varieties stood 12 to 13 feet." After wading through the thick grass for some distance, Bullock and the others found a place where the grass was only knee deep—bare enough for a camping ground. The soil, William Clayton wrote, was "black," looked "rich," and was "sandy enough to make it good to work."

[margin note: SOIL]

Clayton was correct, and the pioneers formed a committee to stake off a piece of ground 40 rods by 20 rods for potatoes and also a suitable place for beans, corn, and buckwheat. Bullock wrote, "At 12 o'clock the first furrow was plowed . . . There were three plows and one harrow at work most of the afternoon. [One] plow got broke. At 2 o'clock the brethren began building a dam and cutting trenches to convey water to irrigate the land. At 4 o'clock the other brethren commenced mowing the grass to prepare a turnip patch."

[margin note: FIRST DAY PLANTING]

Bullock's account, corroborated by others, indicates that the soil could be plowed without first flooding the land and that the plowing continued despite one broken plow. Dam building began after plowing, and there is no evidence that water was turned on to the fields until 24 July. By then a five-acre potato patch had been plowed and ditches made to convey the water. "During the short space between the 23rd of July and the 28th of August," Bullock recorded, "we

8

plowed and planted about 84 acres with corn, potatoes, beans, buckwheat, turnips, and a variety of garden sauce. We irrigated all the land.''[2]

The act of turning water onto the land has sometimes been cited as the beginning of irrigation in the American West—an innovation born out of necessity. However, evidence suggests that the Mormons had anticipated this, having observed irrigation methods in various parts of the world. Apostle Orson Hyde, for example, had reported on irrigation in the Holy Land, Lebanon, Syria, and Egypt. Other members, visiting Santa Fe, had seen Mexicans watering the soil. One member of the Mormon Battalion, Samuel Rogers, reported in his journal for 12 October 1846, "In this country the settlers occupy the valleys near the streams so that they can lead the water upon their fields and gardens as irrigating the land." Another man, Henry G. Boyle, wrote twelve days later that Mexican "land for cultivation is enclosed by ditches, hedges, and adobe walls. On account of the dry seasons, . . . they have to irrigate all this farming land, all their vineyards and orchards, which is done by leading the water from the river through ditches, through all their grain or anything else that is raised or produced." And John D. Lee wrote on 5 October 1846, "They cultivate the valley only and are under the necessity of watering all the stuff they raise."[3]

Howard Egan's journals give interesting details about the pioneers' agricultural activities. On 26 July, he wrote, "At 6 a.m. the

[2] The traditional story of dry land probably came from Clara Decker Young who remembered that the pioneers "found it necessary to irrigate [the land] before plowing." Later, Orson F. Whitney, in *History of Utah*, added, "There was little to invite and much to repel. . . . A broad and barren plain . . . blistering in the burning rays of the midsummer sun. No waving fields, no swaying forest, no verdant meadows to refresh the weary eye, but on all sides a seemingly interminable waste of sagebrush . . . the paradise of the lizard, the cricket, and the rattlesnake."

What it lacked in accuracy, it made up for in mythic imagery, and Whitney's account has become the standard description of the valley the Saints first encountered. In fact, Richard Jackson has suggested that as the story was told and retold, especially during Pioneer Day celebrations and in church meetings, the valley became increasingly desert-like, making the pioneers' accomplishments all the more impressive. Since the salty wasteland was still uncultivated when later migrants arrived, it would have been natural for them to believe that the irrigated farmland had been reclaimed from similar soil. This was not only faith-promoting but could be used effectively to encourage Mormon pioneers who were called to settle the less attractive valleys of southern Utah.

[3] The Mormons even discovered that certain Indians were irrigating parts of the Great Basin. If nothing else, they recognized that their need for water would be constant. With this in mind, they studied irrigation and with their effective organization, cooperative spirit, and program of community control of water resources, effectively used this limited resource on a large scale.

9

bugle sounded for the brethren to collect their horses and cattle to recommence plowing and planting, the team to be relieved at intervals of every four hours during the day." The next day, he continued, "the bugle sounded as usual for the brethren to go to work plowing and planting," and three and four days later "the brethren were engaged as usual plowing and planting. . . . Brothers King, Whipple and myself were sowing turnips, buckwheat, oats, etc."

The soil was fertile, the irrigation program successful. Stephen Markham reported on the evening of 31 July that "thirty-five acres of land have been broken up and planted in corn, oats, buckwheat, potatoes, beans, and garden seeds. About three acres of corn was up 2" above the ground and beans and potatoes were up and looking well." This initial success encouraged continual activity in the fields, weather permitting.

Apostle John Taylor, who arrived in the valley on 5 October, wrote two months later,

> We have plowed and sown since our arrival here about 2,000 acres of wheat, great numbers of plows are incessantly going and are only prevented by the inclemency of the weather which occasionally is too severe. We have put in about 2,000 bushels of wheat, all of which have been drawn for a distance of about 1300 to 1500 miles; we expect to put in the spring about 3,000 acres of corn and other grain, and we have with us almost every variety of seed or vegetables as well as of shrubs, fruits, and flowers.

Unfortunately, the cattle and horses destroyed the crops except for the potatoes. Luckily, the colonists did not have to depend on these crops for survival, and the mild winter and early spring aided their situation. To be sure, there were skimpy meals during the first winter, but the Saints were confident that they could raise adequate crops in the spring.

However, more than plowing, planting, and irrigating had to be attended to. Homes had to be built, the region explored and evaluated. After resting on Sunday, 25 July, Brigham Young organized the pioneers into various committees, each with its own assignment. Some continued to plow, plant, or build forts and houses. Others constructed a road up City Creek Canyon to procure timber, while a few explored the canyons bordering the valley to determine the amount of timber, water supply, altitude of mountain peaks, and the existence of meadows with grazing possibilities.

Ten men were chosen for an exploring expedition the following Monday. Evidently Young and others wanted to make sure that the

[handwritten in left margin: LITTLE CROPS FIRST YR BUT HAD SUPPLIES]

10

spot they had chosen was the most ideal. According to Young's manuscript history, Wilford Woodruff took Young in his carriage and the
group traveled two miles toward the mountains then north five miles.
They climbed to the top of a high hill they named Ensign Peak.
Descending to the foot of the mountain valley, they stopped at a hot
sulphur spring, where Ezra Taft Benson and Willard Richards bathed.
The same day, Joseph Matthews and John Brown crossed the Salt
Lake Valley at its narrowest point. They estimated the valley to be
about fifteen miles wide and reported that the land to the west was
not fertile, nor was there much water. They found a six-year-old horse
which they brought back with them.

The next day, eight apostles were assigned to an exploring party
and were accompanied by six other men, including Samuel Brannan who had just arrived in the valley. Their purpose was to visit the
Great Salt Lake and the mountains west of the valley. They crossed
the Jordan River and traveled twenty miles to a large rock on the
south shore of the lake, which they named Black Rock. They stopped
and bathed in the salty water. When they found they could float on
the surface, they concluded that the lake was one of the wonders of
the world. The following day they explored the south edge of the
lake and Tooele Valley which they judged to be about twelve miles
in diameter. They recognized that the soil was good and that the
land was flat but found little water. Returning to their previous camp,
they spent the night and continued into the Salt Lake Valley the next
day.

As a result of these explorations, Young concluded that they had
already picked the best place to build a community. At a meeting
that evening, a vote was taken and all agreed to locate Salt Lake
City at the site chosen on 23 July. Still, others wished to explore further, and, according to one of his biographers, Young also wanted to
"know every hole and corner from the bay of San Francisco" to colonize every feasible location.

Additional explorations were carried out by Samuel Brannan
and James Brown, the leader of the sick detachments of the Mormon Battalion. Brown was leading a small group to San Francisco,
where he expected to receive the sick detachment's pay. Brannan,
too, was hoping to continue west to join up with the colony he had
left in the Bay area. Brannan and Brown were accompanied by Jesse
C. Little and three companions who wanted to explore the valleys
north and east of the Great Salt Lake. The party first visited Miles
Goodyear's Fort Buenaventura on the Weber River, which they
described as consisting of some log buildings and corrals stockaded

11

with pickets. There were also herds of cattle, horses, and goats, and a small garden of vegetables and a few stalks of corn. Continuing north to the Bear River, Little's group parted company with the California-bound party and turned east into Cache Valley. After traversing the valley from north to south they followed Box Elder Creek back into the Salt Lake region.

Preliminary explorations of Utah Valley were made on 2 August by L. B. Myers and two days later by J. C. Little, Samuel Brannan, and Lieutenant W. W. Willis. A week later, Albert Carrington and two companions briefly explored the Jordan River by boat. Viewing Utah Valley from a low divide, Carrington's party launched their boat toward the Great Salt Lake while one of the men drove the team back to the Salt Lake settlement. They made an enthusiastic report about the appearance of Utah Valley, including the fact that they had caught a number of fish in the Jordan River.

Later, in December, Parley P. Pratt, John S. Higbee, and others more thoroughly explored the valley and lake. They tried fishing with a net but had little success. After exploring the valley for a "day or two," the main company returned to Salt Lake, while Pratt and a companion rode west into Cedar Valley and neighboring Rush Valley, then north into Tooele Valley. They could see the Great Salt Lake at its southern shore, which Pratt had visited earlier. They spent nearly a week hunting, fishing, and exploring.

Prior to Pratt's exploration of the region, Captain Jefferson Hunt of the Mormon Battalion and a party of eighteen men had volunteered to go to southern California to secure seed and livestock. Hunt had just returned with several members of the battalion who had been discharged in California that July. They had made their way to the valley by way of San Francisco and Sacramento. Hunt was well acquainted with ranch owners in the Los Angeles area, and church officials decided to accept his suggestion that he approach them. The route to Los Angeles was new to Hunt's company, and they estimated that they would make much better time than they actually did. Planning on a thirty-day trip, they took forty-five days to reach the Williams Ranch, near present-day Chino. Nearly starved, they were grateful for Williams's hospitality. After resting and bargaining for the desired cattle and seeds, they began preparations for the return trip.

In the meantime, Captain Brown and other members of the battalion had returned from San Francisco. Evidently, the northern route to California was much better known.

12

While some pioneers were exploring and others plowing and planting, a third group of colonists was building a bowery, a row of cabins arranged in the form of a fort, and a wall around the fort. Young's pioneers were not alone in these tasks. On 29 July, they were joined by approximately 152 Mormon Battalion men from the sick detachments that had wintered in Colorado. They were accompanied by approximately thirty wives and fifty children, and by forty-seven Mississippi Saints who had wintered with the battalion families.

Young addressed a general meeting on the evening of the 30th and expressed delight at having the soldiers in the valley, declaring that their voluntary service had saved the Saints from the federal government. He closed the meeting by requesting that the battalion men build a bowery on the temple grounds. They responded the following day and erected a temporary bowery, 28 feet by 40 feet, covered with brush, which provided a shaded place for meetings during the hot August days. This was the first public building in the new city, and it was here on 1 August that the first Sunday religious services involving the three different groups were held. Meeting in both the morning and afternoon, the Saints, according to William Clayton, heard Orson Pratt assert that their location "in the tops of the mountains" literally fulfilled the biblical prophecies of Joel and Isaiah. They also received practical advice from Heber C. Kimball, who recommended the three camps join together in one large camp and begin working unitedly to build houses, corrals, and a fort.

Within a few days, Orson Pratt and Henry G. Sherwood began surveying the city and laying out the streets. Using the spot Brigham Young had selected for a temple as a starting point, they ran a base line on 3 August, and by 20 August a city had been laid out consisting of 135 blocks of 10 acres each, subdivided into eight lots of 1.25 acres. The streets, intersecting at right angles, were 8 rods wide. Three public squares were provided in addition to Temple Square, which originally was planned to contain 40 acres but was later reduced to conform to the other blocks. A site was selected for a fort, and a large group was appointed to begin building the cabins and the wall around it. Lacking timber, the leaders voted to put up a stockade of adobe houses. They soon modified their plan and used logs when possible.

A large group was next assigned to build log cabins and a wall around the fort, "sixty to hoke, twelve to mold, and twenty to put up walls," Howard Egan recorded. Within a month twenty-nine log houses had been built in the fort, each 8 or 9 feet high, 16 feet long,

13

OLD FORT
MORE SAINTS
FIRST CHURCH MTG.
CITY SURVEY

and 14 feet wide. Brigham Young and Heber C. Kimball and their wives moved into their homes on 21 August. A block was set aside for a public adobe yard, and an abode wall was constructed around the three open sides of the fort. Another committee located timber in Emigration Canyon, constructed a road, extracted logs for the cabins, and dug a pit for the whip saw. A boat was made to use on the streams, a blacksmith shop was set up, corrals were built, and a community storehouse was erected. A sense of urgency prevailed, for the Saints were aware that Young and other leaders would be returning to Winter Quarters within a few days and that a large body of new immigrants would soon enter the valley. Anticipating this, leaders sent Apostle Benson with an escort to contact the immigrant company and let them know what they would meet upon entering the valley.

In their 2 August letter, church leaders reported that they numbered "about 450 souls." This estimate seems accurate, since 156 pioneers, including some Mississippi Saints, had entered the valley on 23-24 July, and the Mormon Battalion detachments with their wives and children, numbering about 240 and accompanied by the 47 remaining Mississippi Saints, came into the valley on 29 July. Samuel Brannan and his two companions from California were there also.[4]

Young had been too ill to attend the religious services on 1 August, but on the evening of the 6th Heber C. Kimball rebaptized him as an example to the rest of the camp. The other members of the Twelve followed suit afterwards. All were confirmed at the water's edge and received a renewal of their apostleship. Wilford Woodruff recorded: "We considered this a duty and a privilege as we had come into a glorious valley to locate and build a temple, and build up Zion—we felt like renewing our covenants before the Lord and each other."

The following day, Kimball took advantage of the dam a few rods above the camp and invited his entire "adopted" family to be

---

[4] Some confusion exists about the total number entering the valley in 1847. Church historian B. H. Roberts, basing his calculations on Thomas Bullock's reports, asserted a total of 2,095, but he did not take into account the battalion members from California. Leonard J. Arrington estimated that 1,681 pioneers spent the first winter in the valley, and a church letter of 6 March 1848 reported that the total population stood at "1,671 persons living in 423 houses." There were also some births and deaths, and a few battalion men decided to go back east to their families. In addition, some 250 people who came into the Salt Lake Valley in 1847 returned soon afterwards to Winter Quarters or to California. Thus about 1,930 people could claim the title "Pioneers of '47."

baptized.[5] They, together with a few others, renewed their covenants, making a total of fifty-five who were rebaptized on Saturday, 7 August. The next day, the entire congregation was invited to participate, and 224 men and women responded. Elders Kimball, Snow, Lewis, Goddard, Everett, and Shumway did the baptizing, while Young and the Twelve confirmed. This brought the total number of men and women who were rebaptized by the end of their second week in the valley to 288 out of an estimated 450. Since there were no more than 75 or 80 children in the camp, none of whom would have been rebaptized, some 50 adults apparently did not take advantage of the opportunity to renew their commitment.[6] Rebaptism for renewal of covenants had also occurred at Nauvoo, under the leadership of Joseph Smith.

Church organizational structure was still developing. The Quorum of Twelve Apostles, one of several presiding councils governing the church, had received a vote of confidence in August 1844 and had led the church since then. However, the Council of Fifty, a group of men shouldering political responsibilities, had also been organized and assigned to lead in locating a new place of refuge following the death of Joseph Smith. Since the leaders of this council were also members of the Twelve, the two groups tended to work harmoniously.

During the trek across the Great Plains, Young had announced as "the Word and Will of the Lord" that the camps of Israel should be organized into companies with captains of hundreds, fifties, and tens. A para-military organization was then superimposed upon the Israelitish organization which listed Young as lieutenant-general, Stephen Markham as colonel, and John Pack and Shadrach Roundy

TREK = PARA-MILITARY

---

[5] Kimball had a number of adopted sons—men who had been "sealed" to him as their spiritual and temporal father. According to Howard Egan's journal, after the 25 July meeting, Kimball told his adopted sons, "Most of you here present have become adopted into my family . . . and what is mine is yours and what is yours is your own." Brigham Young evidently used this system of extended families in organizing the contingent that followed the first pioneers into the valley in 1847, and which resulted in Young's sharp reprimand of Apostle Parley P. Pratt when they met near South Pass. Pratt and John Taylor had changed the marching order from family groups to large companies and, of course, had had no way of consulting Young.

[6] This may account for some of the difficulties that developed later that year and may have been one of the motives Young had in suggesting rebaptism initially. Certainly Young was upset by the attitudes of some members of the battalion and their wives, who criticized his handling of monies that had been sent by battalion members to their families. Realizing that the church members in the valley were far from united, Young attempted to bring greater harmony by calling their attention to their religious commitments.

ATTEMPT TO HARMONY

15

LINES OF AUTHORITY CONFUSED DURING FIRST YEAR

as majors. Cutting across this religious and military organization was a family organization based upon the principle of adoption. Many church leaders, such as Young and Kimball, had "adopted" other adults into their extended family before leaving Nauvoo, and such groups were expected to function as a family unit (see also chap. 10). The situation was complicated further by the fact that the battalion men had not been discharged and were still under the command of commissioned officers. Then, too, the Mississippi Saints had not been part of the original pioneer company and tended to function as a separate camp of close-knit families. Little wonder some confusion existed about roles and lines of authority during the first year in the valley.

OBSERVE SABBATH

However, Brigham Young was clearly in charge. Although illness had kept him from leading the pioneers who chose the spot of settlement, his instructions had been followed and he assumed command upon arrival. On Sunday, 25 July, the Saints held a sacrament meeting at which they were encouraged to express themselves. At the close of the meeting, according to his manuscript history, Young announced that they must not work on Sunday for they would lose five times as much as they would gain by it, that they must not hunt or fish on that day, and that no man could dwell among them who would not observe these rules. He concluded: "No one should buy any land who came here, that he had no land to sell; . . . but for every man the land would be issued to him for city and farming purposes, whatever he could till. He might till it as he pleases, but he must be industrious and take care of it."

LAND FREE

Young evidently did not think it necessary to submit his statement on Sabbath labor and land distribution to the Saints for a sustaining vote. Nonetheless, the usual pattern was to seek community support for the leader's decisions. This was true of the selection of a permanent site for the settlement, for the temple site, and for city planning. It was decided to build one house per lot 20 feet back from the street and in the center of the line so that there would be uniformity throughout the city. One advantage of this plan was security should fire break out at any one point. It was further determined that upon every alternate block, four houses were to be built on the east and four on the west side of the square, but none on the north and on the south. The block intervening, however, would have four houses on the north, four on the south, and none on the east or west. Thus, there would be no houses facing each other on the opposite sides of the street, while those on the same side would be about

MAN LOTS WERE LAID OUT

16

8 rods apart, having gardens running back 20 rods to the center of the block. It was moved and carried that there be four public squares of 10 acres each, laid out in various parts of the city for public grounds. "But every man," said Young, "would cultivate his own lot and set out every kind of fruit and shade tree and beautify the city." This plan was submitted to the camp during an evening meeting on the site designated for the temple. Each proposition had already been submitted to the Twelve, and now the entire camp "passed all of the above votes unanimously as they are recorded."[7]

Since the time was rapidly approaching for leaders and others to return to Winter Quarters to prepare for the next pioneer company, a major organizational meeting was held on 22 August. On this occasion Young relinquished his position as presiding officer to Heber C. Kimball. "It is necessary," Kimball then said, according to Young's manuscript history,

> to transact a few items of business, to have a presidency to preside over this place, and to appoint such officers as are necessary to watch over and to counsel them for their well-being. Also the stockade—shall we continue our efforts and concentrate on that, or scatter and every man work for himself? Shall we cultivate the earth in the vicinity of the city or go three or four miles and make farms and fence them so our crops can be secure? Shall we scatter our labors? One man build his house, another fence his lot, another go hunting, and so on. These are matters for your consideration.

After several comments, Young moved that work on the stockade continue and that the labors of the groups be organized and directed. His motion carried unanimously. Then he said, "I move that there be a president to preside over this place." Again, his motion was seconded and carried. "That there be a high council." Seconded and carried. "That all officers that are necessary be appointed for this place." Seconded and carried. "That we call this place The Great Salt Lake City of the Great Basin, North America. That we call the post office the Great Basin Post Office." Seconded and carried. Then Kimball moved to call "the river the Western Jordan." Also seconded and carried. At this point, Young made a classic statement that forms

---

[7] While this appears democratic, it is typical of church leadership in which a council determines a policy, acts on it, and then presents it for an approving vote. It should also be noted that the Mormon leaders did not slavishly follow Joseph Smith's own ideas of city planning but modified them according to their particular circumstances and experiences.

the basis for the Mormon church's theocratic organization. He said, "It is the right of the Twelve to nominate the officers and the people to receive them. We wish to know who is coming in the next company. If Uncle John Smith comes, it is in our mind that he preside." Later in the meeting, the names of the various creeks were decided. Finally, Young asked if the people were satisfied with the labors of the Twelve, who received a unanimous vote of confidence. With this sustaining vote, Young and his party set out for Winter Quarters on 26 August.

Exercising their "right to nominate leaders," the Twelve sent the following letter on 9 September, from twenty miles east of South Pass, after having met immigrant parties led by Pratt and Taylor:

> It is wisdom that certain officers exist among you to preside and attend to the various branches of business that exist, or that may arise during our absence. We would nominate John Smith to be your president with liberty for him to select his two counselors, and we suggest the names of Charles C. Rich and John Young. We would nominate Henry G. Sherwood, Thomas Grover, Levi Jackman, John Murdock, Daniel Spencer, Steven Abbot, Ira Eldridge, Edson Whipple, Shadrach Roundy, John Vance, Willard Snow, and Abraham O. Smoot for a high council, whose duty it will be to observe those principles which have been instituted in the stakes of Zion for the government of the church, and to pass such laws and ordinances as shall be necessary for the peace and prosperity of the city for the time being, if such there need be. We also nominate John Van Cott to be marshal of your city, and Albert Carrington to be your clerk, historian, and deputy-postmaster, and that he keep the barometrical and thermometrical observations daily. We recommend that General Charles C. Rich be the chief military commander of the city, and that a perfect organization be instituted and sustained in companies of ten, fifty, and one hundred.

This proposal was approved on 3 October. But since John Smith's company did not arrive until 25 September, the Saints in the valley were left with no designated leaders for about a month.

When the organization of the Salt Lake Stake (or diocese) was finally completed, the colony's legislative, executive, and judicial affairs were in the hands of a three-member stake presidency and twelve-member high council. Meeting regularly, these fifteen men made laws, provisions for their enforcement, and acted as a court of justice to consider all disputes occurring in the settlement. On 7 November, the city was divided into five wards (or parishes), with

18

the following men selected as bishops over each ward: Joseph Noble, Tarleton Lewis, John L. Higbee, Jacob Foutz, and Edward Hunter. These men were in charge of temporal affairs in their wards and with their counselors formed lower courts of justice.

Much of the high council's time was spent granting permits to build mills and cut timber and attending to the economic welfare of individuals. The first laws established, according to the church's Journal History, were made on 30 November 1847: Every dog owner should secure him during the night under penalty of a fine ranging from one to five dollars; if a dog was reported as a nuisance, the bishop should decide the case and, if the accusations were right, appoint someone to dispose of the animal. It was also recommended that the people build their chimneys at least 3 feet above the roofs of their houses.

This theocratic system of government served the needs of the isolated community but was not without its problems. One of the first difficulties involved the sick detachments of the Mormon Battalion. When they entered the valley on 29 July, they were still officially in the U.S. Army and were subject to their military leader, Captain James Brown. Some battalion men did not like Brown and also resented the fact that Brigham Young had reappropriated their wages for the benefit of the church. Young acknowledged this but asserted that the men had understood this at the time of their enlistment and that the families had voted in favor of it. He pointed out that he had taken care of their families, then said:

> If there are any . . . who do not feel cheerfully to have their funds appropriated for the greatest possible good, as we have proposed, but choose to receive the money in their own hands . . . for their own pleasure, they can have their money, but such a course of conduct will release us from all obligations we are under, to see that they are provided for and taken care of agreeably to our pledges with the soldiers.

Later, Young attempted to mollify the soldiers by telling them that their willingness to join the army had kept the government from destroying the Saints on their march west. According to John Steele's journal, Young then called on the pioneers to share what they had with their battalion brethren. Other soldiers were disappointed that their families had not been brought west with them. On 12 August, William Clayton recorded that several "left the camp secretly [the previous day] to go to Winter Quarters, and this morning others are gone, but it is probable that President Young knows nothing of it

19

yet, although about a dozen are already gone, and the others are preparing to follow them."[8]

Church leaders finally decided that since the term of enlistment for the battalion men should have ended on 16 July, they could probably be mustered out of service. They appointed Captain Brown and a small company to go with Sam Brannan to California to report to U.S. officials there, taking with them the power of attorney for each member to collect the balance of pay due for their services. When Brown returned, the stake presidency assumed control of the money and authorized Brown to purchase Fort Buenaventura from Miles Goodyear for almost two thousand dollars.

Such actions did not promote unity among the Saints, and some soldiers continued to criticize their leaders. In 1849, for example, Brigham Young declared, "Since returning home from the army, most of the soldiers have become idle, lazy and indolent, indulging in vice, corrupting the morals of young females." A case in point was the arrest of six former soldiers for riding their horses into the fort with young women sitting in the saddle with them. The high council, John D. Lee recorded in his diary, voted to cut the men off from the church and fined each of them twenty-five dollars. By the early 1850s, however, church leaders recognized the need to acknowledge publicly the contribution of the battalion, and in February 1855 they sponsored a festival honoring the former soldiers. The sponsoring committee chose for its theme, "The Mormon Battalion—A Ram in the Thicket," recalling Abraham's near sacrifice of his son Isaac in the Old Testament. At the celebration, Young agreed that past differences should be settled and assured the men that they had always been in his prayers.

A more serious problem developed when several former soldiers decided to leave the valley for California with Miles Goodyear. They were apparently led by a man named Weeks, who had become disaffected the previous winter but had accompanied the Saints because he wanted to get to California. When informed that no one would be permitted to leave until the Twelve returned, Weeks rebelled. John Van Cott reported to the high council on 26 December, "Weeks, Gardner, and Babcock had all stated that they would go in the spring, or spill their blood and Babcock had remarked that if it was in his

---

[8] Young evidently felt that the wives of some battalion men were responsible for the dissatisfaction. According to John D. Lee, he once claimed that "they had lied and tattled about me . . . and thereby poisoned and soured the feelings of their husbands." Young even told one man that his wife "possesses a nasty, whining, devilish spirit" and asserted that women should not counsel their husbands.

power he would destroy every Mormon on the earth. Weeks and company said they were getting all the documents they could [against the Mormons] and would get them published."[9] Apostles Parley P. Pratt and John Taylor, who had remained in the valley, both recommended that the men be excommunicated to strip them of all influence and power.

Not all pioneers were devoted, self-sacrificing Saints. But the scribe of these events hastened to add in the Journal History, "As a general thing, the people here are disposed to do right and hearken to council and uphold the authorities, but as is natural under new and untried circumstances, there are few exceptions." Such difficulties prompted the immediate enactment of a number of laws to deal with people who had immigrated with the Saints but were not converted to the church or dedicated to its program of establishing "Zion in the tops of the mountains."

A committee (consisting of Henry Sherwood, Albert Carrington, and Charles C. Rich) that had been appointed to draft laws presented five ordinances for approval on 27 December 1847. The final ordinance concerning vagrants asserted the right of the community to force every person to be employed. The other ordinances concerned disorderly or dangerous persons and disturbers of the peace as well as those accused of adultery and fornication, drunkenness, stealing, robbing, or maliciously destroying property by fire. Persons convicted of such crimes could receive up to thirty-nine lashes on the bare back as well as fines of up to $1,000, depending upon the crime. However, persons convicted of drunkenness, cursing, swearing, foul or indecent language, the unnecessary firing of guns within or about the forts, unusual noise or noises, or any disturbance of the quiet or peace of the community, were required only to pay a fine of not less than twenty-five dollars.

NEW LAWS

Later, in January, two other ordinances were passed addressing violations based on greed and carelessness and reflecting developments in the new community. Ordinances VI and VII read:

HOARDING

> Be it ordained that no person is entitled to more fuel than will last him to the first day of October, 1848, or to more poles of timber than will answer his present fencing or building, unless by permission of the

---

[9] According to the "History of Brigham Young," for 6 March 1848, both Babcock and Gardner, with one son each, left the valley to join a Mr. Walker's party on its way to California. In addition, a Mr. Pollack, who had been excommunicated "on the road," and Hazen Kimball and their families were hoping to intercept Walker's company near Fort Hall.

council, under a penalty of a sum not less than five dollars nor exceeding five hundred dollars, at the discretion of the judge or judges.

Be it ordained that no loose cattle, horses, mules, or sheep shall be permitted to run upon the wheatland, or be driven on the road passing through it; and that the marshal, or any person he deputizes, shall take up every animal thus trespassing; and that the owner of every animal thus taken shall pay twenty-five cents per head to the person who takes them up, and two cents per head a day, for herding, if they require to be herded for the wheatlands and the road through it shall be kept clear of loose animals.[10]

LOOSE LIVESTOCK

Since there were no jails, the high council had to base penalties on some other form of punishment such as whipping and loss of property. The penalties were severe enough to discourage impeding the peace and progress of the settlement, and violations were infrequent during the first winter. In fact, many of the hearings before the high council were based on incidents that occurred during the trek west.

NO JAIL — *FIRST YR PEACEFUL*

Perhaps the most perplexing problem to confront council members was their relationship to apostles Pratt and Taylor. According to the Journal History, Pratt was once criticized during these months for cutting green wood. He appeared before the council voluntarily, not as a transgressor, he said, since he had not been legally notified, but "as moved upon by the Spirit of the Lord and an Apostle of the Lord Jesus Christ," and asked for the privilege of teaching the council about the order of the church. He then asserted that as senior apostle in the valley, he presided over the stake presidency and that it was his "duty to warn, exhort, and admonish" the Saints.

PRATT = GREEN WOOD INCIDENT

Pratt told the council that they had been in darkness all winter and called them to repent. "There had been more jarrings this winter than he had ever known," he reported. "If the Spirit of the Lord had governed the council, he and Elder Taylor would have been referred to more." Regarding the charge of cutting green wood, he admitted that he had done so and fully expected to do so again— that, with only two little boys to help them, he was not able to sustain his fires with dry wood. He acknowledged that he was subject

---

[10] The law concerning animals may have been prompted by an incident involving Albert Carrington's cow. The animal had been found dead by haystacks belonging to two men, both of whom denied any knowledge. High councilmen Sherwood and Grover asserted that "the priesthood had certain power in discovering hidden things" and encouraged the men to tell all they knew about it. Finally John Smith pronounced a curse on the persons who had killed the cow until they came forward and made restitution. According to the Journal History, "it was moved and seconded that the curse stand until restitution was made."

NO FIRST X-MAS DANCE

to the law but felt that the timber law should be altered. John Taylor then rose and said, "I do know that Brother Pratt's teachings this day are true."[11]

Although blessed with a relatively mild winter, the pioneers' life was not easy. There were few diversions, and the people lived austerely. At Christmas, some members felt they should enjoy a little dancing, but Brigham Young and others decided that "it was not proper to engage in dancing at that time, and thus it was not permitted." John Taylor did entertain friends with a dinner and dancing on New Year's Day, but he was careful to clear the festivities with the high council first. Lorenzo Dow Young, who attended the party, reported in his diary, "Our visit was pleasant. The day was spent in [social] chats, and singing and prayer. . . . President [John] Smith blessed our little Lorenzo."

As the winter wore on there was little excess food for entertaining and insufficient strength for dancing. Lorenzo Young recorded that he shared his last bit of flour with a destitute battalion veteran, then traded a pair of oxen for three-quarters of beef which kept his family alive for several weeks. After the beef was gone, he decided to eat the hide: "To prepare a meal, a piece of it was boiled and until it became a glue soup, when salt was added." The thick soup filled their stomachs, but Harriet Young grew weak. Bishop Edward Hunter, learning of Harriet's plight, gave Lorenzo seven pounds of flour which helped her survive until spring.

Hungry pioneers used thistle roots growing along the banks of the Jordan River bottom lands, sego lily roots, and cowslip greens to augment their meager diet. By the end of the year they were looking forward to spring and an early harvest of the garden plants and wheat they had planted the previous fall.

---

[11] Relations between the two apostles and the high council were usually good, but such incidents indicate that lines of authority were not clearly established during the Saints' first winter in the valley. Certainly, the day-to-day struggle to survive in a new location caused some tensions and disagreements, even among men of good faith.

2.
Survival

2ND WINTER HARSH

Although the pioneers had successfully established a base camp by the end of 1847, their survival was not guaranteed. Most immigrants entered the valley in late September or early October, too late to plant or harvest crops, and had to survive on rations. Luckily, the first winter was unusually mild, and no one starved. However, other threats soon developed. A late frost and hordes of crickets would nearly destroy their crops in May and June, while frost, drought, and cattle would destroy crops later that fall. In contrast to their first winter, the winter of 1848-49 would be especially severe. And the discovery of gold in California would tempt many members to leave the valley for richer prospects. Brigham Young, though not present during the cricket attack, would be on hand to face the other dangers and to discourage desertion.

The pioneers had several reasons to feel optimistic as they faced the early spring of 1848. During their first winter several men had built or were in the process of building saw mills to help construct homes and grist mills in anticipation of an early harvest. In their letter of 6 March to Brigham Young, valley leaders reported:

Charles Chrisman has a small grist mill . . . on City Creek. . . . Brother John Neff intends to build a good flouring mill to be ready to grind by harvest if possible. Brother Chase has a saw mill in operation on a spring a short distance from the pioneer garden. Archibald and Robert Gardner have a saw mill nearly ready for sawing on Mill Creek. . . . Brothers Nebeker, Keeler and Wallace are progressing rapidly with a saw mill

25

in the canyon some ten miles north of the city. Brother Amasus Russell has put up a frame for the carding machine near Brother Gardner's saw mills.

Settlers with special skills had been busy making chairs, tables, bedsteads, washtubs, churns, and other items. Others were building fences. Nearly 4,000 rods of fencing had been completed in addition to the wall around the fort. This was especially important since the animals of the companies that had arrived before fences had been built had destroyed nearly all of the crops the previous fall. Still other pioneers were building bridges over the Jordan River and Mill Creek.[1]

A party from Fort Hall visited the valley in December to explore the possibility of establishing trade with the Mormon settlers. John Smith and his two counselors asked the captain to carry a letter to his board of management, in which they described their settlement and prospects for growth as well as their immediate needs. Listing such needed items as "sugar, coffee, tea, bleached or unbleached domestic or cotton cloth . . . colored calicos, broadcloth, cassimeres . . . blankets, iron steel, powder, hardware, [and] leather," they explained that "in case you saw fit to send your goods direct to this place, we . . . will use our influence to turn the channel of trade in your favor." The leaders suggested that the products of their mills could be used as items of trade along with "no inconsiderable share of peltry." Smith and other leaders apparently believed a trading arrangement could materialize to their advantage.

Another source of food became available in the spring as Battalion men brought provisions from California. Early in May 1848, the Lathrop-Hunt party, which had gone to California the previous November to get cattle and seeds, returned. Lathrop reported on 11 May that he "had purchased 200 head of cows, at six dollars per head, [but] . . . had lost forty head on the Mojave, that went back to California." It took the party of nineteen, accompanied by five hired Indians, ninety days to return home. Saying that he had done the best he could, Lathrop presented a bill for $227.91, which the high council agreed to honor. Lathrop's return brought additional

---

[1] Apostle Parley P. Pratt thought about adding to the Saints' meager supply of food by tapping the resources of Utah Lake, which "abounds with trout and various kinds of fish." He volunteered to lead twenty men into Utah Valley to negotiate with the Indians to fish in the lake or to purchase fish. Although the high council authorized Pratt to establish a camp in Utah Valley if he could obtain a satisfactory treaty with the Indians, there is no record that he ever attempted to do so.

livestock to the valley but also twenty more mouths to feed. Less than a month later, on 5 June, Henry G. Boyle, with Porter Rockwell as guide, led into the valley a second contingent of about thirty-five Battalion men (out of eighty-five) who had re-enlisted and served eight additional months in San Diego. They brought wheat and other staples, as well as a band of some 135 horses and mules.

Still, an early harvest was the anticipated remedy to the scanty supplies remaining after the first winter, and the pioneers were quick to take advantage of the mild winter. John Taylor asserted that he had plowed as late as 5 December, and Lorenzo Dow Young wrote on 16 January that "the weather . . . had been warm and pleasant." Parley P. Pratt noted in his journal that the settlers began plowing again as early as 24 February, although in a letter to the *Latter-day Saints' Millennial Star*, published in England, he wrote that "early in March the ground opened and we commenced plowing for spring crops, plowed and planted about twenty acres of Indian corn, beans, melons, etc. My corn planting was completed by 15 May; most of it had done extremely well."

The previous fall, the pioneers had put in approximately 2,000 acres of winter wheat and expected to plant more that spring. They also planned to plant between 3,000 and 4,000 acres of corn and fresh garden vegetables. The high council's 6 March letter to Brigham Young reported that "all of the animals that were permitted to run loose are in fine condition. Many of the brethren are busy in their gardens and many have thriving tomato, cabbage, and other plants ready to set out." As early as 16 April 1848, John Steele wrote that "greenstuff is coming very fast, that wheat, corn, beans, and peas were all up looking grand, grass six inches high that early in the spring."

This optimistic view changed suddenly when a killing frost destroyed almost all of the garden vegetables in late May. The Saints had hardly recovered from that shock when they were confronted with a more serious threat—the invasion of millions of crickets. John Taylor noted crickets in some fields as early as 22 May. Five days later Harriet Young gave the first detailed account: "Today to our utter astonishment the crickets came by the millions sweeping everything before them. They first attacked a patch of beans for us, and in twenty minutes there was not a vestige of them to be seen. They next swept over the peas, then came into our garden and took everything clean. We went out with a brush and undertook to drive them, but they were too strong for us."

27

The next day Isaac Haight recorded, "Frost again this morning. Things killed in the garden such as beans, cucumbers, melons, pumpkins and squash. Corn hurt some and some wheat killed, and the crickets are injuring the crops." On the same day, Harriet Young added, "Last night we had a severe frost; today the crickets have commenced on our corn and small grain. They had eaten off twelve acres for Brother Rosencrantz, seven for Charles, and are now taking Edmund's." The following day the crickets destroyed "three-fourths of an acre of squashes, our flax, two acres of millet, our rye, and are now to work in our wheat; what will the result be, we know not." John Steele, summarizing the previous week, wrote, "There is great excitement in camp; there has come a frost which took beans, corn, and wheat, and nearly everything and to help make the disaster complete, the crickets came by the thousands of tons." The same day, Haight reported, "It was cold and very dry. Crops began to suffer for want of rain. The crickets destroyed some crops eating the heads of grain as soon as the heads are out." Both Steele and Haight feared that the Saints would be forced to leave the valley, and John Young urged that a letter be sent to his brother Brigham, warning him not to bring any more Mormons into the valley that year for fear of starvation.

The pioneers had noticed crickets when they first entered the valley. William Clayton commented in July 1847 that the ground seemed alive with large black insects. Orson Pratt described crickets the size of a man's thumb, and others reported mammoth crickets in the borders of the valley. Some pioneers had recognized the potential threat, but nothing of the magnitude they ultimately encountered. For example, on 29 August 1847, John Steele had written that "his daily labors included planting buckwheat; irrigating crops, killing crickets, etc." Early the next year, John Taylor had noted that crickets and other insects had destroyed much of their spring crops. The pioneers were not entirely surprised to find crickets in their fields in 1848. What they had not anticipated was the effect the mild winter would have on insect survival.

In the face of this threat, the pioneers tried everything imaginable to keep the crickets from destroying their crops. They surrounded their fields with water in irrigation ditches, hoping to drown the insects. When they discovered that crickets were cannibalistic, they piled large mounds of crickets near the borders of their fields to divert others. Sticks, clubs, brooms, branches, and willows were used to knock the black creatures off the plants, and fires were built in long rows in hopes of consuming the insects. Some settlers learned

MILD WINTER → CRICKETS

28

that crickets disliked certain noises, so they pounded on pans and rang bells to try to turn them away from the fields. One of the most unusual techniques was that tried by John Young. He and his brother pulled a rope back and forth across the tops of the grain to knock off the climbing crickets before they could reach the heads of the wheat. But these efforts only stemmed the tide temporarily.

Suddenly, flocks of gulls began landing in the fields and devouring the crickets. It is difficult to determine just when the gulls first arrived and how dramatic their impact may have been. Isaac Haight noted on 4 June that some of the Saints were considering leaving the valley because of the crickets and did not mention the gulls.[2] But five days later the stake presidency informed Brigham Young, "The gulls have come in large flocks from the lake and sweep the crickets as they go, and it seems that the hand of the Lord is in our favor." Thus the gulls may have begun arriving sometime between 4 June and 9 June.

John Smith remembered that the gulls came every morning for about three weeks. He first saw them when he heard their sharp cry. On "looking up," he wrote, "I beheld what appeared to be a vast flock of pigeons coming from the Northwest. It was about three o'clock in the afternoon. . . . There must have been thousands of them. Their coming was like a great cloud; and when they passed between us and the sun, a shadow covered the field. I could see gulls settling down for more than a mile around us." After filling their stomachs, the birds would regurgitate the indigestible parts of the insects and return to the fields for more. It appeared to the pioneers that the birds' main objective was to kill the crickets rather than feed on them. George Q. Cannon, for example, concluded this after walking along the ditches where he "saw lumps of crickets, vomited up by those gulls." Such actions may have seemed unnatural, but the pioneers were grateful that the birds had such voracious appetites. If John Smith's account is correct, the gulls destroyed thousands of insects during a three-week period—enough, in fact, to make the difference between disaster and a respectable harvest.

When the situation seemed to be under control, John Smith reported to Brigham Young on 20 July, rating the gulls as helpers but not as rescuers.

---

[2] Other diarists who did not mention the gulls include Eliza R. Snow, John Steele, Patty Sessions, and Harriet Young. This is also true of Parley P. Pratt, who wrote a detailed account of the summer's events for the *Latter-day Saints' Millennial Star* and also sent a descriptive letter to his brother Orson, who was presiding over the church's British mission.

The crickets are still quite numerous, but between the gulls and our own efforts and the growth of our crops, we shall raise much grain in spite of them. Our vines, beans, and peas are mostly destroyed by frost and the crickets, but many of us have more seed and are now busy replanting. Feel assured that we will still raise many pumpkins, melons, beans, etc. Some of the corn now is growing very fast, as the days and nights are warmer on the whole.

Smith also reported that the fences were nearly up, that the health of the people was good, and that the harvest would probably be much better than anticipated. He concluded, "Everything is as well as could be expected, considering our ignorance of the climate and the crickets and so on. But we are gaining a fund of knowledge and from all such points, and a large majority feel encouraged and well satisfied." Smith's cautious report places things in perspective. Frost, drought, lack of fencing, and irrigation problems, as well as the cricket attack, were all factors in determining the success of the crops. The gulls helped to solve the cricket problem, "along with our own efforts," but they could not aid in solving the pioneers' other difficulties.

When Brigham Young reported to church members in April 1849 on agricultural progress during the previous year, he did not note the gulls at all.

> Most of the early plots were destroyed in the month of May by crickets and a frost which continued occasionally till June while the latter harvest was injured more or less by drought, by frost, which commenced its injuries about October 10, and by the outbreak of cattle. The brethren were not sufficiently numerous to fight the crickets, irrigate the crops, and fence the farm of their extensive plantings; consequently they suffered heavy losses, though the experience of the past year is sufficient to prove that valuable crops may be raised in the valley by attentive and judicious management.

Although little was said about the role of the gulls in saving the crops at the time, the inspirational aspects of the episode were emphasized over time until it came to be regarded as a unique incident in Mormon history. Such an interpretation ignores the fact that gulls and other birds returned regularly each spring to Mormon settlements, devouring crickets, grasshoppers, worms, and other insects. But the episode *was* providential to the colonists who needed food.

The pioneers had psychological needs, as well. They had committed themselves to building their concept of Zion, believing that God had inspired their leaders to choose this location. To have been forced to leave would have challenged their faith and perhaps the

30

unity of the church. Even though the gulls "came late and left early," their <u>presence made a difference</u> and <u>seemed to confirm God's bless-ings</u>. Little wonder that the church later commissioned the Sea Gull Monument on Temple Square and that the gull is Utah's official state bird.

By August 1848 the cricket threat had abated and leaders were able to send a favorable report to Brigham Young and other church officials who were leading a large contingent of Latter-day Saints from Winter Quarters to the Salt Lake Valley. They reported:

> There were some 5,000 acres plowed, planted, and sowed, but owing to the destruction by crickets, grasshoppers, and other insects, we are not able to state how many acres will finally mature their crops. Wheat harvest is over, and the grain is splendid and clean, being mostly in shock and stack. . . . We can raise more and better wheat per acre in this valley than any of us have ever seen and the same with all the other grains and vegetables, etc., that we have tried. The corn looks extremely well, but as in most new countries the worms eat some in the ears though we judge they will injure but little. . . . Green peas have been so plentiful for such a long time that we're becoming tired of them. Cucumbers, squash, onions, peas, carrots, parsnips, and green corn are on our tables as harbingers in their respective departments, and no one has starved, and few have been much shortened for bread and meat, therefore, we feel that the trying time has been passed, and that, too, without any tax on provisions, which some anticipated in the winter.

Other local leaders were equally optimistic. In a 5 September 1848 letter to his brother Orson in England, Parley P. Pratt reported that corn and other crops had done well: "Many of the ears are as high as I can reach. I had a good harvest of wheat and rye without irrigation, though not a full crop, those who irrigated their wheat raised double the quantity on the same amount of land. Wheat harvest commenced early in July, and continued until August. Winter and spring wheat have both done well, some ten thousand bushels have been raised in the valley this season." Likewise, Thomas Bullock reported that Levi Hancock, one of the returning members of the Mormon Battalion, had sown "eleven pounds weight of California wheat on the 14th of April and had reaped twenty-two bushels the latter part of July and had sown half a bushel of English common wheat on an acre and a half, and reaped upwards of twenty bushels. The land," Bullock continued, "then irrigated and produced from the roots a fresh crop, four times the quantity of the first crop. Peas first planted, a good crop ripened, gathered; then planted the same peas, yielded another crop; again a third crop is now growing."

Not all reports were so favorable. Henry Bigler noted that the "corn crop was light and the fodder short," and Isaac Haight wrote that his final wheat harvest was poor. John Steele lamented that his harvest consisted of a "mess-pan full of corn ears," and A. J. Allen produced only five bushels of wheat from his two acres. Apparently the degree of success varied from pioneer to pioneer, depending on irrigation and the impact of the crickets. But the overall harvest enabled valley leaders to fulfill the promise of a harvest festival they had announced the previous Christmas. In a report to the *Millennial Star*, Parley P. Pratt wrote, "On the 10th [of August] we met to a number of several hundred under a large awning to celebrate our first harvest in the Great Basin. We had a feast which consisted of almost every variety of food, all produced in this valley. We had prayer and thanksgiving and music and dancing and firing of cannon together with loud shouts of hosannas to God and the Lamb."

Despite the leaders' optimism, there was reason for concern given the expected increase in population. Approximately fifty-five Mormon Battalion veterans had come into the valley from southern California in May. An even larger number were expected from northern California by early fall, although the recent discovery of gold made it uncertain just how many would arrive. (Eventually, forty-five men and one woman met near Placerville on 1 July and, after two days' preparation, began the long trek to Salt Lake Valley, arriving in mid-October, along with Addison Pratt, who had been serving as a missionary to the Samoan Islands and had joined this group in San Francisco.)

The return of these battalion men caused only a minor increase in population compared to the large groups on their way from Winter Quarters led by Brigham Young, Heber C. Kimball, and Willard Richards. Young's company included 1,229 immigrants, while Kimball's and Richards's were smaller, containing 662 and 526, for a total of 2,417. Fortunately these companies were well supplied with domestic animals as well as a great variety of seeds and plants. Having been in the valley a year earlier, Mormon leaders knew that they could use every plant and animal they could bring. These numbers, plus the Battalion men on their way from California, added to the nearly 1,800 already in the valley as reported by John Smith on 8 August, would total approximately 4,250 valley residents to be provided for during the coming winter.

The Ute Indians, led by Chief Walker, brought several hundred horses for sale into the valley, and some Mexican traders added to the supply. Parley P. Pratt reported that the horses could be used for

32

food, if necessary, and asserted that "our cattle and sheep increase fast." A more welcome source of food was that provided by Captain Grant of Hudson Bay's Trading Post at Fort Hall, Grant kept his earlier promise and brought a train of pack horses into the valley laden with skins, groceries, and other goods.

Despite these attempts to increase the supply of food, the colonists barely survived the winter because of the severity of the weather. Whereas the previous winter had been mild, the winter of 1848-49 was intense. In their first general epistle to the Saints abroad, Brigham Young and his counselors described the weather as follows:

> Excessive cold commenced on the 1st of December, and continued till the latter part of February. Snow storms were frequent, and though there were several thaws, the earth was not without snow during that period, varying from one to three feet in depth, both in time and place. The coldest day of the past winter was the 5th of February, the mercury falling to 33 degrees below freezing point, and the warmest day was Sunday, the 25th of February, with the mercury rising 21 degrees above the freezing point Fahrenheit. Violent and contrary winds have been frequent. The snow on the surrounding mountains has been much deeper, which has made the wood very difficult of access, while the cattle become so poor through fasting and scanty fare that it has been difficult to draw the necessary fuel and many have had to suffer more or less from the want thereof. The winter commenced at an unusual and unexpected moment and found many of the brethren without houses or fuel. Although there has been considerable suffering, there have been no deaths by the frost. Three attempts have been made by the brethren with pack animals or snow shoes to visit Fort Bridger since the snow fall but have failed.

In an effort to conserve their food and to protect their animals from predators, and apparently to promote social life as well, the high council decided to sponsor a massive hunt to eliminate the "wasters and destroyers": "The citizens of this Great Salt Lake City suffered so much annoyance from howling at night, and depredations committed by the foxes, catamounts, ravens, and other animals, that it was considered advisable for rival companies to be organized and destroy the same." John D. Lee wrote that one thousand dollars worth of grain and stock had already been destroyed by the animals. Lee and John Pack were chosen captains of the one-hundred-man teams, and it was agreed that the losers would treat the winners and their wives to dinner. The hunt opened Christmas morning. A point system was established with Isaac Morley and Reynolds Cahoon as judges. Thomas Bullock kept record and was instructed to publish a list of the successes of each individual. The first of February was the deadline for producing evidence of the kill, but this was later extended to 5 March. Animals and birds killed by both companies included two bears, two wolverines, two wildcats, 183 wolves, 499 foxes, 31 mink, 9 eagles, 531 magpies, hawks, and owls, and 1,026 ravens. John D. Lee's team was declared winner, and Thomas Williams was designated individual champion.

Such diversions helped to improve public morale, but as the winter continued, other measures to insure survival and social cohesion were needed. Most important was the institution of a voluntary rationing and community storehouse system. The five city wards were further divided into nineteen, and the newly appointed bishops were instructed to provide for the poor in their ward. Each person with a surplus of food was asked to turn it in to his bishop for distribution among the needy. Brigham Young chose to persuade and appeal to conscience rather than invade homes and wagons to secure the equitable distribution of existing supplies. When members of the high council suggested "passing a law regulating the price of eatables," Young objected and advocated letting "trade seek its own level." Apparently Young did not feel that the situation in January was desperate enough to warrant forced sharing. By 5 February, when the temperature fell to 33 degrees below freezing, however, it was decided that the bishops should "go to every man's house to ascertain the true amount of breadstuff, seed, grain, cows and calves and report at the next session of the Council."

Parley P. Pratt recalled the next year that people suffered from fear more than from hunger and that many who had little or nothing to sell gave to those who had none so that no one starved. Thistle tops, roots, and sego roots "lengthened out the bread," and when winter finally broke, "grass soon came, [and] milk and butter increased."

At a 9 February high council meeting, it was reported that there was a little over three-fourths of a pound of breadstuffs for each person every day until 9 July. Brigham Young said that he felt safe and believed there was more grain in the valley than was turned in. He commented, "If those that have do not sell to those who have not, we will just take it and distribute among the poor and those that have and will not divide willingly may be thankful that their heads are not found wallowing in the snow. There is some of the meanest spirits here among the Saints that ever graced this footstool. They are too mean to live among the Gentiles [non-Mormons]. The Gentiles would be ashamed of them."

After venting his emotions, Young remarked, "Still, if the day should [be] fine next Sabbath, I will talk to the people in public. I know the strongest side are willing to do right." One man, after hearing his leader preach, was reportedly so moved that he confessed to having charged more for an ox than it was worth and offered to make amends.

As the winter progressed, many settlers satiated their hunger with rawhides, sego roots, and thistles. Apparently none, however, followed the Indians in eating grasshoppers and crickets. A number of measures were adopted to cope with the situation. The high council prohibited the use of corn for making whiskey and stipulated that any intended for such use was to be taken and given to the poor. Church officials also wrote to the leaders in Winter Quarters not to send any company west during the summer of 1849 unless they could depend entirely on their own resources and unless they would bring with them enough provisions to last the following winter.

(handwritten margin note: STOP COMMING — MUST HAVE ENOUGH)

Some members advocated more drastic measures. They believed that it had been a mistake to settle in the Great Basin and that they should move to California, which they believed to be superior. The discovery of gold made California even more alluring. A petition from Robert Crow with nine names attached to it was considered by the high council on 24 February. Asking for permission to go to the gold mines, the petitioners promised to pay tithing on all gold they obtained. Brigham Young denied the request and gave the men a scolding, but the idea of moving continued to gather popular support. James Brown remembered:

(handwritten margin note: SOME WANT TO GO TO CALIF.)

> In February and March, as the days grew warmer, the gold fever attacked many so that they prepared to go to California. Some said they would go only to establish a place for the rest of us; for they thought Brigham Young too smart a man to try to establish a civilized colony in such a "God-forsaken country," as they called the valley. They further said that California was the natural country for the Saints; some had brought choice fruit pits and seed and said they would not waste them by planting them in a country like the Great Salt Lake Valley; others stated that they would not build a house in the valley, but would remain in their wagons, for certainly our leaders knew better than to attempt to make a stand in such a dry, worthless locality, and would be going on to California, Oregon or Vancouver's Island. . . . This discouraging talk was not alone by persons who had no experience in farming and manufacturing, but by men who had made a success in their various avocations where they had been permitted to work in peace before coming west. Good farmers said, "Why, wheat was so short we grew here last year,

we had to pull it. Their heads were not more than two inches long. Frost falls here every month of the year, enough to cut down all tender vegetation."

Apparently this deterioration in morale led to an increase in profanity. On 18 March 1849 the Saints agreed that "every man caught swearing should allow his ears to be bored [i.e., required to make a public explanation]." Then in March one diarist reported that about a dozen wagons and families moved to California. Another said that quite a few of the "tares had gone to the gold mines, and some of the wheat had probably gone with them." Many of those already in California elected to remain there rather than join their brethren and sisters, and many in Winter Quarters and Kanesville were skeptical of the future of the Great Basin. There is no doubt that the winter and spring proved trying.

Brigham Young countered this pessimism with powerful rhetoric: "God has shown me that this is the spot to locate His people, and here is where they will prosper. He will temper the elements for the good of His Saints. He will rebuke the frost and the sterility of the soil and the land shall become fruitful. Brethren go to now and plant out your fruit seeds," he declared. "We have the finest climate, the purest water, and the purest air that can be found on earth, and there is no healthier climate anywhere. As for gold and silver and the rich minerals of the earth, there is no other country that equals this, but let them alone and let others seek them. We will cultivate the soil." Such preaching won the day, and with the coming of spring, the people took heart and worked with renewed vigor to make Young's prophecies come true.

An atmosphere of permanence and stability began to prevail when many of the Saints left the fort as early as 19 February to build homes on their city lots. A "February thaw," which caused the collapse of a number of adobe houses on the fort, may have precipitated the early move. The Saints also took advantage of the warm weather to begin work on the Council House. Shortly thereafter, the congregation voted to build a tabernacle, 120 feet by 60 feet, to replace the brush bowery. Enough settlers had established themselves on individual lots by 5 April to request that bishops organize groups to cut ditches and build small foot bridges. Each ward of nine square blocks—90 acres total—was enclosed by a common fence.

Anticipating that more Saints would be coming to the valley in 1849, Brigham Young sent a general epistle to the scattered church on 9 April, in which he reviewed the Saints' accomplishments. He

CALIF — TARES + SOME WHEAT
SWARING — PUBLIC EXPLAINATION

YOUNG RHETORIC CARRIES THE DAY

WARD SIZE

wrote that the inhabitants of the valley would depend completely on the coming season's crops for support but pointed out that there was "an abundance of nutritious roots in the valley so we have no fear of starvation." He continued:

> The scarcity of grain since the settling of this valley has caused the slaughter of a multitude of cattle which leaves room for a fresh supply as fast as opportunity shall present and the emigrating brethren will do well to remember that they are liable to lose many on their journey. Also their cattle are good property after they arrive. There is no fear of their bringing too many cows, young cattle, sheep, oxen, or the choicest breed of stock of any kind to this place. For any of these articles here are better than gold for they will purchase what is to be purchased here when gold will not do it.
>
> There is an extensive variety of grain and seeds already in the valley. That should not prevent the saints from bringing choice seeds from many parts of the earth, for everything good that can grow here is wanted. A large amount of osage orange, cherokee rose tree, and English hawthorne seeds is needed this year for hedges, potatoes for hilling and eating, also lobelia, mulberry, and black locust seed, any amount of unadulterated selesia or French sugar beet would be useful here this season.

In addition to livestock and plants, Young listed other items he considered more valuable than money in the valley, including dry goods, nails, dyes, paints, turpentine, paper, boots, saws, files, screws, sheet tin, cutlery, farming equipment, sheet iron, copper, brass, looking glasses, shoe leather, harnesses, cupboards, and padlocks. Always practical, Young suggested that glass and crockery could be packed in cotton, and that the cotton "would be very useful here." Although there was no danger of starvation in early 1849, there was a shortage of "breadstuffs and there will be a scarcity till harvest which we hope for early in July." Leaders reported that "great preparations were being made for farming the coming season, and more than ten thousand acres will be enclosed and cultivated this summer." A heavy snow fall on 23 May, followed the next day by a severe frost, caused the loss of much of the garden crops, but the settlers simply planted more seeds. By 24 July, food in the valley was abundant.

Because 24 July 1849 marked the second anniversary of the pioneers' entrance into the valley, Mormon leaders decided to stage a mammoth celebration and community-wide dinner. Details of the celebration are worth noting, because they provide a window into the values, attitudes, and concepts of the new settlement.

On 23 July, dinner tables were set up in the bowery, which was extended about one hundred feet on each side to accommodate the "vast multitude at dinner." Brigham Young's flag, which had once flown from the Nauvoo Temple, was hoisted on the east side of the bowery. Captain Daniel Tyler and the artillerists made cartridges for the cannon with seventy-five pounds of powder furnished by some California-bound immigrants. On the morning of the 24th, the set-tlers were awakened by the firing of nine rounds of artillery accom-panied by martial music. Brass bands were then carried on carriages throughout the city. At 7:30 a.m., a large national flag, measuring 65 feet in length, was unfurled at the top of a 104-foot pole. The flag was saluted with the firing of guns, the ringing of the Nauvoo bell, and the playing of airs by the bands.

About 8:00 a.m. the multitude was called together by more music and the firing of guns. Ward bishops arranged themselves along the aisles, each unfurling a banner with an appropriate inscription. Fif-teen minutes later, the Salt Lake stake presidency, the bishops, and the bands went to Brigham Young's home to escort the church lead-ers. The procession started from the President's Home about 9:00 a.m. Marshal Horace S. Eldredge led, followed by the bishops and the brass band. Next followed twenty-four young men, dressed in white, with white scarfs over their right shoulders and coronets on their heads. Each carried a copy of the Declaration of Independence, the Constitution of the United States, and a sheathed sword. One of them carried a banner, reading "The Zion of the Lord." They were followed by twenty-four similarly attired young women, each carry-ing a Bible and a Book of Mormon. One of them held a banner inscribed, "Hail to our Chieftain." They were followed by other groups, each carrying a symbol of loyalty to church and country.

The young men and women sang hymns as they walked, the cannons pounding, the artillery firing, and the Nauvoo bell ringing. When the procession reached the bowery, they were greeted by shouts of "Hosanna to God and the Lamb," and Brigham Young, Heber C. Kimball, and Willard Richards, who comprised the First Presidency, were cheered and invited to sit on the stand. Jedediah M. Grant called the congregation to order, Erastus Snow offered an opening prayer of thanksgiving, and Richard Ballantyne, one of the twenty-four young men, read out loud the Declaration of Indepen-dence and the Constitution. Brigham Young led the crowd in respond-ing, "May it live forever and ever!"

Later, Young addressed the group:

> Why do we not celebrate the 4th of July? The Declaration of Inde-pendence is just as precious to me today as it was twenty years ago! Has

THE 24TH OF JULY CELEBRATION

it not the same validity that it had in 1776? Is it not as good today as it was twenty days ago? We chose this day that we might have a little bread to set on our tables; today we can see the bread, cucumbers, and beets, that we could not have seen twenty days ago. Inasmuch as there are some strangers in our midst, I want you to give them their dinner, for they rejoice to see us happy, and I say they are welcome, heartily welcome.

Several thousand Saints then dined "sumptuously on the fruits of the earth, produced by their own hands, [and] invited several hundreds of the emigrants [to eat with them] even all who were in the valley." While they were eating, a new company of pioneers arrived and were immediately seated at a table. In addition, between forty and sixty Indians joined the festivities.

After dinner, toasts were offered, songs were sung, and the band played several musical numbers. Finally, Young said, "We have had a day of gladness and joy long to be remembered by our children, by the youth, and by the middle-aged. . . . I say to this congregation, be ye blessed in the name of the Lord Jesus Christ. Go your way and never sin no more. The anger of the Lord is only kindled against the wicked." The band then played "Home Sweet Home," followed by more singing. John Taylor offered the benediction, and the pioneers returned home.

In all, it was an impressive celebration. In this way Brigham Young gave public notice that the Saints' two-year struggle for survival in the Great Basin had succeeded and that the Mormons intended not only to stay but to flourish.

3.
The Lure of California Gold

GOLD DISCOVERED

While Brigham Young and other church officials were in Winter Quarters preparing to lead a large group of emigrants to the Salt Lake Valley, other Mormons were involved in events in California that would profoundly impact the church and nation. On 24 January 1848, John Marshall, employed by John Sutter, discovered gold on the American River. News of the find leaked out slowly, but when a Mormon, Samuel Brannan, announced the discovery publicly in San Francisco, the famous California gold rush began in earnest.

Members of both the Mormon Battalion and Brannan's California colony of Mormon immigrants were among the first participants in the gold rush, and several acquired a lion's share of the metal, including the discovery of the fabulously rich Mormon Island. In fact, Brannan, a businessman and entrepreneur who sold supplies to the miners, became California's first millionaire. He was anxious for church members to colonize California rather than the Salt Lake Valley and could have organized a cooperative effort that would have enabled the church to "skim the cream" off the gold areas. With his New Hope colony along the San Joaquin River as an agricultural base and the 4,000 Mormons in Salt Lake Valley or en route to the valley organized as cooperative work crews, the church, Brannan believed, could control sizable areas in the region before the mass migration of gold seekers reached California.

BRANNAN URGED TO HAVE MORMONS CONTROL GOLD RUSH

But such was not the case. Mormon leaders, convinced that their destiny lay in the Great Basin and fearing the divisive effects of

41

gold-lust on their members, opposed such projects and persuaded most Mormons that their future was in colonizing the Great Basin. A few organized groups were permitted to go to the gold fields, and the church profited from gold seekers who passed through their Rocky Mountain settlements, but other than aiding missionary work and financing some colonization, California gold was used primarily for coinage in the Salt Lake Valley and to help finance the migration of Mormon emigrants through the Perpetual Emigrating Fund.

When the Mormons began their emigration from Nauvoo, Illinois, in 1846, their destination was California. The Great Basin, which was part of the Mexican province of Upper California, was to be the site of the first colony, but as Apostle Parley P. Pratt wrote in September 1846, "I expect we shall stop near the Rocky Mountains about 800 miles nearer than the coast . . . and there make a stand until we are able to enlarge and extend to the coast."

Sam Brannan's "Brooklyn Saints" had arrived in San Francisco in July 1846, and the Mormon Battalion was in San Diego by the end of January 1847. Later that same year, the discharged Battalion men had been informed by letter that it might be advisable for those who were unmarried, or who did not know that their families were coming to the Great Basin in 1847, to remain in California and earn money for seeds and other items needed for colonizing the Salt Lake Valley.

Brannan had reason to feel that his group might stay in the San Francisco bay area, for Brigham Young had written to him on 15 September 1845, before Brannan's group had set sail from New York, that he "wished that [Brannan] and his press, paper [later *The California Star*] and ten thousand of the brethren were now in California and the Bay of San Francisco." Young had also notified Brannan as late as 6 June 1847 that "the main [camp] will not go to the west coast, or to your place at present, as they do not have the means." This implied that Young's contingent would have followed Brannan's example, if they had had the means. Young continued in the same letter, "Any among you who may choose to come over into the basin, or meet the camp, are at liberty to do so, and if they are doing well where they are, and choose to stay, it is quite all right." However, after church authorities established the Great Salt Lake Valley as the headquarters of the church, the policy emerged of requiring that all loyal church members gather to that region, help to build it up, and secure it for the church. The strictness with which this policy was practiced can be seen from the following incident, which occurred in late December 1847, a few months after the first group of pioneers entered the Salt Lake Valley.

42

A special meeting of the High Council met at 2 p.m. at Pres. John Smith's house. Parley P. Pratt spoke at some length on the disaffected spirits in the valley. After remarks and testimonies by several of the valley, it was decided that the marshal should stop those who were about starting for California [with Miles Goodyear]. Parley P. Pratt and Henry Sherwood were appointed a committee to inform Miles Goodyear why Samuel Brown, Elijah Shockey and son and Samuel Shepherd and son were stopped.

Dec. 28,—The marshal reported that he took Thomas Williams, Charles Shumway, and Ephraim K. Hanks and went as far south as the last large creek in the valley, and turned back the five persons sent for; they made no opposition. The report was accepted. The persons turned back, reported themselves to Pres. Smith, and were permitted to go on to California with Miles Goodyear.[1]

When word of the gold discovery reached the Salt Lake Valley, the cricket scourge had just begun. This provided an added incentive to abandon the valley. But Brigham Young arrived from Winter Quarters in late September and began vigorously preaching against gold fever.

As early as 17 July 1848, Young warned the pioneers, "The Lord will bless you and prosper you if you will get cured of your California fevers as quick as you can." He explained, in a general letter to all Mormons, dated 12 October 1848, that the Sacramento Valley was unhealthy, that gold was not as valuable as food and drink, and that to become wealthy in precious metals was to court degradation and ruin. He reminded the Saints that the Spaniards had looked for gold and had not only lost their greatness but had almost lost their God, while the English colonists, who had paid attention to agriculture and industry, had become strong and a powerful influence for good. According to James Brown, Young predicted,

> I promise you in the name of the Lord that many of you that go thinking you will get rich and come back will wish you had never gone away from here, and will long to come back, but will not be able to do so. Some of you will come back, but your friends who remain here will have to help you; and the rest of you who are spared to return will not make as much money as your brethren do who stay here and help build up the

---

[1] The policy of trying to discourage desertion appears counterproductive, since the disaffected settlers were no doubt creating problems among the other settlers. One man, a Brother Babcock, reportedly boasted to the high council on 26 December 1847 that "if it were in his power he would destroy every Mormon on earth." Church leaders may have been concerned that many of the disaffected men would leave their families unprovided for. In any case, the policy of trying to keep the settlers from going to California was already established before the gold rush.

43

Church and Kingdom of God; they will prosper and be able to buy you twice over. Here is the place God has appointed for his people.

That fall, Young's scribes recorded in the president's manuscript history that fourteen or fifteen of the brethren from Brannan's colony arrived from the gold country. Some of these were very comfortably supplied with the precious metal, but others had been sick and returned as destitute as they had been when they embarked on the ship *Brooklyn* in 1846. Certainly there was plenty of gold in Western California, the history conceded, but the Sacramento Valley was unhealthy, and the Saints were better off to raise grain and build houses in the Salt Lake Valley than dig gold—unless counseled to do so. "The true use of gold," Young dictated, "is for paving streets, covering houses, making culinary dishes; and when the Saints shall have preached the gospel, raised grain, and built up cities enough, the Lord will open up the way for a supply of gold to the perfect satisfaction of his people; until then," he concluded, "let them not be over anxious for the treasures of the earth are in the Lord's storehouse, and he will open the door thereof when and where he pleases."

Although Young was primarily concerned that Mormons build up the Kingdom of God in the Great Basin, he also seemed convinced that gold mining was not a fit occupation for Mormons and that it would actually be to their economic advantage to remain in the Great Basin and till the soil. "Before I had been one year in this place, the wealthiest man who came from the mines [was] Father Rhodes, with $17,000, [but] could he buy the possessions I had made in one year?" he asked rhetorically in early September 1850. "It will not begin to do it: and I will take twenty-five men . . . who had staid at home and paid attention to their own business, and they will weigh down fifty others from the same place, who went to the gold regions; and again, look at the widows that have been made, and see the bones that lie bleaching and scattered over the prairies."[2] The previous year, on 8 July 1849, Young had exclaimed, "If you Elders of Israel want to go to the gold mines, go and be damned. . . . I advise the corrupt, and all who want to go to California to go and not come back, for I will not fellowship them."

---

[2] Less than two years later, on 24 January 1852, the church-owned *Deseret News* editorialized, "Saints, you cannot go to California, as you have done in years gone by and still retain your fellowship in the Church." And on 16 November 1856, according to the Journal History, Heber C. Kimball recommended that "those who [recently] went to California be cut off from the Church—for their wickedness, their slandering, and their meanness."

44

The impact of Brigham Young's anti-gold rush rhetoric on members of the Mormon Battalion who had participated in the early discoveries must have produced one of the most unusual scenes of the entire gold rush. That these men, who had been engaged in a very successful operation in and around Mormon Island for over two months, would be willing to leave great wealth for a desert wasteland because they felt it was their duty to build up the Kingdom of God must have been incomprehensible to the hundreds of miners who had left their families, jobs, and comfortable homes in search of the shiny metal. Yet it should also be remembered that many of these men had been separated from their families for two years, that gold mining, as they did it, was hard work, that their living expenses were high and that they did not know how long the gold would run.

Not surprisingly, one Mormon who did not "gather to the valley" in 1848 was Sam Brannan. Brannan had arrived in the Salt Lake Valley with the pioneers in July 1847 but had left to return to California in August. Stopping at Sutter's Fort, he had secured permission from Sutter to set up a store at his establishment and left a partner to take charge of it. Thus, when gold was discovered in the region four months later, Brannan was in a position to reap large profits by selling supplies to the miners.

After announcing to the world that gold was being gathered along the American River, Brannan called a meeting of a branch of the church in San Francisco and told them of the rich find at Mormon Island. In a short time, most of the Mormon men in California were at this important site. And Brannan was there to collect one-tenth of all their income as church tithing. According to Mormon miner, Azariah Smith,

> on Tuesday, May 11th [1848], we went up [to the mines] and stayed until May 23rd, when we came down. While at the mines I had very good luck. I gathered nearly $300.00, which makes me in all worth about $400.00. The most I made in a day was $65 after the toll was taken out, which was 30 out of 100, this percentage going to Hudson and Willis, who discovered the mine, and Brannan, who is securing it for them. . . . While there Mr. Brannan called a meeting to see who was willing to pay toll, and who was not, most of the men agreed to pay, while others refused.

Addison Pratt, who was serving as president of the San Francisco branch of the church, added his own version of the experience.

> On our arrival [at Mormon Island] we learned that Brannan had entered into a league with the brethren there, to the effect that all who dug gold there should pay a tax of 30% of all they found. The claim was

45

that this % should go to the Church and from that means obtained, that young cattle should be purchased in California and sent to the valley. I had seen enough of Brannan's tricks to convince me that the church would never see any cattle bought in this manner and considerable dissatisfaction existed among the brethren who had come up from San Francisco over this matter. Many asked me if I intended to pay the % asked. I told them that I considered the demand unjust, and yet if the church could get any benefit from the money, I had no objection to paying it. I saw at once that if I refused to pay the tax, most of the brethren would follow my example. And as Brannan had already collected some means in this manner, I foresaw clearly that his low cunning would naturally lead him to send what means he had already collected to the Church, and then report that if I had not come out against him, he would have been able to send more.[3]

Eventually, such California notables as California governor Richard B. Mason and William Tecumseh Sherman became involved in the dispute. Sherman accompanied Mason on a tour of the gold fields. In his published memoirs, Sherman remembered that a Mr. Clark asked the two men, "Governor, what business has Sam Brannan to collect the tithes here?" Mason responded, "Brannan has a perfect right to collect the tax, if you Mormons are fools enough to pay it." "Then," Clark announced, "I for one won't pay it any longer." Evidently, Brannan used a number of arguments to get the men to pay him some gold, such as Azariah Smith's understanding that Brannan was simply securing Willis and Hudson's claim and Pratt's impression that it was for tithing and to pay cattle for the church. John Sutter's account indicates a third reason. He reported that the "Mormons were being assessed to build a temple to the Lord. Now that God has given gold to the Church, the Church must build a temple." What is apparent is that Brannan used every argument he could think of to get money from the men to increase his own personal fortune.

Meanwhile Brannan continued to send letters to Brigham Young, pledging his loyalty and devotion to the cause and requesting that the president not listen to the complaints of disgruntled members. However, on 5 April 1849, Young sent Brannan a letter that brought

---

[3] Brannan had previously complained to Brigham Young of Pratt's services as branch president, and Pratt's account here provides some evidence of instability. This incident highlights one of the weaknesses of an authoritarian, centralized bureaucracy, for many of the men felt obliged to respect Brannan's appointment as "first Elder" in California, even though they distrusted him and believed he was pursuing unwise and dishonest policies.

matters to a head and drove Brannan from hypocrisy to apostasy. Young informed Brannan that Amasa M. Lyman of the Council of the Twelve Apostles was coming to California with a general epistle to all the Saints and that either the epistle or Lyman would answer the questions Brannan had asked in his letters. After noting that no legal complaints had been filed against Brannan, Young asserted,

> The man who is always doing right has no occasion to fear any complaints that can be made against him, and I hope that you have no cause to fear.
>
> I am glad to hear you say that I may rely on your "pushing every nerve to assist me and sustain me to the last," for I do not doubt that you have been blessed abundantly and now shall have it in your power to render most essential service. I shall expect ten thousand dollars, at least, your tithing, on the return of Elder Lyman, and if you have accumulated a million to tithe, so as to send $100,000.00, so much the better, and may you get two million next year. If you want to continue to prosper, do not forget the Lord's treasury, lest he forget you, and with the liberal, the Lord is liberal, and when you have settled with the treasury, I want you to remember that Bro. Brigham has long been destitute of a home, and suffered heavy losses and incurred great expenses in searching out a location and in planting the Church in this place, and he wants you to send him $20,000 (a present) in gold dust to help him with his labors. This is but a trifle where gold is so plentiful but it will do me much good at this time.
>
> I hope that Bro. Brannan will remember that when he has complied with my request, my council will not be equal with me unless you send $20,000 more, to be divided between Brothers Kimball and Richards, who, like myself, are straightened; a hint to the wise is sufficient, so when this is accomplished you will have our united blessing, and our hearts will exclaim, "God bless Brother Brannan, and give him four-fold for all that he has given us."
>
> Now Brother Brannan, if you will deal justly with your fellows, and deal out with a liberal heart and open hands, making a righteous use of your money, the Lord is willing that you should accumulate the treasures of the earth and good things in time of abundance, but should you withhold when the Lord says give, your hope and pleasing prospects will be blasted in an hour you think not of, and no arm to save [you]. But I am persuaded [of] better things of Brother Brannan. I expect all that I have asked when Brother Lyman returns and may God bless you to this end is the prayer of your brother in the new covenant.

If Young's purpose was to test Brannan's loyalty or call his bluff, it succeeded, for by the time Lyman arrived Brannan had disclaimed all connection with the church.[4] More than two years after Young's letter, Brannan was finally disfellowshipped in San Francisco on 25 August 1851. Among the reasons given at his trial for the action were "a general course of unchristianlike conduct, neglect of duty, and . . . other crimes."

One of the most unusual developments involving Mormons and California gold took place in the fall and winter of 1849-50. Brigham Young, going against his better judgment, permitted a few older leaders to "call" young men of their choice on a "mission" to California to mine for gold. Prominent among these men was Henry Bigler whose diary set the accepted date of the original discovery of gold at Coloma, and George Q. Cannon who later became an influential counselor in the church's First Presidency.

Neither man was especially excited at the prospect of leaving the valley. Bigler, in his journal for 11 October 1849, lamented, "It fills me with sorrow to think of leaving, for I am attached to this place and this people, for they are my brothers and sisters and my friends, and it was with considerable struggle with my feelings that I consented to go." Cannon expressed his own apprehensions twenty years later in a series of reminiscent articles published in the church's *Juvenile Instructor*: "There was no place I would rather not have been at the time than in California. I heartily despised the work of digging gold. . . . There is no occupation I would not rather follow than hunting and digging for gold."[5]

The most detailed and dramatic account of the gold missionaries' call to California is found in Bigler's diary for October 1849. He recorded:

---

[4]There is evidence that Young knew Brannan was gaining wealth rapidly. On 7 December 1848, Young reported that "Brannan had received $36,000 in gold dust for goods" during a seventy-day period. And he knew that the returning battalion men, as well as others in California, had given tithing money to Brannan. In light of reports concerning Brannan's attitudes and activities, it is unlikely that Young expected Brannan's contribution.

[5]A third gold missionary to leave a written record, Albert K. Thurber, felt that the call was given as a test, and although he was not anxious to go, he did not seem as reluctant as Bigler and Cannon. Thurber had come to the Salt Lake Valley with a company of gold seekers in 1849, became converted to Mormonism, and decided to stay in Salt Lake. He obtained work with B. J. Johnson, a local church leader who subsequently called him to the California mines. Thurber and a companion, who was also employed by Johnson and had been called to the gold mission, "worked for one week without mentioning the subject and then decided to go in a short time. Johnson was to fit us out and get one third of what each made and we to receive one third of what he made at home."

48

Monday 8th Makeing preparations today to go on a mission to California to get Gold for Father John Smith,[6] as . . . he is Counciled to fit out some person and send them to the Gold mines and he has called on me to go and is now fiting me out to go with Brother C. C. Rich and others who are sent. . . . Tuesday Oct. 9th This day I settled up all my accounts, paid all my debts, Sold my wheat and a few boards of lumber to Bro. Stanes.

Thursday 11th last evening Father Smith sent for me he wanted to bless me, he then laid his hands on my head and blest me and also Brother James Keeler in the name of the Lord. Brother Keeler is going for Thomas Callister[7] we will go in the same waggon together; about 2 p.m. we was ready. I told Brother Keeler to call by my house with the waggon and I would be ready. I wrote a note and stuck it on the side of my door for my brother-in-law John Hess to [take] charge of some clothing I had left in a sack; at this moment I experienced what I shall not here attempt to describe. I walked back and forth across my floor and my feelings was spent in a complete shower of tears, every thing I looked upon seamed to simpethise with me and say go in peace only be faithful and all will be right. I herd a rattling and looked up and saw the waggon a coming. I hastened to the Curtings of the window and wiped away every tear, and went out to the waggon. I was requested to get in. I refused. I told Brother Keeler I would walk as I wanted to call at the tin shop to buy a canteen, I paid 6 bits 75 cents for one & 2 bits for a quart cup; I then got in the waggon and we drove to Brother Flakes on Cottonwood, about 10 miles. Got thare in the night, all was gone to bed, we mired in the big field. we had to get in the mud and water with our shoulders to the wheels; after a long time we got out all wet and mudy. We called at Brother Chipmans and got some Butter and 2 large fresh loaves of light good wheat bread for which we paid $2 together with a little tin pail to carry our butter in.

Friday 12th This morning we ware detained a little in getting something made. We found that one of our horses was sick, supposed to have a [touch] of the Belly ache, and to carry out father Smith's Blessings we bought a mare of Brother Flakes, paid $20 down and give our note for 100$ with intrest at our Return. At 10 AM we was on the way, went 13 miles and encampt near the Banks of the Jordan.

Bigler and Keeler joined a company of about twenty gold missionaries,[8] with James M. Flake as captain. They left Salt Lake Valley

---

[6] Besides being president of the Salt Lake Stake (1847-48), "Father" John Smith was an uncle to Joseph Smith and the presiding patriarch of the church (1849-54). He was sixty-eight years old in October 1849 and died five years later.

[7] Thomas Callister was John Smith's son-in-law and was twenty-eight years old in 1849. He later became the first president of the Millard Stake.

[8] A reading of Bigler's journal and Cannon's recollections yields the following tentative roster: George Bankhead, John W. Berry, Henry Bigler, John Bills, Joseph

on 11 October 1849 and arrived at Colonel Williams's Ranch (near present-day Chino) on 11 December, after a difficult journey during which they temporarily became part of the "Death Valley" group that attempted to take a short cut to the California mines.[9] While at Williams's Ranch, Bigler recorded a communication from apostles George A. Smith and Ezra T. Benson, which reveals something of the church's attitudes concerning the availability of gold. Bigler wrote on 6 January 1850 that the two leaders wanted the group to raise $5,000 for them so that "their hands may be liberated and be able to return to the fields of labor [missions] and they will pray the Lord to lead the Brethren in some nook or corner where it lays, as for my part," Bigler added, "I shall be glad to help raise it for them and have their prayers and blessings on my head."

The group left Williams's Ranch on 12 January and finally made their way to "Slap Jack Bar" on the middle fork of the American River where they began searching for gold. Bigler's group worked all summer to build a dam across the river. They were so busy that the young diarist was unable to keep a daily account of his activities. Finally, on 23 September, he took the time to vent his frustrations:

> I have exposed myself to both Indians and we[a]ther more than I ever want to do again, living out in the snow and storms and rain without shelter, some of my brethren have died . . . all of my brethren have been sick having been much exposed working in water up to their arms and necks building dams to get a little gold. . . I am tired of mining and of the country and long to be home among the saints.

Two days later, he penned a more detailed report of the summer's experience.

> I have been at work ever since my arrival at the mines which was last February exposing myself living out in the rains and snow, traveling and prospecting, building and repairing dams, working up to my neck in water and for weeks in water up to my waist and arms, having made but little; the expenses overrun the gain. In August I sent $100 to Father Smith by Brother A. Lyman and we expect to finish our claim in a [few] days and then will leave for our fields of labor. . . . The tithing I paid to Brother Rich and Amasa for myself and Brother Smith was $83.60. That shows

---

Cain, George Q. Cannon, Darwin Chase, Joseph Dixon, William Farrer, Peter Fife, James M. Flake, Henry Gibson, James Hawkins, Peter Hoagland, James Keeler, Thomas Morris, Joseph Peck, J. Henry Rollins, Boyd Stewart, Judson Sheldon Stoddard, and Thomas Whittle.

[9] Part of the non-Mormon contingent of this company perished in what has since become known as Death Valley.

how much I have taken from the earth $836, this would appear that I ought to have lots of money, by me, but I have none. I may say at present and it makes the hair fairly stand upright on my head when I think of it.

On 3 October 1850, after finally completing their dam, the missionaries began to reap the rewards of their labors. Bigler described the events as follows:

> Sunday, October 6th. Last Thursday morning we commenced taking out the gold after laboring so long in building and repairing our dam so often, and today we divided the pile, there being twelve shares, $200.00 apiece.
> Sunday, October 13th. Washing gold all week and today divided 444 dollars each.
> Tuesday, 15th the gold has failed, o what a pity.
> Wednesday, 16th divided 92 dollars apiece. We shall make preparations to leave for the Sandwich Islands forthwith.

The decision to go to the Sandwich Islands (Hawaii) resulted from an apparently spontaneous decision reached in mid-October 1850 at "Slap Jack Bar." One morning, according to Bigler,

> the brethren was called together at our tent by Bro. Rich, he stated that he wanted some of us to go on a mission to the Sandwich Islands to preach the gospel, that his opinion was that it would cost no more to spend the winter there than it would here, that we could make nothing in the wintertime in consequence of so much water in the streams, and another thing provisions would be much higher in the mines and it would cost us more money to stay here and make nothing than if we went to the islands and preach, in his opinion it would be the best thing we could do and the best council he could give. . . . Then he called upon ten of us 1 of which was set apart to go to Oragon with Boyd Stewart, and the remaining 9 was set apart as follows, Thomas Whittle, Thomas Morras, John Dixon, myself, Geo. Cannon, Wm. Farrer, John Berry if he wished, James Keeler, James Hawkins. He then laid his hands on us and set us apart for the mission and blessed us in the name of the Lord, and told us to act as the spirit dictated when we got there.

Each of the nine men dutifully accepted his call, landing in Hawaii in December 1850 to begin what would become one of the more successful proselyting projects in Mormon history.

Many missionaries subsequently called to the Pacific islands were apparently advised to go first to the California gold mines to earn enough to clothe themselves and to pay for their passage. Further evidence for this can be inferred from George Q. Cannon's advice in

[margin note, left:] WENT ON MISSION IN WINTER

[margin note, right:] GOLD MISSIONARIES TO HAWAII VERY SUCCESSFUL

the mid-1850s to discontinue this practice. According to Bigler's journal for 18 July 1857, Cannon urged that they "preach their fitout and not go into the mines or hire out to labor in order to raise the necessary means which has been too often the case with the elders in this country while on their missions." Cannon, with his great dislike for gold mining, decided that the wealthy Saints in California could help the missionaries reach their various fields of labor.

Indeed, the church's colonizing effort in San Bernardino had been financed primarily by California gold. When confronted with the necessity of raising $25,000 for a down payment on Rancho del San Bernardino, Apostle Amasa Lyman, who had spent much of the previous year touring the gold fields and collecting $4,000 in tithing and contributions, returned to the gold regions to encourage Mormon miners to invest in the southern California colony. Later, in 1855, about one hundred men were called by leaders in San Bernardino to go to the gold fields to help liquidate the remaining debt.

The gold rush effectively ended the Mormon hope for isolation in the Great Basin. Mormon historian Leonard J. Arrington, in his *Great Basin Kingdom*, estimated that 10,000 people came through the Salt Lake Valley in 1849 and 15,000 in 1850 and that probably 5,000 passed through in 1851. Although most of the non-Mormon gold seekers remained in the valley on the average six and one-half days, many arrived so late in the year that they spent the winter there. For example, approximately 1,000 wintered in the valley in 1850-51. Some were cured of "treasure fever" and chose to remain and make their homes among the Saints. A few even converted to Mormonism and stayed with the body of the church. Others recognized the opportunities that Salt Lake City offered in the fields of business and merchandising.

Whatever the reason, the gold seekers' presence in the region posed some problems. Should church leaders deal with the "Gentiles" and sell them land, produce, and other valuable commodities? Should they permit their sons and daughters to mix with them socially? The general policy was to treat the outsiders kindly, to deal with them if they did not compete with Mormon merchants, but to discourage social contact. The latter policy was almost impossible to administer, however, and soon Mormon girls were marrying outside the faith. Some were able to convert their husbands, or, in some cases, wives, to Mormonism. Some left with new husbands and wives for California. Others, less fortunate, married unscrupulous persons, called "winter saints," who married for a winter of hospitality with in-laws and

52

(margin note, left side: EXCOMMUNICATED)

then deserted their spouses when spring made it possible to continue to the gold fields. On 18 January 1851, eleven men and women were excommunicated for conduct "unbecoming the character of Saints." The first jury trial held in the State of Deseret was called to decide the fate of these so-called "winter saints."

Hoping to encourage the gold seekers to go to California by way of Fort Hall, the First Presidency issued the following epistle on 7 April 1851:

(margin note, left side: ATTEMP TO SEND GOLD SEEKERS TO FT HALL)

> Hitherto, California emigrants have been accustomed to leave their sick in our hands, at a very heavy expense and depart without notice; to turn their teams loose in our streets, and near our city, which has caused so much destruction of crops and grass, so that if we want a load of hay, we have to go from ten to twenty miles to procure it, and drive our cattle a still greater distance to herd the winter; but since the organization of a municipality, quarantine has been introduced, and no animals are permitted to roam within the corporation . . . ; and when the surrounding lands are fenced, the accommodations in our vicinity, for those who travel by multitudes will be small, indeed; and we believe that it will be more convenient for the great mass of travellers to the mines to go by Fort Hall, or some other route north of this, saving to themselves the expense and hindrance of quarantine, and other inconveniences arising from a temporary location near a populous city, where cattle are not permitted to run at large.

On the other hand, the miners also brought material advantages to the valley. The only community of any size on the main route to California, Salt Lake Valley seemed an oasis to the weary gold seekers. Anxious to replenish their supplies before crossing the desert and through the Sierra to California, they willingly paid good prices for all the surplus food and other supplies the Saints could produce. By the time they reached Salt Lake, they were often more than willing to exchange their heavy, costly wagons, and much of their valuable furniture, extra clothing, and luxury items for food, fresh horses, and a lighter wagon.

(margin note, right side: GOLD SEEKERS GOOD BUSINESS)

Such exchanges fulfilled a prophecy by Heber C. Kimball, who had just returned to the valley in the fall of 1848. Brigham Young's first counselor no doubt startled his congregation by declaring that "within a short time, states goods would be sold cheaper in the streets of Salt Lake City than in New York, and the people would be abundantly supplied with food and clothing." According to Kimball's biography, Charles C. Rich, who was present for Kimball's speech, commented that he did not believe a word of it, and even Kimball himself turned to the others on the rostrum when he returned to his seat and confided, "I'm afraid that I missed it that time." Yet Kimball's prophecy was fulfilled within a few months, for not only did the gold seekers sacrifice their personal possessions, many merchants abandoned their heavily laden wagons in order to proceed more rapidly to the gold regions. When word was received that the merchant ships were flooding the San Francisco market with cheap goods, many of the overland merchants were happy to dispose of their goods for whatever they could get out of them. As a result, one contemporary observer wrote in the *Latter-day Saints' Millennial Star* that almost every article, with the exception of tea and coffee, "was selling on the average of about fifty percent below the wholesale prices in eastern cities."

John D. Lee was even more specific about the bargains gained in trade with the California-bound Gentiles when he recorded in his journal that with the first wave of emigrants

Waggons that was rating from 50 to 125 dols. before the Emigration commenced roling in, were sold & traded during the summer & fall of 1849 from 15 to 25 dollars; Harness from 2 to 15 dollars (Per) set. Oxen, Cows, Horse, Mules, &c were sold & exchanged upon the most reasonable terms. Fresh Horses & mules were soon raised to $200 each, so great was the demand for them. Most of the Emigrants abandoned their waggons when they reached the Valley such as had not befor & proceeded with Pack animals. Coffee & Sugar which had been selling at [$]1.00 Per Pint was frequently sold at from 10 to 15 cts.; Bacon the Same; first rate Sacked Hams at 12 1/2 cts. Lb. & Dry goodes & clothing below the State Prices.

According to Arrington, fresh horses and mules, which normally went for $25 or $30, were sold to the miners for as much as $200. Vegetables, too, "brought a first rate price." Mormons were able to buy wagons at one-fifth the normal price and harnesses for about one-third the usual cost.

Another windfall became known as "picking-up expeditions." Mormons profited by traveling east as far as Fort Laramie and salvaging wagons and goods that had been abandoned by the argonauts. John D. Lee remembered frequently finding

Harness, Tools of Every discription, Provisions, clothings, stoves, cooking vessels, Pouder, Lead, & all most everything, etc. that could be mentioned. . . . Very frequent[ly] some 20 or 30 persons would suround the waggon and plead for a memonts instructions, some of them with consternation depicted on their countenances, their teams worn out, wumen & children on foot & som packing their provision[s], trying to reach Some point of Refuse [refuge]. The general cry was, are you from the Mormon

54

city or vally? Yes. What is the distance? Is there any feed by the way? What will be the change to get fresh animals, Provisions, vegitables, Butter, cheese, &c. could we winter in the vally? Do pray tell us all you can that will benefit us, for we are in great distress. Stop & write us a way bill. We will pay you all you ask. Apples, Peaches (Dried), coffee, sugar, Tea, RIce, Flour, Bacon, &c., was often brought & presented. . . . Truly one of the ancient said that the love of money was the Root of all Evil. It was the love of it that has caused thousands to leave their pleasant homes & comfortable Firesides & thus plunge themselves into unnessary suffering & distress. INTERESTING THOUGHT

In the spring of 1850 some Chicago emigrants abandoned "thirty wagon loads of grain which," Arrington explained, "presumably, the Mormons picked up."

In an effort to supply a circulating medium of exchange in the valley, church officials began minting gold coins at a church mint on 12 September 1849 and continued to do so until 1851. (The Saints also used for a time paper notes they had printed in Kirtland, Ohio.) Unfortunately, the minted coins were overvalued by about 10 to 15 percent because they were based on weight only. This led to their being widely regarded as "debased," especially in California, and they eventually were allowed to disappear. Still the coins provided a temporary medium of exchange in the overland trade.

MINTED GOLD COINS

California gold had a more important effect on Mormon church planning. The unexpected security of trading with California-bound emigrants and the infusion of gold and minted currency encouraged church leaders to bring 10,000 new church members from the Missouri Valley and 30,000 new Saints from the British Islands to colonize the Great Basin. The Perpetual Emigrating Fund was organized and ambitious missionary and colonizing programs were launched.

GOLD = PERPETUAL EMIGRATING FUND

Arrington has conjectured that the Mormon economy may have been enhanced by as much as a quarter of a million dollars between 1849 and 1852 as a result of the gold rush. One Mormon writer, Joseph Holbrook, faithfully interpreted the influx of wealth by writing, "And thus in a few years in this desolated part of the mountains we were beginning to enjoy to some degree that which might have taken years had not the Lord provided for the poor saints by His providence in opening up the gold mines in California and inspiring the Gentiles with a lust for gold."

4.
The
Inner Colonies

Trade with gold seekers and the acquisition of some California gold brought unexpected prosperity to the Mormon pioneers. But these were not the only factors prompting church officials to initiate an extensive colonizing program two years after arriving in the Rocky Mountains. Recognizing that the region had only limited fertile soil and water for the thousands of Mormons being urged to gather in the valley, Brigham Young began calling groups of colonists to settle the neighboring valleys. Although church leaders had purchased Miles Goodyear's fort in Ogden and initiated some small settlements in what is now Davis County (between Salt Lake and Ogden), the program that was to bring Young fame as one of America's greatest colonizers was not instituted until the spring of 1849.

This ambitious program resulted in more than one hundred settlements in the Great Basin during the next decade and well over two hundred by 1869. Historians have noted two kinds of settlements in the Mormon colonizing process: the so-called Inner Colonies, which were founded primarily on the basis of contiguity to the Salt Lake Valley, and the less grandiose Outer Colonies, which were established for such specialized purposes as mining, sea ports, and Indian missions. This chapter describes the development of the Inner Colonies during the Mormons' first decade in the Great Basin.

In his study of westward migration in American history, Frederick Jackson Turner observed that the usual pattern was for settlers to

57

move to the next valley or county rather than travel long distances to acquire new land. Although the Mormons countered this pattern when they made their long trek to the Great Basin, they tended to follow the logical practice of moving only as far as the next area of fertile land, once they had established their base colony. True, they established some outlying colonies for special reasons, but the main colonizing pattern was based on contiguity. Only three of the first forty-five colonies were established in areas not bordering the Salt Lake Valley. Not only did the pioneers follow the principle of contiguity as far as valleys were concerned, they established small villages within a few miles of each other in the same valley. Thus Salt Lake City became the base colony, not only for the entire Great Basin but also for a dozen small communities within the valley. In like manner, Ogden, Provo, Tooele, Manti, Parowan, Fillmore, Nephi, and Brigham City became centers of colonization in their respective regions.[1]   CENTERS

City of Zion plan

The Mormons did not settle on individual farmsteads. Following the basic principles, but not the details, of Joseph Smith's "City of Zion" plan drawn in 1833, they settled in forts or small villages and commuted to their farms. In each area, they first worked on cooperative projects—building a fort, fencing in a big field, and constructing an irrigation system. As soon as possible, they acquired individual city lots and built their own homes and farms. They would continue to work cooperatively on irrigation canals, fences, bridges, and other community projects. The City of Zion plan, which called for each village to be laid out on a grid pattern of rectangles, provided ample land for each family to have its own home, orchard, and garden. Wide streets, with homes set back, gave a feeling of spaciousness, and public squares provided areas for schools, churches, public buildings, and parks. Barns were supposed to be on the farms, out of town, but most pioneers found it more convenient to have their domestic animals housed near their homes.

Mormon sociologist Lowry Nelson suggested that the City of Zion plan was devised to prepare people for the Millennium. Whatever Joseph Smith's intent, small communities proved to be particularly well-adapted to the Great Basin. The lack of sufficient water dictated settling in small towns where streams flowed from the canyons. Such

---

[1] Wellsville, in Cache Valley, was colonized in 1856 but was abandoned in the early summer of 1858 as Johnston's Army approached Salt Lake City. Logan, founded in 1859, became the regional center for Cache Valley after the settlers returned to the northern colonies.

58

villages were more easily defended against Indian attacks and provided an enriched social, cultural, and religious atmosphere.

Believing that their leaders were inspired to establish the Kingdom of God, the Mormon pioneers accepted mission "calls" to colonize new areas and usually remained in a colony until they were "released" from their "missions." Often, men who were well established in Salt Lake City or other centers accepted such calls to settle in far less attractive regions. On 3 June 1849, when Brigham Young called several men to the Pacific islands, he asserted that "when the First Presidency ordered a thing, they need not ask any questions but just do as they were told." According to his unpublished manuscript history, Young concluded that his remarks "ended [the meeting] right off," implying that the men did not question their leader. Such attitudes enabled Young and other Mormon authorities to establish colonies throughout the Great Basin using experienced leaders and men and women possessing a variety of talents and skills.

MISSION CALL TO COLONIZE YOU WENT NO QUESTIONS

The first expansion from Salt Lake City was to other locations within the valley and northward into Davis County. Searching for additional pasturage for their animals, Perrigrine Sessions and Hector C. Haight spent the winter of 1847-48 in an area ten miles north of Salt Lake City and, noticing the richness of the soil and the availability of water, encouraged colonists to settle the present towns of Bountiful and Farmington in 1848 and Kaysville in 1849. Pioneers settled Layton the following year. These early settlers were not "called," but Brigham Young later appointed bishops to preside over each community and called other families to build up these settlements.

At the same time, a number of families, led by John Holladay, were establishing a farming community (called Holladay) on the Big Cottonwood Creek, about nine miles southeast of the base colony, with cabins close together in a village. A few months later, in the fall of 1848, John Neff moved his family to the mill he had built on Mill Creek. He was joined by two other mill builders, Robert and Archibald Gardner, who built a saw mill and a grist mill on the stream. Ultimately, sixteen mills dotted the banks of the creek, supporting a community of millers and farmers called East Mill Creek. In addition, the Salt Lake Valley communities of Sugar House, South Cottonwood, West Jordan, and North Jordan all started in 1848, while Brighton, Granger, and Draper were settled in 1849. Clearly, the valley was beginning to fill up.

Settling Ogden in the north was different from the other pioneering assignments because it involved purchasing Miles Goodyear's Fort

Buenaventura which had been established near the confluence of the Weber and Ogden rivers in 1846. Captain James Brown, of the Mormon Battalion, visited the outpost in August 1847 on his way to California to obtain discharge papers and pay for his troops. Noting that Goodyear had a small garden with "beans ripe and corn in tassell," Brown was convinced that crops could be raised in the region. He may not have decided at that time to purchase the fort upon his return from California, but he had plenty of time to think about the location as he made the long trip to San Francisco and back.

Meanwhile, events were taking place that made the purchase of the fort imperative in the opinion of Mormon leaders. Several dissidents and their families had left the Salt Lake Valley in October for Goodyear's establishment, and the prospect of having a non-Mormon settlement inhabited by apostates and Gentiles seemed intolerable to church leaders. Henry G. Sherwood reported that Brigham Young, before returning to Winter Quarters, advised him to acquire the property. However, Goodyear's asking price of $2,000 was high, and a committee, consisting of Ira Eldredge, Daniel Spencer, and Henry Sherwood, unsuccessfully attempted to raise the money.

A few days later, Captain Brown returned from California with $3,000 in back pay for the Mormon Battalion. The Salt Lake High Council, meeting in special session in late November 1847, decided to use part of the money to purchase Fort Buenaventura. The transaction was completed by the 25th, and Goodyear turned over a deed to his land, all of his improvements, seventy-five cattle, seventy-five goats, twelve sheep, six horses, and a cat "in exchange for the sum of $1,950."[2]

Apparently, Captain Brown was able to convince church leaders that he had invested enough of his own money in purchasing Goodyear's fort to justify his taking over the fort and appropriating the livestock. In any case, he sent his sons Alexander and Jesse to look after the newly acquired property early in January 1848. Two

---

[2] Dale L. Morgan's *History of Ogden* discusses the problems connected with the amount of money Brown carried back from California and the amount used to buy out Goodyear. Morgan asserts that only $3,000 was owed battalion members, not $5,000 as is cited in some works. Milton Hunter, in *Brigham Young the Colonizer*, contends that Brown paid Goodyear 3,000 Spanish pesos, worth approximately $1,150, and that Brown paid this out of his own funds earned as a captain in the battalion and from the percentage he charged the men to collect their back pay. Morgan questions this, stating that Goodyear was paid $1,950 from money belonging to the battalion men and that it is not clear why Brown acquired all of Goodyear's stock, "exercis[ing] almost a proprietary interest in the land."

months later, Brown, accompanied by the remainder of his family and several friends, mainly from among the Mississippi Saints, with whom he had become acquainted during their stay in Pueblo, moved to Fort Buenaventura, which they renamed Brown's Fort and later Brownsville.

The little colony was successful in raising a hundred bushels of wheat in 1848, and their dairy products enabled the Ogden pioneers to survive the severe winter of 1848-49 and to share some of their food with the Saints in the Salt Lake Valley. They were not so generous with non-Mormons, however, and Brown refused both food and lodging to Captain Howard Stansbury and his party, who arrived in Brownsville on 27 August 1849 to survey the region. Stansbury was able to secure food from a "neighboring plantation" but was surprised by the inhospitality of the "surly nabal."

Despite some personality problems, Brown became bishop of the LDS Brownsville Ward in February 1849. Later, in September, Brigham Young visited the settlement and recommended that the colony move to a better site, according to Dale L. Morgan, "on the south side of Ogden's Fork at the point of bench land so that waters from the Weber River and Ogden's Fork might be taken out for irrigation and other purposes." The following month, the October General Conference of the church voted "that a city be laid off in Captain Brown's neighborhood." And in August 1850, Young, accompanied by a number of church leaders, traveled again to Weber County to choose a site for the city. He advised the settlers, according to his manuscript history, to "build good houses, school houses, meeting houses, and other public buildings, fence their gardens and plant fruit trees—that Ogden might be a permanent city and a suitable headquarters for the northern country." Young sent Lorin Farr to preside over the settlement. Farr organized a branch of the church and became the first stake president when the Weber Stake was organized in 1851. He built the first saw and grain mills in Weber Valley and was the first mayor of Ogden, a position he held for twenty years without pay.

Ogden became an important center when a road was built through Weber Canyon, a route many immigrants preferred to Emigration Canyon. Thousands of gold seekers also visited the city on their way to California via Fort Hall. Brigham Young directed many of the Mormon immigrants to settle in the area, and by December 1854, according to Dale L. Morgan, Apostle Wilford Woodruff reported that "the county seat of Weber County is a flourishing place containing some 150 families."

Ogden may have appeared to be flourishing to Woodruff, who had seen it in August 1850, but the new settlers were engaged in a daily struggle to survive. Most had moved from their wagon boxes and "dugouts" along the river banks, but their adobe houses and log cabins were decidedly unpretentious. Roofs were of dirt, and doors were hung on wooden hinges. There were no wooden floors until the Burch Saw Mill was built on the site of Riverdale, south of Ogden. In 1851, Luman A. Shurtliff, father of future Ogden leader Lewis Shurtliff, moved one of his wives and three children into a shanty, 10 feet square. His other wives and four of his first wife's children lived in his wagons until he could build another log house which he described as "tolerable, comfortable with no floor." Settlers obtained fuel from sagebrush dug while clearing the land. They made their own soap, candles, homespun clothing, and shoes. Money was in short supply, and almost all trading was by barter. Much energy went into developing canals for irrigating crops. These streams also turned water wheels to run lathes, sugar mills, and other commercial enterprises and were used to supply culinary water to local householders.

Difficulties with Indians (see chap. 6) made a city wall advisable, projected to be "six feet wide at the bottom, eight feet high and thirty inches at the top." The wall was never completed because the need passed, although the possibility of a wall may have contributed to the increased friendliness of the natives. Ogden leaders tried to solve the Indian problem by assigning Indians to families who were to feed and clothe them during the winter and teach them how to cultivate the land more effectively.

Other northern communities were eventually established at Riverdale, Uinta, Brigham's Fort (Lynne), Slaterville, Harrisville, and North Ogden. Wilford Woodruff's December 1854 report described schools in most of these communities and unusual success in farming. Weber County, with Ogden as its center, was an especially bright spot in the church's early colonization efforts in the Great Basin.

The next logical center for settlement was Utah Valley, separated from the Salt Lake Valley only by a low range of mountains but joined by the Jordan River which flowed from Utah Lake northward into the Great Salt Lake. Mormon leaders were reasonably well informed about Utah Valley by Fremont's and others' reports, and they had been warned by Jim Bridger that the Ute Indians, who occupied the area, were a "bad people" who would rob and abuse a man if they captured him. Bridger advised the Saints to settle the Salt Lake Valley which was not occupied regularly by any tribe.

62

Several Mormon groups had traversed Utah Valley in 1847 and in 1848, and Parley P. Pratt had been authorized to establish trade relations with the Utes but without any success. However, the influx of Mormon immigrants in 1849 made it mandatory for the Mormons to colonize additional locations, and Utah Valley was the first to be occupied that year. Control of this valley was necessary if the Mormons were to carry out their plan of establishing a line of colonies to the Pacific coast since Utah Valley was on the direct route from Salt Lake City to southern Utah. The valley also possessed fertile soil, adequate water for irrigation, pasturage for the cattle, and several canyons filled with timber. Fishing opportunities in Utah Lake as well as in the rivers and streams that flowed from the mountains on the east were also important.

A high council meeting held in Salt Lake City on 10 March 1849 voted unanimously that "a colony of thirty men settle in Utah Valley this spring for the purpose of farming and fishing and instructing the Indians in cultivating the earth and teaching them civilization." Three days later, the twenty-nine men called to settle Utah Valley met with Brigham Young to receive instructions and to organize. John S. Higbee, who had explored the valley with Parley P. Pratt in December 1847, was named leader of the group. His brother Isaac and Dimick B. Huntington were appointed as his counselors. Huntington, who had previously gained some knowledge of the Ute language, also served as interpreter. The men who responded to the call, together with their families, made up a company of about 150 settlers.

Higbee's group arrived on the Provo River on 1 April 1849 and two days later began to build a fort on the south bank, about a mile and a half east of the lake. Named Fort Utah, the settlement was completed in about six weeks and served as a refuge from Indian attacks. A cannon was mounted on a bastion in the center of the fort to protect the settlers from the Indians. Farming lands were opened to the south and west, and by May, 225 acres had been cleared.

In September 1849, Brigham Young and his counselors in the First Presidency, Heber C. Kimball and Willard Richards, accompanied by Thomas Bullock, Truman O. Angell, and John S. Higbee and some of their wives, toured the colony to check on their progress. As usual, Young advised the colonists to move to higher ground and selected a spot two miles to the east where the city of Provo is now located. A new fort was constructed enclosing about 11 acres, and a central meeting place, which could serve as a church and school, as well as meet civic and recreational needs, was erected in the middle of the enclosure.

Serious Indian difficulties (see chap. 6) made remaining in the fort advisable. Settlers began building on city lots soon after a survey was completed in 1851 and tried to build a wall around their community. The threat of Indian attacks soon subsided, however, and they never completed the project. Early industries included a grist mill, a carding mill, a pottery factory, a tannery, and a cabinet shop.

In 1852, the Provo settlers petitioned Brigham Young to send Apostle George A. Smith to preside over them, and the church leader honored their request on 17 July of that year. The Saints built a home for Smith and two of his wives, but, although the wives remained in Provo, Smith was busy with other assignments and spent little time in Utah Valley. According to Smith's report to the *Deseret News*, by September 1853

> Provo contain[ed] over two hundred families, three saw mills, one grist mill, one shingle machine propelled by water, one carding machine, and one manufactory of brown earthen ware. There is also a turning lathe for turning wooden bowls, one threshing machine propelled by water power, and two cabinet shops. A meetinghouse, eighty feet by forty-seven, to be finished with a gallery and steeple has been commenced. . . . Provo River affords a great amount of water power for machinery. We occasionally get a taste of trout from Utah Lake, which are very fine.

Within a short time, other settlements were established in the valley. Lehi, Pleasant Grove, Springville, Payson, Alpine, Spanish Fork, Lindon, and American Fork were all founded in 1850; Cedar Fort (in Cedar Valley, west of Lehi) in 1853; Fairfield in 1855; and Salem and Santaquin by the summer of 1857.

With colonies both north and south of the base in the Salt Lake Valley and the Wasatch Mountains to the east, the logical direction for the pioneers' next move was west. The Great Salt Lake lay directly west of Salt Lake City, and a salt desert stretched for miles west of the lake, but Tooele Valley,[3] on the southwestern shore of the Great Salt Lake and stretching southward for twenty-five miles, appeared

---

[3] There is a difference of opinion as to the origin of the name Tooele. The most probable theory is that the area was named after the Indian chief Tuila. Stansbury's map designated the valley by that name in 1849. However, Bancroft, Tullidge, Whitney, and other historians accept the theory that the name resulted from Thomas Bullock's misspelling of "Tule," a reed-like plant growing in the region.

capable of supporting several settlements. The valley had been partially explored by Brigham Young and fellow apostles in July 1847 and had been traversed by Parley P. Pratt on his exploration journey in December that same year. These men had noted that the soil seemed fertile but that there were only small canyon streams to supply water. There was, however, plenty of grass.

On 17 July 1849, Brigham Young, accompanied by about a dozen men, reconnoitered the valley. About the same time John Bernard brought a herd of cattle into the region and discovered that Howard Stansbury, a surveyor for the U.S. government, had built a small adobe house near the most prominent landmark in the north end of the valley (soon named Adobe Rock) during his explorations in the early 1840s. Three months later, Apostle Ezra T. Benson sent Cyrus and Judson Tolman and Phinias Wright into the valley to build a mill. Settling on a large creek in the south end of the valley, they were soon joined by a few others and built cabins on the east side of Settlement Creek, just south of present-day Tooele City.

Benson, assigned by Brigham Young to build both a grist mill and a saw mill in the valley, brought additional settlers into the area, including John Rowberry, who became the leader of the community. A mill was established at Twin Springs (which locals called "E.T.," after Ezra T. Benson), and the valley was used as a herding ground for Benson's livestock. About twelve families spent the cold winter of 1849-50 in the Tooele area.

Difficulties with Indians forced the Tooele colonists to build a fort in 1851. By 1853, a town site had been surveyed, and the people began to settle their city lots, building a mud wall around three sides of their settlement. Like other colonies, when the Indian threat abated, the settlers discontinued building the wall.

Grantsville, some twelve miles west of Tooele, was founded in the fall of 1849, and Lake Vie and Batesville (Erda) were settled in 1850 and 1851, respectively. E.T. City was founded in 1854. Tooele also became the center for colonizing Rush Valley to the south. Clover (Johnson's Settlement) was founded in 1854, Vernon in 1862, and neighboring St. John's, named after early Mormon leader John Rowberry, in 1867.

Manti, in south-central Utah, was also founded in 1849, but since the settlers did not follow the principle of contiguity, its development might be more properly discussed in the following chapter on the Outer Colonies. However, the settlement's initial purpose—civilizing a band of Ute Indians—failed, and the community soon became the hub of numerous settlements in the Sanpete Valley. Thus, it is probably more appropriate to consider Manti as one of the Inner Colonies.

Manti was founded after Walker (or Wakara), a Ute Indian chief from Sanpitch (Sanpete) Valley, visited Salt Lake City in June 1849. He asked the Mormon leaders to send a group of colonists to live near his tribe and teach them to farm and to live as white men did. Some explorers were sent into the valley two months later, and they recommended the present site of Manti for the colony. Church patriarch Isaac Morley was notified during October General Conference that he was called to establish the new colony and that he would be aided by Charles Shumway and Seth Taft. Settlers were selected and notified that they would be expected to leave as soon as possible. By 28 October 1849, Morley left Salt Lake City with the nucleus of a company headed for southern Utah.

As Morley traveled, his company grew and finally consisted of about 225 people, including 125 men and 100 women. They passed by the fertile areas of Utah Valley, continued on to the present site of Nephi, and then traversed Salt Creek Canyon and journeyed into Sanpete Valley, arriving at the site of Manti on 22 November 1849. Unfortunately, the snow began to fall before many houses were built. A few settlers did begin to build log cabins, while others made dugouts, and still others attempted to live in their wagons for a time. Morley advised the people to move to the south side of the hill and make their dugouts there, and it soon became apparent that his advice was sound. Not long after the colonists' arrival, Walker appeared with some 500 to 700 warriors who pitched their tents about a mile away. They stayed near the settlement throughout the winter, showing a friendly attitude towards the Mormons but demanding food. Morley reported that notwithstanding the settlers' meager provisions, they shared their food with the Indians who sometimes cried because of hunger. The snow continued during the winter, making it difficult for the animals to survive.

In his report the following March, Morley said that the group had lost 41 oxen, 38 cows, 3 horses, and 14 head of young stock, which the Indians took for food. The Mormons were able to maintain reasonably friendly relations with Walker's group, although the chief advised them to travel in companies of eight or ten, to keep well-armed, and to keep a good watch at night. Unfortunately, many of the Indians contracted the measles and died. Meanwhile, the colonists had driven their cattle to warm springs two miles south of the settlement, and the men and boys shoveled snow from the grass to help their starving livestock. The cattles' horns were sharpened to protect themselves against coyotes and wolves, but of the 250 head of cattle, only 100 survived.

Because of the severe winter, the pioneers spent most of their time tending fires, taking care of cattle, and trying to stay alive. By 20 February, Morley reported that they had erected twenty houses but that most of the people were still living in tents and in caves. He noted that they were erecting a school house of pine logs which they expected to have finished in a few days. As spring came, the people planted their crops; by May they had 250 acres of wheat, oats, barley, and potatoes. While waiting for their crops to mature, the pioneers were sustained by ten loads of grain collected in Salt Lake under the direction of the city's bishops.

Brigham Young visited the Manti settlement, arriving on 4 August, and on the following day the group chose a site for the city to be established permanently. In the fall 1850 General Conference, Morley was given the right to select additional men or women to join him, and he chose another 100 men and their families. By the end of 1850, Manti was a well-established livestock and agricultural center, with a population of about 365 people. The city of Manti was granted a charter by the legislature of the General Assembly of Deseret on 7 April 1851.

Following Manti's success, Brigham Young encouraged further settlement in the Sanpete Valley. Spring City was settled under the leadership of James Allred and his sons in 1851. Pleasant Creek Settlement, now Mount Pleasant, was established the same year, and Ephraim was occupied during the fall and winter of 1852-53. Many of the settlers were Danish, and towns such as Ephraim and Spring City soon came to be known as Little Denmark. Other early settlements in the Sanpete Valley included Fountain Green, Moroni, Fairview, and Gunnison, all of which were settled in 1859.

The Manti colonists had passed an attractive location on Salt Creek on their way to aid Chief Walker's people. And Brigham Young was well aware that the area immediately south of Utah Valley was on the most direct route to the Pacific coast. In July 1851, Young called Joseph Heywood to "pick up volunteers" to establish a settlement on Salt Creek. Heywood gathered twenty families and began erecting a town they called Nephi. They first surveyed the area in the fall of 1851, and by December Heywood could report to the *Deseret News* that "about 12 houses have been erected: viz. 3 built of adobies, two of willows plastered inside and out, [a] two-story house built of four inch planks, and the balance of logs obtained from a distance of about 10 miles. Our roofs and flooring are principally of lumber cut at Hamilton and Potter's Mills, Sanpete Valley, distance about 30 miles from Nephi." Mona, five miles north of Nephi, was founded by December 1854.

Within a month of the settlement of Nephi, a central colony in the next major valley to the south was being settled by seventeen families under the leadership of Anson Call. Named Fillmore, in honor of the U.S. president who had signed the bill granting territorial status to Utah, the city was almost exactly in the center of the territory. Located in the Great Pauvan Valley which stretches from the rim of the Great Basin on the south to the Utah and Cedar valleys on the north, Fillmore was expected to become the center of a great colonizing effort. The broad expanse of level land caused Mormon explorers to overestimate the location's potential, but even so the area occupied an important site. In addition to its central location, Fillmore was on the direct route to the seaports in southern California.

Brigham Young was so impressed with the reports of the area that he determined to make Fillmore the capital of the territory and signed, on 4 October 1851, a legislative act designating that Millard County be formed and that Fillmore City be the "seat of Government of the Territory." Accompanied by prominent men of the church and territory, Young traveled to the site soon after signing the act to help select the proper location for the capital city. Before leaving, Young advised the colonists to build a fort, which they did, according to Milton R. Hunter, by "erecting their houses in close formation . . . in the shape of a triangle." In his message to the 1851 territorial legislature, Young asserted that the "Pauvan Valley will sustain a large and dense population" and encouraged colonists to settle there to build up the capital city. By 1853, more than 300 church members had occupied the valley which continued to grow.

In addition to homes and public buildings, the settlers were called upon to erect a state house. As conceived, the building would consist of four wings capped by a mammoth dome. The colonists were able to complete the south wing by December 1855 at a cost of $32,000, but changing circumstances kept them from completing any more of the territorial capitol building. The legislature met in the building in December 1855, but this proved to be the only session that would ever meet there. Legislators found life in Salt Lake City more to their liking. A year later Salt Lake City was designated the temporary territorial capital, and Fillmore's role was reduced to being the center colony of the Millard region. Holden was founded in 1855, Meadow in the spring of 1857, and Deseret and Kanosh in 1859.

68

While settlements were being established south of Utah Valley, a few pioneers were pushing north of the Weber settlements into Box Elder County. The first settlement was begun in March 1851, when five families erected cabins on North Willow Creek, some fifteen miles north of Ogden. Eventually naming their settlement Willard, these families were joined by several additional families that fall and the next year. Willard was not destined to become the hub city of the Box Elder region, however, for eight or nine families went a few miles further north to Box Elder Creek and founded Brigham City in the spring of 1851. The little colony was almost surrounded by a group of 500 Shoshone Indians, who appeared to be friendly as long as their demands were satisfied but whose presence was a serious threat to the survival of the colony. Fort Davis was constructed by the fall of 1851, and a larger fort was built in 1853. Nearly all of the colonists spent the winters of 1853, 1854, and 1855 in the fort. Many Scandinavian emigrants were sent to Brigham City during 1852 and 1853, and the community assumed a Nordic atmosphere despite the fact that a Welsh party had been the first to colonize the area.

Apostle Lorenzo Snow's 1854 assignment to lead the Brigham City colony was a turning point in the history of the settlement. Called to gather fifty more families to strengthen the colony, Snow brought not only more settlers but also efficient leadership to the community. He encouraged drama and other cultural activities, as well. But he is perhaps best remembered for later establishing a cooperative association that was responsible for making Brigham City one of the most prosperous and attractive communities in the territory. The region continued to develop, and additional communities were founded at Harper in 1852 and at Perry in 1853.

Wellsville, in Cache County, was chosen as a site for a settlement by Peter Maughan, who had become dissatisfied with Tooele due to a series of dry years there. Traveling from Brigham City, he passed through Box Elder Canyon and emerged into Cache Valley in July 1856. Maughan selected a site in the southern end of the valley, returned to Tooele, and recruited six other families to join him. Most of the settlers were immigrants from the British Isles. Arriving in the valley on 15 September 1856, the colonists were forced to form their wagons into a fort for protection against Indians who regarded Cache Valley as a favorite hunting ground. A fort was completed in 1857, but the community was abandoned in 1858 due to the "move south" when Johnston's Army was approaching the Salt Lake Valley. Before the move south, however, the little town of Mendon was started by Alexander B. Hill and Robert Hill. Colonists returned in the fall, but

69

the following year the city of Logan was founded and soon eclipsed Wellsville as the hub of Cache Valley.[4]

There can be no doubt that the "call" was important in settling communities throughout the territory, but no uniform pattern was followed in calling leaders and settlers. The Davis County settlers called themselves at first, and later Brigham Young appointed leaders and called families to strengthen the settlements. James Brown was assigned to settle the Ogden area by the stake presidency and high council of the Salt Lake Stake while Brigham Young was in Winter Quarters. Brown's call may have resulted from his having volunteered to purchase Fort Buenaventura from Miles Goodyear. The Provo colonists were called individually, but the Tooele colony resulted from the assignment of an apostle to build mills and herd livestock. Isaac Morley was appointed to select a group and lead in the settlement of Sanpete County. Two years later, James Allred was assigned to go to Sanpete and choose a location for his "numerous posterity," resulting in the founding of Spring City. Joseph Heywood was told to "pick up volunteers" to settle Nephi, and Anson Call was assigned to "raise fifty families" to settle Fillmore. Brigham City was founded by volunteers, although Brigham Young began directing Scandinavian groups to settle there as well. Wellsville was founded by Peter Maughan who received permission to leave Tooele and look for a new location. Any of the other Tooele settlers who wished to follow Maughan were given permission to do so.[5] Although colonization was not always well organized, when calls were issued they were taken seriously, and there was some attempt to send certain nationalities to colonize specific areas to avoid language and cultural differences and encourage compatibility.

Additionally, Brigham Young relied on trusted apostles to lead in the colonizing program. As noted, Ezra T. Benson was sent to settle Tooele and Lorenzo Snow was assigned to preside in Brigham City. Charles Rich and Amasa Lyman were chosen to establish a colony in California (see the next chapter), and George A. Smith was called to supervise the iron mining mission. A few years later, Smith,

[4] In addition to the Cache Valley settlements, other early communities were established in high mountain valleys to the east of Ogden, Salt Lake City, and Provo: Wanship in 1854, Morgan in 1855, Peoa in 1857, and Midway and Heber in 1859.

[5] By contrast, the calls to the Outer Colonies were more specific (as is detailed in the following chapter). Men called on Indian missions heard their names called from the pulpit at General Conference. A notable exception (discussed in chap. 5) was when apostles Amasa Lyman and Charles C. Rich had so many volunteers to go to the San Bernardino region that they exceeded their quota.

aided by Apostle Erastus Snow, established the cotton mission in and around St. George (named in Smith's honor). Orson Hyde was assigned colonizing missions in Green River County (Wyoming) and in Carson Valley (Nevada) before being assigned to Sanpete County. And Rich was called to colonize the Bear Lake region after the recall of the San Bernardino colony.

The apostles deserve the recognition they have received for their foresight, but the real leaders of Mormon colonization were the bishops of the respective settlements. In addition to colonizing an area, these men were expected to care for their own families, be responsible for women whose husbands were on missions for the church, as well as care for widows, orphans, and the sick and aged members of their groups. They were also expected to carry out the programs of the church, including presiding at worship services, supervising local schools, collecting and distributing tithing, and watching the morals and spiritual attitudes of their flocks. They were required to organize irrigation companies, build forts, negotiate with local Indians, and promote economic projects for the benefit of the communities. Bishops were usually appointed probate judges and were expected to preside at bishops' courts. They were called to organize cattle drives and raise money and labor for special projects such as building telegraph lines, freighting supplies, and rescuing immigrants. They were expected to provide homes, goods, and employment for new members of the communities until they could establish themselves. Bishops were also expected to set an example to the communities in the matter of plural marriage. New men were chosen to replace recalcitrant bishops who refused to take additional wives. Truly, the bishops were the key players in the colonization of the Great Basin.

Also important were the pioneer women.[6] These wives, mothers, sisters, daughters, and children confronted the same challenges and difficulties as the men. In addition, they bore and raised children, often in primitive conditions without competent medical supplies or doctors. Many women faced these difficulties without the support of husbands, who were sent on proselyting, colonizing, and other specialized missions and were away from their homes for months or even years. Some women, though married polygamously,

[6] True, B. H. Roberts included a chapter in the third volume of his *Comprehensive History of the Church* on "Pioneer Women." But the title is misleading since only two and one-half of the chapter's twenty-seven pages are devoted to the role played by women in colonizing the Mormon communities.

had to <u>fend for themselves</u> to a considerable extent, since their husbands had other wives and families to care for. Tragically, under such circumstances, <u>many women</u> died at an early age, while others lived lives of <u>bitterness</u>, <u>hardship</u>, and <u>disappointment</u>. But from among those who survived emerged a remarkable generation of strong women who became <u>midwives</u>, <u>medical doctors</u>, <u>leaders in womens' rights movements</u>, <u>teachers</u>, and <u>managers of farms</u>, <u>stores</u>, and <u>other businesses</u>. Their lives, examples, and contributions constitute a significant legacy to the Mormon church.

5.
The
Outer Colonies

The first pioneers to settle any distance from Mormon church headquarters were called in the fall of 1849 to travel 135 miles south of Salt Lake City, where they established a colony near Chief Walker's band of Ute Indians. Naming their community Manti, after a Book of Mormon city, they were to assist and prose-lyte the Indians. Settlements were subsequently established in what is now Iron County in 1851, some 265 miles south of Salt Lake City. Later that year San Bernardino, California, more than 600 miles from the center stake, was founded. By December 1854, missionaries to the Indians had founded Santa Clara, Utah, and in 1855 another group of Indian missionaries established a fort at Las Vegas, Nevada, add-ing yet another link in what appeared to be a "Corridor to the Pacific."

Other colonies were established in Green River Valley, Wyoming, in the Salmon River country of Idaho, in the Carson Valley area of western Nevada and at the Colorado crossing at Elk Mountain in southeastern Utah. Unfortunately, with the exception of Manti and the Iron County communities, all of these colonies failed or were in serious trouble by 1857 when the threat of war with the United States government seemed to justify their recall. The motivation behind this ambitious colonial venture and the reasons for its failure form the subject of this chapter.

There is evidence that Brigham Young had initially hoped to create a stronghold in Upper California and in Oregon, including Vancouver Island. Apostle Parley P. Pratt, in a letter to Isaac Rogers, dated 6 September 1845, alluded to such intentions: "I expect we shall stop near the Rocky Mountains about 800 miles nearer than the coast, say, 1,500 miles from here and there make a stand, until we are able to enlarge and extend to the coast." Almost a year later, when asked to furnish a battalion of men to aid in taking California from Mexico in the Mexican War, church leaders saw the request as an opportunity to be the first settlers in that vast territory. "It has always been 'get out of the way Mormons ... we are the old citizens,' " said Brigham Young, according to Apostle John Taylor's journal for 1 July 1846, "whereas if we go and help take the country we will at least have an equal right, I don't want anybody to be in those wildernesses and undiscovered [territories?] before we are.' Eight days later, Pratt wrote, "It is the mind and will of God that we should improve the opportunity which a kind providence has now opened for us to secure a permanent home ... where we shall be the first settlers and a vast majority of the people." Taylor had already asserted in his journal, "If we were to bring in 30,000 inhabitants I do not know but we would be the Old Citizens and I do not know but what we would have a lot of land allotted to us. We would have a great story to tell that we fought for the liberties of the country and our children can say our fathers fought and bled for this country."[1]

After making his initial exploration of Salt Lake Valley, Brigham Young stated on 28 July 1847, according to Wilford Woodruff's journal, that "he intended to have every hole and corner from the Bay of San Francisco known to us." Later, on 9 March 1849, Young wrote, "We hope soon to explore the valleys three hundred miles south and also the country as far as the Gulf of California with a view to settlement and to acquiring a seaport." The extensive territory included in the State of Deseret in 1849 is ample evidence of the Mormon plan to acquire control over an area where "scores of thousands will join us in our secluded retreat." The struggle for survival during the first two years precluded the Saints from carrying out this program, although some exploration of the routes to California was made. But by the fall of 1849, church leaders were ready to begin extensive colonizing efforts, including the inner colonies (previously discussed) and settlements in more distant areas of western North America.

---

[1] This desire to be the first settlers came out of the Saints' earlier difficulties in Ohio, Missouri, and Illinois and prompted their decision to colonize the Great Basin rather than the settled areas of California. Brigham Young's apparent approval of Samuel Brannan's colony remaining in San Francisco and the British Saints' colonizing Vancouver Island indicates that he wanted to establish colonies throughout the West, not just the Rocky Mountains.

74

Before establishing new colonies, Young felt it was necessary to explore the region more thoroughly. Waiting until after the harvest was completed in mid-November 1849, he called a company of fifty men to organize themselves as the Southern Exploring Company under the leadership of Apostle Parley P. Pratt, with William W. Phelps and David Fullmer as counselors. This company was instructed to explore the valleys southward and to find places for settling the Saints in the southern part of the "mountains of Israel." Throughout their journey, they kept a careful and complete record of soil conditions, vegetation, streams, timber, pasturage, and any other information that might assist Brigham Young in determining where future colonies should be established. The small company visited Fort Utah (later Provo) and then traversed Utah Valley and Juab Valley as far as Salt Creek (later Nephi). They then left the direct route to California and followed Salt Creek Canyon into Sanpete Valley, reaching Manti only twelve days after Isaac Morley had arrived with his colonists assigned to help Chief Walker's Utes.

After visiting with the Morley contingent, Pratt and the others continued south and reached the Sevier River, which they estimated to be 149 miles from Salt Lake City. Here they contacted Chief Walker, presenting him with a supply of tea, coffee, sugar, bread, meat, and medical advice. They continued to follow the Sevier River, but by 10 December the temperature had dropped to around 20 degrees below zero and the river had frozen. They managed to make their way into present-day Marysvale and seemed pleased with the valley. As they continued up the Sevier River they discovered an impassable canyon and had to retrace their steps and look for a route across the Wasatch Mountains.

By 20 December, the expedition had made its way through the mountains and camped in the northern extremity of Little Salt Lake Valley. At this point they decided to split into two groups. Twenty men on horseback with pack animals, under Pratt's leadership, planned to explore the Virgin River territory while the remaining men stayed at camp under the leadership of David Fullmer. After leaving Little Salt Lake Valley, Pratt's group emerged into a much larger valley and camped on Muddy Creek, which became the site of Cedar City. They noted that on the southwestern border of the valley thousands of acres of cedars flourished, with an almost inexhaustible supply of fuel in the form of coal underneath. The scribe reported that "in the center of these forests rises a hill of the richest iron ore. Water, soil, fuel, timber, and mineral wealth of this and Little Salt Lake Valleys, are capable of sustaining and employing from

75

50,000 to 100,000 inhabitants, all of which would have these resources more conveniently situated than any other settlements the company had seen west of the States."

Continuing south, the explorers crossed the rim of the Great Basin and descended into Utah's Dixie country where the elevation dropped over 3,000 feet in less than 50 miles and the climate was warm and springlike. The company followed the Virgin River to its juncture with the Santa Clara near present-day St. George where they arrived on 1 January 1850. Having learned from the Indians that the country further south was not promising, they traveled north up the Santa Clara River to rejoin the camp in Little Salt Lake Valley. They ascended the rim of the Great Basin and spent the night in a valley which subsequently became known as Mountain Meadows. On 7 January, they reached Fullmer's camp, which had moved to the present site of Parowan. While Pratt and his companions explored the Dixie country, those left in Fullmer's camp obtained a thorough knowledge of Little Salt Lake Valley and adjacent canyons and mountains. They discovered large quantities of timber and iron ore and were so pleased with the valley that they regretted leaving.

On 9 January, the entire company began the difficult journey home, traveling through valleys that paralleled those through which they had come. They noted an excellent place for settlement on Beaver Creek and also on Chalk Creek, the present site of Fillmore. Unfortunately, snow had begun to fall four days earlier, and on 18 January a foot of snow fell in one night, making it two feet deep on the level. Because of the depth of snow, the group was unable to continue and instead made camp on Chalk Creek. Pratt wrote in his journal:

> Snowing severely. We held a council and finding our provisions would only sustain half of our company til spring, and traveling with the wagons was impossible, we decided upon leaving half the company to winter with the wagons and cattle, the other half with some of the strongest mules and horses should attempt to reach Provo, the southern frontier at a distance of upwards of more than 100 miles. The company that remained were mostly young men without families; my counselor David Fullmer being placed in command.

Pratt's company of twenty men had a difficult time because of the continuing snow storms. Pratt wrote that one morning,

> we found ourselves so completely buried in the snow that no one could distinguish the place where we lay. Someone rising began shoveling the others out. This being found too tedious a business, I raised my voice

like a trumpet and commanded them to arise, and all at once there was a shaking among the snow piles; the graves were opened, and all came forth. We called this Resurrection Camp.

Slowly an advance group made its way into Provo on 28 January, by now entirely without food. The remainder of Pratt's contingent arrived three days later. Both groups continued to Salt Lake City, arriving on 2 February 1850, without any loss of life, having traveled 700 miles during severe winter weather. Members of the company who were left at Chalk Creek with the wagons, oxen, and cattle arrived at Salt Lake City safely the following March.

This company's reports helped determine where colonies should be established. During the next ten years, Brigham Young dispatched colonists to practically every site recommended by Pratt's expedition, and Latter-day Saints were building homes on several of the best sites within the next two or three years. Six months after Pratt's company returned, Young and his counselors had made arrangements to establish a colony in Little Salt Lake Valley on Center Creek (Parowan).

[margin note: A SETTLEMENT AT ALL OF PRATT'S SUGGESTIONS]

Two factors contributed to the desire for a line of settlements stretching from the Salt Lake Valley to a seaport in southern California. The first had to do with the dissatisfaction among Mormon leaders with the immigration route then employed. Many of those from England landed in New Orleans, transferred to river packets sailing up the Mississippi and Missouri rivers, and then made their way west by ox-teams and covered wagons. This was unsatisfactory for a variety of reasons. Transferring from ocean-going vessels to river steamers was expensive, and many immigrants were becoming sick with a strange malady called river fever (probably malaria). Brigham Young, writing in March 1849, added that many immigrants arriving in New Orleans and St. Louis were exposed to bad company and that "few of them reach the body of the church in as good spirits as they started."

Regarding the need for a better immigration route, Young suggested, during a meeting of the Twelve Apostles on 8 March 1849, that if they could find a practical wagon route up the Arkansas or Rio Grande rivers, the immigrants could avoid contact with the "corrupt apostates and Gentiles that swarm the river ports." But this would not solve the health problems. He then suggested that they bring immigrants across the Isthmus of Panama or other Central American country and to a designated Pacific coast port. With this plan, thousands of converts from the British Isles and Europe, who were

[margin note: A MORMON CORRIDOR IDEA]

77

being encouraged to build up the Mormon zion in the Great Basin, could avoid much of the expense and many of the difficulties involved in the immigration routes then used. If they could come by sea to a Pacific port and be met there by Mormon representatives, they could be conducted immediately to a Mormon base and sent from there to colonize the region.

Another development promoting the idea of a Mormon corridor to the sea was the creation of the State of Deseret in March 1849. Alerting Apostle Orson Pratt, the church's mission president in the British Isles, to the possibility of a Pacific port for British and European emigrants, the leaders wrote,

> We have petitioned the Congress of the United States for the organization of a territorial government here, embracing a territory about 700 miles square, bounded on the north by Oregon, latitude forty-two; the east by the Rio Grande del Norte; south by the river lying between the United States and Mexico, near latitude, thirty-two; and west by the seacoast and the California mountains.[2]

The extensive territory claimed by the State of Deseret included the seaports of San Pedro (near Los Angeles) and San Diego, thus providing a Pacific port needed by the leaders for commerce and to expedite immigration.

In the fall of 1850, a company was sent to colonize Iron County with the dual purpose of providing a halfway station between southern California and Salt Lake Valley and to produce agricultural products to support an iron industry. A call for volunteers appeared in the *Deseret News* on 27 July 1850:

> Brethren of Great Salt Lake City and vicinity, who are full of faith and good works, who have been blessed with means, are informed by the Presidency of the Church, that a colony is wanted at Little Salt Lake this fall, and that fifty or more good effective men with teams and wagons, provisions and clothing are wanted for one year.
>
> Seed grain in abundance and tools and all their variety for a new colony are wanted to start from this place immediately after the fall conference to repair to the Valley of the Little Salt Lake without delay. They're to sow, build, and fence, erect a saw and grist mill, establish an iron foundry as speedily as possible, and do all other acts and things necessary for the preservation and safety of an infant settlement.

Apostle George A. Smith was chosen to head the new colony,

---

[2] Initially, church leaders had considered applying for a territorial government of their own, but by August 1849 they had decided to apply for statehood.

and on 27 October he issued a call for one hundred men to accompany him. Three weeks later a notice appeared in the *Deseret News*, giving the names of those who were chosen and calling for an additional one hundred volunteers. Ten days before Christmas, the volunteers rendezvoused at Provo and sustained Smith as president of the company. Traveling to Payson, the group made an inventory which indicated that there were 120 males and 31 females over fourteen years of age, and 18 children under fourteen, for a total of 169 persons. They were supplied with grain, flour, wheat, corn, oats, barley, potatoes, and groceries, as well as a good deal of equipment, some arms, and a sizable number of oxen, horses, mules, cows, and beef cattle. The company left their camp on the Provo River on 16 December 1850 and arrived at Center Creek in Iron County on 13 January 1851. Naming their settlement Parowan, they were joined by other incoming Saints until the population reached 360. They set up winter quarters by placing the wagon boxes in a straight line facing south. A 300-square-foot enclosure of brush reinforced with cottonwoods and adobes provided a fort as well as a corral for the animals. They cleared a field of 500 acres and constructed an irrigation canal. Men acquired ownership of land by drawing for a ten-acre block and were also entitled to a garden plot near the fort.

PAROWAN

A company of English, Scotch, and Welsh miners and iron manufacturers was organized at Parowan to begin manufacturing iron. Selecting a site nineteen miles south, where coal and iron ore were plentiful, they began settling Cedar City on 5 November 1851. By the end of the year, the historian of the Iron County settlements wrote,

> In the midst of semi-hostile savages and guarding, fencing, farming, and exploring, and building houses, mills, and so on, we have had our prayers answered in the preservation of our lives and property. January 1, 1852 came upon us in the estimation of a pleased God. The whole people were called together in a mighty prayer. We thanked the God of Israel for his past blessings upon our labors, and presently called upon him to bless us in the future and to enable us to maintain ourselves in this desert land, to protect us from the Indians, and to accomplish the mission we were sent to perform, namely the manufacture of iron.

While the farmers attended to cultivation, the iron workers turned to furnace building and accumulating supplies for iron manufacturing. A small amount of iron, sufficient for nails to shoe a horse and a pair of andirons, was produced inside the old fort by means of blacksmith bellows. Although the experiment reassured them they could produce iron, it also revealed that the local coal, and its by-product

(margin notes, top left) COAL NOT GOOD ENOUGH FOR MANU OF IRON

coke, were not suited to this purpose. They were forced to gather and use dried pitch pine and charcoal to try to make a fire hot enough for smelting. Despite the problems, the men worked to haul the ore and stockpile heaps of charcoal and pitch pine.

Meanwhile Brigham Young communicated with Mormon agents in England to secure capital for the iron mission. Erastus Snow and Franklin D. Richards succeeded in raising 4,000 pounds sterling for the Deseret Iron Company, organized in Liverpool on 28 April 1852. Young, not yet informed of the success in England, visited the iron colony in Cedar City on 11 May. A superintendent of iron workers and a clerk were elected under his guidance, and work continued until 29 September when the furnace was charged and the entire population gathered in the evening around a huge bonfire. There were short talks, a prayer, and the furnace was fired and the blast turned on. Hours of expectation preceded the crucial moment when tapping would reveal the success or failure of a year's hard labor. The next morning, the furnace was tapped and "a small quantity of iron run out which caused the hearts of all to rejoice. Hosanna, hosanna, hosanna to God and the Lamb rang through the wilderness to announce the first iron production west of the Mississippi. Before nightfall a committee of five was riding hard towards Salt Lake City, carrying samples of the iron ore to Brigham Young."

At the same time, Richards and Snow had left England for Utah, where they reported to Young on their work organizing the Deseret Iron Company. He approved what had been done and advised them to go to Iron County and reorganize the iron program. By November 1852, the two apostles were in Cedar City and purchased the entire operation for $2,865.65. They also appointed new supervisors and encouraged James A. Little and Philip K. Smith to open coal mines to fuel the furnace. Within ten days after Little and Smith commenced work, they found several veins of coal. One vein of special richness was traced for several miles along the precipitous side of the mountain far above the valley. A road to this deposit was constructed at a cost of $6,000. It now appeared that all factors necessary for the production of iron were available and that they could begin to produce iron cheaply and rapidly. Unfortunately, such was not the case.

(margin note, left) FALSE HOPES

The outbreak of war with Chief Walker's Utes in July 1853 suspended operations, as colonists had to defend themselves. Two months later, the industry received another blow. Floods swept down Coal Creek, carrying bridges and dams with it. The torrent forced down huge boulders—some weighing twenty to thirty tons. The site

(margin note, lower left) INDIANS WAR FLOOD

of the ironworks was inundated to the depth of three feet. Large amounts of charcoal, lumber, and wood were carried away, and the remaining property was greatly damaged.

By April 1855, the iron workers had built a large furnace and were able to make as much as 1,700 pounds of good iron in twenty-four hours, but they were short of laborers and called for an additional 150 men. Brigham Young volunteered to send two teams and teamsters and called for others to go to Iron County. The company continued to function, but circumstances, over which the Saints had no control, finally caused the failure of the iron industry.

FINALLY IRON WAS A FAILURE

Extremely cold weather in 1855-56 hampered the process of manufacturing. Coal Creek was frozen, and snow lay so deep in the canyons that workers could not secure coal for three months. Additional expenses for new machinery were too great for the young company which had made no profits. In September 1857 the Mountain Meadows Massacre occurred (see chap. 14). Cedar City, with a population of between 400 and 900, had furnished most of the men participating in the massacre. In shame and despair, people began leaving the community, and the iron works soon closed down. The following year Johnston's Army brought a considerable amount of iron products into the territory lessening the demand for the manufactured product. The Deseret Iron Company was disbanded. Cedar City continued to survive even after the iron failure because the settlement also enjoyed an excellent agricultural location. Although almost half of its inhabitants moved, the community became a center for agricultural activity in Iron County.

A few months after the iron missionaries had settled Parowan, they were visited by a large company of Latter-day Saints led by apostles Amasa Lyman and Charles C. Rich, who had been assigned to establish a Mormon colony in southern California near a Pacific port. Lyman had previously been sent to California in the summer of 1849 to look after the church's interests and to work out a political compromise with the Californians; and Rich had been called to organize a stake in the San Francisco Bay region. Arriving in California in December 1849, Rich carried a letter from Brigham Young instructing both men to investigate the conduct of Samuel Brannan, collect delinquent tithes, receive donations for the Perpetual Emigration Fund, and

> take into consideration the propriety or impropriety of continuing to hold an influence in western California by our people remaining in the region, and if so, to gather them into healthy locations in communities

together, that they might be able to act in concert and receive instructions with facility; otherwise, to gather up all that are worth saving and return to the valley with all speed.

Lyman was also instructed to obtain information regarding good locations for a chain of settlements from Salt Lake to the Pacific Coast.

After spending several weeks contacting church members in the gold fields, Lyman and Rich reported to the First Presidency that "the only suitable place for a colony of the brethren is in the southern part of the state." Consequently, on 23 February 1851, a number of missionaries were called to establish a settlement in southern California.

Young recorded his reasons for such a colony in his journal:

> Elders Amasa M. Lyman and C. C. Rich, with some twenty others, having received my approbation in going to Southern California, were instructed by letter to select a site for a city or station, as a nucleus for a settlement, near Cajon Pass, *in the route already commenced from this place to the Pacific*; to gather around them the Saints in California; to search out the best route, and establish as far as possible the best location for stations between Iron County and California, in view of a mail route to the Pacific, to cultivate grapes, sugar cane, cotton, and other desirable fruits and products; to obtain information concerning the Tehuantepec route, or any other across the isthmus, or the passage around the Cape Horn, with a view to the gathering of the Saints from Europe; to plant the standard of salvation in every country and kingdom, city and village, on the Pacific and the world over, as fast as God should give the ability.

As far as Young was concerned, the colony got off to a bad start when the pioneers gathered at Peeteneet Creek (later Payson) to prepare for their journey. Instead of a small company of twenty or thirty, Young found 437 volunteers. He was so upset to find "saints running to California, chiefly after the God of this world," that he was unable to address them.

Disappointment also awaited the pioneers in California. When Lyman and Rich arrived at Isaac Williams's Chino Ranch, which earlier had been offered for sale at a reasonable price, they found that Williams had increased the amount. In desperation, they abandoned the Williams's ranch and agreed to pay the Lugo brothers $77,500 for their Rancho Del San Bernardino and immediately left for northern California to contact Mormons in the gold fields to secure funds for a down payment. Subsequent payments, with significant interest penalties, plagued the community for the next six years. Ultimately, Young recalled the apostles who had acted as trustees and persuaded Ebenezer Hanks to take over their obligations.

Despite the inauspicious beginning and heavy indebtedness, the San Bernardino community prospered, attracting many of the men and women who had migrated to San Francisco with Sam Brannan, as well as former Mormon Battalion soldiers and a few Saints from the gold fields. A church estimate for 1856, reported in the *Western Standard*, put the population of the San Bernardino colony optimistically at 3,000, making it the second largest Mormon colony in the West.[3] Benjamin Hayes, a non-Mormon from Los Angeles, visited the settlement in 1854 and gave the following report:

> This city continues to flourish steadily. It is certainly one of the best, if not the very best tract of land in California; well-wooded, with abundance of water, and the soil adapted to every species of culture. This year the wheat was raised in a common field, amounting to near 4,000 acres, and averaging thirty-two bushels to the acre. They have a fine flouring mill in operation and the streams from the mountains might turn the machinery of the largest manufacturing town in the whole world. This rancho alone would comfortably sustain 100,000 souls and the neighboring ranchoes as many more. At least one hundred new buildings have been put up within the last four months, principally adobe—some of them very fine. We noticed particularly the mansion of President Lyman and the new hotel of our excellent host, Bishop Crosby. Already about two-thirds of the city lots have been sold. There is a great demand for mechanics, particularly carpenters, whose wages are $3.00 per day. Very soon they expect to begin building with brick.

Despite this prosperity, Brigham Young discouraged Utah Saints from going to California. In a letter to John Eldridge in July 1854, Young wrote, "If it so be that nothing else can satisfy your feelings but to go to San Bernardino, why go—and do the best you can, and do not complain if you see the day that you wish to return to this country more, and are less able than now."

In March 1855, Young made one attempt to relieve the San Bernardino colony of debt by trying to organize a cattle drive in Utah, as described in the following circular to all church leaders and members in Utah:

---

[3] The 1860 census identifies Salt Lake City as having a population of 8,100; Provo, 2,030; Ogden, 1,463; and San Bernardino, 567. This raises some question about the accuracy of the church's estimate four years earlier, as well as the percentage of Mormons who refused to return to Utah in 1857-58.

Owing to the scarcity of money in that country [San Bernardino], and the hardness of the times, our brethren having no prospect of being able to meet this debt in time to save the ranch, we have, therefore assumed to help them raise the required amount.

It is to this end that we address this circular to you, that we may receive your assistance to accomplish this object.

We propose to drive sufficient cattle to California in order to obtain the means that we cannot raise in this Territory, and make up the deficiency the brethren of the ranch cannot supply; and we wish the brethren to let us have money, cows and oxen as they can spare, either on tithing or as a loan until the property of the ranch be made available to refund it.

Apparently there was little positive response to this request for there is no record of such a drive being made or of Young's ever having pursued the project further. The debt remained, as evidenced by the call at the June conference in San Bernardino for men to go "to every county in California and preach the gospel and to raise $35,000.00, the amount yet due on the mortgage."

By this time, the colony was also suffering from other problems, which became so serious that Brigham Young called his apostles home and wrote the colony off as a failure several months before he became aware of the approach of the U.S. Army. These difficulties included a California court's ruling that allotted the colonists less than half of the land they had purchased, troubles with squatters, apostasy—because of differences over the governance of the colony—difficulties with the Indians, and anti-Mormon sentiment because of polygamy.

Young, in addressing the church's 1857 April conference in Salt Lake City, shared his feelings on the situation. According to the *Deseret News*, he explained:

We are in the happiest situation of any people in the world. We inhabit the very land in which we can live in peace; and there is no other place on earth that the Saints can now live without being molested. Suppose for instance, that you go to California. Bros. Charles C. Rich and Amasa Lyman went and made a settlement in Southern California, and many were anxious that the whole church should go there. If we had gone there, this would have been about the last year any of the Saints could stay there. They would have been driven from their homes. Were he here to tell you the true situation of that place, he would tell you that Hell reigns there, and it is just about time for himself and every true Saint to leave the land.

84

Prior to this prediction, Young had informed Lyman and Rich that they had been called to serve the church in Europe and were required to wind up their affairs in San Bernardino. After they left, no leader was sent to replace them. A few months later, when word was received of the approach of the U.S. Army, orders were sent to "forward the Saints to the valleys as soon as possible," thus ending official church connection with the colony.

This was a particularly tragic loss to the church because a number of the colonists refused to obey the call to return. An estimated 5 percent of those who obeyed the church leaders returned to San Bernardino within a year or two, including stake president Seeley. Those who remained were regarded as "apostates," and no effort was made to reclaim them. Apparently, Young sensed from the start that southern California was no place for a large colony of Saints and permitted it to grow without giving it strong support, especially after the need for a Pacific port colony diminished.

The establishment of San Bernardino proved to be important to the Mormon corridor. With a base on the Pacific and a midway settlement in Iron County, the corridor's key stations were in place. Provo, of course, was directly on the route, and by the summer of 1851, Lehi, American Fork, Pleasant Grove, Springville, Spanish Fork, Salem, Payson, and Santaquin had also been established in Utah County. Nephi and Mona in Juab County were settled before the end of 1851, as was Fillmore in Millard County. Paragonah and Harmony in Iron County were both established in 1852. However, there was still a 375-mile stretch without colonies between Harmony and San Bernardino. Nothing was done about this until 1855, when at April conference thirty men were called to establish an Indian mission at Las Vegas Springs. This was a strategic location on the route to southern California and was a logical part of any plan to connect Salt Lake City and San Bernardino.

George Washington Bean wrote in his autobiography he understood that the colonists would "teach those wild Piede Indians the blessings of peace and industry and honesty and kindred principles." Isaac Haight, president of the Cedar City Stake, after visiting with the missionaries en route to Las Vegas, wrote to Erastus Snow as follows:

> From the knowledge that I have of most of the men who compose that mission, I feel sanguine that much good will be done to better the condition of these poor and degraded sons of the desert, not only their temporary condition, by teaching them how to plow, plant, sow, etc.,

85

and raise their own living without depending upon the precarious means of subsisting on the little game that exists in the sterile regions, and of killing the cattle and horses of travelers, but also in their spiritual condition, by delivering them from the gross superstition of their fathers and bringing them to a knowledge of the covenants that the Lord made with Abraham, Isaac and Jacob, with Lehi, Nephi, and Moroni.

This indicates that the work with the Indians was probably uppermost in the missionaries' minds since no mention was made of a Mormon corridor.

En route to Las Vegas Springs, the missionaries met Rufus Allen and four members of the Southern Utah Indian Mission who had been sent to explore the Colorado and were waiting at the Muddy River for the missionaries in order to cross the desert with them. Bean reported that members of Allen's group were baptizing Indians by the hundreds and giving them new names such as Thomas, Rufus, and Isaac.

After arriving at the springs and choosing a location for a fort, the missionaries built a bowery and held their first Sabbath meeting. President Bringhurst said that he hoped the Elders would feel the responsibility of their mission and would remember "to set an example before the Lamanites of sobriety and industry and in short, everything requisite to civilize and enlighten the degraded sons of promise."

Brigham Young wrote to the Las Vegas missionaries counseling them to be patient with the Indians and asserting that he would rather abandon the mission than pursue "such a course as will lead to angry and hostile feelings at every little annoyance caused by their folly, theft, etc." Church leaders decided to strengthen the mission by sending twenty-nine additional men called at a special conference on 24 February 1856. The circumstances leading to the call were related by Apostle Heber C. Kimball in a letter to his son William.

There has [sic] been courts in session here for weeks and weeks, and I suppose that one hundred and fifty or two hundred of the brethren have been hanging around; with the council house filled to the brim. This scenery continuing for a long time, one day brother Brigham sent Thomas Bullock to take their names, for the purpose of giving them missions, if they had not anything to do of any more importance. So brother Brigham counseled me to make a selection—for Los [sic] Vegas some thirty . . . another company of forty eight to go to Green River . . . thirty five or so to Salmon River. . . . These are all good men but they need to learn a lesson.

86

Thus many of the missionaries assigned to Las Vegas Springs were reluctant. Life at Las Vegas was further complicated by the arrival of lead-mining missionaries under Nathaniel V. Jones. Jurisdictional disputes between Jones and Bringhurst led to Bringhurst's disfellowshipment. The miners succeeded in smelting only about 9,000 pounds of lead because they were handicapped by lack of water and food, by threatening Indians, and by the presence of a substance which made the ore very hard. The missionaries guess that the contaminant was silver was verified later when the rich Potosi silver mines were discovered.

Released from their mission, the mining missionaries started for home on 18 February 1857, and the Indian missionaries were informed that they were free to return home on 23 February. Some stayed on until September when it was decided that the "mission should be dropped on account of the thieving disposition of the Indians."

The failure to maintain a colony at Las Vegas was a sign that the dream of a Mormon corridor had been forsaken, since this desert oasis was the most strategic location between the Virgin River and California. That Brigham Young recalled apostles Rich and Lyman without replacing them was further evidence. In fact, on 29 January 1855, in a letter to Parley P. Pratt, Young wrote, "I am not particularly disappointed that there is no place in California for the gathering of the Saints. If the whisperings of the Spirit are to come to the Valley of the mountains, it is a happy whispering to you, to them, and very satisfying to me."[4] In Young's April 1857 conference address, he admitted that it was time for every true Saint to leave California and "gather" to the stronghold in the Great Basin.

Thus, within a period of six years, Young's vision of a 700-square-mile empire stretching from the Rocky Mountains to the Pacific Ocean, with colonies established on a line from the Salt Lake Valley to a seaport, had dwindled to an isolated stronghold in the Great Basin. Other than the financial and legal problems already discussed, what factors led to the abandonment of this dream?

(margin note: LAS VEGAS ABANDONED)

---

[4] Two days later, Young advised Charles C. Rich, "Your Gentile neighbors will steadily continue to increase upon your hands, [and] . . . either the Saints will imbibe the spirit of the world and strike hands with the enemy of all righteousness, or the two spirits will come in contact with each other and mobocracy will be the consequence." He recommended that Rich and Lyman sell out and return to "these peaceful vales" as soon as possible.

In addition to the local problems in San Bernardino, Mormon immigration officers in Europe had been unable to charter ships willing to sail around Cape Horn to a Pacific port. Nor were they able to make arrangements for crossing the Panama or other Central American country. And since the railroads were extending their lines into Iowa, it seemed more advantageous to have the European Saints land in one of the eastern ports such as Boston or New York City and take the train directly to Iowa, where they could be outfitted for a relatively easy trip to the Salt Lake Valley. This lessened the need for a colony near a Pacific port, although such a port could continue to aid the Saints coming from Australia and the Pacific islands, as well as missionaries going to and from the Pacific and Asian missions, and could provide a base for securing supplies from ships docking in San Diego or San Pedro.

Another factor leading to the abandonment of the corridor was the rejection of the State of Deseret by congress and the creation of the Territory of Utah in 1850, whose territorial boundaries encompassed a much smaller region than that claimed by Deseret. The California ports were not to be part of Mormon territory.

Brigham Young's emotional attachment to the Great Basin may have been a third factor. Although he talked of colonizing large areas, he became convinced that God had led him to the Salt Lake Valley and that the future of the church lay in the Great Basin. Returning to it in 1848 from Winter Quarters, he never left it again. His winter trips to St. George, though technically beyond the Great Basin, were certainly part of the region.

But perhaps the principal reason for abandoning San Bernardino was that already discussed—the recognition that the Saints would not be the "old settlers" of California, as they had once hoped, and that they could not survive in areas they did not dominate. Also, the fear expressed in an 1855 letter to Charles C. Rich that the Saints would begin to "strike hands with the enemy of all righteousness" if they remained in California may have also caused Young to reconsider his plan.

Even as Young was retreating from his dream of planting colonies "all the way to the Pacific," he became involved in a colonizing venture in Carson Valley. Although within the Great Basin and part of Utah territory, Carson Valley was 400 miles west of Salt Lake City and was already settled by non-Mormons.

Despite regular contacts with Carson Valley from the time of James Brown's visit there in September 1847, Mormon leaders had not tried to colonize the region. During the summer of 1850, a small

88

trading post known as "Mormon Station" was established on the Carson River where the city of Genoa, Nevada, was later located. But the name "Mormon Station" was misleading, because it is doubtful that any of the seven partners who established the post were devout Mormons. They were part of a group of eighty men who had left for the California gold fields in April 1850 with Abner Blackburn as guide. Blackburn had been with Captain Brown in 1847 and had gone back to the gold fields with his brother Thomas in 1849. The Blackburn brothers' parents were Mormon, and Abner had been a member of the Mormon Battalion. However, they were out of harmony with Young's policy and were certainly not acting for the church when they helped establish "Mormon Station."

When trade dwindled, the partnership dissolved, and the two Blackburns and Hampton Beattie decided to go to Salt Lake by way of Fort Hall. They arrived in Salt Lake City in October 1850 and spread word about the attractiveness of Carson Valley, including Blackburn's story that there was gold in the area. This information interested Mormon merchants John and Enoch Reese, who made plans to set up a trading post in the valley. Arriving at "Mormon Station" in June 1851, John Reese bought out a Mr. Moore who had acquired it from the seven partners a few months earlier. Reese prospered but became apprehensive when he heard that Mormon leaders planned to set up a civil government in the region. He then began actively promoting the annexation of the valley by California.

It was not until 1855 that Mormon leaders showed any active interest in Carson Valley,[5] and by that time it was too late for Mormons to become the original settlers since numerous non-Mormons already occupied the area. Carson County had been created in January 1854 by the Utah Territorial Legislature but was attached to Millard County for "election revenue and judicial purposes." The act authorized Brigham Young to appoint a probate judge, and on 17 January 1855 he wrote to Orson Hyde, asking him to take the position and to serve as ecclesiastical leader of the Mormon community as well.

Hyde, accompanied by ten or so colonizing missionaries, arrived at Mormon Station in June 1855 and was favorably impressed by the Reese establishment. He wrote to Young on 19 June that "this

---

[5] The lack of Mormon influence in the area may be seen in a letter printed in the *Deseret News*, in July 1853 by a prominent Mormon visitor, Edwin D. Woolley, who reported, "It is the most God-forsaken place that ever I was in, and as to Mormonism, I can't find it here. If the name remains, the Spirit has fled. I have my doubts whether Mormonism can exist in the country as far as I have been."

country has been neglected quite long enough if Utah wishes to hold it. It is a great and valuable country." Hyde also recommended the establishment of a settlement in Ruby Valley as a half-way base which would enable the Mormons to control the area and to explore the valleys to the north and east.[6]

Hyde eventually established a mill and became involved in other economic enterprises, both for himself and in behalf of the church. He became convinced that the only way the Mormons could survive in the region was to gain a balance of power politically and urged Young to send more colonizing missionaries to achieve control. Young responded by calling about one hundred "missionaries" and their families in April 1856.

The colonizing group, numbering approximately 250, left for Carson Valley in mid-May and most reached their destination by 2 July. Their arrival increased the fears of non-Mormon settlers who had already expressed opposition to Mormon dominance by petitioning that the region be annexed to California. Matters worsened when Mormon officials tried to help John Reese collect debts from non-Mormons, who resisted. Hyde felt that Reese's claims were questionable and urged him to cease litigation. When Reese continued to "refuse counsel," he was excommunicated.

On 16 October 1856 Hyde wrote to Young, describing the attitudes of the Gentile citizens towards the Mormon settlers.

> The old citizens, that is a portion of them, have become highly mobocratic. They are going to regulate all matters. They are going to lynch the assessor and collector till he pays back any taxes that he may have collected and costs that have been paid in any law case must be refunded. No man that is a Mormon can live who has more than one wife, everything must be regulated; and to this end they are said to be enlisting the Indians. They already have from six to ten, and they say they intend to bring 300. This is the talk.

Hyde's solution was for church leaders to send more men, but when he received a letter authorizing him to appoint a new probate judge

---

[6]Hyde indicated that he felt a church representative should stay in the valley throughout the winter and agreed to do so if Young would send him a wife. He wrote, "If you think it is not wisdom for anyone to come to me from the Lake, may I get one here? . . . Women are scarce here and good ones are scarcer still!" One of Hyde's plural wives, Mary Ann, joined him in Genoa for the winter and helped to establish a homestead. Later, Hyde proposed to leave Mary Ann with her sister, since he had "taken up a good ranch that will do for both" and did not know what "my future destiny may be."

ORSON HYDE

90

and return to Salt Lake City, he quickly settled his affairs and left the valley on 6 November 1856, never to return.

Hyde's successor, Chester Loveland, was instructed on 3 January 1857 to be "wise and prudent" and to live in peace and without contention. If that were impossible, the missionaries should dispose of their property and return to Salt Lake. Young made it clear that he did not intend to send any more "missionaries" to that region.

A period of uncertainty followed, one filled with rumors that the missionaries would be called home soon. Young informed Loveland on 3 June that "you were not and are not recalled from your mission, only as in all places and at all times if there be any who would rather not stay, let them return to this place." But Young's letter was not received until August. By 5 September the missionaries had received word that they were all recalled due to the approach of the U.S. Army.

Young was probably ill-advised to try to control Carson Valley after it was already inhabited, and he seems to have recognized this when he heard of the resistance to actions of elected Mormon officials. This would be the last of the major colonizing ventures under Brigham Young, although Indian missions would be established in 1855 at Elk Mountain (Moab), Fort Lemhi, Fort Bridger, and Fort Supply. The next two chapters examine the relationship between the Mormons and the original settlers of the Great Basin—the Indians.

6.
The Mormons
and the Indians
—Ideals versus Realities

Ｗhen the Mormons moved into the Great Basin, they not only occupied Mexican land but invaded Indian territory. Because they believed in the Book of Mormon, which claimed to be a history of the ancestors of the American Indians, they had sympathy for the Indians.[1] Previous experience with various tribes in the midwest had taught the Mormons to avoid contact whenever possible, but the Mormons were confident that one day they would convert the Indians and live peacefully with them.

Initial contacts with the Indians were friendly, but as Mormon colonies extended into neighboring valleys,[2] the natives began to

---

[1] The Mormons were not the first to suggest that the American Indians were remnants of the tribes of Israel. However, their belief in the Book of Mormon convinced them that the Indians were descendants of the tribes of Ephraim and Manasseh, had migrated to America in three different groups, and had spread through the land. The Book of Mormon detailed the story of the ancestors of the American Indians, who had once been a "white and delightsome" people and had developed a great civilization. Sin and wickedness had brought warfare, and eventually the white-skinned people had been exterminated. Those left, known as Lamanites, had been cursed with a dark skin and became savages. But they were also a people of promise, for the Book of Mormon contained a prophecy that the gospel of Jesus Christ should be declared among them and "be restored unto the knowledge of their fathers, and also to the knowledge of Jesus Christ. And then they shall rejoice; for they shall know that it is a blessing unto them from the hand of God; and their scales of darkness shall begin to fall from their eyes; and many generations shall not pass away among them, save they shall become a white and delightsome people" (2 Ne. 30:6). Believing themselves also to be of Israelitish origin, the Mormons regarded the Indians as blood brothers and believed that it was their duty to bring this knowledge to them.

[2] The Mormons had been warned by explorer and trader Jim Bridger to avoid

resist the intrusion. Their resistance threatened the existence of the Mormons who were, in their words, "a thousand miles from nowhere." On the frontier the Mormons acted much like other Americans in the east and in the south: they occupied Indian land, killed resisters, and called upon the federal government to remove the Indians to another part of the region.

In August 1846, while the Mormons were camped near the Missouri River, Brigham Young remarked at a high council meeting that "it was his impression that the committee should not enter into any specific agreement with the Indians, but to endeavor to create a friendly feeling and to have a meeting at a future time. We should not invite them into our camp but we can go and see them." He suggested that the Indians be paid for the use of their land only if they asked for it.

The Mormons' primary contact during the trek west was with the Omahas at Winter Quarters who stole between $3,000 and $5,000 worth of horses and cattle from the Saints, according to Brigham Young. Although angered by the attack, Young counseled against killing the Indians. At a conference in March 1847, just before leading the pioneers west, Young said that it was wrong to feel hostile toward the Indians, the descendants of Israel, who might periodically kill a cow, an ox, or a horse. It was their way of life to kill and eat. But if the Omahas persisted in robbing and stealing after being warned, then the Saints would be justified in whipping them.[3]

Such evidence suggests that the pioneers approached the Salt Lake Valley feeling benevolent toward the Indians as well as determined to avoid trouble. Unfortunately, the desperate circumstances the Mormons faced in colonizing the region made accommodation difficult and led to conflict during their first two to three years.

It is unclear how many Indians were in the Great Basin when the Mormons arrived. Some estimates place the number as high as 35,000, while others are considerably lower. Andrew Neff's analysis, based on Brigham Young's report as territorial Indian superintendent, projected a native population of approximately 12,000, not

the Utes around Utah Lake. Bridger described them as vicious savages who would "torment whites if possible but who would not resist large groups of whites." So church leaders avoided making a settlement at the fertile valley to the south for almost two years.

[3] Young also pointed to an unfortunate double standard. Some Saints, who knew better, would also sometimes steal. Mormons might forgive this, yet fellowship a man who would kill an Indian for stealing.

counting the Navajo, Hopi, or other Indians in the Grand Canyon and Arizona regions.[4]

The largest Indian group was the Utes. They had divided into eastern and western bands sometime before 1848. The western Utes occupied the eastern two-thirds of what is now the state of Utah, situating themselves south of the Shoshone, north of the San Juan River, and east of the southern Piutes. They were divided into smaller bands known as the Uintahs (in northeastern Utah), the Timpanogus (around Utah Lake), the Pavantes (around Fillmore and the Silver Lake area), the San Pitch (in the same general north-south area but ranging further east), and the Weeminuche (in southeastern Utah and across the border into Colorado). The Navajo had moved from northwestern New Mexico and northeastern Arizona into the region of Utah south of the San Juan River and traded regularly across the river with some of the Utes. Further south into the Arizona region were the Hopis and the Havasupis.

Most of these Indians had had contact with white men before the Mormons came. Those in the south and central parts of Utah had been in almost constant contact with Spaniards from Mexico, beginning with Escalante and Dominguez in 1776 and perhaps even a few years earlier. Following the Spanish padres' expedition, parties of traders came regularly into the Utah region and developed flourishing trade along the Old Spanish Trail, often taking Indian women and children captive and selling them into slavery in Los Angeles and Santa Fe. Beginning in the 1820s, mountain men and fur traders moved through the region and made alliances with Indians of the Rocky Mountains and Great Basin, frequently intermarrying with the women of the various tribes. Annually after 1825, fur rendezvouses were held in the Rocky Mountains, and hundreds of Indians, especially Utes and Shoshones, attended these gatherings and engaged in gambling, bartering, athletic contests, and in general revelry.[5]

KNEW WHITES

---

[4] Most of the Indians of the Great Basin spoke the Shoshonean language, a branch of the Uto-Aztecan language family which includes languages spoken by the Hopi, Pima, Papago, Yakki, Comanche, and some of the other tribes in Mexico and the American southwest. In addition, the northern Shoshone, the western Shoshone (known as the Goshutes), the southern Piutes, and the Utes all spoke Shoshonean. Northern Shoshone were located in what is now northern Utah, southern Idaho, and Wyoming. The Goshutes and other western Shoshone were located in northwestern Utah (west of the Great Salt Lake) and in northeastern Nevada. The southern Piutes were in southwestern Utah, southern Nevada, and in northern Arizona.

[5] The first four rendezvouses were held in the Utah area of Henry's Fork on the Green River, in Cache Valley, and at the southern end of Bear Lake. Cache Valley

Ultimately forts were established in the region, and these became gathering places for Indians in the area.[6] Government explorers, including Bonneville and Fremont, also made contact with the Indians in the region. The results of these contacts are difficult to measure. Some Indians, especially the Utes, became involved in horse stealing raids on California ranches and also became addicted to alcohol and other vices. The food supply diminished as the Oregon, California, and Old Spanish trails developed, the Indians becoming even more dependent upon the encroaching whites.

INDIAN DEPENDENT ON WHITE

Most of these Indians were poor, seed-gathering peoples. As no single locale provided a dependable food supply, most groups, especially the Shoshone, Goshutes, and Piutes, moved from place to place. They never learned how to store surplus food, and the search was constant. Only small groups could survive in a given area, thus precluding the development of large tribal organizations. A small family unit was the basic Indian group. This kept cultural development at a minimum compared with other North American Indian groups. Such conditions also made large-scale resistance to the Mormons unlikely.

The Salt Lake Valley was a fortunate choice for the first Mormon settlement. No Indian group occupied the valley, although the Shoshone claimed it and the Utes were often in the valley to trade with the Shoshone. Soon after their arrival in July 1847, the Mormons met Indian parties filtering into the valley—some to trade and others to satisfy their curiosity. On 27 July, Howard Egan wrote that "after breakfast, two Indians of the Utah tribe came to camp somewhat slightly clad in skins and quite small in stature. Jay Redding exchanged a gun for a pony. They gave us to understand by signs that there was a large party about 40 miles from here." That afternoon, five or six more Indians came into camp and stayed during the night.

A few days later, an event occurred that demonstrated some hostility between the Shoshone and the Utes. An altercation ensued over the alleged theft of a horse. Andrew Neff's account maintains

---

was the favorite wintering place of the mountain men and was selected as the rendezvous site in 1826 and in 1831. Although the supplies did not arrive in 1831, the whites made contacts with the Indians. An 1834 rendezvous at Ham's Fork on the Green River happened in what was known as Utah Territory. It was not uncommon for Indian women to be bartered on such occasions, and mountain men often vied with each other in adorning their Indian wives with colorful clothing and trinkets.

[6]Most prominent were Fort Rubidoux on the Uintah, Fort Davey Crocket at Brown's Hole on the Green River, and Fort Bridger at Black's Fork on the Green River.

[left margin: UTE VS SHOSHONE]

that two of the three Indians accused of theft were killed. Almost immediately, the Mormons were apprehensive about associating with people who killed each other over such minor incidents. Furthermore, the Shoshone appeared displeased because the Mormons were trading with the Utes. They claimed the land was theirs and that the Utes were interfering with their rights. With sign language, they indicated they wanted to sell the land for gun powder and lead.

Heber C. Kimball, acting head of the pioneers while Brigham Young was still recovering from his illness, addressed the pioneers on 1 August, advising them not to trade or sell their guns and ammunition to the Indians. He announced a new and far-reaching policy regarding land ownership. Whereas Young had said in Winter Quarters that "if they want us to pay for occupancy of their land, we will pay them and they should not touch our property and we will not touch theirs," Kimball now discouraged Mormons from paying the Indians for their land. "If the Shoshone should be thus considered, the Utes and other tribes would claim pay also," he asserted, concluding that "the land belongs to our Father in Heaven and we calculate to plow it and plant it and no man shall have the power to sell his inheritance for he cannot remove it. It belongs to the Lord."

[right margin: INDIAN POLICY]

[left margin: SHARE? CONNECT & SHARE]

Thus the Mormons occupied the land without compensating the owners. Of course, the Mormons intended to convert the Indians both to their religion and to a more civilized way of life—planting crops and raising cattle, horses, and other domestic animals—thereby hoping to share the limited land in the watered valleys of the Wasatch and the Great Basin without difficulty. At the same meeting, the settlers voted "not [to] trade with or take any notice of the Indians when they come in to camp," emphasizing the separateness of Mormon policy over fairness. *SEPARATENESS > FAIRNESS*

It is not certain what the Indians' attitude toward the Mormons was during the early days of July and August 1847; however, there probably was no unified feeling. Certainly the Indians were curious and hoping to benefit from the whites. But they had no way of knowing the extent of colonization that the Mormons were contemplating. Edward Tullidge, in his history of Provo, asserted that a large number of Utes were in Spanish Fork Canyon when the pioneers came into the Great Salt Lake Valley and that one of their leaders, Chief Walker,[7] advocated attacking the group immediately and wip-

---

[7] Walker was a successful Ute chief, having learned much from the mountain men. He had made trips into California to barter for horses, stealing a good number in the process, and had brought his people a considerable degree of economic prosperity.

ing them out before they could get established. Walker was reportedly overruled by an older leader, Chief Sowette, who had to flog Walker to bring him into line with a more peaceful policy.

Brigham Young may not have known about Walker, but he had been informed about the Utes by Jim Bridger, who asserted that the Mormons could "drive out the whole of them in twenty-four hours." Young said he "felt inclined not to crowd the Utes until we have a chance to get acquainted with them" and, for that reason, said it would be better to settle in Salt Lake Valley rather than around Utah Lake. By settling some distance away, the Saints would be less likely to be disturbed but would have a chance to form an acquaintance with the Utes and hopefully establish peaceful relations with them.

The Mormon leaders decided to build a stockade or fort to keep the Indians out. After Young and other Mormon leaders had left the valley to return to Winter Quarters, Young wrote a letter to those remaining in the valley: "When the Lamanites are about, you will keep your gates closed and not admit them within the walls. So far as you come in contact with them, treat them kindly but do not feed them or trade with them or hold familiar intercourse with them within the city. But if you wish to trade with them, go to their camp and deal with them honorably."

In September 1848, Walker and several hundred Utes appeared in the Salt Lake Valley with several hundred head of horses for sale. Evidently, they did not feel the Mormons represented enough of a threat to preclude trading with them. And the Mormons, although apprehensive, were nonetheless eager to placate animosity on the part of the Utes.

An unfortunate incident occurred early in February 1849. Apparently fourteen horses and several head of cattle were stolen in Tooele Valley and taken to Utah Valley. A posse of thirty to forty men, informed about the location of the Indian thieves by a friendly Indian, surrounded the Indian party near present-day Pleasant Grove, and killed all four warriors. This first hostile contact between Mormons and Indians ran counter to Brigham Young's policy that Indians should not be killed for stealing. The following day the posse returned along with the squaws and children of the slain.

More serious difficulties developed as the Mormons expanded into neighboring valleys. In places such as Ogden, Provo, Tooele, and Manti, Indians resisted colonization and confrontations took

---

Walker was also engaged in the slave trade and periodically raided the camps of the southern Piutes to seize their women and children to sell into slavery.

place. The most serious occurred in Utah Valley. In early 1849, when Mormon leaders sent a group of about 150 to colonize Utah Valley, two Ute chiefs, Old Elk and Walker, urged an attack on the settlement. Brigham Young told the colonists to be careful, not to make them any presents, to be friendly, to teach them to raise grain, and to order them to quit stealing.

The summer of 1849 was relatively peaceful, as far as Mormon and Indian relations were concerned in the Utah Valley. However, on 15 October, the Mormon leader in the valley, Isaac Higbee, wrote that the Indians had been troublesome for several weeks. One man had been shot at, two animals had been killed, and some corn had been stolen. Young repeated his previous counsel to build a fort, attend to their own affairs, and leave the Indians alone. He emphasized the policy of separation when he commented, "If you would have dominion over them for their good, which is the duty of the Elders, you must not treat them as your equals. You cannot exalt them by this process. If they are your equals you cannot raise them up to you."

A few months later, Young was persuaded to reverse his policy of benevolence and peacefulness. Early in January three Mormons accosted an Indian nicknamed "Old Bishop" (because he resembled Bishop Horace Kimball Whitney), accusing him of stealing a shirt that belonged to one of the three men. When he resisted, they attacked and shot him. They then opened his abdomen and filled it with rocks and placed the body in the Provo River. After this, the men boasted about what they had done. When the Indians found the body, they threatened to destroy the Mormon community. Without telling Brigham Young of the murder, Alexander Williams informed him of the Indian attacks.

Once again Young asserted that the Mormons should be tolerant. However, Isaac Higbee decided to travel to Salt Lake City to gain permission to lead a punishing expedition against the Indians. He met with Young, his counselors, the militia commander, Daniel H. Wells, and with Parley P. Pratt, who had just returned from southern Utah. Pratt supported Higbee, arguing that the only alternatives to a military expedition were abandoning the valley or leaving the settlers to be destroyed. Higbee added that every Mormon man and boy in the valley had voted to exterminate the Indians. Young considered the colony in Utah Valley a necessary link along the route to California and a key example of the Mormon resolve to occupy every fertile valley in the region. He was supported by Captain Howard

Stansbury of the U.S. Army and head of the topographic engineers surveying in Utah at the time.

On 2 February 1850, Young explained to the General Assembly of the State of Deseret that an extermination campaign would be carried out against the Utah Valley Indians and ordered that all Indian men were to be killed but that women and children would be saved if they behaved. Six days later, a voluntary force of militia from both Salt Lake and Utah Valley laid siege to about seventy Indians on the Provo River. After two days of fighting the Indians withdrew, leaving eight dead, including one woman whose legs had been severed by cannon shot. The wounded and sick retreated up Rock Canyon, but the main body reportedly fled to the Spanish Fork River. Daniel Wells then joined the militia with orders from Young "not to leave the valley until every Indian was out."

A relentless pursuit ensued. One party entered Rock Canyon and found eight or ten Indians, including Big Elk, dead from wounds or illness. Another group pursued the main body of Indians to the south of Utah Lake where they killed five and took the rest prisoner. The following morning, 15 February, all seventeen prisoners escaped to the frozen lake. One by one they were overtaken and killed. Then, to conclude what was certainly one of the most brutal incidents in Mormon history, their heads were cut off by a U.S. Army surgeon, aided by two of the Mormon militia men, ostensibly for scientific or medical research. Later, a local force of twenty-three men was sent out when Indian campfires were spotted nearby. These men came upon twenty-four Indians who had found the bodies of their friends. Despite hostile attitudes, the two groups negotiated a peace settlement at Fort Utah.

Evidence suggests that Young was increasingly pessimistic of ever converting the Indians to Mormonism and that he was concerned about the future of Mormon colonization. On 7 May, he told colonists in Utah Valley that the "older Indians would never enter into the New and Everlasting Covenant but that they would die and be damned." He admonished the people to mind their own business and that the Indians would do the same. "If they come and are not friendly, put them where they cannot harm us."

Five days later, Young expressed an equally pessimistic view. Although the Indians did not represent a significant danger Young said that he did not "want to live among them and take them in his arms until the curse is removed from them. This present race of Indians will never be converted. It mattereth not whether they kill one

100

another ott or [if] somebody else does it. And as for our sending missionaries among them to convert them, it is of no use."[8]

Young's primary reason for the change of policy is best noted as follows: "[The Indians] must either quit the ground or we must. We are to maintain that ground or vacate this. We were told three years ago if we don't kill those Lake Utes they will kill us. Every man told us the same. They all bore testimony that the Lake Utes lived by plunder and robbing. And if we yield in this instance, we have to yield the land." This was the crux of the matter. The Mormons were intent on building a new Zion in the region. They had hoped that the Indians would be converted and benefit from the Mormon occupation of their valleys. But since they were not willing to do this, the policy of benevolence and fairness would be changed. With no further talk of purchasing the land, Mormon leaders sent a worldwide appeal for colonization: "We want men, brethren come from the states and the nations. Come and help us build and grow until we can say enough, the valleys of Ephraim are full." At a public meeting calling for young men to occupy the San Pitch Valley, Young explained that he wished "to take possession of all good valleys." Later, he admitted that when the Saints first entered Utah "we were prepared to meet all the Indians in these mountains and kill every soul of them if we had been obliged to."

In April 1849, before the extermination in Utah Valley, Brigham Young, Heber C. Kimball, Willard Richards, and interpreter Dimick B. Huntington met with Chief Walker and twelve of his tribe. According to Young's manuscript history, Walker first asked for some tobacco, which was given to him. Then Huntington said, "Walker wants us to go down to his land and make a settlement. He wants to know how many moons before we will go [to his villages] and build at his place. He will do what we want him to do."

After passing the pipe of peace around, Walker said, "I am friendly with the Snakes, they are at peace, I can go among them. A few of the Snakes and Timpani Utes will not hear. I never killed a white man. I was always friendly with the Mormons. I hear what they say and remember it. It is good to live like the Mormons and their children. I do not care about the land but I want the Mormons to go and settle it." Young replied, "We want some of your men to

---

[8] He also believed "that old Bridger is [wishing] death on us and [that] if he knew that 400,000 Indians were coming against us, and any man were to let us know, he would cut his throat [to keep him silent]." Young felt that Bridger and other mountaineers were the real cause of the Saints' problems with the Indians.

CHIEF WALKER & YOUNG

come and pilot some of our men through to your place in the fall. We will school your children here if they are willing to go to school and in six moons we will send a company to your place. We have understanding with the Goshute and the Wanship about this place. It is not good to fight with the Indians. Tell your Indians not to steal. We want to be friendly with you. We are poor now, but in a few years we shall be rich. We shall trade cattle with you." Walker answered, "That's good." Young continued, "We will build a house for you and teach you and your tribe to build houses for yourselves. You can pay us your own pay." Walker responded, "My land is good, no stones, high timber."

The two leaders suggested how they might help each other. Then Walker said that the Timpanogus, or Timpini, Utes killed his father four years ago, that he had recently retreated from Utah Valley, and that he would be friendly to the Mormons and would welcome them to live near his villages. Young agreed to give the Indians some ammunition and hats, then asked, "Are you ready to go in peace? A good peace go with you. We want a good peace that our children can play together." Walker replied, "Good." The counsel finally concluded, and Young later remarked, "I gave the Indians half an oxen and the people commenced trading with them."

Young carried out his promise (see chap. 4). However, Walker was a difficult man to control. Despite the fact that he was baptized a Mormon on 24 March 1850, Walker was on the warpath less than a year and a half after meeting with Young. That summer a band of Shoshones raided a Ute camp and stole several horses. Walker planned a retaliatory raid and asked for support from a Mormon militia. His request was denied, and Walker rode off with his warriors to do bloody battle with the Shoshone raiders. Upon his return, Walker and his band made a gruesome demonstration in front of the fort at Manti. They then decided to move north and attack the Provo settlement. However, rebuffed by another chief, Walker called off the attack and withdrew.

Later, in mid-September 1850, another Indian was killed by a Mormon for stealing. This time it was in the Shoshone country near Ogden. Retaliation was immediate and vicious. A Shoshone chief, Terikee, was caught stealing corn and was shot by a Mormon farmer, Urban Van Stewart. The Indians retaliated by burning Stewart's house and grain. They then murdered a nearby millwright and threatened to massacre all of the settlers and burn the property unless Stewart was turned over to them for punishment by nine o'clock the next morning. A large militia force immediately rode to the scene. The Indians were outmatched and fled, and the incident was terminated without further bloodshed.

Apparently, these activities reconfirmed to Brigham Young that there was no way the Saints could live in peace with the Indians. On 20 November 1850, he wrote a letter to the church's representative in Washington, D.C., John M. Bernhisel, requesting that he attempt to have the Indians removed from the region by the federal government. Young explained,

It is our wish that the Indian title should be extinguished, and the Indians removed from our territory Utah and that for the best of reasons, because they are doing no good here to themselves or any body else. The buffalo had entirely vacated this portion of the country before our arrival; the elk, deer, antelope and bear, and all eatable game are very scarce, and there is little left here . . . Naked Indians and wolves . . . are annoying and destructive to property and peace, by night and by day, and while we are trying to shoot, trap and poison the wolves on one hand, the Indians come in and drive off, butcher our cattle, and steal our corn on the other, which leaves us little time between the wolves and the Indians to fence and cultivate our farms; and if the government will buy out and transplant the Indians, we will endeavor to subdue the wolves, which have destroyed our cattle, horses, sheep and poultry by the hundreds and thousands.

After noting some of the Indian atrocities, Young wrote:

Do we wish the Indians any evil? No we would do them good, for they are human beings, though most awfully degraded. We would have taught them to plow & sow, and reap and thresh, but they prefer idleness and theft. Is it desirable that the barren soil of the mountain valleys should be converted into fruitful fields? Let the Indians be removed. Is it desirable that the way should be opened for a rapid increase of population into our new State or Territory, also to California and Oregon? Let the Indians be removed, we can then devote more time to agriculture and raise more grain to feed the starving millions desirous of coming hither.

For the prosperity of civilization, for the safety of our small route, for the good of the Indians, let them be removed.

Young recommended that the Indians could be sent to the Wind River mountains

where fish and, at least part of the year, buffalo abound, to the Snake River where there are fish and game, to the eastern slope of the Sierra Nevada between the northern and southern routes to California where no white men lives and where forests and streams are plentiful, or to the western slopes of the Sierra Nevada above the dwellings of the whites where elk and other game are abundant.

When it became clear that the Indians would not relinquish their lands peacefully, Mormons resorted to the solution of James Monroe and Andrew Jackson—remove the Indians, by force if necessary. Young's recommendation was never acted upon. Bernhisel, who knew that Utah had already been made a territory and that Young had been appointed governor and would probably be appointed super-intendent of Indian Affairs, decided to talk to Young in person in the spring of 1851.

Although Young was appointed governor on 9 September 1850, he was not appointed Indian superintendent until the following Feb-ruary. Still he became aware of both appointments about the same time. He learned that he had been named governor in January 1851, and was informed the following month that Congress had extended the Intercourse Act over Utah and that he was being appointed ex-officio superintendent of Indian Affairs. The new territory, compris-ing approximately 186,000 square miles, included all of the present states of Utah and Nevada (except the southern tip near the Las Vegas area), the part of Colorado west of the crest of the Rocky Mountains, and the southwest corner of present-day Wyoming.

The Intercourse Act of 1834 provided Superintendent Young with an Indian agent and as many subagents as needed. United States president Millard Fillmore appointed Jacob H. Holeman as Indian agent and Henry R. Day and Steven B. Rose (a Mormon) as subagents. Before the arrival of the agent and subagents, Young divided the territory into three agencies or administrative units, each to be super-vised by one of the newly appointed officers. These units included the Uintah Agency (supervised by Rose), which took in all of the Snakes and Shoshones within the territory and all of the other tribes east of the Great Basin. The Parowan Agency (supervised by Hole-man), included all of the territories lying west of the eastern rim of the Great Basin and south of the southern boundary of the Pahvant Valley. Day's responsibility included the Pahvant Valley and all of the territory west of the Shoshone nation and north of the southern boundary of the Pahvant. Young's action seemed rational, but fol-lowing their arrival the agents criticized the new superintendent, feeling that he should have waited for them before outlining boundaries.

104

THE MORMONS AND THE INDIANS

The following letter from Holeman to the commissioner of Indian Affairs, dated 1 September 1851, foreshadowed the future pattern of interaction:

> I can take the opportunity of again stating to you as my fixed opinion that with Governor Young at the head of the Indian Department in this territory, it cannot be conducted in such a manner to meet with the views of or do justice to the government. He has been so much in the habit of exercising his will which is supreme here, that no one will dare oppose anything he may say or do. His orders are obeyed without regard to their consequences and whatever is in the interest of the Mormons is done whether it is according to the interest of the government or not.

Holeman noticed that trouble was brewing between the Mormons and the Indians because of the Mormon program of colonizing the more fertile areas of Utah. He wondered whether the Mormons should be allowed to move onto the rich hunting and fishing grounds occupied by the Indians:

> I find much excitement among the Indians in consequence of the whites settling and taking possession of their country, driving off and killing their game and in some instances driving off the Indians themselves. The greatest complaint on this score is against the Mormons. They seem not to be satisfied with taking possession of the valley of the Great Salt Lake, but are making arrangements to settle the rich valleys and best lands in the territory. This creates much dissatisfaction among the Indians and excites them to acts of revenge. They attack immigrants, plunder and commit murder whenever they find a party weak enough to enable them to do so, thereby making the innocent suffer for the injuries done by others.

Holeman sent his report directly to the commission without channeling it through Brigham Young's office, promoting additional antagonism.

Further difficulties developed when non-Mormon agent Henry R. Day joined territorial chief justice Lemuel H. Brandebury, territorial secretary Broughton D. Harris, and associate justice Perry E. Brocchus to withdraw from the Utah territory in protest. These men gave as their reasons the lawless and seditious conduct of the inhabitants of Utah, and Day said specifically that he could "no longer take the abuse that was being given to the United States and its officials by the Mormons." Holeman remained and not only complained of the Mormons taking Indian lands but also accused Young of using his office and government funds to further Mormon colonization. He alleged that government money was being used to buy presents

105

for the Indians in areas the church wanted to settle. Young, he complained, made it clear to the Indians that the Mormons were their friends and that the federal government was their enemy. "It seems to me officially," Holeman concluded, "that no Mormon should have anything to do with the Indian."

In the first few months of his superintendency, Young thus found himself deserted by one agent and opposed by another, who would try to undermine every request Young made on behalf of the Indians in his territory. As a result, Mormon programs were under-financed and criticized, and the Indians themselves were neglected. The Utah territory received only .03 percent of total federal appropriations earmarked for Indians in the United States and its territories. During the same period no lands were reserved for Indians in Utah, although throughout the country over 19 million acres were put into reserve. Of course, Utah Indians were not as numerous, but they were entitled to more help from the government than they received.

Another problem was Indian slavery. As already indicated, a slave trade was conducted over the Old Spanish Trail that came through much of Utah since the early 1800s. Walker and his band raided weaker tribes, taking their children and sometimes their wives as prisoners and selling them to Mexicans. As early as November 1851, the *Deseret News* called attention to a party of twenty Mexicans in the San Pete Valley, trading for Indian children. In his book, *Forty Years Among the Indians*, Daniel Jones wrote that when this party of traders arrived in Utah Valley, Brigham Young was notified and came to Provo. According to Jones, who acted as interpreter,

Mr. Young had the law read and explained to them showing them that from this day on they were under obligation to observe the laws of the United States instead of Mexico. That the treaty of Guadaloupe-Hidalgo had changed the conditions and that from this day on they were under the control of the United States. He further showed that it was a cruel practice to enslave human beings and explained that the results of such business caused war and bloodshed among the Indian tribes. The Mexicans listened with respect and admitted that the traffic would have to cease. It was plainly shown to them that it was a cruel business which could not be tolerated any longer and as it had been an old established practice they were not so much to blame for following the traffic heretofore. Now it was expected that this business would be discontinued. All seemed satisfied and pledged their word they would return home without trading for children. Most of them kept their promise, but one small party under Pedro Leon violated their obligation and were arrested and

INDIAN SLAVERY

106

brought before the United States court, with Judge [Zerubabbel] Snow presiding.

The Mexicans were found guilty and fined. The fines were afterwards remitted, and the men were allowed to return to their homes.

Stopping the slave trade embittered some Indians. Some of them attempted to sell their children to the Mormons. Jones related one graphic incident. Arrapine, Walker's brother, insisted that because the Mormons had stopped the Mexicans from buying these children, the Mormons were obligated to purchase them. Jones wrote, "Several of us were present when he took one of the children by the heels and dashed his brains out on the hard ground, after which he threw the body toward us telling us we had no hearts or we would have saved its life."

Incidents such as this led the Legislative Assembly of the Territory of Utah on 7 March 1852 to pass an act legalizing Indian slavery. The purpose was to induce Mormons to buy Indian children who otherwise would have been abandoned or killed.[9] It provided that Indian children under the proper conditions could be legally bound over to suitable guardians for a term of indenture not exceeding twenty years. The master was required to send Indian children between the ages of seven and sixteen years to school for a period of three months each year and was answerable to the probate judge for the treatment of these apprentices. As a result of this act, many Mormon families took small Indian children into their homes to protect them from slavery or from being left destitute. John D. Lee, for example, wrote in his journal about a group of Indians who "brought me two more girls for which I gave them two horses. I named the girls Annette and Elnora."

Negro slavery was also permitted in the territory, but the pioneers had passed no similar rules about the treatment of blacks, certainly

---

[9] The Mormons had first confronted the problem of buying Indian children soon after their arrival in the Salt Lake Valley. Children were brought into the pioneers' fort as early as the winter of 1847-48, and Indians said that they were war captives and would be killed if not purchased. The Mormons bought one of the children. Two more children were brought to the fort under the same threat, and the Mormons bought both of them. Charles Decker bought one of these two, Sally Kanosh, who was later given to Brigham Young and raised in his family. Speaking with church members in the Iron County Mission, Young advised them to buy children and teach them to live a good life. According to the Journal History for 12 May 1851, Young said, "The Lord could not have devised a better plan than to have put the saints where they were to help bring about the redemption of the Lamanites and also make them a white and delightsome people."

not the requirement that they be schooled. However, blacks were not permitted to be sold to others without their own consent.

The Mormons evidently hoped that Mexican traders would soon learn that they were no longer welcome in Utah. Soon, however, a trader from New Mexico boasted to Brigham Young of having 400 Mexicans on the headwaters of the Sevier River. This trader was selling arms to the natives and was presumably purchasing children to be sold into slavery. As a result, Young announced early in 1853 that he was sending thirty men south through all of the settlements surveying the country and directing the inhabitants to guard against sudden surprise. They were also authorized to arrest and keep in close custody any strolling Mexican party, those associating with them, and any other suspicious person or party. The presence of Mexican slave traders quickly subsided.

Young has been credited with the statement that it was cheaper to feed the Indians than to fight them. However, this was not his policy during the Saints' first years in the Great Basin. No doubt Young had great compassion for the Indians, but his letters to the chiefs advised against idleness and dependency. He was convinced that "he who is idle shall not eat the bread nor wear the garments of the laborer." Young's policy was never to give an Indian anything without letting him work for it.

When Young sent Isaac Morley's company to Sanpete County to settle near Walker's group, he realized that the Indians would be unhappy if the Mormons took over their valleys and hoped to demonstrate that a Mormon presence could mean a dependable food supply, even during the winter. In the spirit of this commitment, Young visited the Sanpete, Pahvant, and Parowan valleys in late October and early November 1851 and appointed James Case, Anson Call, and John C. L. Smith to inaugurate a farming program among the natives. Young's program was not officially sanctioned by the federal government, even though Washington apparently provided funds for its support.[10] The beginning salaries of Case, Call, and Smith were $300, $365, and $500 per year.[11]

Young wanted to develop a similar program for the Shoshone. He was especially anxious to do this because Mormon immigrants were coming through Shoshone country in the Green River area by

___

[10] Not until after 1858 did the church organize Indian farms which were clearly detached from federal support.

[11] Call was called to the Pahvantes on 23 October 1851; Smith to the Piutes near Parowan on 13 November 1851; and Case to the Utes on 3 November 1851.

Fort Bridger and were being menaced by Indians influenced by mountain men. These men had married Indian women, had become members of their tribes, and were surviving by controlling the ferries
over the Green River. Young was convinced that such men, including James Bridger, were encouraging the Indians not only to resist
Mormon immigration but to steal their cattle and attack the immigrants and settlers. In his annual report for 1851, Young wrote that
he and others had met with the Shoshone chief and had smoked in
token of lasting friendship. They had met also with the Utes and had
asked both groups if they would like to have the Mormons settle by
them and teach them how to farm.

By 29 September 1852 Young received Chief Washakie's personal, though reserved, welcome to settle on the Green River lands.
Acting on this, Young sent a letter with Dimick Huntington to some
of the Mormon immigrants who were coming west in 1852, asking
them to stop over on the Green River and to establish a permanent
settlement. A small group under Huntington's direction stopped on
the Green River in the late summer of 1852. However, the Indian
agent, Jacob Holeman, visited the region and reported to his superior that the chief in council at Fort Bridger had asserted that they
intended to drive the whites from their lands immediately. Unless a
compromise was possible, he feared bloodshed. When Young learned
of this, he wrote, ''If some of our people would go out with the Indians on their trips hunting and get acquainted with them and with
their chiefs, then a good influence might be exerted among them
which would not be in the power of anyone else to counteract. But
we must wait for the present, therefore all of you come back and let
things take their course a little longer.''

Things remained relatively quiet during the winter of 1852–53.
But in 1853 two important developments caused farming to cease
temporarily and involved the Mormons in military action against
Walker in central Utah and against Bridger and mountain men in
the Green River country. Young had continued to work with Walker
and the other Ute chiefs and had baptized a number of them. In fact,
in June 1851, Young's scribes recorded that Indian chiefs Walker,
Sowette, Arrapine, and Unhwitch were ordained Elders.

Nevertheless, Young was aware that the priesthood was not having much impact on the Indians and knew that Walker and others
were upset that Mormons were moving into the valleys along the
Wasatch Mountains and were stopping the slave trade. Hearing of
these attitudes Young dictated to his scribes on 18 May 1853, ''I shall
live a long while before I can believe that an Indian is my friend

109

when it would be to his advantage to be my enemy." Young was referring to Walker who in July 1853 led an outbreak known as the Walker War. A trivial altercation in Springville ended in the death of an Indian, and Walker led his band on the warpath, killing twelve white men during the nine-month feud. The number of Indians killed equaled the number of whites slain.

Walker's action caused fear among the Mormon colonists and an estimated $2 million in losses. The territory accumulated a $70,000 deficit, personal losses accounting for the rest. None of the personal losses were compensated, but the U.S. congress appropriated $53,512 for territorial losses. By the end of October 1853, the "war" was over except for a few minor incidents in the southern part of the territory. Formal peace was signed the following May at Chicken Creek (south of present-day Nephi) between Young and Walker, who died less than a year later and was buried at Meadow Creek.

During the Walker War, another incident occurred in the territory which complicated matters for the Indians, the federal government and the Mormons. On 26 October 1853, U.S. Army captain John W. Gunnison and seven men under his employ were killed near the Sevier River while surveying a railroad route. Army colonel Edward Steptoe was sent to investigate the murders and reported that a member, or members, of an immigrant train en route to California had killed the father of a prominent chief and wounded two other Indians. The Indians retaliated by taking revenge on the first whites they encountered, the innocent Gunnison party. This atrocity was committed by the Piutes of Chief Kanosh's tribe. Kanosh, one of the most friendly of Indians, had been baptized into the Mormon church and ordained an Elder.

Eventually, Kanosh was told to turn over the killers. He agreed but only turned over old and decrepit members of the tribe, hardly the attackers. An unusual trial was held in which a good deal of antagonism surfaced between the Mormons and Colonel Steptoe and his army officials. Three Indians were convicted and sentenced to prison. Steptoe, disgusted with the experience, later turned down the invitation to be governor of the territory, leading his troops instead to Oregon.

Meanwhile, as a result of the Walker War, Brigham Young revoked all licenses to trade with the Indians in the territory. He felt that this was the most prudent course to pursue until peace was restored. Otherwise he could not prevent the selling of guns, powder, and lead to the enemy. Although the Walker War did not extend into Green River Valley, the revocation of all trading licenses did.

Thus Jim Bridger and other mountain men were forbidden to trade with the Indians. However, when Mormon traders returned from the region in the early fall of 1853, they reported that Bridger was not only trading with the Indians but selling them powder, lead, and liquor, and was supposedly inciting them to kill the Mormons as well. Believing such reports, Young decided to arrest Bridger.

Sheriff James Ferguson received a court order to lead a 150-man posse to Fort Bridger to arrest the mountain man, to bring him back to Salt Lake City for trial, and to confiscate his weapons. The posse arrived at Fort Bridger in late August 1853. Despite several days of searching, they could not find Bridger. His Indian wife claimed she did not know where he was, but apparently he was hiding in nearby mountains. Posse members occupied Fort Bridger and confiscated the goods they deemed dangerous. William Hickman reported that no ammunition was found but that the whiskey and rum, of which Bridger had a good stock, was "destroyed by doses."

The posse then went to the Green River where they killed two or three mountain men and captured several hundred head of livestock. Ferguson left James Cummings with twenty men in possession of Fort Bridger. The men remained there until mid-October when they also returned home. Shortly after the posse left the fort, Bridger returned with John M. Hockaday, a government surveyor, and began a survey of the country claimed by Bridger. On 6 November 1853, the survey was completed, and soon afterwards Bridger left the area permanently for his home in Missouri.

Thus the first few years of Mormon colonization proved disastrous for the Indians. Hoping to profit from the Mormons, the Indians soon found themselves overwhelmed by pioneers moving onto their hunting and camping territories. Reacting by stealing and by threatening the colonists, the Indians came to be regarded as threats to Mormon survival. Despite the Mormons' initial good will, the two cultures were too dissimilar to accommodate each other, and in the early clashes, both groups lost. Finally, after seven difficult years, Mormon leaders decided to try new methods of accommodation: Indian missions and farms.

111

7.
Indian Missions
and Farms

The Walker War and other difficulties convinced Mormon leaders that they needed a more effective program to deal with local Indians. Hence during October 1853's semi-annual General Conference a series of Indian missions was announced. The Green River Mission was functioning by mid-November, and the southern Utah missionaries were organized the following April. Although the Green River Mission had failed by July 1854, and the southern Utah mission enjoyed only limited success, church leaders decided to call new missionaries in April 1855 to return to the same area. The Indian missionaries also traveled north to the Shoshone, Bannock, and Flathead territories, southeast to Elk Mountain (Moab), southwest to Las Vegas, and west to White Pine and Carson Valley. However, most of these missions were unsuccessful, and those that survived were discontinued when the U.S. Army approached the region in the fall of 1857.

At the close of the October 1853 conference Apostle Orson Hyde, who had been assigned to organize an Indian mission, read the names of thirty-nine young men selected to participate in the newest colonizing expedition. Church leaders must have viewed this particular call with some urgency because the missionaries were instructed to leave in less than two weeks. Perhaps they realized the danger of sending men into the high mountains around Fort Bridger with winter coming and wanted them to be established before the cold set in. Despite the urgency and the difficult prospects, the men accepted the call and, according to Hyde, left in high spirits. James Brown, chosen to be one of the leaders, recorded the purpose of the mission:

> [To] build an outpost from which to operate as peacemakers among the Indians, to teach civilization to them, to try to teach them to cultivate the soil, to instruct them in the arts and sciences if possible, and by that means prevent trouble for the frontier settlements and the immigrant companies. We were to identify our interest with theirs and even to marrying among them if we would be permitted to take the young women of the chiefs and leading men and have them dress like civilized people and educated. It was thought that by forming that kind of alliance we would have more power to do them good and to keep peace among the adjacent tribes and also with our own people.

PURPOSE

Brown also indicated that they were expected to thwart the mountain men, who were believed to be inciting the Indians to attack the Mormons and the government. *STOP MT MEN*

Three important points should be noted in Brown's report. First, no definite place was designated for the colony, only that it be somewhere near the Green River and the Indian tribes. Second, the main purpose of the mission was to establish good relations with the Indians, not necessarily to convert them to Mormonism. They were to work with the Indians, to civilize and educate them, to make farmers out of them, and also to gain their confidence. The third purpose was to upset the schemes of the mountain men. Since plural marriage had recently been publicly announced as a practice of the church, the missionaries were advised to take Indian wives, if possible.

PURPOSES

The Indian missionaries could not assemble until 1 November, when they met at the Council House at Salt Lake City. The company leader was John Nebeker, who would act as president and captain; John Harvey was chosen counselor and lieutenant; James Brown was named second counselor and lieutenant. Brown explained that the dual designation as military and ecclesiastical officers was made so that they could act in a military capacity if required. But the more important calling was the church office. The officers were blessed and set apart by three apostles, and the members of the company were told that they would also be blessed if they prayed and did their duties.

The men arrived at Fort Bridger about two weeks later and found the post occupied by twelve or fifteen mountain men who "seemed to be very surly and suspicious of us." Brown added that "many of our party could feel the terrible influence and made remarks about

114

it.'' The missionaries were informed that two mountain men had fought a duel with butcher knives the night before and that both had been killed and thrown into a common grave. The missionaries traveled one and a half miles above Fort Bridger and camped at Black's Fork that night. They awoke to find that it had snowed about six inches. According to Brown, they planned to move to Henry's Fork, because the Ute Indians were coming to spend the winter there. However, when they learned that there was a band of between seventy and one hundred desperadoes near Henry's Fork, they changed their plan and appointed a committee to search out a spot for a temporary location.

While the advance company was scouting a location, Orson Hyde was in the Salt Lake Valley recruiting additional missionaries. He reported to the *Deseret News* that "in less than two weeks' time I had fifty-three young hardy men well fitted out with large supplies of everything necessary, twenty-six wagons from two to five yoke of oxen, many milk cows, mechanics of all sorts and kinds, necessary tools and implements in abundance [as well as] much clothing, leather, nails and so on." This group was led by Isaac Bullock as captain, William Muir as first lieutenant, William Prince as second lieutenant, and John L. Dunnion as surgeon.

By the time the second company arrived in Fort Bridger on 25 November, the first company had left Black's Fork and passed over the divide in a southeasterly direction, traveling along Smith's Fork to keep away from the mountain men as much as possible. A site-selection committee followed a creek to a point where the water came down the foothills. There, between the forks of the stream, they chose a spot for winter quarters. They then returned and made their report, which the captain accepted. The camp moved to the new site on 27 November. The second group, with fifty-three men, came into the camp on the 26th. Thus a joint company of ninety-two men, all well-armed, moved to the location that came to be known as Fort Supply and began to build a post on 27 November.

Brown reported that they named a committee to superintend the erection of the blockhouse, which was ready for occupancy in two weeks. This was not an hour too soon for the weather was already cold and threatening. According to W. W. Sterrett's 23 December report, leaders then sent eight men with four wagons back to Salt Lake City when they discovered the flour would not last until spring. The wagons became irretrievably lodged in snow banks less than a mile from the summit of Big Mountain and were abandoned there.

A rider was sent for help, and the seven men on foot were subsequently rescued. No attempt was made to furnish Fort Supply with food and equipment until spring.

Given the outcome, the settlers might reasonably have questioned the wisdom of the call so late in the year. The missionaries certainly could not have planted crops, nor could they have done any missionary work. They exerted every energy just to survive the cold and the danger from unfriendly Indians and mountain men. According to Brown, they had not been settled long when some of the mountain men paid them a visit. Although the mountain men applauded the Mormons' energy and enterprise, they expressed some envy and caused the missionaries to feel unsafe, especially when the latter realized that there was such heavy snow between them and the Utah settlements. They frequently heard that the Utes were threatening to attack them from the southeast. As a result, the settlers continued their military organization and regular guard duty. This annoyed most of the men, who had to spend cold nights on guard for fear of Indian attacks.[1]

The missionaries were fortunate in having the services of mountain man and Mormon convert Elijah B. (Barney) Ward, his Shoshone wife Sally, and their children. Ward was a guide and Indian interpreter. His wife Sally had been married to a French trapper, Baptist Exervid. Exervid, however, had died and left a daughter, Adalaide, whom Ward cared for. Ward and his wife agreed to teach the missionaries the Shoshone language during the winter of 1853–54. In addition, six other Indians wandered into the camp and aided in the study of the Shoshone language and customs.

During the winter, only six of the missionaries made progress in Shoshonean. Of these, four were chosen by Orson Hyde to make first contact with the Indians. These men—Elijah Ward, Isaac Bullock, James S. Brown, and James Davis—left in mid-April to visit the Indian camps. Chief Washakie received the elders cordially. During the council meeting the tribal leaders listened to the Mormons' message and to a letter from Apostle Hyde. In it he said, "Our young men are learning to speak your language. They want to be united with your people and a number of our men want to marry wives from your people and live with them and live in your country." The

[1] Orson Hyde visited the group on 8-9 December and brought them some mail. He applauded their work, then set out on his return trip. As one missionary later reported, "everyone felt blessed by his visit." Before leaving, Hyde wrote a letter to Chief Washakie explaining the purpose of their mission and once again offering to marry their women and to teach the Indians to farm.

116

chief did not rebut the message but objected to the marrying of Indian women:

> We have not got daughters enough for our own men, and we cannot afford to give our daughters to the White men, but we're willing to give him an Indian girl for a White girl. I cannot see why a white man wants an Indian girl. They are dirty, ugly, stubborn and cross. And it is a strange idea for white men to want such wives. The white men may look around though and if any of you can find a girl that would go with him it would be all right, but an Indian must have the same privilege among the white men.

With this the council ended.

The missionaries continued their journey to the surrounding camps, visiting one band of Shoshone led by White Man's Child. Here they found the Indians under the influence of mountain man L. B. Ryan, who claimed that the Mormons had robbed "his bottom dollar" and talked revenge. On 1 June they reached the middle ferry where they found Mormon officials who had been sent to the Green River Valley in the spring of 1854 to serve as county officers. These included Judge W. I. Appleby, prosecuting attorney Hosea Stout, and Sheriff William Hickman. Captain Holly, who ran the ferry, and his family were also there. The mission had achieved very little. No baptisms were performed, and little had been done to influence the Indians except for Washakie's band which was already friendly.

Brown and the other missionaries returned to Fort Supply on 11 July to find that morale had declined and that many of the men had deserted the mission. The remaining missionaries began planting crops early in May even though the weather was still cold and farming difficult. Hosea Stout, who visited Fort Supply at this time, wrote in his journal, "It is the most forbidding and God-forsaken place I've ever seen for an attempt to be made for a settlement. Judging from the altitude, I have no hesitancy [in saying] that it will yet prove a total failure. But the brothers here have done a great deal of labor . . . Elder Hyde seems to have an invincible repugnance to Fort Supply."

Because so many missionaries left, the organization collapsed, and by July all of the men were released, except possibly a few who volunteered to harvest the crops. John Pulsipher, whose brother Charles was one of these, wrote, "Many of the men were discouraged and dissatisfied and Elder Hyde was not with them and they thought it was a hard, lonesome place, so the next July they were all released to go home unless some wished to stay and save the crops." Not many stayed.

117

The missionaries in southern Utah were more successful. This group had been called at the October conference, and a party of twenty-three had been chosen to labor there. Apostles Parley P. Pratt and Orson Hyde organized the men into a company at Salt Lake City and appointed Rufus C. Allen, age twenty-six, to be president, with David Lewis as first counselor and Samuel F. Atwood as second counselor. Having just returned from a mission in Valaparaiso, Chile, Allen felt prepared to direct a proselyting enterprise among the natives. Jacob Hamblin, a noted Mormon scout and Indian interpreter, was another member of the company. The party left Salt Lake City on 4 April 1854 and arrived at a settlement called Harmony in southwestern Utah, twelve days later. At that time some twelve to fifteen families were located there under the leadership of John D. Lee. This group had been sent to southern Utah on a colonizing mission two years earlier by Brigham Young and had already done some work among the natives. The missionaries spent about a month with Lee, and then both groups moved north about three miles to construct a fort.

On 5 June 1854, Allen, Hamblin, and others started south to visit the various native groups. Their first day out, they met a small, friendly band of Indians and had an interview with Chief Toquer. The next evening they reached the Rio Virgin and came upon another camp of Indians. The women and children hid themselves in the brush. No doubt they feared being taken as slaves.

The following night, the missionaries camped on the Santa Clara River and found a large group of Indians. There were about 250 Indian men but very few children, since most had been taken captive. The Indians had heard about the missionaries and treated them cordially. The Mormons found that the Santa Clara natives were farming in a primitive way but did have patches of wheat, corn, squash, and melons near their village. Allen informed them that they had been sent there by the "big captain," Brigham Young, and that they would teach them how to farm in a better way. They explained their gospel message, and eleven of the Indians were baptized. A short time later, the missionaries returned and succeeded in baptizing fifty more Indians. They spent the remainder of the summer of 1854 visiting the various native groups in the region.

By special appointment, Hamblin was sent alone among the Indians in November to keep them from disturbing travelers on the southern route to California, a task he accomplished successfully. The next month, Allen called Hamblin, Thales Haskell, Ira Hatch, Samuel Knight, Augustus P. Hardy, and others to leave Harmony and make

SANTA CLARA

118

a permanent settlement on the Santa Clara River. They were instructed to take their families and to build homes. Apparently Harmony had insufficient water to accommodate a large group of settlers, and Santa Clara was a more favorable location for missionary work.

Arriving at Santa Clara in early December, the missionaries chose a site about five miles northwest of its confluence with the Rio Virgin. It was a narrow valley, necessitating the division of the land into small tracts, but the colonists became very productive farmers. They erected a log cabin on the upper end of the present site of Santa Clara, constructed a dam across the creek, built canals, and made preparations for irrigation. Chief Tut-se-gab-its and his tribe, numbering about 800, aided the Mormons. By spring, the dam, about 100 feet long and 14 feet high, was completed and about one hundred acres of land was prepared for planting. The Mormons and the Indians cultivated the land jointly and shared the produce equally. Hamblin reported that "we've raised melons and had the privilege of disposing of them ourselves. I don't think the Indians ever took any without leave." The settlers enjoyed good relations with the Indians, although some of the older natives complained about changing their customs. "We must be Piutes," they said. "We want you to be kind to us. It may be that our children will be good, but we want to follow our old customs."

[margin note: MOSTLY GOOD RELATIONS W/ PIUTES]

In July 1856, Apostle George A. Smith visited the missionaries with instructions to build a fort in case the Indians should cease to be friendly. A few months later the fort, one of the best in Utah at the time, was completed. Amasa Lyman, returning from San Bernardino in May 1857, wrote that "the brethren in this place have built a stone fort 100 feet square inside of which are some crude cabins in which its occupants reside at the present. They seem to have some good land and cultivation with and for the natives with whom there seems to exist a good feeling at present."

Allen was released as president in August 1857, and Hamblin was appointed to succeed him. Brigham Young, in a letter to Hamblin, urged him to continue the conciliatory policy towards the Indians. "Omit promises when you are not sure you can fill them and seek to unite the hearts of the brethren on that mission. Let all your direction be united together in the holy bonds of love and unity. Do not permit the brethren to part with their guns and ammunition, but save them against the hour of need." Young composed this letter in August 1857 when he was aware of the approach of Johnston's Army.

[margin note: YOUNG'S COUNCIL]

Besides being effective with the missionaries and Indians around

Santa Clara, Hamblin was also helpful to immigrants and to Mormons returning from San Bernardino. Several of the families from San Bernardino settled in Santa Clara, helping to strengthen the settlement.

The success of the southern Indian mission at Santa Clara encouraged Mormon leaders, who were determined to expand the Indian missionary program the following year. At April conference in 1855, a number of missionaries were called to the different Indian missions. The initial report was: Shoshone Mission, 17; Elk Mountain, 34; White Mountain, 22; Carson Valley Mission, 9; Northern or Flathead Mission, 27; and Las Vegas Mission, 30. The same report mentioned only eight missionaries called to the English mission which gives some idea of the emphasis placed on work among the Indians that year. Apparently additional numbers were added, since the Elk Mountain Mission later reported that forty men were called.

Least successful of these missions was the White Pine Mountain Mission near the present Nevada-Utah boundary. E. G. Williams on 11 June 1855 wrote a lengthy account to Heber C. Kimball of the trials of missionaries going to White Mountain, such as locating potable water, "the same being found only in out-of-the-way places known to Indian guides who accompanied them." Williams also described the Indians' fear of the missionaries and the missionaries' own attempts to instill confidence. Williams claimed to have been the first white man to ascend White Mountain. After making a limited effort to establish a mission among the Goshutes or Western Shoshone in the area, the missionaries returned home and reported that the project was impractical.

The Elk Mountain Mission also proved short-lived. President Alfred N. Billings was appointed to head the forty-man group that met in Manti on 21 May 1855. They were well supplied with wagons, oxen, cows, horses, pigs, dogs, chickens, food, and tools. Following the Old Spanish Trail and Gunnison's route, the missionaries reached the Green River where they met some of the Indians. Billings told them "our business was to learn them the principles of the gospel and to raise grain." The missionaries had difficulty getting their cattle across the Green River in the little boat Billings had brought. He wrote, "We worked nearly two days in trying to swim more cattle, and only got twenty-five over. We then took two at a time and towed them over with a boat. Many of them would not swim a stroke and some swam back." One large fat ox broke its leg, which one missionary thought a good thing because they needed beef. Completing a twenty-day journey, the group reached the Colorado River. After selecting a place for a fort, the missionaries held a meeting and then retired to the river where they baptized the converts.

The settlers experienced some opposition from the Indians, who could not understand why the white men were building a fort if they intended to be friends. A few days later, Ute chief Arrapine came into the camp carrying mail to the missionaries. He also preached to the Indians, speaking first in Ute and then in Navajo. Arrapine had been ordained a Mormon Elder and his message was favorable to the Mormons. Other Indians spoke in favor of the Mormons, and within a week fourteen men and one woman were baptized. On 19 August, a letter from Brigham Young to Billings instructed him that a few missionaries were to be left to defend the fort but the rest were to live with the Indians.

Despite their success in baptizing many of the natives, the missionaries were unable to convince them not to steal. By 20 September, Billings reported that the Indians had taken "all of the beets, part of the turnips, part of the potatoes, all of the squash, and all of the melons. The corn had been cut and hauled into the fort in effort to save it." Three days later some Indians attacked the fort, killing three missionaries, wounding Billings, and setting fire to the missionaries' winter supply of hay and corn. At this point the decision was made to abandon the mission. Mormon leaders made no subsequent attempt to revive this mission.

The pattern established at Elk Mountain was repeated in other Indian missions. The missionaries had to support themselves by farming and chose the most fertile Indian land. Knowing they were isolated and believing they were dealing with savages, they built forts to protect themselves and fences to protect their property. In so doing they became unwanted outsiders in valued lands and traditional gathering places. Initially, the Indians seemed friendly, and some would be baptized. But they were not willing to accept the Mormon message. Certain tribe members became dissatisfied. When they attempted to steal produce and other supplies, the missionaries retaliated, sometimes resulting in death.

This was the pattern of the Las Vegas Mission (see chap. 4) and the Lemhi settlement in northeastern Idaho. The choice for the location of the Lemhi Indian mission is puzzling. The manuscript history of Brigham Young for 8 April 1855 designates this particular mission as the Northern or Flathead Mission. John Bluth, who wrote the first significant history of the mission, maintained that the missionaries were instructed to settle among the Flathead, Bannock, or

121

Shoshone Indians, or anywhere the tribes would receive them. When the missionaries arrived at Fort Hall, in Bannock territory, they came under the influence of Niel McArthur, an ex-Hudson's Bay Company man who had spent the previous winter on the Salmon River and recommended the valley as an excellent place for missionary work. Apparently this was also a place where three tribes converged at various times for salmon fishing and other purposes. Although not an ideal place for a settlement, Lemhi was selected as a site for a fort. Initially, these missionaries faced the same problem as those in the Elk Mountain, Las Vegas, and southern Utah missions—survival.

After making their way into the Salmon River region, the missionaries built a fort and began to cultivate farming land. Only after spending the winter in the region did they ask to bring their families from Salt Lake and to colonize the valley. There is no evidence that Brigham Young decided to make Lemhi a permanent colony until after his visit in May 1857. At that time, he proposed to send more settlers and encouraged the building of a new settlement two miles from the fort. Fields were divided into individual plots. Before this, the missionaries had cultivated a common field.

The colony continued until unexpected events led to its abandonment. The approach of the U.S. Army, and Mormon resistance to it, caused whites in the Lemhi region to be apprehensive, and this effected the Indians. The burning of the government supply train by Mormon raiders led to the fear that Mormons in the Lemhi region might engage in similar activity. One group of mountaineers reported that the Lemhi Mormons were saying that Brigham Young would save the republic and be made president of the United States. The Mormons' relationship with the natives deteriorated until, on 25 February 1858, an estimated 280 Indians raided the fort, driving off the cattle and killing and wounding some of the defenders. Messengers were sent to Salt Lake City for help, and the missionaries were instructed to abandon the colony. One hundred and fifty men, who were sent to rescue the colonists, arrived the next month. The exodus began immediately, thus ending the Salmon River Mission.

Although nine missionaries were called to the Carson Valley Mission, only a minor part of the colonizing effort took place in Carson Valley. The work among the Indians there was mostly unsuccessful and was soon discontinued. There was also a group of missionaries appointed to the Cherokee Mission, but this was different from the other Indian missions. Four men labored with the Cherokees

122

and succeeded in establishing a branch of the church in present-day Oklahoma.

The apparent failure of the first Indian mission to the Green River Valley did not discourage church leaders. In fact, only a month or two after the Fort Supply missionaries had left, James Brown reported that he had received a letter from Orson Hyde, dated October 1854, asking him to go on a mission to the Shoshone during that winter. Brown reported to Salt Lake headquarters but learned that the Indians had gone so far into the buffalo country that it would be inadvisable for him to follow them. He returned to Ogden where he spent the winter trading with the Indians and gave lessons in the Shoshone dialect.

At the April 1855 General Conference, Brown was appointed president of the newly organized Green River Mission and his former missionary companion Isaac Bullock was designated captain. Brown left Salt Lake City on 10 May, arriving at Fort Supply seven days later. He found that seven Elders had arrived ahead of him and were busy planting crops. Apparently the missionaries had been instructed to gather at Fort Supply rather than organize in Salt Lake City, and they arrived at different times. John Pulsipher, who did not leave Salt Lake until 17 May, reported that when his party arrived there were already twenty missionaries at Fort Supply. Pulsipher and the others benefitted from the building efforts of the first Green River missionaries.

The first meeting of the group was held on 27 May; Pulsipher was appointed clerk and historian of the mission. He reported that seven missionaries, including Brown, were assigned to seek out the Indians while the rest were to raise their standard of living, if possible, and to teach any Indians that might call at the fort.[2]

Brown's group met with Chief Washakie and the subchiefs early in the summer of 1855. They explained their mission and presented to the Indian leaders a letter from Brigham Young offering friendship, trade, and a promise to give instructions in farming methods. When they handed the Indians a copy of the Book of Mormon, some of the subchiefs declared "the book no good to the Indian," indicating that they wanted something to eat and wear, not a book.

---

[2] Apparently the purpose of the second Indian mission was different from that of the first. In 1853, Orson Hyde's instructions had emphasized peaceable relations with the Indians and attempts to civilize them. However, the 1855 missionaries seemed more intent on preaching Mormonism. Perhaps they had decided that the earlier goal could be accomplished more effectively by first converting the Indians.

Washakie, however, picked up the book and reportedly exclaimed, "You are all fools. You are blind. You cannot see. You have no ears, for you do not hear. You are fools, for you do not understand. These men are our friends. The great Mormon Captain, Brigham Young, has talked with our father above the clouds, and he told the Mormon captain to send these good men here to tell us the truth not a lie." Washakie continued speaking of the Indians' need to change and adapt to a more stable existence. He also expressed his desire to learn the ways of farming and continue trade with the Mormons. This attitude was manifested many times during the following years.

At Fort Supply the Indians were instructed whenever they came to visit and trade. Pulsipher's journal expresses a common sense attitude as to the amount of information given the natives. "On the 9th of August 30 Indians visited for a week, they danced and feasted. August 12, Sunday about 40 Indians attended church and were taught all the missionaries thought they could remember." Toward the end of summer, the first fruits of the proselyting mission were produced: four baptisms—Mary, Corger, Sally Ward, and an Indian boy named Corsetry—all Shoshone. These included the first women of that tribe to accept the Mormon faith.[3]

In August 1857, because of war with surrounding tribes, the Shoshone had been driven together for protection. On 18 August, fifty to sixty of them came to Fort Supply. According to Isaac Bullock, they "were very friendly we made them a dinner while it was being preferred I preached to them the Book of Mormon writings of their Fathers." Bullock and the other missionaries told the Indians that the approaching federal army was coming to punish the Mormons because of the Book of Mormon and the church's doctrine of polygamy. According to Bullock, "this excited the Indians, for said

---

[3] Most of the missionaries realized that the greatest missionary tool would be converted, baptized Indians, who could preach to their own people. For example, Friday, an Arapaho who visited Fort Supply, was singled out for two reasons: he seemed interested in Mormon doctrine and he could both understand and speak English well. Isaac Bullock noted,

Yesterday we received a visit from Mento Supa or Black Bear in company with Friday and some 40 other braves of the Arapaho Tribe. They are on their return from a fruitless chase after the Euwinta Tribe. They said they were two days without food. We fed them bountifully after which we preached to them in English as Friday understood the English language well, he interpreted to them. We instructed them concerning the Book of Mormon, the nature of our mission, etc. We told them about the good feeling we entertained for all the Red Men, counciling them to be at peace with all tribes, etc. etc. They manifested a good friendly feeling towards us and we believe their visit will be productive of good . . . We believe Friday would make a good missionary as he was 7 years in St. Louis.

they we have more than one wife. If they are mad at you and are going to fight you because you have many wives what will we do?''

But the missionaries also experienced some trouble with the Indians. Bullock, who replaced Brown as head of the mission in December 1855, wrote to George A. Smith that "it is a busy time here now and the Indians are coming all around us. We have our grain to harvest, potatoes to dig and crops to secure and with all our care and diligence the natives are bound to have a share." Referring to Brigham Young, Bullock quoted Tababooindowestay, a Shoshone chief, that the Indians believed "they had much to complain of Brigham. Said they, says the Buffalo, Elk, Deer, Antelope, and little prairie dogs, all of the Shoshonee meat was going to decrease and they must go to farming. And the Mormons were poor and coveted their victuals meaning flour and meat. . . . Brigham had given them nothing." Continuing, Bullock explained, "They camped 12 miles from our Fort, and ordered us to bring a wagon load of potatoes and also one of flour, as if they were lords and were to be obeyed. They demanded a beef, some flour and other articles of George W. Boyd, who is in care of Fort Bridger and he had to fork over, after which they are not satisfied but went to Jack Robinson's, a mountaineer, and shot one of his best work oxen."

In another letter to Smith, dated 20 October 1855, Bullock described the problem that arose between the Indians and settlers. One person would promise something to the Indians without informing the other settlers. This was usually done to get rid of the Indians who could become a nuisance. Bullock wrote that a band of Indians had come to the camp three weeks earlier and

> demanded a present of potatoes and wheat from Bro. Brown telling him that he had promised it to them. He told them he had made no such promise. They told him that he lied and were very bold and impatient. There had been a promise made to them by Bro. Pulsipher before they went into the valley that when the leaves fell the potatoes and wheat were ripe if they should come we would give them some wheat and potatoes that grew on their land. This promise was made in Bro. Brown's absence and he knew nothing of it. Bro. Pulsipher having the charge of affairs made this promise to get rid of them until the crops were mature for they were grapling the potatoes before they were as big as hazel nuts.

This lack of communication usually led to the Indians' stealing or destroying crops. Bullock noted, "Just about this time three braves, two young bucks and one little chief come to where Pres. Brown

125

was standing at the bars and wanted to go through he said they might if they would keep the path and not run over the grain. They pushed through and went galloping over the wheat saying it was good to run over Mormons' grain." Often the settlers allowed the Indians to have food from the fields. Yet when the settlers went to the fields to pick the crops, the Indians would take advantage of the situation by ravaging the fields and becoming angry if asked to stop. Bullock wrote, "I went to dig some potatoes for the Chief as I had promised him some he went along with me nearly his whole band followed and commenced grapling all round me. I spoke to the Chief to see what his people were doing he very carefully replied that he had no eyes and could not see them."

Usually the settlers ended up taking precautions against attack from the Indians.

> A strong guard was placed around the fort and kept up all night. . . . Our horses were sent out next morning with a guard to place where if any enemy was to come they could see the enemy before it would get to them and if they saw any dust or appearance of Indians that the guard should run the horses into the corral in the fort. About one or two O'clock a large dust rose in the distance pretty soon here comes the guard full charge with the horses the cry was the Indians are coming. Orders to arms . . . Every man was to his post expecting every moment to hear the war hoop cry from the guard house, which all most stopped our hearts from beating.

Such alarms were often false or the Indians had second thoughts about attacking the fort. On several occasions, the Indians were accompanied by the Indian agent to the fort to settle the differences between the settlers and the Indians. Summarizing the relationship between the Indians and Mormons, Bullock observed, "At times they manifest the most friendly feelings imaginable and at other times they are hostile. As you can see that we have to exercise the greatest patience imaginable to get along with them."[4]

Brigham Young had proposed a program for Indian farming in the Green River Valley in a letter to Washakie on 1 May 1855. He admonished the Shoshone to accept the Mormons' help in farming and livestock grazing, assuring the Indians that

---

[4] On 24 July 1856, the missionaries held a celebration and invited several Indians to participate. One feature of the procession was a troop of twenty-four young Indians dressed in buckskin pants, blue shirts, and moccasins, with a banner proclaiming, "We shall yet become a white and delightsome people."

We will not disturb you when you make farms and settle down. But now no matter where we settle you feel it is an infringement upon your rights. But it is not so. The land is the Lord's. And so are the cattle and so is the game. And it is for us to take that course that is best to obtain what he has provided for our support upon the earth. Now we raise grain and stock to last us year after year and work to do so. But you depend upon hunting wild game for your support.

Young explained that hunting was best for the Shoshone when they did not go too far into Sioux and Pawnee country. He continued that times were changing, that the Shoshone should locate on good land and raise grain and stock and live in houses and quit rambling about. Citing the examples of the Creek and Cherokee, Young observed that "now many of them are very rich and have good comfortable houses and plenty of property. If you do so, the Lord will be pleased with and bless you which I desire with all my heart." Washakie reacted favorably and said finally, "We will build houses by their houses, and they will teach us to till the soil as they do. Then when the snow comes and the game is fat, we can leave our families by the Mormons and go and hunt and not be afraid."

At the same time the missionaries were establishing themselves, Mormon leaders were negotiating for the purchase of Fort Bridger, which they acquired on 3 August 1855. Louis Robison had been appointed church representative in the negotiations and also headed the Indian mission there. In a letter to Daniel H. Wells, dated 5 August 1855, Robison reported that the mountain men had controlled Fort Bridger until spring 1855, when Bridger sold the outpost to the Mormons. The Mormons did not take possession of the fort until it had been legally purchased, but after 3 August the Fort Supply missionaries had an ally in the Green River Valley.

Fort Bridger was a traditional gathering place for the Indians and played an important role in promoting Mormon missionary work among Shoshone and Bannock. Food supplies were maintained at the trading post so that the physical needs of the natives could be met. This promoted friendship and confidence necessary to advance the missionary program. The mountaineers made one last effort to provoke the Indians to rebel against the Mormons in 1855. But the following year Louis Robison arrived in Salt Lake City to report that peaceful relationships had been established again. Isaac Bullock, writing from Fort Supply the following June, told Young that Washakie was glad for their presence and would accept additional settlements on their land. Young sent a reply stating, "We are glad that Washakie and his band feel so well satisfied in regards to our settling upon his land. Let all the brethren pursue a uniform course toward them of friendship and peace. Continue to conciliate them, and force them by your kinship to love you. This will not only gain but maintain peace and goodwill toward each other.''

Young was quick to capitalize on the peaceful nature of the Shoshone and the leadership of Washakie. Young's letter of 11 August 1856, written in his capacity as superintendent of Indian Affairs, advised William Hickman

> to meet with the Shoshone Indians and to hold a council with Washakee and his principal men during which you will endeavor to inculcate friendly feelings and give such instructions which will have a tendency to induce the Indians to abandon their wandering and predatory mode of life and induce them to cultivate the earth and to raise stock for subsistence. You will also seek to impress upon their minds the benefits of civilized existence and of their locating themselves so that schools may be established among them. You will seek to conciliate them toward each other and with other tribes as well as toward the whites with whom it is believed that they have ever been at peace and friendly. In the distribution of presents you will collect as many of the Indians together at Fort Bridger as you can and call to your aid Mr. Louis Robison of that place and Isaac Bullock of Fort Supply.

Acting on this request, Hickman, Bullock, and Robison reported on 19 August 1856 to Young that they had had a conference with Washakie and his tribe.

Following the arrival of the Indian goods at Fort Bridger, Isaac Bullock of Fort Supply sent Joshua Terry in search of Washakie and his band and

> found them high up on the Bear River on the eve of starting to this place. Terry informed that William A. Hickman was at Fort Bridger with presents for them. On the 16th, Washakee and his band arrived here. We smoked, had dinner, and gave them a beef after which we had a treaty or council with Washakee and some 15 of his braves. We explained the nature of Hickman's coming and by whom sent. Good spirit seemed to prevail and after much conversation adjourned to the next day at which time Washakee was notified that he should have another beef and also his presents as sent by Governor Young per William A. Hickman and Isaac Bullock. Seemed to render good satisfaction to all of the Indians present.

The letter also described how the presents were distributed and commented upon the friendliness of Washakie and his people, on the order that prevailed during the presentation of the gifts, and on a long speech by Washakie.[5]

Indian relations at Fort Bridger were quiet during the remaining months of 1856 and into early summer of 1857. In the latter part of June, Washakie and a small band of Shoshone visited the fort. Robison wrote, "They feel first rate toward us. A more friendly feeling I've never seen manifested among the Indians." Washakie and his men left soon after when a war party of forty Arapaho visited the fort. They had been warring against the Utes under the leadership of Chief Friday. Robison described the Arapaho as "the finest looking Indians that I have ever seen. They had a good interpreter with them belonging to the nations, so we had a good chance to talk with them." He said that the Indians were very hungry and that he killed a cow for them and gave them some flour and other things. The Indians were apparently anxious to have Robison meet them on the Platte River at the mouth of the Sweetwater to trade during the coming winter. By the summer of 1857, it seemed apparent that the Indian mission was successful in pacifying the Shoshone and that the missionaries might be able to extend their influence to the Arapaho.

In 1854, Brigham Young instituted a program of establishing Indian farms and appointing men to be agents (sometimes called Indian farmers). These men were expected both to teach the Indians how to farm and to be an agent with the Indians in trade and commerce. The idea had been suggested by Major George W. Armstrong, an Indian subagent, in the summer of 1854. Young elaborated his proposal more fully in an official communication, dated 23 November 1855, to the recently arrived Indian agent, Garland Hurt.[6] In his letter to Hurt, Brigham Young said,

---

[5] This orderly conduct did not always prevail, as evidenced by a letter from Robison to Daniel Wells just four days later. Robison reported that Washakie and a group of his people came to the fort for a spree. Robison tried to intervene in a fight between Washakie and one of his tribesmen and was hit several times in the face by Washakie. Washakie forced Robison to supply him and his favorites with whiskey. Robison estimated that the Indians consumed about 20 gallons of liquor before Washakie pronounced that "they should drink no more." The next morning the Indians quarrelled over a proposed attack on the Utes. Washakie opposed the action but became enraged at his own mother's defiance of his orders and stabbed her in the side with a butcher knife. Some of the braves proposed to kill Washakie for the rash act, but it was decided to wait to see if his mother died. The Shoshone chief left the post with his family, and Robison reported that Washakie's mother was still alive three days after the altercation.

[6] Hurt had succeeded subagent B. E. Betell, who had replaced Agent Holeman in late 1853. Armstrong settled in Provo and took over the eastern division while Hurt was assigned to the western agency.

I think there should be a small reservation in each of the following counties to-wit, Utah, Juab, San Pete, Millard and Iron. The reason is obvious why these counties should furnish a reservation for the natives. They are already there and would feel it a grievance to entirely leave the scenes of early childhood and cherished memories although willing to be somewhat circumscribed in the usual haunts and wanderings, comparatively small tracts of land suitable for cultivation will be sufficient for all practical purposes. They should also be connected with extensive hunting grounds which in this mountainous country there will be no difficulty attaining.

After suggesting specific locations, Young said that there "should be a farmer at each point whose business should be not to farm for the Indians at the expense of the government, as is too often the case, but to teach them to farm, raise grain, cattle, etc., and to keep and preserve property."

This program was not new (see chap. 6). Young had designated three men to work with the Indians as farmers as early as 1852, but now a more concerted program was instituted. Unfortunately, for both Indians and Mormon settlers, the non-Mormon Indian agents suspected Young's motivation and failed to cooperate fully with his recommendations. Hurt sent a secret communication to the U.S. Commissioner of Indian Affairs, dated 2 May 1855, complaining that at the recent Mormon conference a large number of missionaries had been assigned to preach and work among the Indians. Hurt feared that these missionaries might create a distinction between themselves and other Americans and suggested that the act to regulate trade with the Indians be invoked to prevent the Mormons' mission. Hurt's superiors evidently felt that the communication was important enough to forward it to the Secretary of the Interior.

Meanwhile, Brigham Young, as ex-officio superintendent of Indian Affairs, and his subordinates proceeded on their own to settle Utah's Indian problems along humanitarian lines. Young's quarterly report, dated 30 June 1856, summarized the achievements: "Farming is being successfully conducted on three of the Indian reservations made by Agent Garland Hurt, namely on Corn Creek in Millard County; on Twelve Mile Creek in San Pete County; and near the mouth of Spanish Fork, Utah County." He then expressed his ambitions for the Indians: "It is to be hoped that these laudable efforts will be crowned with the desired success and that the redmen will be successfully induced to maturely contribute to their own support, and . . . steadily advance themselves in the habits, means and appliances of civilized life."

130

In the area supervised by Subagent Armstrong, a report credited the Mormons for a successful Indian policy. On 30 June 1856, Armstrong wrote that since his last report he had visited various bands of the Piede Indians south of Fillmore City in Iron County and also those in Washington County. He reported that those on Church Creek, though few in number, operated a small farm aided by some of the citizens of Cedar City, made fences, and were preparing the ground and planting corn. They appeared pleased with the prospect of raising grain and vegetables for their own subsistence. However, they needed the necessary tools to pursue their work even on a small scale. A few implements had been loaned by the citizens of Cedar City, and Armstrong took a number of other implements to give them. On Wood Creek he found many of the Indians engaged in the same manner. Assisted by the citizens of Fort Harmony, he was convinced that Indians could become self-supporting.

A year later, Armstrong made his annual trip to the southern areas of the territory and reported that the Indians were doing better and that improvements had been made on the Indian farm. He had visited Indian locations in Fort Harmony, Santa Clara, and the Rio Virgin River, Washington County. He also reported on a band of Ute Indians under Chief Ammon on the Beaver River. With one yoke of cattle and an old plow from Beaver City, they had cleared about twenty acres of bottom land near the river and had plowed and sowed a number of acres in wheat. Armstrong said that the wheat was two inches high and had been irrigated once. Water ditches were functional. The agent presented Ammon with various tools, as well as blankets and clothing. Later he visited the farm and found that Ammon's people had used the tools to clear twelve additional acres and to plant them with corn and potatoes.

Young's successor as superintendent of Indian Affairs was Jacob Forney, who confirmed the wisdom of his predecessor when he stated that "the agricultural experiment is the only available means of ameliorating the condition of the Indians in this territory as game enough could not be found to subsist for one year." Forney described the three farms that had been opened under Young's direction and asserted that improvements exceeded $15,000. The San Pete Farm was the second farm within the boundaries of the Ute tribe and was well watered, timbered, and had a sufficiency of good grazing lands. For these reasons, it was a more desirable location for a reserve than Spanish Fork. Forney added that on "this farm there are 95 acres of land under cultivation and will produce this year about 1200 bushels of wheat besides small quantities of corn and potatoes." In addition, Kanosh, chief of the Pahvantes, had visited Forney, requesting, not paint and beads, but tools and a farmer to guide their farming activities at Corn Creek where eighty acres of wheat had been raised during the 1858 season.

While these attempts were being made to help the Indians in southern Utah, several bands in northwestern Utah and southern Idaho were almost ignored or neglected.[7] One group, under Chief Pocatello, wintered near Kelton on the northwestern point of the Great Salt Lake, and four other bands lived along the Bear River. A seventh group occupied areas in Cache Valley near the juncture of the Logan and Little Bear rivers. These Indians did not represent a threat to Mormon colonization during the early years, since the Mormon program was directed more to the south. But as the Mormons began to fill in the valleys north of Ogden, the Northwestern Shoshone became more hostile. Late in 1854, one band under Chief Little Soldier established a winter camp near Ogden and began stealing cattle and cutting fences for fire wood, asserting that "the grass that cows eat and the wood from which the fences are built belongs to the Indians." Young tried to keep these northwestern Shoshone on friendly terms, meeting with seven of their chiefs in September 1854 to distribute presents to them. And while Mormon settlers occasionally asked the Indians to join them for 24 July celebrations, they still found it difficult to "feed rather than fight them."

Another development was important in conjunction with Mormon/Indian relations prior to 1857-58. Young founded the Brigham Young Express Company in 1856 to establish colonies twenty to fifty miles apart where colonists could raise grain and provide supplies for immigrants coming to Salt Lake Valley. Part of the program was also to work with the Indians near these settlements. As a result, the Indian agent in the Platte River area protested to the federal government that the Mormon colonies jeopardized his control of the Indians. This accusation added to the suspicions already circulating in Washington, D.C., that the Mormons constituted a threat to the nation, especially in their effort to proselyte the Indians and to convince them that Americans were their enemies, Mormons their friends.

---

[7] These were later identified as the Northwestern Shoshone by anthropologist J. H. Steward, who described the various bands and located the winter camps.

This was one of the factors leading to the Utah War which also proved disastrous for the Indians. In the south they became involved in the Mountain Meadow Massacre (where John D. Lee was an Indian farmer) and other depredations, encouraged, in a sense, by the Mormon need for help in resisting the approaching army. In the north, they took advantage of the army's approach to "get even" with the Mormons who had encroached on their lands.[8] Demands that the Mormons feed large groups of Indians became so onerous that the Saints began to demand government aid and supported the idea of government reservations. The tragic Bear River battle, subsequent Mormon attempts at missionary work and farming programs, and the reservation solution are discussed in chapter 17.

[8] Jacob Forney was convinced that the Northwestern Shoshone had been "true to the government" and believed that the presence of the army implied government sanction for the attacks on Mormon colonies.

8.
Pioneer
Economics

O_f the many dictionary definitions of economics, the following probably best describes the Mormon situation during the pioneers' first decades in the Rocky Mountains: "Any practical system in which the means are adjusted to the ends." In an 1859 General Conference address, Brigham Young clearly restated the pioneers' "ends" when he avowed, "Our faith must be concentrated in one great work—the building up of the Kingdom of God on Earth." Believing that the advent of Christ's millennial reign on earth depended upon their establishing an acceptable nucleus of the kingdom, Young and other leaders instituted a wide variety of programs to achieve their desired goal. These included the colonization efforts discussed in earlier chapters; proselyting missions to the United States, Canada, the British Isles, western Europe, and elsewhere; and organized emigrating systems to "gather" the converted to the Great Basin to help build the kingdom.

The "means" to achieve these ends were primarily the volunteer labor and donations of Mormon converts, the wealth acquired and developed in colonizing the Great Basin, and the economic "windfalls" brought into the region by gold seekers and U.S. Army contingents. These means were collected primarily through the tithing system of the church and were administered by leaders to support public works, agricultural programs, merchandising, banking organizations, industrial developments, and transportation and communication systems—all of which were designed to build the earthly kingdom and make it self-sufficient.

135

To understand Mormon economic activities during this period, one must be aware of certain concepts and beliefs held by the Latter-day Saints. First, they believed that Christ's millennial reign was imminent—likely to begin in their lifetimes—which engendered tremendous energy and a willingness to sacrifice. It encouraged them to accept calls to leave settled communities and valuable property to begin building the kingdom in other areas; to labor with primitive, half-civilized Indians; or to leave families and travel to distant parts of the world to warn the inhabitants of "the impending doom."

Second, there was no division between the spiritual and the temporal in Latter-day Saint philosophy, for with God all things are spiritual. According to Mormon historian Leonard J. Arrington, church members were taught that "digging canals, tending herds, cultivating crops and constructing telegraph lines, railroads, and factory-buildings were acts of religious devotion fully equal in God's sight to prayer and worship." The construction of a water ditch was as much a part of Mormonism as water baptism, and the redemption of the land was as important as the redemption of one's soul. Some observers have asserted that because all things were spiritual, ultimately nothing was spiritual; that Mormonism became most proficient at developing practical, material programs; and that this was the essence of the religion. Whatever the case, few would question the fact that religious devotion enabled the Latter-day Saints to accomplish an economic miracle in the Great Basin.

Another important concept in discussing Mormon economics was the idea that the "earth is the Lord's" and that men and women are only stewards of their property, not absolute owners. This enabled the "Lord's representatives" not only to take Indian lands without compensation but to dictate policies concerning land distribution and use; control of natural resources such as water, timber, and mineral wealth; and the accumulation and distribution of surplus wealth in order to promote unity, equality, and self-sufficiency.

It is difficult to know how extensive a kingdom the church leaders believed must be established to usher in Christ's reign on earth. As noted previously, Brigham Young initially wanted to colonize much of the southwestern part of the United States but gradually was forced to modify his plans. It is unlikely that Young and others had clearly or even fully defined what needed to be accomplished, only that the world had to be warned, the faithful gathered to Zion, and the nucleus of a self-sufficient kingdom established. Planned villages filled with hard-working, God-fearing Latter-day Saint families engaged in building homes, chapels, and temples would continue until God decided

136

that the time was right for his son's reign on earth. Those who paid tithing to the church were promised that they would not be consumed by the fires that would destroy the wicked at the Second Coming.

Instituted in July 1838 to replace the largely unsuccessful law of consecration and stewardship, the Law of Tithing was officially accepted by church members in 1841. As initially implemented, it required that members donate to the church the equivalent of one-tenth of their possessions at the time of their conversion and one-tenth of their annual increase thereafter. Because of the unsettled conditions and the fact that many pioneers experienced a decrease rather than an increase during the trek west, the system proved rather ineffective during the early years, from 1846 to 1849, even though efforts were also made to collect donations in England and elsewhere.

Collecting tithes was also difficult because more than 70 percent of all donations were made in agricultural produce or livestock, both of which were difficult to care for during migration. Some collections were made in the Salt Lake Valley in 1848 and 1849, but an effective system was not established until 1850, when a General Tithing Office and Bishops' Storehouse was built in Salt Lake City and an elaborate network of local tithing houses was organized in each community. Church farms were located at strategic points to care for the herds of horses, cattle, and sheep received by the Presiding Bishop as tithing.

In his landmark study of the Mormon financial system during this period, *Great Basin Kingdom*, Arrington found that five different kinds of payments were used, including property, labor, produce and stock, cash, and institutional tithing. Since one-tenth of a convert's possessions at the time of his or her conversion was required, the initial donation was more likely to be paid in the form of property or livestock. Because the system had not functioned effectively in Winter Quarters, or during the early years in the Great Basin, members resolved in the September 1851 General Conference to require that each member to donate one-tenth of his or her assessed property at that time, regardless of earlier contributions. According to the account in Brigham Young's unpublished manuscript history, the resolution included a time limit, a threat of excommunication, and some millennial warnings:

> Conference also voted to commence anew with their tithing and consecrations and that within 30 days the saints should make a consecration of one-tenth of his property and one-tenth of his interest or increase ever

137

after and that those who will not thus tithe themselves be cut off from the church. A fire is kindling in the earth and who can quench it. A light is shining and who shall extinguish it. The nations of the earth are fearing and trembling. Fire burns and the light dazzles but they know not what to make of it. God has set his hand to restore Israel and the remnants of Ephraim. They know it not. The oldest and most powerful governments are shaken to their center and the kings know not the cause. The way is fast preparing for the introduction to China, Japan, and other nations.

Such appeals must have been effective. Four and one-half years later, on 30 April 1852, church leaders reported that they had received during the preceding four and one-half years $244,747.03 in tithing (mostly property) and $145,513.78 in loans and from other sources, for a total of $390,260.81. During this same period they had expended $353,765.69, which left a total in church reserves of $36,495.12.

Tithing in the form of labor involved donating every tenth day toward various church building projects, such as forts, meetinghouses, irrigation canals, roads, and other public works. The bishop was in charge of these projects when they were local; otherwise the trustee-in-trust or superintendent of public works directed the work. The church thus employed several hundred men each year in the Salt Lake City area and proportionately fewer elsewhere.

Arrington's detailed study of the tithing system in northern Cache Valley revealed that 15.4 percent of all donations were in labor. Some wealthier members paid their labor tithing by hiring others to work on church projects in their behalf. Others, craftsmen for example, used their own merchandise as tithing. This merchandise, in turn, supported the men on the public works projects. "We would not wish our tradesmen to leave their shops to work out their labor tithing in common labor with the shovel, the pick, and etc.," explained the local superintendent of public works. "We want them to pay their tithing in the kind of labor they are constantly employed at, and the products of this we can place to an excellent use."

Produce and stock tithing forced each local bishop and branch president to set up a tithing house with adjoining barns and corrals. The Cache Valley study showed that 71.8 percent of tithing paid was in the form of stock and produce. Thus the local bishop was required to collect, store, evaluate, and distribute local products. Eventually, the Mormon tithing house served its community as a storehouse, a merchandising establishment, a bank, a manufacturing plant, and, in some cases, an inn. This type of operation required a great deal of the local leader's time and energy. The church soon allowed the

138

B.P. PAID FOR WORK OR KEEPING STOREHOUSE

bishop to keep as recompense a certain percentage of the tithing collected.

Produce and stock tithing was used to take care of local Saints in need, such as widows, the elderly, the handicapped, and families of men who were on missions. It was also used to help Indians in the region. The policy of "feeding rather than fighting" was implemented only after the Mormons' first few years in the Great Basin (see chaps. 6 and 7). Men who were called to labor on church and public buildings or to colonize a new region were permitted to draw needed food from the nearest tithing office. Much of the produce and stock tithing was forwarded to the General Tithing Office in Salt Lake City where it was converted into cash by sales to local citizens or by organized stock drives to California where prices were much higher.

WHERE GOODS WENT—

As surplus goods over and above tithing donations were turned in for credit or in exchange for some needed items, the bishop was required to set a price on the commodities. In order to facilitate exchanges and to pay those who were spending their full time on church-sponsored building projects, a form of paper money called "tithing scrip" was printed. Thus the church had a kind of internal monetary system. The churchwide tithing organization made it possible for a man in England to make a donation in Liverpool and have his family receive the equivalent value from the Tithing House in Salt Lake City or in some smaller community.

Cash tithing in the form of U.S. currency or in the currency of the locality where members resided or in gold dust was especially welcome, since there was a constant demand for items that could only be purchased in the east or on the west coast. In Cache Valley the cash donations during the period 1863-1900 averaged only 12.8 percent of the total tithing paid.[1]

Another important source of income was the Perpetual Emigrating Fund (PEF) Company. Organized in 1849 to aid church members in Iowa to migrate to the Great Basin, the PEF used monies donated by church members for the specific purpose of aiding emigration. In theory, the recipients of the aid would repay the loan, thus making it possible to use the money to aid other converts to come to Zion. These contributions were in addition to the tithing donations described above.

WAS AN ADDITIONAL DONNATION

---

[1] Institutional tithing was a levy on the profits of shops, stores, and factories. This did not become an important source of income for the church until after 1869 and the advent of the transcontinental railroad.

In 1850, the PEF began raising funds to help approximately 30,000 members in England emigrate. Contributions by wealthy converts and tithing paid by European members were used to establish the fund, which was also augmented by the commissions LDS agents received from shipping lines. Brigham Young even contributed the ten dollars per case he received from granting church divorces—a contribution which gradually amounted to more than $16,000. Contributions were gathered from the Mormons who were seeking gold in the California gold fields. But the principal source of revenue was in contributions made by members already established in the Great Basin. Most of these donations were "in kind" and were collected by or delivered to block teachers and bishops throughout the territory. Through the PEF, church leaders assisted more than 51,000 Mormons to migrate to the Great Basin by the end of the 1860s.

The accumulation of community wealth in the tithing houses enabled church leaders to offer new immigrants immediate employment through the organization of Public Works. The office of Superintendent of Public Works was established in January 1850, with Daniel H. Wells designated head of the organization. Prominent in military, civic, and church affairs, Superintendent Wells served effectively throughout the 1850s and 1860s, employing an average of 200 to 500 men during the 1850s. These men were first employed in a carpenter's shop, a paint shop, a stone cutter's shop, a blacksmith shop, and an adobe yard. Later a machine shop, a foundry, and a nail factory were added. Ultimately Wells was called to supervise a variety of enterprises such as a paper mill and a sugar factory as part of the Public Works.

This organization not only enabled the immigrants to find immediate employment but also utilized their skills in building needed edifices. The Council House, the old Tabernacle, the Social Hall, the Endowment House, a bath house at the warm springs north of the city, a General Tithing Store, and a storehouse, as well as a number of other walls, residences, schools, and church buildings were all built in the 1850s.

The desire for self-sufficiency led Brigham Young to subsidize a number of floundering industrial experiments. These resulted in the loss of sizable sums of tithing money, many hours of hard work, and some additional private funds. Pottery, paper, sugar, wool, iron, and lead industries were all attempted during the Saints' first decade in the Great Basin, and while some of them enjoyed a measure of success, all must be classified as unsuccessful if judged by the goal of economic growth and self-sufficiency.

140

Perhaps the most dramatic example of the church's involvement in industrial experimentation was the attempt to supply the sugar needs of the region by developing a beet-sugar industry. This involved not only investing substantial capital in machinery and a building for a sugar refining factory but also encouraging the farmers of the region to engage in the difficult task of raising and harvesting sugar beets.

The program began in typical Mormon fashion, with the leaders sensing the need and "calling" someone to address that need. Isolated as the Mormons were, it soon became apparent to Young that purchasing enough sugar at 40 cents per pound to satisfy the needs of the growing population in the Great Basin would require an expenditure of $270,000 in 1852 alone. Of course this sum would only increase as more members emigrated to the region. Attempts to find substitutes by boiling parsnips, carrots, beets, and watermelons proved unsatisfactory. Appeals for ideas to solve the problem led Apostle John Taylor, then in Europe, to investigate the sugar beet industry in France. Aided by a young convert from the Isle of Jersey, Phillip De La Mare, Apostle Taylor became convinced the sugar industry could succeed in Utah. The Deseret Manufacturing Company was organized under Taylor's direction. Several converts put up capital for the company, including De La Mare, who invested approximately $5,000, and Isaac Russell, a Scottish ship builder, who subscribed in excess of $40,000, not all of which was in ready cash. They secured "1200 pounds of the best French beet seed" and ordered the necessary machinery from a Liverpool manufacturer. They sent the seed to the Salt Lake Valley so that a beet crop would be ready when the refining machinery arrived. They enlisted several men who could operate the factory and sent them with the machinery on the ship *Rockaway* in March 1852.

After this promising start, the story of the venture is filled with heartache and failure. Following a seven-week ocean voyage, the machinery arrived in New Orleans, where the investors were required to pay a heavy duty. Church agents took care of this and also purchased heavy Santa Fe schooners to transport the wrought-iron fabrications across the Great Plains and Rocky Mountains to the Mormon Zion.

Crossing the plains was long and difficult, but after arriving in the valley no one could be found to assemble and operate the machinery. Handicapped by delays in erecting the factory and pressed by eastern creditors for payments of debts, the investors called on

SUGAR BEET INDUSTRY

141

Brigham Young to assume their obligations and take over their properties under the Public Works supervision. Repeated attempts were made between 1853 and 1855 to refine the beet juice, but these were unsuccessful. On 29 March 1855, according to Young's unpublished history, it was announced that "the sugar works have stopped for a season, having ground over 23,000 bushels of beets into molasses during the seven weeks they were operating."

By 1856 the industry was entirely abandoned and Young turned to sorghum cane as a source of molasses that would satisfy the inhabitants. This enterprise cost the church and investors at least $100,000 and the beet growers themselves an additional $50,000. Ironically, in 1890 the Utah Sugar Company, owned by the Mormon church, succeeded in refining beet-sugar in Lehi, Utah, thus establishing what would become one of the leading industries in the region.[2]

The high cost of these industrial ventures, plus increased expenditures in emigration programs and colonizing efforts, led church leaders to reinstate the "higher" law of consecration and stewardship in 1854. As Arrington has noted, the failure to receive funds from the federal government for territorial governmental costs and a disappointing response on the part of the Saints in California to their leaders' appeal for financial help may also have contributed to the decision.

The program required church members to deed all of their property to the trustee-in-trust of the church who would then assign each member an inheritance, or stewardship, according to his or her needs. In practice, the forfeiture of personal wealth was often just a good will gesture on the part of the member, since most usually received back as an inheritance the same properties donated to the church, with the right to pass them on to their heirs or to retain them if they should leave the church. However, church leaders did acquire the right to control surplus more effectively and gain some wealth for immediate needs. Young himself listed his property to be consecrated to the church at $199,624. This was a considerable sum to have

---

[2] The attempt to establish an iron industry followed a similar pattern. Calls to serve were made by church leaders, companies were organized, money was invested, expert iron makers were recruited, and colonies were established to support the workers. High grade iron ore and coal were available in the immediate vicinity. Everything seemed right for the successful production of the much-needed product. But, as previously noted, a series of misfortunes, including floods, droughts, grasshopper attacks, Indian troubles, and finally the Mountain Meadows Massacre, all contributed to the failure of a promising industrial enterprise.

[margin notes: "1st ATTEMPT COSTLY & FAILURE" ; "1890 A SUCCESS" ; "REASONS TO RE INSTATE THE "HIGHER LAW"" ; "THE WAY THE PROGRAM RAN"]

acquired in six years and demonstrates the inequality that had become evident in the valley.

Proposed and promoted in 1854, the consecration movement was delayed until 1855 when the following printed form was distributed among the Saints:

> Be it known by these presents that I, _____, of _____, in the County of _____, and Territory of Utah; for and in consideration of the good will which I have to the Church of Jesus Christ of Latter Day Saints, give and convey unto Brigham Young, Trustee-in-Trust for said Church, his successors in office and assigns, all my claim to, and ownership of the following described property. . .

While approximately 40 percent of the 7,000 heads of families in the territory deeded their property to the church, none of the property was actually taken over by the church, and the program was abandoned in 1857 with the approach of Johnston's Army. For non-Mormons, the movement was evidence of an oppressive theocracy "snuffing out all prospect of free enterprise and private property in Utah." Congress had not yet passed laws granting land ownership in Utah, and non-Mormons threatened to oppose passage of such legislation if the Mormon church confiscated its members' property.

But there were other reasons for postponing the redistribution of wealth. The grasshopper attacks in the summer of 1855 wiped out whatever surplus food existed in the region, and the drought that followed made survival essential. Depending on the locality, the fall 1855 harvest was less than one-third to two-thirds of previous harvests. These natural disasters were followed by a bitterly cold winter—the worst the colonists had experienced since coming to the Great Basin. Heber C. Kimball estimated that about half the cattle in the territory died as a result of the snow and severe cold.

The following summer the Saints experienced another bad grasshopper attack, and the 1856 harvest was less than that of 1855. So the Law of Consecration and Stewardship of the mid-1850s suffered the same fate that it had experienced in the 1830s, and for a similar reason: it simply was not given a chance at success. However, it did stimulate the spirit of self-sacrifice and helped to increase public willingness for greater contributions to the public purse.[3]

---

[3] Although 40 percent of family heads manifested a willingness to live the "higher" law, three-fifths failed to comply with the request. This brings into question the seriousness of the millennial expectations of the members and their dedication to the building of the Kingdom of God. Such reluctance may also have been a factor in

The attempt to obey the law of consecration also led to a practice that still remains in the Mormon church: "fast offerings" (see chap. 10). During the winter of 1855-56, church leaders asked members to fast for twenty-four hours on the first Thursday of each month and to contribute the food thus saved to help the poor. Fasting was a time-honored practice for purifying the soul and communing with God, and when combined with a free-will offering to less fortunate brothers and sisters and with a "testimony" meeting in which the Saints could give extemporaneous expressions of thanksgiving and religious conviction, the monthly "fast meetings" became an accepted regular practice among the Mormons.

One of the factors leading to the industrial experiments of the 1850s and 1860s was the high cost of freighting goods from the Missouri River to the Great Basin. Brigham Young proposed and organized a large freighting and colonizing company, one that could dominate the transporting of people and materials as well as the U.S. mail from the Missouri River to the Mormon communities. Known as the Brigham Young Express and Carrying Company (BYX Co.), the organization proposed to establish a series of colonies—mile-square villages, complete with farms, mills, shops, storehouses, corrals, and other needs for community living, approximately fifty miles apart all the way from Salt Lake City to Beaver Creek, Nebraska (about 100 miles west of Winter Quarters and near the juncture of the trail north from Independence, Missouri). This company was to enable immigrants coming from Europe to make the trek to Salt Lake Valley in greater safety, less expensively, and in greater comfort. It was also to reduce the cost of freighting needed supplies for the building of the kingdom and bring added income if the U.S. mail contract could be obtained.

Using Fort Bridger and Fort Supply as support stations, Young called men to begin settlements in Nebraska and Wyoming. Once again, the limited resources of the people were tapped to carry out this far-sighted plan. Responding to church leaders' requests, 400 men and women contributed labor, livestock, provision, and

Young's inability to push the program successfully. Young's usual approach was to threaten excommunication, as he did in 1851 when he called for obedience to the Law of Tithing or in 1855 when he called the people to a voluntary rationing program. But when 60 percent of family heads failed to comply with the program of consecration and stewardship, Young may have decided to give the plan some second thoughts.

supplies. Leather makers furnished boots, shoes, harness leather, saddles, and cushions. Other craftsmen supplied additional items. The contributions of individual Mormons ranged from "1 pair socks" to quilts to a revolver to "tithing office pay." Merchants traded their wares for surplus donations or church "tithing pay." From February to July 1857, the total value of all donations to the BYX Co. amounted to approximately $107,000.

Young succeeded in securing a four-year mail contract in October 1856, and it appeared as if the plan would actually succeed. But there was opposition from Indian agents along the route, and because some settlements would be on Indian lands this was a serious matter. But Young, in characteristic fashion, pushed ahead with the project, counting on the obvious advantages to the government to nullify any opposition. Unfortunately, a more serious obstacle was developing in Washington, D.C. President James Buchanan, convinced that the Mormons were in rebellion against the federal government, cancelled the mail contract, appointed a new governor to replace Young, and ordered U.S. troops to Utah to see that his orders were carried out. This action, which is discussed in greater detail in a later chapter, brought an end to the BYX Co. and an accompanying loss of money and manpower. This ended a promising program.

It seems clear that Young was the moving force guiding and directing the economic program of the church during the Saints' first twenty years in the Great Basin. This might be expected since he was governor of the territory, Indian superintendent, and president of the church. But he was also trustee-in-trust of the church, having been appointed by General Conference vote in 1848.

When the church was incorporated by territorial legislative action in 1851, its charter limited the power of the church to acquire and hold property only by "the principles of righteousness or the rules of justice" and provided that such property "shall be used, managed, or disposed of for the benefit, improvement, erection of houses for public worship and instruction, and the well being of the church." As the sole trustee, with twelve "assistant trustees," Young had tremendous power in administering church funds. He often promoted favorite projects in his own name when he was really acting as trustee-in-trust, and using church funds without consulting other church leaders. For example, when requesting funds from Congress to construct a road from South Pass to Carson City, Nevada, Young "offered to furnish 300 miles of the road if a daily express were provided." Arrington suggests that Young did this "presumably as trustee-in-trust," but the distinction was not always clear. After Young's death, it was difficult to settle his estate because his own business affairs were intermeshed with church finances. The Anti-Bigamy Act of 1862, denying the church the right to hold property valued in excess of $50,000, forced church leaders to acquire church properties in their own names, but this only accelerated the pattern established by Young.

Young's record of failures during the 1850s must have been discouraging, not only to himself but to many of the Saints who lost sizable sums of money or property and many hours of hard labor under primitive colonizing conditions. But the programs were conceived with a desire to benefit the church and its members as well as to build up the kingdom and were carried out by and large with intelligence, courage, and fortitude. Despite all, the pioneer colonists survived, largely due to the employment opportunities and public works sustained by tithing funds and the vision of a theocratic utopia. Like many great leaders, Brigham Young was responsible for both the church's successes and failures.

B YOUNG- IN CONCLUSION

9.
Church
Organizational
Development

While colonizing efforts demanded time and energy, Mormon leaders never lost sight of their real purpose: the establishment of the Kingdom of God on earth. This required ecclesiastical organization. During their first years in the Rocky Mountains, the three-member First Presidency was firmly established as the leading quorum of the church. An extension of the Quorum of the Twelve Apostles, the First Presidency worked effectively with the apostles, while the Quorum of Seventy continued to struggle to find its role and the Presiding Bishopric became identified and stabilized only after a period of some confusion. The Presiding Patriarch, an office based on lineage, served as a comforting and guiding influence.

Stake presidencies and high councils continued to function as they had in the pre-Utah period. However, ward bishoprics assumed a much more important role, especially as the number of settlers continued to grow. Their duties included presiding over weekly sacrament services and also exerting control over such priesthood activities as visiting the Saints at home each month (variously called block teaching, ward teaching, or home teaching). Sunday schools and a reactivated Relief Society were auxiliary organizations, but neither assumed the importance that it was to gain in later years. These first decades were a time of stabilization.

The First Presidency, dissolved at the time of Joseph Smith's death in June 1844, was not formally reorganized until after Brigham

Young had led the majority of church members from Nauvoo to Winter Quarters in 1846 and the pioneers to the Great Salt Lake Valley in 1847. Young served as de facto leader for the majority of church members by virtue of his position as president of the Twelve Apostles, which was sustained as the governing quorum of the church on 8 August 1844.[1]

Upon his return to Winter Quarters in the fall of 1847, Young began to sound out the members of the Twelve about organizing a First Presidency composed of members from within their ranks. Some of the apostles initially opposed the move, fearing that their authority would be diminished as a result, and three meetings ended without a decision. However, a fourth meeting on 5 December 1847, in Orson Hyde's home in Kanesville, Iowa, resulted in Young's being sustained as president, Heber C. Kimball as first counselor, and Willard Richards as second counselor. The Twelve's action was sustained by the church at a conference on 27 December in Kanesville and in other conferences held in Salt Lake City and in Manchester, England.[2]

The First Presidency, as initially reorganized, was little more than an extension of the Twelve. Although the Twelve did not actually set the First Presidency apart for their positions until twenty years after the death of Brigham Young, since 1847 the senior member of the quorum with the longest period of continuous service in the quorum has been named the new president. The quorum voted on the reorganization, so technically it was not an automatic appointment; however, this vote was, and is, *pro forma*.[3]

(Left margin, vertical text: 1st PRES ORGANIZED)

[1] Since Smith had not clearly designated a successor or given an apparently consistent formula for choosing a new leader, the church faced a serious crisis when its prophet was martyred. In fact, according to D. Michael Quinn, Joseph Smith had designated a number of possible successors at different times and suggested eight patterns for choosing a new leader. Young had directed the completion of the Nauvoo Temple, administered temple endowment and sealing rituals, and instructed Apostle Wilford Woodruff to obtain foreign copyrights to church publications in the "name of Brigham Young, President of the church of Jesus Christ of Latter-day Saints."

[2] Quinn suggests that the absence during the December 1847 meetings of dissident apostles Lyman Wight, William Smith, and John E. Page made it possible to secure a unanimous vote from the quorum. There is also evidence that both Parley P. Pratt and John Taylor, who were in the Salt Lake Valley, had previously expressed some opposition to the idea of reorganizing a First Presidency.

[3] At least two subsequent attempts were made to deviate from this pattern—one in 1877, the other in 1887—but both were rejected by the majority of the Twelve. Several problems also developed in regards to seniority in the quorum. Prior to the October 1861 General Conference, Wilford Woodruff's name appeared before John Taylor's, since he was the older of the two. However, Taylor had been ordained an apostle four months prior to Woodruff. Young chose to reverse this order at the

Young's first presidency functioned more effectively than those organized by Joseph Smith. With the single exception of Smith's older brother, Hyrum, every member of the first presidencies organized by Smith either apostatized or was excommunicated. Young's counselors, on the other hand, were tested friends and close relatives. Richards was Young's first cousin, and Kimball was not only a long-time personal friend but he and Young shared several in-law relationships through polygamous marriages.

The three men operated as a unit until Richards died at the age of forty-nine on 11 March 1854. He was succeeded by Jedediah M. Grant the following 7 April. Grant, who had been the first mayor of Salt Lake City, was still a young man when he died after only two years in the presidency. He died at the age of forty, after leading the church through a vigorous period of introspection and self-criticism known as the Mormon Reformation (see chap. 11). His place was filled by Daniel H. Wells on 4 January 1857. Kimball served as first counselor until his death in 1868 and was succeeded by George A. Smith. Smith had served as an apostle since 1839 and had been one of the most successful colonizers in the Great Basin.

If the First Presidency was an extension of the Twelve, then the Quorum of the Twelve Apostles was the source that produced and directed church leadership. As Young said on 26 June 1865, "Tomorrow it will be twenty-one years since Joseph Smith was killed, and from that time to this the Twelve have dictated, guided and directed the destinies of this great people." Despite his having organized the First Presidency, Young still considered himself president of the Quorum of the Twelve and that his being president of the church resulted from his being senior apostle.

Originally designated as a "traveling high council," with jurisdiction only in areas outside the organized stakes, the Twelve had been given increased recognition and authority by Joseph Smith, especially during the Nauvoo period. The proselyting success of the apostles in England and the loyalty of some of the quorum members

October conference, and Taylor's name was placed ahead of Woodruff's. Fourteen years later, and two years before Young's death, Young again changed the order of the Twelve when he pointed out that both Orson Hyde and Orson Pratt had either been temporarily excommunicated or suspended from the quorum and had consequently lost their seniority. Taylor, Woodruff, and George A. Smith had been set apart as members of the quorum during Hyde's and Pratt's "brief and painful separations" and so were placed ahead of the two apostles, both of whom outlived Young and would probably have succeeded him as president if the adjustment had not been made.

149

to their prophet during times of crisis had contributed to the ascendancy of the Twelve during the succession crisis that followed the prophet's death.

Eight (nine, counting Young) members of the Twelve supported Young after Smith's death. Apostles William Smith and John E. Page had been excommunicated in 1845 and 1846, respectively, and Lyman Wight was disfellowshipped in 1848 when he failed to respond to the call to go west. But Heber C. Kimball, Orson Hyde, Parley P. Pratt, and Orson Pratt, of the original Twelve, and later additions John Taylor, Wilford Woodruff, George A. Smith, Willard Richards, Amasa M. Lyman, and Ezra Taft Benson all played prominent roles in leading the church west and in colonizing the Great Basin. Their leadership added greatly to the prestige of the Twelve during the pioneers' first twenty years in the Rocky Mountains.

Some problems of authority did inevitably arise. During the early months of 1848, for example, while the pioneers rationed their food and continued their building projects, some of their leaders became involved in a jurisdictional dispute. As noted in chapter 1, when Young left the valley in late August 1847, he indicated that John Smith was to preside as stake president, with Charles C. Rich and John Young as counselors. A high council was also organized. Young did this, knowing that in two or three months, apostles Pratt and Taylor would arrive in the valley. Evidently, Young expected the stake organization to recognize Pratt's and Taylor's higher position in the hierarchy. However, neither Pratt nor Taylor felt that their authority was being respected by the stake presidency or high council.[4] When Young returned to the valley in September 1848, he attempted to clarify the issue. In so doing, he left the way open for varying interpretations.

According to his manuscript history for 16 February 1849, Young said, speaking of the duties of the president of the stake:

He should take charge of all the affairs of the stake, spiritual and temporal, under the direction of the first Presidency. It is his privilege to call on the Presidency, the Council of the Twelve, the High Priests, the different Quorums, or any man in the Stake to assist him. . . . The Twelve are not ruling authorities here, they are subject to the authorities of the Stake and the High Council and are to observe every law and ordinance as would any member of the Church, the same as if they had not office. If

[4] Pratt, in particular, was chafing under criticisms he had received both on the trip across the plains and in the valley and finally felt it was his duty to assert his superior position.

150

the First Presidency are absent and the Presidency of this Stake or the High Council are in transgression, then if the Twelve or any one of them be there, it is his right and duty to step in and say, "I am the man to lead you." And if the High Council think they are as big as he, let them call the people together and he can wield the power and the Word of the Spirit as he pleases in magnifying his office. If the people are given up to wickedness and will not harken to him then he can bid them good-bye and leave them in the hands of the devil and God. The High Priests are a local quorum to fill up the travelling quorum when needed.

Young thus attempted to subordinate the Twelve to local authorities in matters of local concern but left the way open for any member of the Twelve to assert his authority and to demonstrate his power if the occasion demanded. Young seemed to be reflecting his experience in the 1844 succession crisis.

By the end of 1847, four vacancies existed in the Quorum of the Twelve. Three members had been called into the First Presidency and Lyman Wight had been dropped from the quorum for "dishonor[ing] the Holy Priesthood" by publishing a pamphlet against the Twelve. On 12 February 1849, Young, his counselors, and four of the Twelve met and ordained Charles C. Rich, Lorenzo Snow, Erastus Snow, and Franklin D. Richards to fill the vacancies.[5] Young then said, as reported in the official minutes of the Twelve, "Brother Heber and I have now ordained twelve apostles and we expect to ordain no more. Joseph never ordained one. Oliver Cowdery and David Whitmer did it. It then fell on the Twelve. They have been ordained by us. If any more come in they will be ordained by the Quorum and not by us as we have done our work. Seven of the twelve were here."[6]

Shortly after this meeting, Amasa Lyman and Charles Rich were sent to California, George A. Smith was called to the Iron County Mission, Lorenzo Snow was called to "open the door of the Gospel in Italy," Erastus Snow was sent to open the Scandinavian Mission, John Taylor was called to France, and Franklin D. Richards was sent to England—first to assist Orson Pratt and then to replace him when Pratt felt it was time to return to Utah. Each of these men showed remarkable ability in difficult situations and no doubt enhanced the prestige of the quorum in the eyes of church members.

---

[5] Orson Hyde, assisted by George A. Smith and Ezra T. Benson, was "presiding over the Church in the Pottawattomie land"; Orson Pratt was in Europe; and Wilford Woodruff was in the North American British Provinces.

[6] Only six apostles were present. Young later ordained George Q. Cannon and three of his own sons to the apostleship.

151

George A. Smith represented the southern Utah settlers in the territorial legislature, helped to survey a city plat for Provo and established part of his family there, served as military commander for the military district "south of Utah mountains" during the Walker War, went to Washington, D.C., in 1856 with a constitution of the proposed State of Deseret, and later led settlers to St. George, which was named for him. In 1868, six years before his death, he became a member of the First Presidency.

According to his own report, Lorenzo Snow set out on

> my mission to Italy, established the gospel in that country and also in Switzerland and the Island of Malta and sent missions to Calcutta, Bombay, and the East Indies and returned home after an absence of nearly three years. Built me a good home in Salt Lake City and was then appointed to superintend the settlement of Box Elder. Laid out a city which we called Brigham City. Built a large flour mill and a public hall for meeting 45 to 60, two stories high, above the basement [and] which when completed will cost perhaps $30,000.

This beginning enterprise ultimately led to the most successful communitarian enterprise in pioneer Utah.

Lyman and Rich presided at San Bernardino until they were called to serve in the European Mission in 1857. Due to uncertainties regarding the Utah War, they did not leave for Europe until May 1860. After serving in Europe, Rich returned to his families but was soon called to colonize the Bear Lake region. Lyman drifted into Spiritualism, was deprived of his apostleship in 1867, was excommunicated in 1870, and died seven years later.

Orson Hyde, after returning from Iowa, was called to colonize the Green River country in Wyoming in 1853 and was then asked to serve as probate judge and leader of the church in Carson Valley, Nevada, in 1855. He fell into disfavor with Young as a result of his activities in the Nevada colony. Young even referred to Hyde as "a stench in my nostrils" and insisted that Hyde "had no more right to lead the twelve than a dog." However, when Hyde returned from Carson Valley, he entered into the Mormon reformation crusade with vigor and was called to fill many speaking assignments by Young. He subsequently incurred Young's wrath again by presuming to start a conference meeting when Young was late in arriving and took a "tongue lashing from Brigham on that occasion." Later he was called to preside in San Pete County, where in died in 1878.

Ezra T. Benson presided over the church in Cache Valley, while Orson Pratt, John Taylor, Wilford Woodruff, and Franklin D. Richards served in various capacities in the Salt Lake Valley and in immigration and mission assignments.

Perhaps most tragic was the case of Parley P. Pratt. Called to preside over the Pacific missions, Pratt went to California in 1851 where he set the church in order, including disfellowshipping Samuel Brannan. He then attempted to open missionary work in South America, traveling to Chile where he labored under great difficulty. Returning home, he tried to aid a recent convert, Eleanor McLean, whom he had met in California. Finally, Pratt married her even though she had not been legally divorced from her first husband. Trying to help her secure her children, Pratt was waylaid by her first husband and his friends near Van Buren, Arkansas, and was shot and stabbed to death in 1857. He was replaced on the Twelve by George Q. Cannon, a nephew of John Taylor. Cannon had distinguished himself as a missionary in Hawaii and as editor of the *Western Standard*, a Mormon newspaper published in San Francisco.

Only two other men were added to the Quorum of the Twelve during these early years, and both were called and ordained in rather unusual circumstances. Joseph F. Smith, a son of Hyrum Smith, was only twenty-eight years old when Brigham Young ordained him to the apostleship. According to the official minutes:

> July 1st, 1866. Sunday Afternoon in a prayer circle. After we were dressed in our priesthood garments, Elder John Taylor offered the opening prayer, then Brigham Young offered a prayer with great spirit and power. When we had finished, President Young arose from his knees and took off his apron with an intention apparently of undressing. Of a sudden he stopped and exclaimed, "Hold On, should I do as I feel it? I always feel well to do as the spirit constrains me. It is in my mind to ordain Elder Joseph F. Smith to the apostleship. And to be one of my counsellors." And then called on each one of us for an expression of our feelings and we individually responded and it met our hardy approval, and we then offered up the signs of the priesthood after which Elder Joseph F. Smith, knelt upon the alter and taking off his cap we laid our hands upon him, brother Brigham being mouth and we repeated after him in the usual form. We said, "Brother Joseph F. Smith, we lay our hands upon your head in the name of Jesus Christ and by the virtue of the holy priesthood to ordain you to be an apostle in the Church of Jesus Christ of Latter-day Saints and be a special witness to the nations of the earth and seal upon your head all the authority and power, and keys of this holy apostleship and ordain you to be a counsellor unto the first Presidency of the church and the kingdom of God upon the earth. These blessings we seal upon your head in the name of Jesus Christ by the authority of the Holy Priesthood. Amen." After the ordination, Brother

153

> Brigham said that this is the first time that any person has been ordained in this manner. . . . After we had finished upstairs we descended into the historian's office and wrote this statement which we signed about 20 minutes past 6 in the afternoon of Sunday July the 1st, 1866. Signed, John Taylor, Wilford Woodruff, George A. Smith, and George Q. Cannon.

Smith was not set apart as one of the Twelve until 8 October 1867 when he replaced Amasa Lyman who was dropped from the quorum at the same time.

On 15 April 1864, Young, Taylor, and George A. Smith met for prayers. The minutes record that Young said,

> I am going to tell you something that I have never before mentioned to any other person. I have ordained my sons, Joseph A., Brigham, and John W., apostles and my counsellors, have you any objections? Brother Taylor, George A. Smith said that they had not that it was his own affair and they considered it under his own direction. He further stated that in ordaining "my sons I have done no more than I am perfectly willing that you do with yours and I am now determined to put my sons into active service in the spiritual affairs of the Kingdom and keep them there just as long as possible, that you have the same privilege." Signed John Taylor, and George A. Smith.

Brigham Young, Jr., was ordained on 4 February 1864 by his father but was not set apart as a member of the quorum until 9 October 1868. At that time he replaced George A. Smith who had been called to the First Presidency. Young evidently ordained his son John at the age of ten and again at the age of nineteen. John Young served in the First Presidency from 1873 to 1877 but was never admitted to the Twelve, nor was his brother, Joseph, who died in 1875.

The office of Presiding Patriarch was unfilled at the time the pioneers came to the Rocky Mountains.[7] William Smith, brother of Joseph Smith, had claimed the right to be ordained by reason of his relationship to Joseph and Hyrum. Although acknowledging Smith's right to the patriarchal office, Young did not ordain him until 24 May 1845, only after Smith had satisfactorily explained his questionable conduct in the eastern states where he had evidently entered into and performed plural marriages. Soon afterwards, however, Smith published a pamphlet against the Twelve and was rejected as

---

[7] The office of Presiding Patriarch was the only hereditary office in the church and was confined to the descendants of Asael Smith, grandfather of Joseph Smith. In the three cases that follow, William Smith was a brother, "Uncle" John Smith an uncle, and John Smith a nephew to the prophet.

Presiding Patriarch by a conference assembled on 6 October 1845. Excommunication followed thirteen days later.

The office was not filled again until 1 January 1849 when "Uncle" John Smith, president of the Salt Lake Stake, was ordained by Young and Kimball. Then sixty-eight years old, John Smith was highly respected by church members. In addition to his other church callings, Patriarch Smith gave some 5,560 patriarchal blessings which were recorded in seven large books. Five years later, sensing his own death, Smith dictated the following statement to church scribes, as recorded in the Historians' Office Journal, in mid-May 1854: "Father John Smith, patriarch, does not wish the brethren who meet in the council house to pray for him to live, for I know it is the will of the Lord to take me to himself when he pleases and I want him to do it in the best possible manner for my ease and comfort. By his request, John Smith, patriarch." He died at 10 minutes past 11 p.m. on May 23, 1854, a few days after making this request.

Smith was succeeded as Presiding Patriarch by John Smith, son of Hyrum Smith, on 18 February 1855. Only twenty-three years old, Smith had lost his mother in 1837 and his father in 1844. Commenting on Smith's life at the time of his ordination, Young said, according to his manuscript history,

> John Smith, son of Hyrum and Jerusa, was born in Kirtland, Guana (now Lake) County, Ohio, September 22, 1832. When in his twelfth year, his father, the patriarch, was massacred at Carthage. In consequence of the persecution of the Church and the circumstances of his family, his opportunities of attending school were very limited. He labored diligently to attend to the wants of his father's family. In manner, he was very diffident and he possessed no tact for public speaking. In the canyons and on Indian expeditions he was always found on hand by his brethren.

John Smith acted as Presiding Patriarch until his death in 1911 but was often threatened with dismissal because he habitually used alcohol and tobacco.

The Seventy had difficulty finding a definite role in the church during the Saints' first two decades in the West. Members played a prominent part in the Mormon Battalion, and Levi W. Hancock, one of the seven presidents of the Seventy, emerged as spiritual leader of the group, although he held the lowly rank of Musician, 3rd Class, which was about the same as Private. Seventy-eight members of the Seventy were listed in Brigham Young's 1847 pioneer company. As quorum members helped to colonize the West, they settled in different communities, and leaders found it difficult to keep in contact with members, since each quorum of Seventy retained their members no matter where they lived.

The seven presidents of the Seventy, who made up the presiding officers of the Seventy, were veterans of church service when they came to Utah. Joseph Young, brother of Brigham, had been ordained one of the first presidents in 1835 and continued in that office until his death in 1881. Levi W. Hancock, also called to the Seventy in 1835, served until his death in 1882. Henry Harriman and Albert P. Rockwood were ordained in 1838 and served until their deaths in 1879 and 1891. Zera Pulsipher was also ordained in 1838 but was released in 1862 because he "transcended the bounds of his priesthood in the ordinance of sealing," according to church historian Andrew Jenson.

Perhaps the most dynamic leader of the group was Jedediah M. Grant, who was ordained in 1845 and served until he was called to the First Presidency in 1854. Benjamin L. Clapp was also ordained in 1845 but was rejected in 1852, reinstated in 1853, threatened with being dropped again in 1856, and finally excommunicated in 1859. Horace Eldridge replaced Jedediah Grant in 1854 and was included with most of the other presidents in a public criticism at the October 1856 conference when Brigham Young threatened to drop all of the leaders except his brother Joseph. This was at the height of the reformation when a number of leaders were publicly criticized and threatened. The leaders survived these threats and continued to prepare their members to be missionaries. Approximately 70 percent of all missionaries between 1860 and 1870 were Seventies.

Jacob Gates and John Van Cott, a cousin of Orson and Parley P. Pratt, were chosen to replace Benjamin L. Clapp and Zera Pulsipher, completing the roster of men who served as the seven presidents during these early years. Van Cott, although of Dutch extraction, had served two missions in Scandinavia and was looked upon as the Scandinavian representative in the church hierarchy.

The fifth and final quorum organized in the church was the Presiding Bishopric. According to Michael Quinn, "Of all the units of L.D.S. hierarchy, the historical development of this office has been the most complex and least understood." This lack of understanding, particularly about the relationship of the Presiding Bishopric to the First Presidency, continued after the Saints arrived in the Great Basin. Newel K. Whitney functioned during the early to mid-1840s as General Bishop along with Vinson Knight and William Miller. When Knight died and Miller became disaffected while crossing the plains,

Whitney emerged as Presiding Bishop and was sustained as such in 1847.

Initially, Whitney served in the bishopric alone. But on 6 September 1850, Brigham Young and Heber C. Kimball were sustained as his counselors. Whitney died two weeks later, and the experiment of unifying the office of Presiding Bishop with the quorum of the First Presidency ended. P B + F. P.

Edward Hunter replaced Whitney on 7 April 1851, serving without counselors until the following 8 September. At that time Young called Nathaniel H. Felt and John Banks as traveling presiding bishops under Hunter. A month later, Young called Alfred Cordon to be a "traveling bishop to preside over other bishops." All of these men were sustained as "assistant presiding and traveling bishops among the people" in the April and October conferences of 1852 and also in April 1853. Despite these appointed assistants, Young and Kimball were, according to Young's manuscript history, called as Hunter's counselors on 11 April 1852 and were unanimously sustained by the conference.[8]

From October 1853 to October 1856, however, Hunter served without assistants or counselors being sustained with him at General Conference. Felt, Banks, and Cordon had all been released in October 1853. Leonard W. Hardy and Jesse C. Little were sustained as first and second counselors in the Presiding Bishopric at the October 1856 conference and continued to serve with Hunter through the 1860s.

Since the church was financed by tithes, and about 80 percent of tithing was contributed in "kind" or labor, the Presiding Bishopric had a major task in managing these products. The General Tithing Office and "Deseret Store" in Salt Lake City became the merchandising center of the territory and, as previously noted, played an important role in colonizing the region.

John Smith, Charles C. Rich, and John Young served as the presidency of the Salt Lake Stake from 3 October 1847 until 1 January 1849. Together with the high council, these men constituted the governing body of the church in the valley during the difficult months of early settlement. They not only presided in religious affairs but were required to make laws, to punish offenders, to settle disputes,

---

[8] Quinn has written that Young and Kimball were apparently never presented at General Conference as counselors to Hunter, but Young's manuscript history is clear. Hunter was also named at the time as assistant trustee-in-trust for the church.

to regulate economic affairs, and to organize a military force to protect the settlements against Indian attacks. They proved to be effective leaders, even though apostles Parley P. Pratt and John Taylor felt that they had failed to create an atmosphere of harmony and confidence.

This stake presidency was broken up on 1 January 1849 when Young, Kimball, and Grant called on John Smith and ordained him Presiding Patriarch. Charles Rich was called to be an apostle, and John Young was ordained president of the High Priests. Smith was succeeded as stake president by Daniel Spencer, who was chosen on 12 February 1849. Five days later, Spencer helped to ordain David Fullmer and Willard Snow as counselors. Isaac Morley was chosen to head the high council. Brigham Young charged Spencer to be responsible for both the temporal and spiritual welfare of the Saints under the direction of the First Presidency and gave him to understand that he had the right to call on any member of his stake, apostle and prophet alike, to aid in building the kingdom. Spencer served as stake president until his death in late 1869. Between 1847 and 1869, nine stakes were organized. The longest tenure for any stake president was Daniel Spencer's twenty years, while the shortest was Charles C. Rich's four months.

One of the unique aspects of stake government was Brigham Young's tendency to appoint members of the Quorum of the Twelve to serve as stake leaders as well. Lorenzo Snow, Ezra T. Benson, Charles C. Rich, Franklin D. Richards, Brigham Young, Jr., Orson Hyde, and Erastus Snow all served as area leaders. Young decided to end this practice just before his death in 1877.

Perhaps the most important and critical change in church organization involved the duties of bishops. During the Nauvoo period, the city had been divided into geographical units, called wards, and bishops had been appointed to preside over them. However, a bishop's duties were primarily temporal. All members of the church in a geographic area, from various wards, met together for preaching services. This pattern was followed during the first years in the valley. Brigham Young, or another of the general authorities, was typically the speaker, and matters of concern to the community were usually discussed. Apparently, preaching services were held in the forenoon and afternoon, with the evening reserved for quorum meetings, high council trials, and other gatherings. These general meetings in the Bowery, Council House, or Tabernacle were held during most of these early years. However, ward bishops also evidently held preaching and sacrament services.

158

At first, the city was divided into five wards. But on 16 February 1849, the valley was divided into four wards south of the city and east of the Jordan River, one ward west of the Jordan River, and three wards north of the Great Salt Lake and east of the Jordan River. Six days later, the city was divided into nineteen wards of nine blocks each. Edward W. Tullidge asserted, in his *History of Salt Lake City*, that "each of the nineteen wards developed . . . before the regular incorporation of the city, like so many municipal corporations, over which the bishops were as chief magistrates or mayors."

Leonard J. Arrington, writing about the career of an important and influential Salt Lake bishop, Edwin D. Woolley, summarized the general and specific duties of the typical bishop: He "saw that the ward was fenced in to protect the garden and orchards in the ward from roving livestock"; that "a ward school was built and operated"; that a ward Sunday school was organized; and "supervised dances, musical, and theatrics each winter after the harvest." He "introduced and directed programs, collected tithes and contributions, gave counsel, relayed doctrinal pronouncements and policy decisions," solicited volunteers for "economic and gospel missions"; and "raised his ward's quota of laborers on the public works, teamsters to 'go east' to pick up immigrants, laborers to work on temples, produce for various church causes, and cash to buy such items as telegraph wire." He "performed marriages, conducted funeral services, promoted women's work by organizing a ward Relief Society, and directed the work of what they called the Lesser Priesthood (Aaronic Priesthood)." He "counselled young people, old people, and in fact all members of the ward"; "directed the activities of the ward, both temporal and spiritual"; was "their representative in dealing with Church officials, city officials and territorial officials"; and their "advocate, defender, promoter." Finally, he was "a mediator, arbitrator or conciliator. Any difficulties between neighbors or ward members which could not be settled by the parties concerned—and there were many—were to be settled by the bishop. He might conduct a bishop's court in which testimony would be taken, statements and affidavits read, and the bishop would make a decision which would be binding upon the parties involved."

Bishops were not paid. Instructing the bishops in 1856, Brigham Young acknowledged that they sometimes complained they had no time for their own family responsibilities. Specifically, some of them had said that they had to reserve time to go get wood and poles from the canyon, attend to their farm, and make repairs on their own houses. Young always insisted that their work as bishops came first.

"Let it take up all your time," he said, "and trust in God for a living." "If you do your duty," he said, "the Lord will open up your way so you will be rewarded."

Unfortunately, not all bishops lived up to their callings as indicated in Young's sermon delivered on 15 June 1856:

> I have proof ready to show that Bishops have taken in thousands of pounds of tithing which they have never reported to the general tithing office. We have documents to show that Bishops have taken in hundreds of bushels of wheat, and only a small portion of it has come into the general tithing office; they stole it to let their friends speculate upon. If anyone is doubtful about this, will you not call on me to produce my proof before a proper tribunal? I should take pleasure in doing so, but we pass over such things in mercy to the people.

This, of course, may be little more than typical Young rhetoric. Still, it should not be surprising that some bishops failed in their calling; what is impressive is that so many succeeded in light of their other duties and the problems they faced in supporting their own, often large, families. During the years 1847 to 1869, more than one hundred bishops were appointed, and they frequently served twenty years or more. Edwin Woolley, for example, was called to be bishop of the Salt Lake Thirteenth Ward in 1854 and served until his death in 1881, a period of twenty-seven years.

One of the difficulties bishops had to deal with was their relationship to priesthood quorums. For example, the Melchizedek Priesthood quorums, except the Seventies, were organized on a stake basis (as is the case in the Mormon church today) and held their own meetings. The bishop had no authority to deal with such quorums. The Seventies were organized as units of the church, had a wide organization, and were not subject to stake jurisdiction. Bishops were assigned to be in charge of the Aaronic Priesthood quorums and to serve as president of the Priests' quorum, but even here there were some jurisdictional disputes and misunderstandings.

Only two of the church's auxiliary organizations functioned during these two decades. The Sunday School was started by Richard Ballantyne in December 1849 in his own home with fifty children in attendance. The idea soon spread throughout the region, but each group operated independently. Not until 1872 did the church unify the activities of the separate groups with the Deseret Sunday School Union. The Sunday School was intended primarily for young people, and adult classes were not organized on a churchwide basis until the twentieth century.

160

The second auxiliary organized during this period was the Women's Relief Society. Based on the Nauvoo Female Relief Society of the early 1840s, the Women's Relief Society was established in 1867 and presided over by Eliza R. Snow, one of the most influential women in pioneer Utah. Relief Society members aided the poor, avoided luxuries, assisted in the operation of cooperative stores, and supported home industry. They also encouraged the organization, beginning in 1869, of Retrenchment Societies among young, usually single, women. These societies were eventually grouped together and became known as the Young Ladies' Mutual Improvement Association. Members promoted frugal, practical economic and cultural activities and advocated women's suffrage and equal rights throughout the settlements.

After an initially unstable period following their arrival in the Great Basin, church leaders settled on a program of steady ecclesiastical development. The First Presidency assumed control of church affairs and governed the various settlements and missions through the leadership of the Quorum of the Twelve Apostles and, to some extent, the Presiding Bishopric. Stake presidencies and high councils supervised the members in the stakes; bishops exercised the most direct influence over the day-to-day lives of the pioneers. Eventually the general and local leadership stabilized, and the kingdom was ruled in an increasingly orderly fashion.

10.
Religious
Doctrines
and Practices

W hen its members entered the Great Basin in mid-1847, the Mormon church had existed only seventeen years— hardly enough time to establish uniform religious doctrines and practices. Plural marriage, which emerged in Nauvoo, Illinois, was practiced openly in the Rocky Mountains and in 1852 was publicly announced and defended. The closely allied doctrine of celestial or eternal marriage continued to develop, as did the temple ordinances for the living and dead, including the endowment.[1] The extending of family ties through adoption back to Adam survived the trek west, as did rebaptism, which was also practiced in Nauvoo. Observance of the Word of Wisdom both increased and declined during these early years, depending upon the time and situation. And because of the injunction to preach the gospel to all the world before the Second Coming, missionary work expanded to include the Middle East and Orient.

Plural marriage was an important practice during the Saints' first twenty years in the West. Joseph Smith had initiated this complex marriage system in Nauvoo and perhaps even earlier in Kirtland, Ohio, but only a few trusted church leaders had been allowed to practice it before 1847. When Smith secretly introduced the

---

[1] The temple endowment is a ritualized drama of the creation, fall, and redemption of Adam, during which its participants make specific promises regarding obedience to the commandments and loyalty to the church, together with learning various passwords and other signs they believe will one day enable them to enter into the celestial, or highest, kingdom of heaven.

163

NAUVOO
VERY FEW

practice to the Twelve Apostles and others in 1841, he told them to take extra wives or be damned. According to Mormon genealogist Richard Horsley, less than 100 men took plural wives during the Nauvoo period, and in almost every case they were "veterans" of the church, having been members for more than five years.

Fearing public exposure, Mormons who entered into plural marriage were told to keep the practice secret and to deny it publicly. This policy continued after the Saints left Nauvoo in 1846. In England, church leaders denied rumors that the church sanctioned polygamy as late as 1851. However, keeping plural marriage secret was difficult in Winter Quarters and during the exodus west, and little reason for secrecy existed once the pioneers had settled in the Great Basin. Captain John W. Gunnison, who had been in the Salt Lake Valley since 1849, wrote in his account of the Mormons in 1850 that "many have a large number of wives in Deseret is perfectly manifest to anyone residing among them and indeed the subject begins to be more openly discussed informally and it is announced that a treatise is in preparation to prove by the scriptures the right of plurality by all Christians if not to declare their own practice of the same."

With the influx of non-Mormons into the valley during the California gold rush and the appointment of territorial officials, church leaders realized they could no longer keep the practice secret. The federal officials who returned to Washington, D.C., claiming that they could not work with the Mormons, were among those who first reported that the Mormons were practicing plural marriage, leading Brigham Young and other leaders to publicly announce and defend the practice. A special conference of the church was called on 28 and 29 August 1852, ostensibly because a large number of missionaries were being called to various parts of the world and leaving in August was more convenient than leaving in October. However, on the forenoon of the second day, Elder Orson Pratt[2] stated that he had been called upon to address the people on the "Plurality of Wives."

FIRST PUBLIC
ANNOUNCEMENT

Pratt argued that over four-fifths of the world accepted plural marriage and gave evidence from both the Old and New Testaments

---

[2] In 1842 Pratt had been temporarily suspended from the Twelve because he opposed polygamy and believed that Joseph had propositioned his wife. However, after considerable struggle, he came to accept plural marriage under certain circumstances as sanctioned by God. Pratt eventually married a number of wives and sought evidence from world history and the scriptures to justify the practice.

164

that the biblical prophets accepted and practiced polygamy. Pratt even asserted that Jesus may have been a polygamist, pointing to the relationship he seemed to have with Mary, Martha, and Mary Magdalene. In addition, Pratt pointed out the sociological advantages of polygamy—that it gave every woman the right to be a wife and mother and that there was therefore no place for prostitution in the Mormon scheme of things. He concluded by saying that he believed the United States would not, under the present form of government, condemn the Mormons for their religious teachings: "The Constitution gives privileges to all the inhabitants of this country—the free exercise of their religious notions and the freedom of their faith and the practice of it. . . . And should there ever be laws enacted by this government to restrict them from the free exercise of this part of their religion, such laws must be unconstitutional."[3]

The immediate impact of the church's disclosure is difficult to judge. Certainly antagonism ensued, and many editorials were written against the Mormons. The announcement even occasioned some dismay among foreign church members[4] and outraged the general population of the United States. In fact, polygamy was used to argue against popular sovereignty in the discussions of the Kansas-Nebraska Act (see chap. 13).

Mormon polygamy, unlike polygamy in other cultures, developed rapidly, without the usual societal norms and institutions for regulating its practice. Thus no limit, formal or informal, was imposed on the number of wives a man might have. Neither did a strictly prescribed method of gaining additional wives exist. As a result, several Mormon leaders married large numbers of wives in a short period. Writing in the mid-1850s, John Hyde, Jr., a Mormon apostate,

---

[3] In commenting on the necessity of Pratt's discourse, early twentieth-century Mormon historian B. H. Roberts wrote that the church owed such a public disclosure because "it had been a matter of wide knowledge within the Church for some time that such a principle was not only believed in but practiced by many leading Mormon officials. Yet none to whom this knowledge had come felt at liberty to make a public proclamation of the doctrine. . . . In the absence of an official announcement," Roberts concluded, "plural marriage had become a source of embarrassment. Justice to the women involved in the system, moreover, also required an official proclamation, for their standing must have become equivocal had the announcement been delayed much longer."

[4] T.B.H. Stenhouse, in *Rocky Mountain Saints*, asserts that many excommunications followed the announcement, but B. H. Roberts's more careful study indicates that there were about as many excommunications in the six months prior to the announcement as in the six months after. Nevertheless, from 1850 to 1854, some 15,000 excommunications took place in England, evidence of significant unrest, whatever the reason.

described Salt Lake City's downtown section not far from Brigham Young's Lion House and Beehive House:

> A very pretty house on the east side was occupied by the late J. M. Grant and his five wives. A larger barracks-like house is tenanted by Ezra T. Benson and his four ladies. A large but mean-looking house to the west was inhabited by Parley P. Pratt and his nine wives. In that long dirty row of single rooms half hidden by a beautiful orchard and garden lived Dr. Richards and his eleven wives. Wilford Woodruff and his five wives reside in another large house still farther west. Orson Pratt and some four or five wives occupy an adjacent building. And looking toward the north we see a whole block covered with houses, barns, gardens and orchards in the east [for] Heber C. Kimball and his eighteen or twenty wives and their families.

Hyde did not mention Young's Beehive House and Lion House, where eighteen to twenty of his wives lived.

Numerous wives was the exception rather than the rule. Mormon researcher Stanley Ivins, in his study of 1,784 polygamist men, found that 66 percent married only one extra wife. About 22 percent had three wives, and only about 7 percent had four. This left a small group of less than 6 percent who married five or more women. Ivins wrote that "the typical polygamist, far from being the insatiable male of popular fable, was a dispassionate fellow content to call a halt after marrying one extra wife, required to assure him of his chance to salvation."

Nor was there an established courtship pattern. Some men married widows or young girls who had no other relatives. Some married girls who were living with their family as maids. Some asked their wives to help them choose, while others became involved in romantic courtship, often causing heartache to their other wives. Everything seems to have depended on the feelings and the situation of the people involved. Often, the men married sisters because the wives found it easier to get along together. In fact, Mormon sociologist Kimball Young's study, *Isn't One Wife Enough?*, found that as many as 20 percent of men taking additional wives married sisters. Often when these men married additional wives, the sisters refused to accept them or left the marriage rather than tolerate an "outsider."

How the wives were housed also varied. Some plural families lived under one roof. In others, each wife lived in a separate house. At times, families were spread throughout the city or even the region.

SEPARATE HOUSE

Gradually a rule was established that no man could marry into polygamy unless he could support an extra wife in a separate household. But this rule was never really followed or enforced. Theoretically, all of the wives in the family were to be equal. In practice the first wife was usually more powerful because she was the only "legal" wife. She was supposed to give her permission before her husband married other wives, for example. Kimball Young's study indicates that when a man took several wives, he consulted the first wife but often not his other wives. Although the first wife enjoyed legal status, the second or later wife was often younger, more beautiful, or benefited from the romance of the courtship.

The percentage of Mormons involved in polygamy is difficult to ascertain. Studies by Young, Ivins, and Nels Anderson indicate that about 10 to 15 percent of eligible males were polygamous, and since each had at least two wives, a fairly sizable percentage of Mormons were involved in plural marriage—perhaps as high as 40 to 60 percent. Ivins found in his study that the percentage increased whenever the federal government threatened the practice. Leonard Arrington, in *Great Basin Kingdom*, argued that church pressure was the strongest motive for polygamy and that the rate of polygamous marriages rose whenever religious reformations took place or the Mormons were threatened economically. The classic example is the Mormon Reformation of 1855-57 when a tremendous amount of pressure was exerted on men to marry polygamously. Apostle George A. Smith wrote that by 1857 there was hardly an unmarried girl in the territory who had reached her fourteenth birthday.

YOUNG WIVES

SUCCESS RATE

The success of such marriages is an open question. According to Kimball Young, 53 percent of the cases he examined were either highly successful or reasonably successful. One-fourth were moderately successful, and only 23 percent were rated as having considerable or severe conflict. There is evidence, however, that this may be too optimistic because Brigham Young granted a large number of divorces during this period. Between 1847 and 1859 Young authorized 517 divorces, practically all of which were from polygamous marriages. These divorces involved church officials, including Young himself, Heber C. Kimball, Willard Richards, John Taylor, Wilford Woodruff, John Smith, John and Phineas Young, Orson Spencer, William W. Phelps, Benjamin Johnson, and John M. Bernhisel. Many of these had probably been marriages of convenience, involving women who had been disassociated from their first husbands or disowned by their families. Some had no one to take them across the plains or give them a home after they reached the Great Basin. Many of these

failed marriages began without a real chance for developing mean-
ingful relationships between the partners.[5]

Despite difficulties, many plural families succeeded in establishing good relationships and in raising well-rounded, intelligent children. Many of the wives loved each other and each other's children
and were able to function well in this system. Nonetheless, plural
marriage was a constant source of difficulty with the outside world
and ultimately one of the factors leading to the so-called Utah War
(chap. 14).

Beginning in Nauvoo, Mormons believed that marriages performed by the necessary authority, or priesthood, would last for all
eternity. Eternal marriage for Mormons implies all the joys of the
wedded state, including parenthood. According to B. H. Roberts,
"Man's heavenly home was to be upon the earth after it had become
sanctified and made a celestial sphere. His relations with his kindred and friends were to be of such a nature to satisfy the longings
of the human heart, for society, for fellowship, and needed only the
revelation of this marriage system to complete the circle of his promised future felicity." In Mormonism men and women are spirit children of God capable of achieving godhood themselves. To do so they
must enter into "the new and everlasting covenant of marriage."
Thus sealed for eternity, Mormon couples will one day procreate
spirit children, organize worlds, and people them with their own offspring.

This and other ordinances can only be performed in Mormon
temples—although when temples were not available some ordinances
were performed elsewhere.[6] The Nauvoo Temple was completed
while the Mormons were preparing to leave Illinois and used heavily
from 1845 until the Saints left in 1846. The fervor with which the
temple was completed indicates the extent of the Mormon belief in
the necessity of temples and temple ordinances.

On 28 July 1847, just four days after the pioneers entered the
Great Salt Lake Valley, Brigham Young designated an area for a new

SUCCESS

---

[5]Some of these marriages undoubtedly were also entered into because of the
belief in an impending millennium. Convinced that Jesus Christ's reign on earth
would begin soon and that a man's kingdom would be based on the number of wives
and children he had, men might enter into such marriages without planning very far
into the future. It was a time of dislocation and adjustment, and it is easy to understand why so many marriages failed.

[6]For example, Addison Pratt, who had not received his endowments in the Nauvoo
Temple, was taken to Ensign Hill, just northeast of Salt Lake City, on 21 July 1849 for
that purpose. Brigham Young's scribes noted in his unpublished history that Ensign
Hill had been specially dedicated that day for the giving of endowments.

temple on City Creek. This site was later approved and meetings were held on the location. During the April 1851 General Conference, construction was officially authorized, and on 9 October 1852 church members voted to use only the best materials available. Groundbreaking ceremonies took place on 14 February 1853, and then in an impressive celebration, the corner stones were laid on 6 April.

After Brigham Young opened the conference session with song, prayer, and some remarks, a parade formed and marched through a line of guards to the southeast corner of the temple grounds. Young then intoned, "We dedicate the southeast corner stone of this temple to the most high God. May it remain in peace until it has done its work, until He who has inspired our hearts to fulfill the prophecies of these holy prophets that the House of the Lord shall be reared in the tops of the mountains shall be satisfied and say, 'It is enough.' " Similar services were held at each of the other cornerstones. However, it would be forty years before the temple would be completed. So for a time these ordinances were performed in the Council House or in Brigham Young's office until a temporary Endowment House could be erected.

Conducting these ordinances in the Council House proved increasingly difficult because the building was used for a variety of purposes, including offices for federal officials. Church authorities decided to construct a temporary building for administering ordinances where they would not be observed by the growing non-Mormon community. The architect was Truman O. Angell, whose first blueprint of the floor plan was completed in March 1854. By 11 September, the foundation was finished, and three months later the rafters were going up. Angell called the project the temple protem or pro tempore, meaning temporary temple. It was not until the early part of 1855 that the phrase 'endowment house' was used.

On Saturday, 5 May 1855, eight years after Joseph Smith began performing endowment ceremonies in Nauvoo, Brigham Young and other church leaders dedicated the new building. The prayer "was done by first naming each room separate, then the material of each part separate from stone to lumber, from adobes to sand, including every kind of material from the foundation to the chimney top." After the dedication, ordinances were administered until five in the afternoon when three couples were sealed. As they progressed through each stage of the ceremony, initiates stepped up to the next room. Though simple, the Endowment House contained all of the rooms

169

modern LDS temples have and served as a structure for temple ordinances during the Saints' first three decades in the region.

The primary ordinances performed in the Endowment House included sealings of living couples; sealings by proxy for the dead; sealings between couples in which one partner was living and the other dead; endowments for the living; and second anointings (a "higher blessing" confirming the blessings of godhood upon its recipients). Only near the end of the pioneer period, beginning in July 1867, were baptisms for the dead performed in the Endowment House. Brigham Young decreed that until the Saints completed a regular temple, certain ordinances could not be performed, including sealings between both living and dead parents and children and endowments for the dead. "We can just administer so far as the law [of God] permits us to do," Young insisted.[7]

By refusing to seal children to parents, Young temporarily curtailed a program that had emerged in Nauvoo and played an important role in colonizing the Great Basin—that of adoption. Many adoptions were performed in the partially completed Nauvoo Temple beginning in 1845. Not only were children sealed to parents, but men adopted other adults into their family. Adoption was usually restricted to apostles, who believed that in the Millennium they would be adopted into a family system that extended back to "Father Adam."[8] Seventy-four percent of those adopted, excluding natural children and relatives, were linked to Heber C. Kimball, Willard Richards, John Taylor, or Brigham Young. Most of those adopted were young couples in their twenties and thirties, although some were in their forties. Some of the adopted would become well known Saints, but only one or two ever occupied positions of first rank in the church.[9] According to Mormon historian Gordon Irving:

[7] Prayer meetings and instructional meetings for departing missionaries were also held in the Endowment House. Most prayer meetings were general weekly gatherings; however, some were meetings of the First Presidency and Twelve Apostles. The first instructional meeting was held on 5 April 1855, shortly before the building was dedicated. Following the day's services, Heber C. Kimball lectured to "about 15 brethren who were immediately going on missions." Missionaries were also set apart in the Endowment House.

[8] For a time during the mid-nineteenth century Mormons regarded Adam as a god who stood at the head of the human race and to whom they would ultimately be sealed as members of an eternal patriarchal family unit. This complex belief is usually referred to as the "Adam-God theory." It was never systematized into a consistent and understandable theology and was never adopted as an "official" doctrine of the church.

[9] One who achieved some prominence was John D. Lee, who was adopted by Brigham Young. On occasion he even signed his name John D. Lee Young. Writing

170

The circumstances of 1846 made such a practical application of the adoption doctrine particularly appealing to the Church leadership. Apart from problems of member loyalty left over from the succession crisis which had followed the murder of Joseph Smith, the Church was also faced with the confusion inherent in breaking up of homes and moving en masse to an unsettled wilderness. People had to be moved; supplies had to be found; camps and temporary cities had to be located and established; morale, not to mention faith, had to be maintained; and always present was the uncertainty of the Church's future course. In the midst of turmoil, uncertainty and weariness, Mormon leaders were sufficiently impressed with the potential of adoption, already part of the Mormon doctrinal system, as a unifying force to take seriously its this-worldly implication. So in what can be viewed as an experiment, the organization of Mormon society along family lines was tried out on a small scale within the families of the leaders. Part of this experiment was the expansion of the adoptionary system to include a large number of people. As there was no temple in the wilderness, there could be no further formal adoptions. This difficulty was overcome by treating persons desiring to join one's family as though they had already received the temple sealing. Later, when a temple could be built, they would go through the formal ceremony.

Hosea Stout recorded in his journal on 13 July 1846 that Apostle Orson Hyde had announced that "all who felt willing to do so to give him a pledge to come into his kingdom when this ordinance could be attended to." The Mormon concept that one's status as a god in the next life would be determined by the number of descendants encouraged recruitment. Apostle George A. Smith admitted in February 1847 that he had "electioneered with all his might to get people to join him." And Wilford Woodruff, in his journal, described the creation of several of these extended families:

Brigham Young went with his company or family organization of those who had been adopted unto him or who were to be and organized them into a company which . . . may yet be called the tribe of Brigham. They entered into a covenant with uplifted hands to heaven with President Brigham Young and each other to walk in the commandments of the Lord. President Heber C. Kimball organized his family company consisting of about 200 persons in the council house.

later, Lee noted, "I was adopted by Brigham Young and was to seek his temporal interests here and in return he was to seek my spiritual salvation. I, being an heir of his family, was to share his blessings in common with other heirs." Thus sons were to give their fathers the benefit of their labor and fathers were to offer their adopted children not only security in the next world but counsel and direction in this one as well.

171

Woodruff organized his own family company of forty men, mostly heads of families, who entered into a covenant with "uplifted hand to heaven to keep all the commandments and statutes of the Lord our God and to sustain me in this office."

When Brigham Young was having trouble with some of his family over plural marriage, he called them together for a lecture followed by dinner and a dance. The Heber C. Kimball family, as a general rule, met on Sundays for sermons and the sacrament. Kimball's family also held parties and dances. However, difficulties began when it became apparent that not all adopted members enjoyed the same status. For example, jealousy surfaced among Brigham Young's adopted sons and in John D. Lee's family. Part of the difficulties between adopted sons and fathers arose when men who had been adopted into families felt that they were working only for their adopted father and were not building up a kingdom for themselves. George Laub, one of Lee's adopted sons, wrote that on a trip to Missouri to buy grain, one of Lee's other sons refused to return the corn purchased there to him, swearing that "he was not going to be a negro for John D. Lee any longer and he was going to work for himself." Laub and Lee quarrelled several times over Lee's keeping too large a portion of the fruits of his sons' labors. Eventually Laub appealed to Brigham Young to be released from this relationship.

After 1848, adoption began to decline. Still, relationships which had already been established continued, and some new ones were formed on a temporary basis while awaiting the completion of a temple. Nineteenth-century Mormon historian Edward Tullidge believed that adoption explained how some pioneers distributed land upon entering the valley. Adoption also continued to influence personal relationships. Gradually, as memories of unpleasant experiences faded, members began speaking again of adoption. For example, in 1860, Brigham Young maintained that adoption was a glorious doctrine but that the people were not ready for it. However, after the completion of the St. George Temple and the death of Brigham Young, adoption was reintroduced and practiced until the 1890s.

Another important religious activity during this period was missionary work. During his temporary absence from home, a man's family would have to survive without him by running the farm or business enterprise themselves. Wives managed to survive with help from relatives, friends, and church leaders. One early missionary venture included men from the gold fields (see chap. 3) who were sent to the Sandwich Islands in the fall of 1850. Although five of the ten missionaries, including the mission president, became discouraged and left, George Q. Cannon learned the language rapidly and was able to publish the Book of Mormon in Hawaiian. Subsequent missionaries were either accompanied by their wives or later joined by them. The mission was successful for the first few years, but with the coming of Johnston's Army, the missionaries were called home, leaving some 4,000 converts to fend for themselves. Many came under the influence of Walter Murray Gibson, an opportunist who attempted to set up his own kingdom in the Hawaiian Islands.

The most remarkable aspect of missionary work during the 1850s was the call of hundreds of men to distant parts of the world to proclaim the gospel when, at the same time, Brigham Young was encouraging people to gather to Zion. Not surprisingly the church sent many of these missionaries to the United States, Canada, and Europe, especially the British Isles. But missionaries were also sent to countries where missionaries had never labored before. Because of their belief that the gospel must be preached to all the world prior to the Second Coming, church leaders sent missionaries to Gibraltar, the Middle East, India, Ceylon, China, and South Africa despite the need for manpower in the Great Basin.

Perhaps the least successful of these endeavors was Parley P. Pratt's mission to South America. Pratt was called in February 1851 to the Pacific Islands, lower California, and South America. He arrived in California in March, and under his supervision a second group of missionaries was sent to the Hawaiian Islands. Pratt also announced he wanted to send Elders to New Zealand and Australia, while he would visit Chile and South America. Accompanied by one of his wives and Rufus Allen, Pratt's small contingent took up residence in Valparaiso, Chile, where they remained for several months but had little success. A revolution was then in progress, and restrictive laws about religion made missionary activities impossible. Pratt also found the language difficult and never felt competent to preach in Spanish. Finally he was forced to return, hungry and sick, without making any contacts for the church.[10]

Other missions were launched at the special August 1852 conference when plural marriage was first publicly announced. Orson Spencer and Jacob Oats were sent to Prussia but found it almost impossible to work there. Edward Stevenson and Nathan Porter

---

[10] Pratt sent John Murdock and Charles W. Wandell to Australia in October 1851, and they were able to organize a branch of the church in Sydney on 4 January 1852 with thirteen members. This mission was reasonably successful, and some missionaries, including the nine sent to Australia in 1852, extended the work to New Zealand and Tasmania (then called Van Diemen's Land).

arrived in Gibraltar but encountered difficulty even though Stevenson had been born there. They attempted to extend the work into Spain, but apparently without success. One of the most ambitious yet fruitless efforts was in Hindustan in northern India. Nathaniel B. Jones, Robert Skelton, Samuel Woolley, William Fotheringham, Richard Ballantyne, Truman Leonard, Amos Milton Musser, Robert Owen, and William F. Carter held a conference in Calcutta in April 1853 but found it impossible to work with the Hindus. They found a few "Rice Christians," who were willing to change their religion if they were paid, reasoning that if they left their own religion they would be excluded from their families and castes and would have no livelihood. Ultimately the missionaries began to visit places where British army outposts were located and succeeded in converting some British soldiers.[11]

These ventures seem to demonstrate some wastefulness considering the need for these men to be at home or to work among English-speaking peoples. But church leaders were motivated by a conviction that the Millennium was imminent and that their duty was to bear witness of the restored gospel to all the world before the end. While the men who were willing to undertake such assignments deserve credit, the misery of their families during their absence, and the need for them at home, these activities seem questionable in retrospect.

One of the distinguishing marks of modern Mormonism is the Word of Wisdom. This revelation, announced by Joseph Smith on 27 February 1833, advised the Saints to avoid alcoholic beverages, tobacco, and "hot drinks" (which was later interpreted to mean tea and coffee), except for medicinal purposes. The Word of Wisdom included other dietary rules such as "eating the fruits in the season thereof" and eating meat sparingly, primarily in times of cold and famine.

Although this has become an important part of Mormonism, and observing the Word of Wisdom is required of members to hold church

---

[11] This was not the first time Mormon missionaries had been sent to India, for Lorenzo Snow had sent missionaries there from Europe in 1850-51; and one or two were still there when the new wave of missionaries arrived. Eventually the missionaries came home, some by way of England, thus completing an around-the-world journey. Other missionaries were sent to Hong Kong in April 1853, some to Siam in 1852. Unable to go to Siam, some of these moved to Ceylon. Missionaries were sent to South Africa and the West Indies in 1853, and still others to British Guiana. Some went to the Island of Malta where they established several branches. One, a "floating branch," consisted of a group of British soldiers and sailors assigned to the Mediterranean Sea.

offices and to go to the temple, Mormons did not strictly observe the Word of Wisdom prior to their move west. Since it was not given as commandment, members tended to regard it simply as good advice.[12] On their trek west the Saints were instructed to bring tea and coffee and to have some alcohol, primarily for medicinal purposes. The menu for the first Thanksgiving Day in the Salt Lake Valley listed tea, coffee, and wine. For Brigham Young, Mormon sociologist Nels Anderson has explained, the virtues of the Word of Wisdom were "precious, but secondary."

Still Young would periodically threaten the Saints with excommunication if they did not abide by the revelation. As early as February 1850, the *Millennial Star* reported that the subject had caused dissension in various branches, and the *Deseret News* declared, "We recommend a thorough perusal of the Word of Wisdom to the Twelve, high priests, elders, bishops, priests, teachers, deacons, brethren and sisters of the Church of Jesus Christ of Latter-day Saints. And that the officers present the subject before the Church and decide whether they are sent forth in the wisdom of heaven or by the folly of man." The following year, Young, Heber C. Kimball, Parley P. Pratt, and others met to pray and decided to renew their commitment to the Word of Wisdom.

Despite this meeting, no extant evidence demonstrates that leaders made any strong effort to encourage obedience until the September 1851 General Conference, when Young took action. On 9 September, according to the *Frontier Guardian*, church patriarch John Smith urged that all members not use tobacco and other harmful substances. Young then arose and put it to a vote, calling on the sisters to raise their right hand in support. The motion carried. Young next put the motion to "all of the boys who were under 90 years of age." It too carried. Young commented, "The Lord bears with our weaknesses. We must serve the Lord and those who go with us will keep the Word of Wisdom. If the high priests, and seventies, and elders, and others will not we will sever them from the church. I will draw the line and will know who is for the Lord and who is not. And

---

[12] Joseph Smith, for example, did not object to drinking beer and wine on occasion and may have once smoked a cigar after lecturing on the Word of Wisdom, supposedly to teach people to follow his teachings rather than his example. On another occasion, he reported that some of the brethren had been drinking whiskey but that when he investigated the complaint, he "was satisfied that no evil had been done. And I gave them a couple of dollars with directions to replenish the bottle to stimulate them in the fatigues of their sleepless journey."

175

those who will not keep the Word of Wisdom, I will cut off from the church."

A number of church leaders have concluded that the Word of Wisdom was made a commandment at this time. Yet a perusal of sermons during the 1850s and 1860s leads to another conclusion. Clearly the Word of Wisdom had not become obligatory at this time. A later acceptance date seems more logical for several reasons. Young himself did not strictly adhere to the Word of Wisdom until the early 1860s. Jules Remy, a French adventurer, observed Young preparing a "quid of Virginia Tobacco" in late September 1855, and seven years later Young publicly alluded to the fact that he had only recently overcome habits contrary to the Word of Wisdom. Also, Young said as late as 1861 that he never chose to make observance of the Word of Wisdom a test of church fellowship. Finally, a catechism prepared during the Mormon Reformation only asked members if they had ever been drunk, not if they drank tea, coffee, beer, or light wines.

In fact, Young was surprisingly lenient with many older Saints who were addicted to tobacco or hot drinks and realized that they would have a difficult time abstaining. However, appeals were made to the younger generation to live the Word of Wisdom. Young and George A. Smith were particularly zealous in their efforts to persuade the youth not to follow their parents. Smith felt that it was disgraceful for any man younger than thirty-five to use tobacco. Young expressed his view on young tobacco users as follows:

> If the old fogies take a little tobacco, a little whiskey, and a little tea and coffee, we wish you boys to let it alone. Let those have it who have been longer accustomed to its use. It is far better for these my brethren who are young and healthy to avoid every injurious habit. There are a great many boys here who are in the habit of chewing tobacco. They should stop it. Take no more. They are better without it. Some may turn around and say, "Father do you think so?" Yes, let the old folks have it, but you young smart gentlemen, let it alone.

Mild infractions, especially drinking tea and coffee, were apparently no cause for concern. Hard liquor—and the question of whether or not it should be imported—was a more serious problem. Still the *Deseret News* recommended building a city brewery, and Young himself manufactured liquor for what he called rational purposes. However, Heber C. Kimball admonished individual Saints not to sell beer and strong drink unless counselled to get a license. Kimball disdained the selling of intoxicating liquors without proper counsel. On one occasion he related seeing in vision the armies of heaven.

176

According to Kimball, this army was composed of righteous saints who had not sold whiskey or established distilleries.

One can only surmise to what extent the Word of Wisdom was observed by lay members. Observations by four non-Mormons who travelled through Utah suggest that the Mormons were considerably more moderate in the use of alcohol, tobacco, tea, and coffee than their contemporaries. Franklin Lane in 1850 noted that the Mormons did not use intoxicating drinks. S. N. Carvalho spent ten weeks in Salt Lake City in 1854 and was impressed with the lack of grog shops and the fact that he never saw a drunken man. Perhaps more accurate notes were taken by William Chandless and Jules Remy in 1855. Chandless had eaten dinner with a Mormon family. He commented on the absence of tea and coffee and noted that this was the only family he had seen rich enough not to obey who still followed the advice. Remy, perhaps the most sage observer, noted:

> Although there are neither grog shops nor dealers in any kind that drinks can be met with, it does not necessarily follow that the Saints refrain from the moderate use of spirits or fermented liquors. No command compels them to reject certain productions of nature or of art. It is true that Joseph Smith in a sermon on the Word of Wisdom counselled true believers to abstain from the use of fermented drinks and tobacco and recommended such abstinence as a means of arriving at perfection. The more fervent do abstain, with this view, but occasionally they make no scruple about the use of moderate drink. Many of them take beer to make which they cultivate hops in the valley, others drink wine when they can get it and, some even indulge in whiskey which they distill from the potato.[13]

Gradually Young's rhetoric became stronger. In an address reported in the *Deseret News*, he rebuked the Saints for boiling their grains to make liquor when the poor were going without food. He also stated that if Christ were to come to the valley some poor devil would step up with a bottle of liquor and offer him a drink. In the April 1855 General Conference, many brethren, including Young, spoke on the Word of Wisdom. George A. Smith, another strong preacher, declared to the Provo Seventies just a few days before conference that they should all observe the Word of Wisdom and not

---

[13]Remy later observed that Mormons were more temperate than most societies and used coffee and tea less than other staples. He added that "the majority abstained from fermented or spiritous liquors either voluntarily . . . or on account of their poverty." He concluded by pointing out that the tobacco habit was less usual among them than in other parts of the union.

use any tea, coffee, tobacco, or spiritous liquors. At conference, Smith said,

> When a Mormon elder comes up to me and wants to get a little counsel and if his breath smells as if he had swallowed a still house, it is all I can possibly do to remain near enough to him to hear his story. He necessarily wishes to come close to me, as such men are sure to have a secret they wish to whisper, and the breath is offensive then I am forced to retire. When I am called to counsel to the man who is indulging in these intemperate practices I feel at a loss to know whether my counsel is going to do him good or harm or whether he will pay any attention to it after he gets it.

Bishops' courts for drunkenness are reported in Lorenzo Hatch's journal for November 1858 and in A. G. Allen's journal for the following month. About this time, Young lamented, "It is a pity that the Latter-day Saints who live here who say that they have embraced the gospel of eternal life and are willing to sacrifice all for their salvation or give up all for Christ should be bought over by a gill of whiskey." The following year, Lorenzo Brown recorded,

> October 1st, carried to Brother Daniel MacIntosh a letter that he was disfellowshipped by the council of his quorum. At home all day, October 2nd, 4 p.m. quorum meeting, approved the action taken by the council and he was unanimously disfellowshipped by the quorum for repeated drunkenness. This has been a time of serious trial for me and a source of much reflection as he is beloved by many, if not all, not as much by others than by myself, yet there was no other course to be taken.

Brown later recorded that MacIntosh wrote a letter of apology, promising never again to get drunk, and was reinstated in the quorum. Later he was again disfellowshipped. William H. Kimball, president of one of the seventies' quorums and oldest son of Heber C. Kimball, was also disfellowshipped for drunkenness.

Generally speaking, very few Saints were ever cut off completely; most were handled by their quorums and simply disfellowshipped. Of the total number of sermons given on the Word of Wisdom between 1847 and 1869 and reported in the *Journal of Discourses*, only one occurred in 1848, none in 1849 or 1850, one in 1851, none in 1852 or 1853, four in 1854, nine in 1855, two in 1856, one in 1857, and none in 1858 or 1859. Brigham Young spoke on the subject most often; George A. Smith was next. These two leaders spoke on the Word of Wisdom more than anyone else.

Another practice during the Saints' first years in the Great Basin was fasting and using the food saved to help the less fortunate. On

FASTING—

Sunday, 30 May 1847, while still en route to the valley, Howard Egan wrote in his journal, "Tomorrow is set aside as the last Sunday was, for fasting and prayer." Sunday lent itself to the practice since the pioneers did not travel on Sundays and could more easily fast when not engaged in vigorous activity. Apparently not until 1849 were fast days regularly observed. Thursday, 26 April 1849, according to the Journal History, was set aside as a fast day, and the following Thursday was also a day of fasting. At the April 1852 General Conference, Young announced that from "henceforth we should hold meetings regularly each Sabbath at 10 a.m. and 2 p.m. and in the evening several quorums of the priesthood would assemble to receive instructions. On Thursdays the brethren and sisters would come together at 2 p.m. for prayer and supplication and on the first Thursday of each month at 10 a.m. for the purpose of fasting and prayer." This pattern was followed until November 1896 when the First Presidency decided that Fast Day would be the first Sunday of the month.[14]

Mormons had always been admonished to give to the poor; but not until 1855-56 did this become associated with fast meetings when Mormons were asked to bring their "fast offerings" to the meetings.[15] Sources for 1856 are replete with evidence that members brought donations for the poor to monthly fast meetings. The scribe of the Salt Lake Eighteenth Ward recorded on 7 February 1856 that "meeting opened by prayer by Brother George Works, Saints who met for fasting and prayer and who brought corn beef and cabbage and seed for the relief of the poor bore their testimonies, and the

[14] Evidence suggests that fast meetings on the first Thursday of each month were observed throughout the entire church. Some historians believe that fast day resulted from the prolonged drought, the grasshopper attacks of 1855-56, the severe winter, heavy immigration, and the great number of miners on their way to California. B. H. Roberts quoted George A. Smith that "In all of these times of scarcity, measures were taken to supply those who were unable to furnish themselves. The fast day was proclaimed for the Church on the first Thursday of each month, and the food saved in that way was distributed among the poor and thousands of persons who had abundance of bread put their families on rations in order to save the same for those who could not otherwise obtain it."

[15] During the early years, little was written to address the question of the length of an acceptable fast. Scriptures counselled that fasts customarily last from evening to evening. The instructions to the Saints at Nauvoo had also been to fast for one day. To fast from evening to evening implies that the fast should last approximately twenty-four hours, or two meals. An acceptable fast offering would thus comprise two-thirds of one's daily allowance of food. Mormons still compute fast offerings in this way. Mormons still participate in other fast day observances which became common during this period, including blessing children, bearing testimony, and attending to ward business.

meeting was closed by prayer." During this year some wards even instituted two fast days a month. However, many members seemed to resent this, and the practice was discontinued after a few months. By 1857, fast days had become a permanent institution in the church.

Thus by 1860, many of the doctrines and practices of the church were stabilizing. Plural marriage was defended as an important teaching. The endowment as a key to eternal marriage was emphasized, and temple building had begun. Adoption and the Word of Wisdom both had periods of importance and decline. And although missionary work fell off, the practice of fasting and using the food to benefit the poor became an increasingly important facet of church membership and loyalty.

11.
The Mormon Reformation

The Mormon Reformation, an outburst of religious fervor and evangelical activity in response to an emotional call for retrenchment, reached its climax during the fall of 1856, continued through the following winter, and was largely dissipated by June 1857. It was a sudden phenomenon, promoted primarily by Jedediah M. Grant, and began to decline with his untimely death in December 1856. At its peak, it resulted in a large scale program of rebaptism and rededication to religious principles, including personal cleanliness and a concern for orderliness in homes and communities.

At first the Mormon approach to conversion and repentance was intellectual rather than emotional. While there was some emphasis on the gifts of the spirit, including the gift of tongues, healing, and prophecy, such beliefs did not result in widespread emotional outbursts. Most Mormon preaching tried to demonstrate that Mormonism harmonized with the scriptures and fulfilled biblical prophecy.

Mormon leaders had always emphasized obedience to church commandments, and when Brigham Young was about to return to Winter Quarters after bringing the initial pioneer company to the Salt Lake Valley, he counselled followers to rededicate themselves to the gospel and be rebaptized. The pioneers were constantly reminded that their primary purpose was to establish the Kingdom of God and that they were now in the desert because they had failed to usher in the Millennium in Jackson County, Missouri. In April 1852 General Conference, Young complained that the Saints were not dedicating

their lives to the Lord and that this was the cause of their evil practices, evil speaking, and evil thinking. Such evil, Young felt, must be
done away with by people covenanting "to prepare for the coming
of the Son of man." Young further hinted that perhaps the members
did not want to be righteous for if they did they would bind the Devil.
If they united their hearts in the church and Kingdom of God, they
would live to see the Millennium.

At the dedication of the Salt Lake Temple cornerstones, the Saints
heard predictions that this temple would provide a place for Christ's
return. Parley P. Pratt explained the vital role of the temple, then
called for "a thorough repentance and reformation of life" and promised if the Saints "fail not to keep the commandments in the Church
as it is established in peace and security of the mountains, it will
never be prevailed against by its enemies and oppressors." A year
later Heber C. Kimball asked whether it was "not high time that
there should be a reformation? We must be of one heart and one
mind just as though we were one man. Before this people can enter
into the celestial world, there must be a great reformation among
them."

Speaking in May 1855, Orson Pratt complained that some of the
new immigrants were too complacent, that they needed hardships
to make them more dedicated. According to Pratt, earlier Saints had
learned to submit when the Lord decided to chastise them. But the
newer Saints were careless and called on Jesus only in time of need.
When the Saints lived in Jackson County, they felt that the end was
near. Now, Pratt lamented, "they have gone to the other extreme. . . .
The people think of everything else but the redemption of Zion . . . I
will give you my opinion so far as the revelations go in speaking
of this subject. I think the event is nearer than this people are
aware of."

Such calls to repentance were persistent during the first decade
in the Great Basin. However, the rhetoric intensified following the
appointment of Jedediah M. Grant as second counselor in the First
Presidency on 7 April 1854. Grant, from the moment he joined the
church in 1833, was involved in a crusade that consumed him and
which, he believed, deserved the same commitment from others.
Dull, spiritless preaching, he feared, was the cause of much spiritual
sickness among the people. He believed that his abilities as a ser-
monizer were supernaturally produced and criticized some of his
colleagues for their preaching, calling on them to find the fire within
themselves. If he could not chastise the corrupt world, he would pil-
lory the Saints for their attachments to it. He was not interested in

182

the past but in an immediate future in which the pure dreams of the sacred were real.

Before Grant's call to the First Presidency, he was mayor of Salt Lake City but not a prominent leader in the church. Indeed, Young's selection of Grant in the spring of 1854 to fill the vacancy left by Willard Richards must have surprised many. Despite Grant's personality and proven dedication to Mormonism, other men would have seemed more logical choices for the vacancy. But the affinity between Young and Grant could not be measured. During the succession crisis, Grant's loyalty to the Twelve had withstood the assaults of such schismatics as Sidney Rigdon, Benjamin Winchester, and even Grant's brother-in-law, William Smith. In addition, Young appreciated men of practical grit and realized that the tall preacher possessed certain charismatic qualities that would demand the fealty of bishops and seventies, even apostles. This relationship between Grant and Young was crucial during the Mormon Reformation.

Certainly the specific contours of the reformation can be traced to Grant's psyche despite his deference to Young's leadership. Young allowed Grant to lead in this matter, from preaching sermons to writing reformation catechisms. Young was not losing control of his vigorous young counselor but rather demonstrating his support and affinity for Grant's work. But even the most controversial reformation doctrines were a common part of Grant's pre-1856 dogma, and Grant's character was stamped indelibly upon the movement.

A 13 July 1855 sermon in Provo previewed the demands Grant would make on church members. "The Church needs trimming up," he warned, "and if you will search, you will find in your wards certain branches that had better be cut off. The Kingdom will progress much faster and so will you individually than it will with those branches on, for they are only dead weights to the great wheel . . . I would like to see the works of reformation commence and continue until every man had to walk the line." His concluding admonition summarized his basic message: "Purify yourselves, your houses, lots, farms and everything around you on the right and on the left and then the spirit of the Lord can dwell with you."

Brigham Young in his late 1855 sermons often complained of conditions among the Saints and spoke of the need for reform. He stressed the importance of maintaining "home missionaries" in each of the wards and stakes to root out evil locally. When one of these home missionaries was accused of overzealousness, Young supported him. He said it was more likely that the Saints would confess too little than too much. Still nothing in Young's own teachings or activities foreshadowed the dramatic call for reform the following year.

Another grasshopper attack and drought made the pioneers' economic situation precarious in 1855–56. Heber C. Kimball reportedly said that this was the tightest time he had known since arriving in the valley. Writing to George Q. Cannon on 3 April 1856, Brigham Young reported that many persons were living almost entirely upon roots and "until we are blessed with another harvest there will be more or less a pinch for provisions. Myself as well as nearly everybody around me have rationed their families to half a pound per day. By frequent fastings we save considerable amounts and this allows us to give to the poor. I pray to heaven that we may have a plentiful harvest. We understand that the prospect is for a large immigration this season." Still he insisted that the Saints were healthy and that peace prevailed.[1]

These reports do not reflect a sense of crisis. But a week later Grant accompanied Joseph Young of the First Council of Seventy and four home missionaries to a 13 September 1856 stake conference in Kaysville, Davis County, and began calling for introspection, reform, and rebaptism in earnest, marking the beginning of the Mormon Reformation. In fact, the *Deseret News* reported the events of this important conference under the heading "Great Reformation."

In the Saturday evening session, Grant spoke on faith, repentance, and baptism. The following morning he addressed topics that were to become the theme of many sermons during the reformation. Saying that he brought a simple message from Brigham Young, "Saints, live your religion," he asserted that "the Lord will not hold parents guiltless who neglected to inform the minds of their children."

---

[1] Young's letters during this period mention drought and worms on the corn and potatoes. Writing to John Taylor in June, he said, "To tell you the truth, it is with great difficulty that things seem to grow." But in a July letter, Young simply said, "Times are dull, money is scarce, but we have peace and quietness, health and joy." Writing on 30 August, he noted:

Notwithstanding the drought and consequent low water, the wheat in most places throughout the territory has yielded beyond expectation and for the year we should have ample. Potatoes, for some reason, will probably make light crop, but beets, carrots, and other edible roots together with squashes are promising a plentiful yield and also the fruit trees in bearing near the benchland. You are aware that this community is mostly so peaceful, orderly and industrious it affords but few items of what the world calls of thrilling interest.

He added the following 4 September 1856, "The wheat has turned out pretty fair and other crops are flattering . . . There will be none, however, to spare, but peace prevails with all the natives and we have a general time of health."

Grant called on members to obey their covenants, observe cleanliness in their persons and dwellings, set their families in order, cultivate their farms and gardens, and keep only that land they could attend to. He concluded by praying that those who did not feel to do right might leave the territory and that "those that did not come forward to do their first works, that is, repent and be baptized, let them be unto you as heathen men and publicans and not numbered among the Saints." Joseph Young remarked that he supported Grant's sentiments, observing that the spirit of avarice would only lead the people to apostasy.

During the afternoon meeting, Grant again called on the people to repent and be baptized for the remission of their sins and advised the teachers in each ward to report to the bishop at least once a month on the standing of the members. After calling on others to speak, Grant himself discoursed at length on the Saints' need to purify themselves, their lands, their houses, their persons, and to dedicate themselves and their substances to the Lord. He called for a vote in response to his query whether they were willing to renew their covenants. Their assent was unanimous. The conference adjourned after Grant's and Young's Sunday evening addresses but reconvened the next morning for rebaptism. The early morning meeting began with further addresses by Grant and Young, who then called on twelve ward teachers to speak. During the meeting, other home teachers administered to and blessed members in a nearby school room. Grant concluded by calling upon all home missionaries to arise and bless the people.

Speaking of this event six weeks later, Grant reported that when they went to Kaysville to preach, they found a

> dark and dull spirit there which was not very congenial to our natures. Brother Joseph Young felt life in him and was full of the spirit and after staying a couple of days he said to me, "Brother Grant, they feel cold and I guess we'd better go to Farmington and preach there and go home." After awhile I said to him "Do you know how I feel about it? In the name of the Lord, Jesus Christ, I will never leave this land until this people surrender. I will hang the flag of the Lord Jesus Christ on their doors, and there shall be a siege of forty days. Then let every man storm the castle and rule against the bulwarks of hell, and let every elder throw the arrows of God Almighty through the sinner and pierce their loins and penetrate their vitals until the banner of Christ shall wave triumphally over Israel. Shall we give up and let the wicked and ungodly overcome us? No in the name and by the power of God we will overcome

185

them. We will cleanse the inside of the platter and have Israel saved through the name of Jesus Christ and by the power of his word."

Later, Grant tried to credit Brigham Young with instituting the reformation. Although Young had sent him to the conference with a typical charge to tell the people to live their religion, Grant said that when he arrived he felt like baptizing them and confirming them anew into the church.

Following Kaysville, Grant and companions traveled five miles southeast to Farmington to hold an evening meeting in the upper room of the courthouse. They called on members to join the reformation and asked if they would be rebaptized. The whole assembly "arose as with a sudden rush." An estimated six hundred persons were rebaptized and reconfirmed members of the church. During an afternoon sacrament service, while the bread was being broken, Grant asked if all present could fellowship those who had been rebaptized. All hands raised in union. While the sacrament was passed, a number of sick members were administered to.

The next week, Grant and Joseph Young were in Salt Lake City. Along with members of the First Presidency, they preached the reformation to members at the bowery. According to his unpublished history, Brigham Young delivered two sermons. "I feel to call upon this congregation and know whether any of them or whether all of them wish salvation," he said. "If they do, I have the gospel of salvation for them and I call on the people to know whether they are friends of God or only of themselves individually." He then called for all to stand who were willing to have the gospel preached to them. He continued:

When we get the baptismal font prepared that is now being built, I will take you into the waters of baptism if you repent of your sins, if you will covenant to live your religion and be saints of the most high . . . . We need a reformation in the midst of this people. We need a thorough reform, for I know that very many are in a dozy position with regards to their religion. I know this as well as I should, if you were now to doze and go to sleep before my eyes. Are you losing the spirit of the gospel? Is there any cause for it? No, only that which there is in the world. You have the weakness of human nature to contend with. Will you spend your lives to obtain a seat in the Kingdom of God, or will you lie down to sleep and go down to hell?

Three days later, on 24 September, Grant and Joseph Young were back in Davis County, this time in Centerville. After a day of preaching Grant was not satisfied with the response of the people and said that he thought it best to postpone rebaptism so the people could prepare their minds and be benefited by the sacred ordinances. He then instructed the bishop and ward officers to cut off every person who would not keep the commandments and put his house in order. The bishop was required to appoint a fast day for 16 October and to keep a correct account of "all that do and those who do not attend the fellowship meetings which are to be held every Sunday up to the day appointed to hold the fast." Grant then adjourned the conference until 16 October.

After leaving Centerville, Grant and Young continued south to Bountiful for the next conference. Grant addressed the meeting, claiming that the people were as cold as ice, that they had been in a deep sleep and were still asleep. He reprimanded their slackness in assembling for meetings and surmised that they were in a state of apostasy. Young bore testimony to the truth of Grant's remarks. Others joined in the same spirit, and Grant "showed the people wherein they had sinned and the necessity of an entire immediate reformation and called upon all to repent and to turn to the Lord their God with broken hearts and contrite spirits." He then expressed his conviction that over half of the people had never been converted. The following Monday morning after asking the congregation some questions, Grant said that he did not feel free to baptize the people in their present condition but requested the bishop and his counselors to work with ward members and when prepared he would come and baptize them.

While in Bountiful, Grant decided to resume the conference at Centerville and sent several of the home missionaries there to complete the reformation. Special conferences were in session at both Centerville and Bountiful on 28 September. Grant was pleased that the spirit he had experienced the previous Friday was gone and asked the people to come forward on Monday morning to renew their covenants by baptism. Then he returned to Bountiful and after some preaching moved the meeting to the water's edge. After singing, 231 persons were rebaptized.

At the same time Heber C. Kimball was telling Saints in Salt Lake "there is a reformation proposed and has already commenced in the north. The people there are repenting, that is they say they repent and many have gone forward and been baptized for the remission of their sins. But brethren and sisters you may go forth and be baptized and say you repent and receive the laying on of hands, and if ye do not repent and lay aside your wickedness, you will go to hell." Reporting on this, Wilford Woodruff, in a letter to Orson Pratt, wrote:

The Presidency of the Church have commenced a great reformation among this people in the valleys of the mountains. I have never heard as strong a sermon delivered to the people as have been preached unto them of late. The presidency are weighing the people in the balance and are calling all men to repent and be baptized for the remission of sins. President Grant has gone into the northern counties and is preaching and baptizing whole wards and building up churches. I presume the same course will be followed in the wards of this city. The people begin to feel more than ever that they are dealing with the spirit and power of God in the holy priesthood. Yes, the Latter-day Saints begin to feel that they are dealing with a spirit that can reach the hearts, know the thoughts and intents thereof and try the souls of men. The people are called to sanctify themselves before the Lord that we may be prepared for the work of our God.

A baptismal font, which had been completed near the Endowment House, was dedicated on 2 October, and the following Sunday the reformation continued in earnest. Members of the First Presidency and several home missionaries addressed crowded meetings at the bowery during both the morning and afternoon. At 5:30 p.m. the people gathered at the new baptismal font and a great number were rebaptized and afterwards reconfirmed under Grant's direction.

The semi-annual General Conference of the church convened a few days later on 6 October. The reformation took second place during the opening session to the more pressing matter of arranging relief for the Willie and Martin handcart companies endangered because of early snows near the Sweetwater River, Wyoming. However, Wilford Woodruff said that the Presidency

> had called upon us to reform our ways, to renew our covenants, and commence to live the lives of Saints. . . . You may take the twelve and the seventies and the high priests and all the other quorums except the First Presidency. They have been more or less asleep. I believe the First Presidency have been awake or they would not have known that we were asleep. And they now think it is time for us to awake and arise from our slumbers, and I feel so too.

After other comments, Woodruff concluded: "I believe the majority of the people are ready to wake up. . . . For the day has now come when we must awake and become the friends of God. We must not allow anything to stand between us and our God or we shall be cut off."

188

Two weeks earlier Brigham Young had lashed out at women for complaining and offered to release all of them, including his own wives from their marriage vows unless they would "round up their shoulders and accept their lot in life and quit whining and agree to live the gospel." At the conference, according to his manuscript history, Young again took up the offer, "I wish to fulfill the promise which I made two weeks ago. I then told the people or females that I would release them at this conference. And I will do so on certain conditions, and that is that you will appear forthwith at my office and give good and sufficient reasons and then marry men that will not have but one wife." He added:

> When you go home tonight, we want every man and woman and every child that comes to this meeting to wash themselves with pure water inside and out and come here that the Holy Ghost may dwell with you and your brethren. Then you will hear the words of the Lord. As soon as you are released from this meeting, go home and wash yourselves, and already many of you would do well to have a tub and soak overnight and perhaps by morning you would get the scale off. While that is a rather hard story, it is true. I believe that is all I have to say to this congregation.

Young's advice echoed a favorite theme of Grant, who was concerned with cleanliness. He insisted on cleanliness of person as well as of home and yard. This refrain became a powerful theme of the reformation. On 7 October, Heber Kimball warned the people not to leave early or talk or make noise and suggested that the police "crack the heads" of the offenders.

In the evening, Woodruff and Grant met with the Quorum of the Seventy. The seven presidents of the Seventy were present, Joseph Young presiding. Young spent the early part of the meeting transacting quorum business. Calling for support for the reformation, he received a weak response. This infuriated Grant, who arose and said, "I feel there are some things that grieve me." Young asked if it would not be well to send the presidents of the Seventy out. He said:

> No, they would preach the people to sleep, then to hell. Now this shows me that the Presidents of the Seventies, the First Seven Presidents are asleep . . . This body of counselors are guilty of great sins, either of omission or commission. I would advise Joseph Young to cut off his counsel and drop them and appoint men in their stead who are full of the Holy Spirit and who will act with him, assist him now and will take up his counsel. Look at them! Now here is Brother Levi Hancock. Why he will fiddle-diddle de fiddle de do, fiddle de dum and tweedle de dee. Now he

might preach a month and there would be no more spirit of God in it than there would be in a cabbage leaf. Now if you would preach this people to sleep and to hell, you are guilty of some great sins either of omission or commission. You have either committed adultery or some other sins and you ought to be dropped. Here is Brother Harriman. Now if you will preach the people to sleep and to hell you are guilty of some great sins—either of commission or omission.

Grant continued, rebuking and criticizing Albert Rockwood, Zera Pulsipher, and H. L. Eldridge. He stressed that he did not care where the men came from, only that they possessed the Holy Ghost. After he finished, some of those present, including Levi Hancock and Benjamin Clapp, defended themselves. All the presidents of the Seventy, except Joseph Young, offered to resign.

Woodruff wrote in his journal that Grant continued this policy of accusing people to their face of being lethargic. Woodruff seemed to be greatly impressed with Grant. Speaking of a meeting on 16 October 1856, Woodruff wrote in his journal:

> Jedediah Grant preached in the power of God. He is a quiver in the hands of the Almighty among the people. He took up Bishop Hoagland, his two counselors, then the teachers, then the ward and all the people in it and took a look at them in the light of truth, the candle of the Lord. The whole body was searched with scrutinizing eye and all sins rebuked by the power of God. He left as soon as we got through speaking and was followed by Elder F. D. Richards who bore testimony to the words which had been spoken.

Other leading men also began to criticize their brethren publicly. For example, on 19 October Brigham Young reported that he had received a letter from Orson Hyde in Carson Valley and accused the apostle of writing things "day after day against God, our religion, and the people, for a few dimes." Young asserted that Hyde "ought to be cut off from the Quorum of the Twelve and the Church. He is no more fit to stand at the head of the Quorum of the Twelve than a dog. His soul is entirely occupied with a few dimes and it is much more in his eyes than God, heaven and eternal life. He is a stink in my nostrils."

On 27 October Woodruff met with Grant and all the home missionaries. When asked what course he thought they should pursue, Grant said, "We should do as though there were no missionaries before. I want you to go through this territory and I want you to do as God wants you. Go prepared for battle when it is necessary. Jerk men up by their names, wake up their bishops and all presiding officers and then the people." He continued,

Now we want to know what all men are doing through this territory. The people are dirty and filthy. We want to reform this thing. Many do not treat their children right. They use them roughly. Now if a man has the spirit of God he will use his children well and treat them kind. I can tell you that children are very sensitive and the great men they meet with have a great effect on them and we want you to see that the people are employed. The reason we prosper in this city more than any other is that we labor. I went to Taylorsville with Joseph Young, and the people were so dead, so bad, that Bishop Joseph wanted to go home. And I told him that I would not go until I converted the people, and I stayed until I'd done that. Then I conquered the people in the city of Bountiful. I preached until the spirit stayed with us for a few days. But at first the bishop was asleep. And when you go to a place, treat the people right, and get the spirit of God, you will know all what is going on. And when you go to a place to preach, people don't get into Noah's Ark or into the City of Enoch. Just tell the people what you want them to do.

Following the conference, home missionaries continued to call people to repentance and to renew their covenants by rebaptism. Some went to West Jordan, some to American Fork and Pleasant Grove in Utah Valley. Presidents Young and Kimball continued to give sermons in the bowery on the reformation. For example, on 2 November, Young said:

If the people in their present situation and mode of dealing in this city, say nothing of those out of the city, all go to work now and have meetings and call upon God to get the spirit of the reformation, but to sing and pray about doing right without doing it, instead of singing themselves to hell, and at the same time make people feel enough on the subject to put away their filth and be clean. If you want me to speak smoother, do better and keep cleaner. Were I to talk about God, heaven and angels, or anything good, I could talk in a more refined style. But I have to talk about things as they do exist among us.

A climax to the early stages of the reformation was reached on 3 November 1856 when the First Presidency called for a priesthood meeting at the Social Hall. Presidents Young, Kimball, and Grant were on the stand, as well as several of the apostles and Joseph Young, senior president of the Seventy. During this assembly a catechism was introduced, which was to become an integral part of the reformation. The following description of the meeting is from John Powell, one of the participants. He wrote:

191

After singing and prayer, Brigham Young had the doors locked. He then said, "I am about to question the brethren and I charge them in the name of Jesus Christ to answer the truth. Those who cover up their sins, the curse of God shall be upon them." He then drew from the breastpocket of his coat a long slip of white paper and read the following questions, calling upon the brethren to answer them as they were put. 1. Have you shed innocent blood, or assented thereunto? 2. Have you committed adultery? 3. Have you betrayed your brother? 4. Have you borne false witness against your neighbor? 5. Do you get drunk? 6. Have you stolen? 7. Have you lied? 8. Have you contracted debts without the prospect of paying? 9. Have you labored faithfully for your wages? 10. Have you coveted that which belongs to another? 11. Have you taken the name of the Lord in vain? 12. Do you preside in your family as a servant of God? 13. Have you paid your tithing in all things?

To all of these questions, the brethren answered. Then Brigham Young commented, "There are some brethren who have confessed sins they have not done. I am happy to say that there is not as much sin as I expected." He said that if the brethren repented and sinned no more, they would start with a clean page, but if they sinned again, their former sins would be accounted unto them. "At this meeting," Powell concluded, "I saw the power of the Priesthood and felt the same as I had never saw or felt before."

As the reformation progressed, the catechism grew longer until some versions contained as many as twenty-six questions, including a question about bathing regularly. This catechism and later editions were copied and sent throughout the church. Visiting home teachers were instructed to gather the family together and catechize each member. Sometimes they did this in front of the others, sometimes privately. At Fort Supply, the men were divided into four groups and catechized individually by four leaders. If members answered the questions honestly and agreed to repent of their sins and to be rebaptized, they were promised that they would start with a clean slate. Many people felt relief from the guilt of past sins. But, for others, the catechism was an invasion of privacy and greatly resented.

Grant continued to call the people to repentance and spent hours in the baptismal font rebaptizing people, often in very cold weather. Tragically, on 19 November, Grant took sick, apparently from pneumonia. Four days later, Woodruff, Kimball, Franklin D. Richards, Daniel H. Wells, and others went to his home, laid hands on him to bless him, and rebuked the sickness. On the next day the First Presidency laid hands on him. Two days later, on the 26th, Woodruff

192

recorded that he called on Grant and found him very sick. "I laid hands on him and prayed on him and rebuked his disease." Woodruff continued to call on him, and on 29 November Grant said that he had spent the worst night yet. He reported that the

> devil had worked hard all night to kill his body but the brethren laid hands on him many times and rebuked the devil, but the devil would lay upon him a strong hand from his feet to his head and all through his stomach and rib cage and at the time, it seemed as though he would crush his body. Brother Grant, though very weak, would rebuke him for an hour at a time from limb to limb and rib to rib. It was perfect warfare all night, but he is easier this morning.

On 1 December, Woodruff reported that Grant's "lungs appeared to fill and no power to raise anything from them. It appeared that he could not live, but a short time." Brigham Young sent him some food and he seemed to relish it, but Woodruff reported that this was a death appetite. When informed by the doctor that Grant had finally passed away, Woodruff wrote:

> We immediately went into the house and found his wives and children weeping bitterly. As I gazed upon his clay tabernacle without his spirit I felt to exclaim, "A mighty man of Zion is laid low. A valiant man in Israel has fallen." I felt that a great champion in the kingdom of God was taken from us. We felt his loss deeply. For two months it seemed as though he had been hurried to close up his work. He had been preaching for several months, calling on the people to repent. His voice had been like a trump of an angel of God and he had labored night and day until he was laid prostrate with sickness. He has shot the arrows of the almighty with great power.

The funeral was held on 4 December to praise the man who had spearheaded the reformation.

Two days later, Woodruff continued what Grant had begun by disagreeing publicly with his home ward bishop, Abraham Hoagland. Hoagland had called upon some of the home missionaries to preach to the Gentiles, but Woodruff felt this was unwise. Hoagland responded that he presided over the Fourteenth Ward and was sending the teachers to preach to the Gentiles. When he sat down a confused teacher asked, "What shall I do?" Woodruff answered that he should not go to the Gentiles. However, Hoagland insisted, "Go!" Woodruff then told the teachers to "obey your Bishop for he says he will take the responsibility upon himself." After the meeting Woodruff went to Brigham Young and related what had happened. Young immediately sent for Hoagland. Both men talked the incident over and Young told him the Twelve held the keys of the Kingdom of God and all the world. No bishop presided over any of the Twelve. Hoagland confessed his error and went home.

The following day, 7 December, Young received a letter from Orson Hyde who wanted a hundred men sent to Carson Valley because he anticipated a fight with the Californians. Young said he wished all the men, including Hyde, were at home and would not send him on another mission again because he had lost the spirit of his office. According to Woodruff's journal, Young was sorry that members of the Twelve and others did not feel the spirit of their office.

By 29 December, Hyde had returned from Carson Valley, and at a meeting Young, after complementing two apostles, said, "But as for you, Brother Hyde, I will say that if you do not magnify your calling better than you have done, I shall object to your standing where you do if nobody else does, for you have not had the spirit of your calling upon you. You have been trying to build yourself up and not the kingdom of God." Woodruff added, "Yes, Brother Hyde, the Quorum of the Twelve feels this and has felt it for a good while and we want you to take hold and lead, as you are our president. We want a leader and if you will magnify your calling, we will be with you."[2] These accusations must have pained Hyde, but he seemed to accept them and was soon promoting the reformation.

Woodruff's journal after December 1856 gives the impression that the reformation was on the wane in the Salt Lake area. People were catechized and confessed, and soon most were rebaptized, apparently believing that their past sins had been forgiven.[3] On 8 March, Woodruff attended a meeting during which Young alluded to the city of Enoch and its inhabitants, which Mormons believe was physically removed from the earth because of righteousness. Young suggested that within 125 years the Saints along with the portion of the earth they occupied would be separated from the wicked.

---

[2] Young also criticized Orson Pratt and said that if he did not take a different course in his philosophical writings and speculations he would not stay long in the church.

[3] Some outbursts still occurred. On 18 February, for example, Woodruff quoted Kimball saying, "I don't want to see the President of the Seventies on the stands until they get more in the spirit of God for they are dead and the Seventies have to receive their food through them." (Kimball sounded as Grant had a few months before.)

Although the reformation declined in the Salt Lake and central Utah regions after the death of Jedediah Grant, it spread to outlying regions of the church for a time. One development involved the territorial legislative assembly meeting in Salt Lake City. After the Christmas recess, the House went into the Council Chamber where Heber C. Kimball preached to them. One participant remembered, "Nearly all the members spoke, all being filled with a testimony. The meeting lasted until dark. The power and testimony of the Elders of Israel exceeded anything I have seen in many a day. It was truly a pentecost." Four days later, both houses of the legislature met and Kimball required every member to repent of his sins and be rebaptized before transacting any business. They then passed a resolution that they would all repent and forsake their sins and be rebaptized. Preparations followed and all members repaired to the Endowment House, where they were rebaptized and reconfirmed under the hands of the Twelve and the Seventy.

Word of the reformation spread also to the church's missions. Brigham Young wrote to Silas Smith in Hawaii, "Quite a reformation is springing up among the Saints in many parts of the territory, and we hope and trust that it will extend to all the settlements. A general awakening to the interests of Zion and their own condition is much needed. And we are happy that it has commenced and is rapidly extending. Many have renewed their covenants in the waters of baptism."

On 30 October 1856, the First Presidency sent a letter to John Taylor in New York criticizing him for his financial activities and calling on him to start a reformation there:

> Arouse yourself first, get the Holy Ghost, and be filled with it and pour it out on the people. Preach evenings, make appointments in various branches and fill them, make the elders feel the fire in you and make them labor. Ordain elders and send them out to every ward of the city, to every nook and corner thereof. Humble yourself before the Lord and cause all the saints to do likewise. Preach life and salvation unto the elders and unto the people and then make them do the same. Be lively in things of God and make all the elders do the same.

On the same day, Orson Pratt in England was called to inaugurate a similar reformation: "Listen, there is a great reformation needed in England, Scotland and Wales. The Saints are dead and we do not drink at the living fountain. The fire of the Almighty is not in them. And we make the same observation regarding the elders who

195

are sent to preach."[4] Erastus Snow, head of the church in St. Louis, received a letter dated 31 October, calling for a reformation there. Charles C. Rich and Amasa Lyman, in San Bernardino, received a similar letter on 4 November:

> We have stirred up quite a reformation in these valleys among the Saints. They had measurably gone to sleep, and strange as it may appear, we found that a reformation was essential to the happiness and salvation of the people. They do not live their religion. Brethren, let the reformation extend to your places well and see if you can get the fire of the Almighty kindled in your midst.

Chester Loveland, who replaced Orson Hyde as leader in Carson Valley, received a letter on 3 January 1857, urging him to remain in the valley unless things came to a point that they could not live there in peace without contention: "The reformation continues its influence among the people; meetings are frequent and well attended; people seem determined to sanctify themselves before the Lord and, henceforth, live their Holy religion."

Andrew Dunningham, branch president in Florence, Nebraska, reported that by the early part of February 1857 they had appointed home missionaries for each ward in the city,

> who have been visiting the saints in their homes and have been putting a list of questions to them which we had drawn up for this purpose and the great reformation as a result. Self-examination, confession, restitution, repentance are effective for good here. . . . We desire sincerely a similar operation in the Spirits among the Saints abroad. We have had no dancing, no theatrical presentations this spring; yet the Saints enjoy themselves more in their religious assemblies which are numerously attended. A number of local leaders made similar reports, that they had withheld the sacrament, cancelled dancing, cancelled theatricals and spent their energy in meetings in which there was a good deal of self-examination and confessions.

Repentance was the key theme, but cleanliness was also emphasized. Meeting at the Seventeenth Ward in October 1856, Brigham Young said:

> It is your duty to keep clean. I've given the teachers a new set of questions to ask the people. I say to them, "Ask the people if they keep clean.

---

[4] Ezra T. Benson, in England, estimated that not more than half of the Saints in Great Britain were willing to renew their covenants and be rebaptized. The sacrament was withheld from the Saints for several months "to afford them time and space for repentance and restitution."

196

Do you wash your bodies once a week, when circumstances will permit? Do you keep your dwellings and outhouses and dooryards clean? The first work of the reformation with some should be the cleaning of filth away about their premises. How would you like President Young to visit them and go through their buildings and examine their rooms, etc.?'' Many houses stink so bad that a clean man cannot live in them nor hardly breathe in them. Some men were raised in stink and so were their fathers before them. I would not attempt to bless anybody in such places.

Taking the sacrament also became more significant. On 9 November 1856, Young said:

I forbid all unworthy persons from partaking of the sacrament. If such do partake of it, they shall do it on their own responsibility and not on mine. In partaking unworthily a person is corroding and destroying himself, not me. This ordinance is administered on conditions of your living in righteousness and your hearts being true to your God and to your brethren.

He continued, ''Do I feel as though I wanted to dance? No, I never want to go forth in the dance until the spirit of the Reformation is right among the people. Neither do I want to see any man or woman partake of the sacrament when they are living in open rebellion against God, against his governments, and his servants.''

Another doctrine emphasized during this period was plural marriage. Many Saints were urged to live polygamy, and this push resulted in considerable competition for wives. The competition became so intense in some places that men volunteered to go on missions to find new wives. On 5 March 1857, one man writing from Fillmore reported that in that town ''there were 56 single men besides all the married ones that were anxious to get more wives, and only four single women. Now, sir, would it not be a good policy for me to go on a mission to the states or England if you thought best. I know of some good women in the states of my own baptizing that might be got, besides many more.'' Brigham Young's correspondence files are filled with requests for permission to marry more wives. Philo T. Farnsworth, writing from Beaver on 26 March 1857, inquired, ''Is it my privilege to take a couple more wives if I can find some free girls? If so, I thought I'd come up this summer when you get home from your trip north.'' One of the more unusual requests involved a woman whose husband was unable to father a child. Young instructed her to council with her husband to see if he would permit some good brother to take his place so that she might conceive, adding that if she, her husband, and the bishop all agreed and kept the affair secret, there would be no sin in it.[5]

The most extreme teaching to emerge during the reformation was that of blood atonement. Jedediah Grant, after talking about unrepentant sinners, asserted in the *Deseret News* for 1 October 1856:

> There are men and women that I would advise to go to the President immediately and ask him to appoint a committee to attend to their case. And then let a place be selected and let that committee shed their blood. We have those amongst us that are full of all manner of abomination. Those who need to have their blood shed where water will not do, their sins are of too deep a dye. You may think that I am not teaching Bible doctrine, but what says the Apostle Paul. I would ask how many covenant breakers there are in this city and in this Kingdom? I believe that there are a great many and if they are covenant breakers we need a place designated where we could shed their blood.

He continued, "Brethren and sisters, we want you to repent and forsake your sins. And you who have committed sins that cannot be forgiven through baptism, let your blood be shed. Let the smoke ascend that the incense thereof may come up to God as an atonement for your sins."

Brigham Young repeated the doctrine and approved of it:

> I know when you hear my brethren telling about cutting people off from the earth that you consider it as strong doctrine, but it is to save them, not to destroy them. And after talking about the children of Israel in the wilderness, I do know that there are sins committed of such a nature that if the people did understand the doctrine of salvation they would tremble because of their situation. And furthermore I know that there are transgressors who, if they knew themselves and the only condition

---

[5] One of the more distressing developments was the number of men asking Young for permission to marry girls too young to bear children. To one man at Fort Supply, Young explained, "I don't object to your taking sisters named in your letter to wife if they are not too young and their parents and your president and all connected are satisfied, but I do not want children to be married to men before an age which their mothers can generally best determine." Writing to another man in Spanish Fork, he said, "Go ahead and marry them, but leave the children to grow." A third man in Alpine City was instructed, "It is your privilege to take more wives, but set a good example to the people, and leave the children long enough with their parents to get their growth, strength and maturity." To Louis Robinson, head of the church at Fort Bridger, Young advised, "Take good women, but let the children grow, then they will be able to bear children after a few years without injury." Another man in Santa Clara was told that it would be wise to marry an Indian girl but only if she were mature. Still another man wanted Young to counsel him concerning a sister who proposed to give him her twelve-year-old daughter.

upon which they can obtain forgiveness, would beg of their brethren to shed their blood, that the smoke thereof might ascend to God as an offering to appease the wrath that is kindled against them and that the law might have its course. I say further, I've had men come to me and offer their lives to atone for their sins. It is true that the blood of the Son of God was shed for sins through the fall and those committed by men. Yet men can commit sins which it can never remit. As it was in the ancient days, so it is in our day. And though the principles are taught publicly from the stands, still the people do not understand them. Yet the law is precisely the same. There are sins that can be atoned for by an offering upon the altar as in ancient days. And there are sins that the blood of a lamb, or a calf or turtledoves cannot remit, but they must be atoned for by the blood of the man.

Although Young, Kimball, and Grant all preached blood atonement in theory, no presently reliable evidence demonstrates that it was practiced officially. Still, the blood rhetoric fueled anti-Mormon exposes for decades.

As might be imagined, this type of introspection and enthusiastic preaching put the fear of God into the hearts of many. As the Saints began to repent of their sins Young had to shoulder an additional burden by personally listening to many confessions and responding to bishops for his advice. Despite his rhetoric, he could be remarkably generous. Grant himself noted, "Brigham Young is more forgiving and generous [than I]. I would cut you off whereas Brigham Young is willing to forgive you this type of thing." An example is the case of a Fillmore bishop who wrote on 10 December 1856 that he had been in hell for eight years because of his transgression—"unlawful communication with the opposite sex"—and said that he would do anything—even die—to atone for his sins. Similarly, Isaac Haight, a stake president in Cedar City, wanted to know how to advise a man who had confessed to adultery in Winter Quarters. He had married the woman, but, Haight said, "I think he has deeply repented of his sin and says that if the law of God requires his blood to be spilt, he will." Then Haight asked, "Will you tell me what to say to him, because in answering this it will answer many of like nature." Clearly, the reformation was working among many who were searching their hearts and confessing their sins.

In all, however, it is difficult to evaluate the impact of the reformation upon the Mormon church as a whole. While there seems to have been some excesses, such as withholding the sacrament for long periods, preaching blood atonement, taking very young girls into plural marriage, and the fervor of trying to get extra wives, the positive results are not as easily identified. Whether the houses were cleaner, and the people bathed more regularly, or were more industrious, honest, and devout, is difficult to judge. Certainly the pioneers committed themselves to be better Saints, but just how effectively these resolutions were carried out remains unclear.

12.
Beginnings of Civil Government

Determining the feelings of Mormon leaders toward the United States government during these first twenty years in the Great Basin is difficult. Bitter because federal officials did not help them in Missouri and Illinois, Brigham Young and other authorities called on members to "leave this wicked nation" and led them to settle in Mexican territory. Yet at the same time they furnished a battalion of men to help in the campaign to take California and notified U.S. president James K. Polk that they intended to apply for admission into the union if they settled in the Great Basin.

Initially, church leaders wanted to apply for "a territorial government of our own" and chose a representative to carry their petition to Washington, D.C. Changing their plans, however, they soon formed the State of Deseret and sent a second representative to the nation's capital. As part of the Compromise of 1850, the Territory of Utah was created. Brigham Young, upon learning of his appointment as territorial governor, began to organize the territory before the arrival of non-Mormon officials. This led to a confrontation that alienated several federal appointees. They returned to Washington convinced that the Mormons were religious fanatics dominated by a theocratic priesthood, whose leaders practiced polygamy, were corrupting the Indians, and were disloyal to the United States.

Whether the Mormons were loyal to the United States at the time of their exodus from Illinois is especially difficult to assess. There had been little contact between the Mormons and federal officials prior to 1845, but church leaders blamed the federal government for failing to protect them from antagonistic state governments. Martin Van Buren's assertion to Joseph Smith in 1839 that "your cause is just but I can do nothing for you" demonstrated to Mormons the federal government's weaknesses. Thus, Apostle Orson Pratt could write in 1845, without reprimand, "It is with greatest joy that I forsake this Republic," and call on all Mormons "to get out of this evil nation by next spring."

Negotiations between the Council of Fifty[1] and the Texan government (1844-45) reveal that the Mormons at least contemplated the possibility of leaving the territorial limits of the Union. Brigham Young, in a general epistle to members "scattered abroad throughout the United States of America," asserted during the fall of 1845 that removal beyond the boundaries of the U.S. would be a test of orthodoxy: "If the authorities of this Church cannot abide in peace within the pale of this nation, neither can those who implicitly hearken to their wholesome council. A word to the wise is sufficient." The move into Mexican territory in 1847 and negotiations with Great Britain for permission to colonize Vancouver Island demonstrate that these were not idle threats. Later, when the church was threatened by the approaching federal army, Young expressed similar feelings: "The time must come when this kingdom must be free and independent of all other kingdoms. Are you prepared to have this thread cut today?"

However, an equally strong case can be made for Mormon loyalty to the United States. Some scholars feel that disloyal statements

---

[1] On 11 March 1844, three and one half months before his death, Joseph Smith organized a group of men to help establish the political Kingdom of God on earth. Based on a revelation which Smith claimed to have received as early as 7 April 1842, this group was designated formally as "The Kingdom of God and His Laws and the keys and powers thereof the judgment in the hands of his servants" but was generally referred to as the Council of Fifty. In simple terms, the council was to be a political organization that would rule the world at the Second Coming. It was to work in close cooperation with God's church on earth but would not be identical with it. Most of the council's members held high church positions, but non-Mormons, at least at the beginning, served on the council as well.

The most difficult aspect of the Council of Fifty was its secrecy. Since the LDS church does not presently make any of the council's official records accessible, scholars have to piece together evidence from journals, letters, sermons, etc., and cannot always be certain when men were acting as members of the Council of the Twelve Apostles or Council of Fifty. Still, the evidence seems clear that the Council of Fifty played an important role in colonizing Utah and that by 1849 council members spearheaded an attempt to set up a state government to maintain their political independence within the confines of the United States.

were made in times of exasperation and usually directed toward government officials rather than the country itself. Expressions of loyalty, love of country, admiration for the Constitution, and willingness to fight for the country are certainly more numerous in the records than contrary ones. For example, in a letter addressed to President James Polk, dated 9 August 1846, Young wrote:

> While we appreciate the constitution of the United States as the most precious among the nations, we feel that we had rather retreat to the deserts, islands, or mountain caves than consent to be ruled by governors and judges whose hands are drenched in the blood of innocence and virtue, who delight in injustice and oppression.

Six years later, on 4 July 1852, Daniel H. Wells reiterated the loyalty of the Saints:

> Because demi-gods have arisen and seized the reigns of power, should we relinquish our interests in that country made dear to us by every tie of association and consanguinity? Those who have indulged such sentiments concerning us have not read Mormonism, . . . for never, no never, will we desert our country's cause. Never will we be found arrayed on the side of our enemies although she herself may cherish them in her own bosom. Although she may launch forth the thunderbolts of war which may return and spend their fury upon her own head, never, no never will we permit the weakness of human nature to triumph over the love of country. Our devotions to her institutions were handed down to us by our honored sires and made dear by a thousand tender recollections.

Such patriotic statements could be multiplied. The fact is that the Mormons felt a dual loyalty to the Kingdom of God and to the United States, and in most situations, the two did not conflict. But if a choice had to be made, the Saints' first loyalty was, and would always be, the Kingdom of God.

In fact, the divine origin and destiny of the United States was a basic Mormon concept. Mormons believed that God had intentionally hidden America from the rest of the world until the proper time to open it to a new race of religious seekers. Mormonism was to culminate that grand plan. "The United States of America," wrote Apostle Parley P. Pratt, "was the favorite nation raised up with institutions adapted to the protection and free development of the necessary truths and their practical results, and that great prophet, apostle, and martyr, Joseph Smith was the Elias, the restorer, the presiding messenger holding the keys of the dispensation of the fullness of times." Without the United States, Pratt continued, this would not have been possible, for the grain of mustard seed—the nucleus of the Kingdom of God—needed a land of free institutions where such organizations could be developed and protected. No other country provided the necessary conditions. The government of the United States, like all man-made governments, would ultimately fail and the Kingdom of God take over.[2]

More important than examining statements of Mormon loyalty are the actions the Saints took to establish a civil government in their new refuge. Although the United States had defeated Mexico, and both nations had signed the Treaty of Guadalupe-Hidalgo on 2 February 1848, ratification had not taken place when the first contingent of church members left Winter Quarters for the Great Basin that April. Apostles George A. Smith and Ezra T. Benson, who remained behind, wrote their leader as follows:

> If you find it wisdom to petition Congress for annexation as a state in the American union or for territorial privileges, send a petition to us by some of the brethren coming from your place next Fall or as soon as is convenient, and if you do, we would suggest the appointment of a delegate to Congress with credentials of his election by the people as the bearer of this petition. If the petition is favorably received, he might be admitted to the floor of the lower house. If not, he would be considered the accredited agent of the people and be heard in any of the committee rooms. As the Mexican Congress has refused to ratify a treaty of peace with the United States, which government may finally have jurisdiction over the basin, is impossible for us at present to tell. But we are in possession of the soil of our destiny with the independence, should Mexico maintain her old lines. We are not particularly in favor of either plan but are willing to abide by your better judgment and are willing to use our humble endeavors to the utmost in carrying out any project you may desire for the establishing of the "Kingdom of God and His Laws."

Smith and Benson seemed more concerned with the welfare of the Kingdom than with loyalty. In a later letter, they listed advantages of having "legal communication with the United States" but warned against a territorial government.

By the time Smith's and Benson's letter arrived, most of the members of the Council of Fifty had arrived in the Salt Lake Valley and decided to act along different lines. Called to assemble on 9 December 1848, council members elected to apply for a "territorial government of our own," implying that officers would be chosen from

---

[2] Such perceptions are best interpreted in light of the Mormon belief that Jesus Christ would return to earth and usher in his millennial reign soon and that he would recognize the Mormon church as the nucleus of his earthly kingdom.

the Mormon leadership. An official petition was drawn up, and John M. Bernhisel was chosen to secure names on the petition and carry it to Washington, D.C. When Bernhisel left on 3 May 1849, the document bore 2,270 signatures, including those of Brigham Young and other Mormon leaders.

While Bernhisel was securing the signatures, the Council of Fifty decided to organize a civil government and to draft a constitution. They convened on 4 March 1849 to plan a constitutional convention, which would meet the following day, and that the election of officers should be held on 12 March. But no constitutional convention met. Instead, the Council of Fifty disregarded the new constitution, which specified that elections were to take place in May, and held elections on the date the council itself had originally designated, 12 March. The single slate of officers reflected a theocratic pattern of church organization. The ballot also included some officers not listed in the constitution of the State of Deseret and omitted some that were listed. Both the constitutional convention and constitution seem to have been little more than a facade to mask the beginnings of the political Kingdom of God under the name of Deseret.

The new General Assembly of the State of Deseret met in July 1849 and selected Almon W. Babbitt to carry its petition for statehood to Washington, D.C. Since Bernhisel was already on his way with a petition for territorial government, difficulties seemed inevitable. But when Bernhisel called on Thomas L. Kane in Philadelphia, Kane persuaded him that there was no hope of obtaining a territorial government "of their own" and that he should direct his efforts toward obtaining statehood. This, of course, coincided with Babbitt's instructions, and the two delegates unified their efforts.

Unfortunately, the church's application for statehood was doomed to defeat. Utah became part of the Compromise of 1850, which admitted California into the Union as a free state and created Utah and New Mexico as territories with the right to decide by popular sovereignty whether they would be slave or free, as a gesture to the South.

Even if a controversy over slavery had not been raging in Congress at the time, the admission of Deseret would have nevertheless been unlikely. The proposed territory embraced almost one sixth of the total territory of the United States, including most of southern California. Also, Deseret's population fell far short of the 60,000 people required by the Northwest Ordinance for statehood.

Although the State of Deseret's application was rejected and the Utah territory was formed on 9 September 1850, a Mormon state government, functioning since March 1849, continued to serve until

April 1851 when the territorial government took over. Since Brigham Young had been governor of the state and now was appointed territorial governor, little changed at first.

Following early exploration and colonization of the region, the following seven counties were organized and their boundaries set by the General Assembly: Salt Lake, Weber, Davis, Tooele, Utah, Sanpete, and Iron. Five cities were incorporated and chartered by the State of Deseret, including Great Salt Lake City, on 17 January 1851, and Ogden, Provo, Manti, and Parowan, on 6 February. The counties had no governing officials but were merely units of the state and served as legislative and later judicial districts. Church leaders appointed men to preside in these areas until cities were chartered and elections held. In Salt Lake City, officers were appointed by the governor and legislature on 19 January. The first regular election was held the following April, and all of the appointed officers retained their positions except two councilmen. The city was divided into municipal wards represented by aldermen; the tax rate for the city was fixed; and other necessary officers such as treasurer, marshal, and assessor were appointed. This procedure was followed in the other settlements in the State of Deseret.[3]

The State of Deseret also set up a judiciary. Civil courts replaced the high council and bishop's courts of the "theodemocracy." The latter courts had been adequate during the first years, but with the "gold rush" to California, legal disputes developed which church courts could not resolve. A church court might render a fair decision, but in a case involving Mormons and non-Mormons, a decision was almost certain to be condemned as partial, especially if the non-Mormon lost. This problem was not entirely solved by the establishment of civil courts, because the chief justice and associate judges were all church leaders, and the magistrates of the lower courts were primarily ward bishops. But despite claims of prejudice and unfairness, the courts continued to render an important service to Mormon settlers and people passing through the territory.

The courts frequently adjudicated claims of property rights and ownership of articles. Often such cases resulted from quarrels occurring within emigrant wagon trains. Captain Howard Stansbury, who came to the Salt Lake Valley in 1849, seemed favorably impressed by the work of the courts:

---

[3] One of the most interesting enactments of the State of Deseret was the founding of the University of Deseret on 28 February 1850, which eventually developed into the University of Utah.

The decisions were remarkable for their fairness and impartiality, and if not submitted to, were sternly enforced by the whole power of the community. Appeals for protection from oppression, by those passing through their midst, were not made in vain; and I know of at least one instance in which the Marshal of the State was dispatched, with an adequate force, nearly two hundred miles into the Western desert in pursuit of some miscreants who had stolen off with nearly the whole outfit of a party of emigrants. He pursued and brought them back to the City, and the plundered property was restored to its rightful owners.

Lieutenant John W. Gunnison, a government surveyor in Utah in 1850, reported a similar experience: "Of the parties organized in the States to cross the plains there was hardly one that did not break into fragments and the division of property caused a great deal of difficulty. Many of these litigants applied to the courts of Deseret for redress of grievances, and there was every appearance of impartiality and strict justice done to all parties."[4]

During this period, the church's representative John Bernhisel[5] was promoting the appointment of Mormons or men known to be friendly to the church to the newly created territorial offices. Bernhisel recognized the need for diplomacy in order to secure the territory a corps of friendly officials. He wrote:

> I have labored with my pen and otherwise used my best endeavors to obtain a consummation so devoutly to be wished and I am gratified to be able to inform you that my efforts were crowned with complete success. What I wished was that the 37th parallel should form the southern and the crest of the Rocky Mountains, the eastern boundaries. These limits were established just before the bill was ordered to be engrossed. For more territory, I dare not venture to ask lest we receive none exterior to the basin.[6]

---

[4] Some of the main claims of unfairness were made by emigrants charged with damaging the property they were passing over on their way through the different communities. In discussing this problem, Gunnison wrote, "Again, the fields in the valleys are imperfectly fenced, and the emigrants often trespassed on the crops. For this, a good remuneration was demanded, and the value being so enormously greater than in the States, it looked to the stranger as an imposition and an injustice to ask so large a price." The difficulty of raising crops may account for the difference in value placed upon the damaged gardens.

[5] Church leaders were particularly fortunate in their choice of Bernhisel as their representative in Washington. He had been able to counteract the negative influence of Almon W. Babbitt who had alienated members of both parties during statehood negotiations.

[6] Bernhisel also noted that two of the church's old enemies, Missouri senators Thomas Benton and David Atchison, offered no opposition. Benton showed a kind disposition and favored a Utah territorial bill, and Atchison remarked that he was

Bernhisel must be credited not only for securing territorial government and sizable territorial boundaries but also securing the appointment of Brigham Young as governor, along with three other Mormon officials. Immediately after the passage of the Omnibus Bill that created the Territory of Utah, Bernhisel had an interview with President Millard Fillmore regarding territorial officials. Of that meeting he afterwards wrote to Young:

> He (Fillmore) is quite favorably disposed and I entertained but little doubt of your appointment. He inquired whether you would support the administration if you should be appointed and I replied that I thought that you would. The names of the following gentlemen have also been presented; Willard Richards for secretary of the territories, Zerubabbel Snow for Chief Justice, Daniel I. Miller of Iowa as one associate justice and Joseph L. Heywood for Marshall. The names of the other associate justice and the United States attorney I will give you in my next. Mr. Snow was baptized again last winter. Mr. Miller is not a member of the Church though friendly and is known to John Smith, patriarch and others. I have strong hopes that the whole ticket will be appointed. The president has requested my views in writing of the gentlemen whose names I presented to him for officers and I shall comply with his request tomorrow.

Despite Fillmore's friendliness, his appointments were disappointing to Bernhisel, who wrote to Young on 9 November, expressing his deep regret that his recommendations had not been followed and suggesting that his lack of legal training may have been the reason for this.

News of the appointment of territorial officers reached Great Salt Lake City on 27 January 1851 in a copy of the *New York Tribune* which came to Utah via Los Angeles. Young was on a preaching tour at the time, so Daniel H. Wells, the chief justice of Deseret, went to Davis County at the head of a body of cavalry and a brass band to inform Young of his appointment as governor. Although the news was not official, Young felt that it was reliable enough to justify taking office. So on 5 February 1851, he took the oath of office as chief executive of Utah territory.

In addition to his appointment as governor, Young was also designated superintendent of Indian Affairs. Other officials appointed by Fillmore were: Broughton D. Harris, as territorial secretary; Lemuel H. Brandebury, a non-Mormon, as chief justice; Perry E. Brocchus, a non-Mormon, as an associate justice; Zerubabbel Snow,

---

impressed that Utah had "asked for a government and was willing to take what we chose to give her."

a Mormon, as an associate justice; Joseph L. Heywood, a Mormon, as U.S. marshal; and Seth M. Blair, a Mormon, as U.S. Attorney.

The 1850 act provided for a territorial legislature and a delegate to Congress. Since representatives to the legislature and to Congress were elected by the people, they were chosen by the same theodemocratic process that had governed the State of Deseret. According to Mormon historian D. Michael Quinn, "Up to 1890 the [LDS] General Authorities were the source of first approval for every political nomination in Utah that they regarded as important." This included appointments recommended to the governor by the legislative assembly.

Members of the thirteen-member territorial Council and twenty-six-member House of Representatives were for many years unanimously elected. The presiding officers of the two bodies were usually members of the First Presidency or Council of the Twelve Apostles, and most of the members belonged to the Council of Fifty. Annual forty-day sessions of the legislature, beginning in December, were usually peaceful. One year the session was completed "without the occurrence of a negative vote on any question or action."

The territorial delegates to the U.S. House of Representatives were quasi-ecclesiastical appointments. Bernhisel and his successors for more than forty years were selected and set apart by the First Presidency, and no elections for the office were contested until non-Mormons filed a candidate in 1867, twenty years after the Saints had arrived in the region.[7]

Although much smaller than the proposed State of Deseret, the territory over which Brigham Young presided was extensive. It was bounded north and south by the 42nd and 37th parallels; the summits of the Rocky Mountains and the Sierra Nevada completed the boundaries. Estimates place the Indian population from 12,000 to 35,000. If the more conservative figure is taken, then whites and Indians were almost equal in number when the territory was born. But whites increased rapidly, while the displaced natives decreased until the mid-twentieth century. Fueled largely by the "gathering" of the Latter-day Saints, the population of Utah territory was reported

---

[7] There is evidence that the delegates were chosen to match the political majority in Washington and that they sometimes changed their party when that majority changed. At the local level, competition for city or county offices occasionally occurred, but partisan elections did not characterize Utah politics until the Liberal and People's parties were organized in 1870. Church leaders regularly selected candidates for mayor and city councilmen in Salt Lake City, Ogden, and Provo, and no candidate without their approval was elected to any of these offices until 1889.

by the decennial censuses to be 11,380 in 1850; 40,273 in 1860; 86,786 in 1870; 143,963 in 1880; and 210,779 in 1890.

Young's relationship with the non-Mormon officials was damaged from the start when he began a census and called for an election of legislators before the arrival of the non-Mormon officials. Since the Secretary of State was supposed to supervise the census-taking and certify the validity of the election, Young appeared to have acted precipitously.

However, the non-Mormon territorial officials were slow in arriving. Chief Justice Brandebury arrived on 7 June 1851, and Secretary Harris, with Indian agents Stephen B. Rose and Henry R. Day, reached Salt Lake on 19 July, accompanied by Mormon representatives Almon W. Babbitt and John M. Bernhisel. Unwilling to wait for Secretary Harris's arrival, Young instructed his assistants to begin taking the census on 14 March 1851. He felt this was necessary in order to establish legislative and judicial districts and was anxious that an election be held so that territorial representatives could travel to Washington before inclement weather developed. Although the first Monday in August had been designated as election day, Young suggested that the election be held in May in Iron County while he was visiting there. He recommended that Bernhisel be named territorial representative, which recommendation was followed.[8]

Although Secretary Harris was too late to participate in the census, he and fellow officials arrived in time to witness the 24 July celebration and to hear some vitriolic comments directed toward both the federal government and the late U.S. president, Zachary Taylor. The principal speaker, Daniel H. Wells, reviewing Mormon history, charged that "in the following winter and spring of 1846, the Church, in accordance with the provisions of said treaty, left their homes, and in the most inclement season of the year, amid storms of snow, with their families, crossed the ice of the Mississippi, and pursued their journey westward, not knowing where or when they should find a resting place." He asserted that the Mormon Battalion had been called to leave their families and make a 2,000-mile journey on foot across deserts, that the country had called them to do this but had not protected them from ruffians who plundered their property, robbed them of their rights, waylaid them, and murdered them "while

---

[8] Other irregularities upset the new Secretary of the Territory. When Joseph L. Heywood received his commission as U.S. Marshal in April, he immediately filed his bond with the Secretary of State of Deseret with instructions that it be delivered to the Secretary of the Territory "when he arrived." Apparently this never happened.

under the safeguards of their pledged faith. That country that could have the barbarity under such peculiar circumstances to make such a requirement could have no other object in view than to finish by utter extermination the work they had so ruthlessly begun."

Brigham Young followed by suggesting that those who worked against the Saints would die an untimely death and end up in hell, a reference to Zachary Taylor. Other speeches of the day, and in religious services throughout the remainder of the summer, invariably criticized government officials while at the same time professing love for the Constitution and the government.

Associate Justice Perry Brocchus did not arrive until 17 August, accompanied by Apostle Orson Hyde. They had been waylaid by about 300 Pawnee Indians who had robbed them of their supplies, including most of their clothing. Brocchus had expressed his willingness to serve as territorial representative and was disappointed to learn that Bernhisel had already been chosen. Less than three weeks after his arrival, he antagonized the entire community by a speech made at a special conference of the Saints on 8 September 1851. An exact transcription of the judge's speech is not extant, but the following synopsis of it was included in Brigham Young's manuscript history. Reportedly, Brocchus

> regretted to hear in our midst such expressions as that the United States were a stink in our nostrils. He was pained to hear it said that the government of the United States was going to hell as fast as possible. He said that if the people of Utah could not offer a block [of marble which was being solicited from every state and territory] for the Washington Monument in full fellowship with the United States, it were better to leave it unquarried in the bosom of its native mountain. He directed a portion of his discourse towards the ladies, and libertine as he boasted himself, strongly recommended them to become virtuous.

Brigham Young replied:

> Judge Brocchus is either profoundly ignorant, or willfully wicked, one of the two. There are several gentlemen on this platform who would be glad to prove the statements referred to in relation to him, as much more, if I would let them have the stand. His speech is designed to have political bearing. If I permit discussion to arise here, there may be either pulling of hair or a cutting of throats. It is well known to every man in this community, and has become a matter of history throughout the enlightened world, that the government of the United States looked on the scenes of robbing, driving, and murdering of this people and said nothing about the matter, but by silence gave sanction to the lawless proceedings. Hundreds of women and children have been laid in the tomb prematurely in

consequence thereof, and their blood cries to the Father for vengeance against those who have caused or consented to their death. George Washington was not dandled in the cradle of ease, but schooled to a life of hardship in exploring and surveying the mountains and defending the frontier settlers, even in his early youth, from the tomahawk and the scalping knife. It was God that dictated him and enabled him to assert and maintain the independence of the country. It is the same God that leads this people. I love the government and the Constitution of the United States, but I do not love the damned rascals who administer the government.

I know Zachary Taylor, he is dead and damned, and I cannot help it. I am indignant at such corrupt fellows as Judge Brocchus coming here to lecture us on morality and virtue. I could buy a thousand of such men and put them into a bandbox. Ladies and gentlemen, here we learn principle and good manners. It is an insult to this congregation to throw out such insinuations. I say it is an insult, and I will say no more.

After some reflection, a mellowed Young sent the judge a conciliatory letter suggesting an exchange of apologies:

B. Young to P. E. Brocchus Great Salt Lake City, September 19, 1851.

Dear Sir, —Ever wishing to promote the peace, love, and harmony of the people, and to cultivate the spirit of charity and benevolence to all, and especially towards strangers, I propose, and respectfully invite your honour, to meet our public assembly at the Bowery, on Sunday evening next, at 10 A.M., and address the same people from the stand that you addressed on the 8th inst., at our General Conference; and if your honour shall then and there explain, satisfy, or apologize to the satisfaction of the ladies who heard your address on the 8th, so that those feelings of kindness which you so dearly prized in your address can be reciprocated by them, I shall esteem it a duty and a pleasure to make every apology and satisfaction for my observation which you as a gentleman can claim or desire at my hands.

Should your honour please to accept of this kind and benevolent invitation, please answer by the bearer, that public notice may be given, and widely extended, that the house may be full. And believe me, sir, most sincerely and respectfully, your friend and servant,

Brigham Young. Hon. P. E. Brocchus, Asste. Justice.

P.S.—Be assured that no gentleman will be permitted to make any reply to your address on that occasion.

Brocchus refused the invitation, asserting that his speech "in all its parts were the result of deliberation and care" and that he did not feel he had said "anything deserving the censure of a justminded person."

Rebuffed, Young gave vent to his anger in two letters sent a day apart in which he emphasized Brocchus's insults to the ladies. Brocchus decided to vacate the territory but before leaving told the governor that he wanted to "bury the hatchet, shake hands and forget the past." He also asked Young to apologize to those whom he might have offended. Young announced the apology in a meeting the following day, 28 September, and two days later informed Brocchus by letter that his apology would be accepted if he agreed to control his tongue and cease to vilify "those who must everlastingly be your superiors."

Other difficulties involved Young and Secretary Harris. The secretary was ruffled over the action of the governor before and after the officers arrived in the valley. Specifically, he was not satisfied with the census, the apportionment of counselors and representatives to the territorial legislature, and the way the election was handled. Young, ever the pragmatist, justified the alleged irregularities on the basis of practical necessity.

Young waited upon the disgruntled officers and was told they were determined to return to the states. Harris wanted to take the $24,000 entrusted to him for legislative expenses and also the territory's seal and legal documents. Young immediately tried to block Harris's intended actions. The legislature was hastily called to meet on 22 September. With only five days notice, every legislator except a representative from Iron County was present. Two days after the legislative session opened, a joint resolution authorized the territorial marshal to take into his custody the public properties and all monies the secretary had in his possession.

To counter this move the non-Mormon officials turned to the branch of government under their control, the territorial supreme court. The secretary sought an injunction from the court to block the marshal from obtaining the public properties and monies. This injunction was granted. Upon learning the court was in session, Young prepared a request for an advisory opinion on his duties and those of the secretary, and instructed Attorney Seth Blair to file a petition to force an opinion on the matter. On that same day, 28 September, Brocchus and Brandebury, along with Harris and Indian Agent Day, left for the states.

Young recognized the danger a negative report from these officials represented and immediately dispatched a letter of explanation and defense to U.S. president Millard Fillmore. Dated 29 September 1851, Young's report detailed his activities since receiving his appointment as territorial governor, with supporting documents.

He defended his census and call for a territorial election before the arrival of Secretary Harris. Although Harris had been appointed in the fall of 1850, Young pointed out, he had not arrived in the territory until August 1851.

Young also reported that when he learned the federal officials were unhappy and that Harris was planning to return east with the $24,000 set aside to pay territorial legislators, he had hastily convened the territorial legislature. The legislature had voted to take into custody all of the funds and property belonging to the territory and authorized the marshal to obtain those funds and properties from the secretary. However, Harris, working through the territory's supreme court, succeeded in nullifying the legislature's actions.

After criticizing the "runaway officials" for this action and for failing to make an honest attempt to carry out their duties, Young suggested that the president use better judgment in future appointments. He asserted his intention to discharge every duty pertaining to his office and declared himself grateful for any instructions from President Fillmore. He also took the opportunity to assert his loyalty and that of the Mormon people to the basic principles of their country:

> It has been and is said of myself and the people over whom I have the honor to preside, that they frequently indulge in strictures upon the acts of men who are intrusted with governmental affairs, and the Government itself sometimes does not wholly escape. Now, sir, I will simply state what I know to be true, that no people exists who are more friendly to the Government of the United States than the people of this Territory.
>
> The Constitution they revere, the laws they seek to honor. But the non-execution of those laws in times past, for our protection, and the abuse of power in the hands of those intrusted therewith, even in the hands of those whom we have supported for office, even betraying us in the hour of our greatest peril and extremity, but withholding the due execution of laws designed for the protection of all the citizens of the United States: it is for this we have cause of complaint, not the want of good and wholesome laws, but the execution of the same, in the true meaning and spirit of the constitution.

Young concluded by reporting that it was rumored that the "runaway officers" had been sent to Utah with "private instructions" to spy on the Mormons and misrepresent them in order to prejudice the minds of the people against them. If this is true, Young wrote,

> better, far better would it be for us, to live under the organization of our Provisional Government, and entirely depending upon our own resources, as we have hitherto done, until such time as we can be admitted as a

State than thus to be tantalized with the expectation of having a legal government which will extend her fostering care over all her offspring. In fancy, if ever, it is necessary to assist the rising state.

Young added a bit of advice on the appointment of new territorial officers, suggesting that Fillmore choose men who reside within the territory and have an "extended knowledge of things as well as of the elementary and fundamental principles of law and legislation."

Young's letter was an able defense of his actions and a bold statement of the church's position in its relations with the federal government. That such a defense was needed is demonstrated by the antagonism that was created against the Mormons following the report of the returning officials and the subsequent public announcement by church leaders of the practice of plural marriage.

13.
Church
versus State

The early years of territorial government in Utah were difficult ones for both Mormon and federal officials. Unfavorable reports by former territorial chief justice Brandebury, former territorial secretary Harris, former associate justice Brocchus, and former Indian subagent Day increased federal worries about granting Utah territorial status. The public announcement of plural marriage in 1852 only exacerbated concerns about the appointment of Brigham Young as governor. United States president Franklin Pierce tried to solve the problem by appointing a new governor, but after spending some months in Utah on an army assignment prior to taking office, his appointee declined. Young continued to serve by default, without a definite term.

Mormonism became a subject of national politics when opponents of popular sovereignty used polygamy to illustrate the dangers involved in permitting local voters to decide moral issues. Further adverse national publicity came to the region when the newly organized Republican party campaigned for the presidency in 1856 with a promise to "rid the nation of the twin relics of barbarism, slavery and polygamy." Democrats reacted by condemning polygamy but defending slavery. Despite Utah representative John M. Bernhisel's efforts to stem this adverse tide, misunderstandings, personality conflicts, and unwise actions by federal and Mormon leaders alike led to confrontation. This cold war threatened to erupt into a hot one.

217

The official report of Brandebury, Harris, Brocchus, and Day that the Mormons were immoral, disloyal fanatics led by a despotic priesthood was heard in Congress and publicized throughout the nation. Brocchus claimed that he and his companions had been compelled to leave Utah because of the lawless acts of Governor Young and his followers. He said that the Mormon church controlled territorial affairs, disposing of public land and exacting onerous taxes. Specifically, Brocchus charged that Young had misappropriated $20,000 in federal funds originally appropriated to build a territorial capitol building. Territorial representative John Bernhisel denounced the Brocchus report in the House on 10 January 1852, maintaining that it contained grossly exaggerated, if not false and perverted statements, and challenging the Speaker of the House or the president to appoint a commission to investigate the charges.

President Millard Fillmore invited Bernhisel to visit him in April 1852, telling him that he hoped to do justice to the Mormons while still fulfilling his duty to the government. He did not join in the current prejudice against the Mormons and felt that everyone had a right to worship God according to his conscience. Fillmore asked Bernhisel if he supposed there was any truth to the report that the Mormons had set up a government for themselves. Bernhisel assured him that this was not true. About mid-April, Fillmore, wishing to discuss the matter further, sent a note to Bernhisel, who called again on the president, finding him sympathetic and understanding.

Early in May, Bernhisel had yet a third interview with Fillmore, this time to discuss the appointment of territorial officers to replace those who had left in September 1851. Soon after the interview Bernhisel wrote to Brigham Young that it was "his solemn conviction that the president honestly and sincerely desired to do what is right toward us. He is a noble, high-minded accomplished gentleman. The more intimately I become acquainted with him the more he excites my respect and admiration."

Young wanted Willard Richards, Heber C. Kimball, and Orson Hyde to replace the "runaways." Hyde was even nominated to replace Brocchus, but the Senate refused to confirm the Mormon apostle, "not because he was a Mormon, but because he was not a regular-bred lawyer." Lazarus Reid was named territorial chief justice; Benjamin Ferris, territorial secretary; and Leonidas Shaver, territorial associate justice. Bernhisel seemed pleased with the appointments, assuring Young that although non-Mormons they were different men than their predecessors. He urged the governor to see

PRESIDENT MILLARD FILMORE

that they were kindly received in the valley, adding that the president did not want "the good people of Utah [to] get into difficulty with these runaway officers."

On 9 July, Bernhisel wrote from Washington that the runaway officers had been beaten on every point, although the Brocchus affair had prompted the first significant rehearsal in Congress of Mormon peculiarities. Bernhisel worried about Young's inability to understand how sensitive the Saints' situation was as well as the president's attitude that God would take care of them no matter what. Bernhisel wrote to Young that the slightest jar might result in his removal as governor. He said, "If there shall be another flare up we shall be utterly ruined here as regards to obtaining of appropriations or even retaining any offices in our territory." He then suggested "that no pains nor effort be spared to cultivate the most friendly relation between the new appointees and the authorities and people of Utah. In order to attain and maintain so desirable a state of things, it may frequently become requisite to exercise great patience and forbearance—to 'stoop to conquer as the play says.' "

Young seemed unworried and advised Bernhisel to "be of good courage doctor, for all is right. Do not permit anything that may occur discourage you in the least. Go ahead never doubting although the sun and all else may appear dark around you." Using aides and secretaries, Young compiled a 92-page open response to the accusations of the departed officials, dated 11 June 1852, and sent a copy of it to the president. Entitled "Beating Against the Air," the document contained specific details to refute the accusation that Young had misappropriated $20,000. The Brocchus report maintained that Young had seized the money to pay church debts. According to his unpublished manuscript history, Young had publicly announced several months earlier, in January:

> The $20,000 received from Congress for the erection of public buildings for the territory has been appropriated by the governor and the legislative assembly so far as it will go in the purchase of the State House of Deseret in this city which was built by the church of Jesus Christ of Latter-day Saints at the expense of $45,000. This is to be the seat of the government of territory until suitable buildings can be erected in Fillmore City which is designed as the permanent locality of the capital. Our present state house has two spacious halls for the general assembly and four rooms suitable for public or executive offices.

In a later communication with the U.S. Secretary of the Treasury, Young explained that the State House of Deseret was the only

suitable building in the territory and that it was too late in the season to build another capitol. The church might have rented the building to the territory, but Young thought it would be "more economi-
cal to purchase a portion of the existing State House conditionally."
Young concluded, "This I did in all good faith and out of the exercise of my judgment and backed up and sanctioned by the assembly."
Territorial officials would proceed with the building of a capitol in
Fillmore and would sell the purchased portion of the State House
back to the church upon the completion of the Fillmore building.

The remainder of Young's mammoth letter rehearsed Mormon
history. On page 7, Young stated it was well known that polygamy
was practiced by the Latter-day Saints. This was three months before
the church's official announcement, but apparently Young realized
that the practice could no longer be concealed or denied. Bernhisel
was understandably dismayed at this announcement. Willard
Richards sent word to Bernhisel that the revelation on polygamy
dictated by Joseph Smith to scribe William Clayton in 1843 would
soon appear in print. Bernhisel complained to Young, "I shall have
to fight the battles of the last session all over again." Bernhisel felt
that statehood, appropriations, and all that he had hoped to accomplish in Washington were now threatened. He was convinced that
the Brocchus report would seem more credible and feared that "not
one in a thousand will be convinced that the doctrine is at all consistent with chastity or even morality, much less that it is a pure and
righteous one. I know and dread the scenes through which I shall
have to pass this coming winter and I could fervently pray in the
language of our blessed Saviour that this cup might pass from me."

Bernhisel was further upset that apostles Orson Pratt (in Washington, D.C.), John Taylor (in New York), and Erastus Snow (in St.
Louis) were publishing Mormon newspapers defending polygamy.
Pratt's periodical, *The Seer*, announced in its 21 December 1852
prospectus:

> The doctrine of celestial marriage or marriage for all eternity is believed
> in and practiced by the Saints in Utah territory and will be clearly
> explained. The views of the Saints, in regard to the ancient patriarchal
> order of matrimony or the plurality of wives as developed in a revela-
> tion given through Joseph Smith the Seer, will be fully published . . . in
> the very first number. Also, the celestial origin, pre-existence of spirits
> and so on. It is hoped the president-elect, honorable members of Con-
> gress, the heads of the various departments of national government, the
> high-minded governors and legislative assemblies of the several states

and territories, the ministers of every religious denomination, and all inhabitants of the great republic will patronize this periodical.

Although Mormon disclosures of polygamy elicited Congressional denouncements, the issue was overshadowed by a larger controversy. Legislation introduced into Congress in 1854, resulting in the Kansas-Nebraska Act, focussed debate on the principle of popular sovereignty.[1] Hoping to solve the problem of the transcontinental railroad route, to increase the value of his own property in and around Chicago, and to placate southern Democrats on slavery, Illinois senator Stephen Douglas championed the creation of two territories that would decide the slavery issue on the basis of popular vote. But Douglas was disturbed by the existence of polygamy in Utah. For if popular sovereignty could license slavery it could also license polygamy, and Utah would certainly vote to legalize plural marriage—an argument against popular sovereignty. Still, as distasteful as polygamy was, slavery was the more burning issue. Thus while debates raged in the nation's capital, comparative peace and quiet reigned in Utah.

POPULAR SOVEREIGNTY

The new officials had only a brief tenure in their offices, but not because of any unfriendliness on the part of the Saints. Both Reid and Shaver became ill and were dead within the year. Ferris chose to move on to California after six months; both he and his wife later wrote books about their experiences in Utah. Their successors, named by Fillmore's Democratic successor, Franklin Pierce, included Chief Justice John F. Kinney, a friendly non-Mormon, and Associate Justice George P. Stiles and Territorial Secretary Almon W. Babbitt, both apostate Mormons.

During the absence of the runaway officials, the territorial legislature in 1851-52 passed a law extending the jurisdiction of local probate courts, thereby lessening the influence of federal district courts. The act stipulated that in probate courts, "by the consent of

---

[1] Popular sovereignty, or squatter sovereignty as it was sometimes called, was particularly the property of northwestern Democrats and was advocated by the man who would emerge as their leader, Illinois senator Stephen A. Douglas. An unusually adroit manipulator, Douglas and other western politicians faced a problem that challenged their best talents. Their constituents wanted to keep slavery out of the territories, and party chiefs had to assure that it would be banned, but they also desired to win national elections. Douglas in particular hoped to be president, and this meant that the party had to be held together as a national organization, that the southern wing not be goaded into withdrawing. Popular sovereignty was a subtle doctrine conceived to satisfy both sections. It proposed that Congress should neither exclude slavery nor encourage its expansion. Instead, its status would be decided by the people of each territory through their territorial legislature.

the court and the parties, any person may be selected to act as judge for the trial of any particular cause or question, and while thus acting he shall possess all the powers of the district judge in the case." This was intended to promote the social custom of settling difficulties by arbitration rather than litigation as well as to expand home rule by local officers.

The judges of the probate courts, one in each county, were elected by the legislative assembly but commissioned by the governor to hold office for a term of four years and until their successors were elected and qualified. In addition to probating wills, administering the estates of deceased persons, and determining the guardianship of minors, and mentally retarded and insane persons, probate courts had power to exercise in their respective counties original jurisdiction, both civil and criminal, in chancery and at common law, when not prohibited by legislative enactments. As a result, the local probate courts, usually with bishops as the presiding judges, were able to handle practically all criminal and civil cases that arose in the territory, leaving district judges and territorial supreme court judges with little to do.

During the summer of 1852, Brigham Young wrote to Bernhisel to begin seeking statehood for Utah. "Whereas we are only a territory," Young wrote, "we are now a state, a sovereign independent state in our organization. We ask admission into the union upon an equal footing with the original states. The reason for our preferring the state to a territorial government is that we are separated from the appointing power." Bernhisel, following Stephen Douglas's advice, did not attempt to present Utah for statehood. It seemed incredible to Bernhisel that Young would push for statehood so soon after the public announcement of polygamy.

Newly elected President Franklin Pierce decided to replace Young as governor. Although he said he wanted to do what was best for Utah, he refused to take the advice of Chief Justice Kinney and Bernhisel to re-appoint Young. Pierce believed that there was too much prejudice against the Mormons to allow Young to continue in office and decided to appoint an army officer, Colonel E. J. Steptoe, who was in Utah on a special assignment.

Steptoe had been sent to Utah in the summer of 1854 and had arrived with his command in Salt Lake City on 31 August with two specific assignments. One was to explore the possibility of a military road to California; the other to investigate the murder of Lieutenant John W. Gunnison and his party. Steptoe commanded about 175 soldiers and 150 employees. He decided to winter his 1,000 head of horses and mules in Rush Valley, ten miles south of Tooele, and to locate his troops in the Salt Lake Valley.

After renting several large buildings in Salt Lake City, including Wilford Woodruff's valley house, Steptoe began to carry out his duties. He apparently had no prior knowledge that he was being considered for an appointment as Utah's governor and did not receive notification of this until he had been in the territory for several months. The letter notifying him of the appointment was dated 21 December 1854 and informed him that the official commission was on its way. This did not arrive until the following March, and by that time Steptoe had decided to accompany his troops on their road survey assignment to California.

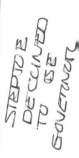

STEPTOE DECLINED TO BE GOVERNOR

In the meantime Steptoe had joined Judge Kinney and several prominent non-Mormons in signing a petition requesting that Brigham Young be re-appointed. The petition was accompanied by a long list of Mormon signatures as well. After signing this petition, Steptoe concentrated his efforts on the arrest and trial of Gunnison's murderers. Some historians have wondered why Steptoe turned down the opportunity to be governor. The obvious answer is that he realized it would be very difficult to preside effectively when Young was the overwhelming choice of the inhabitants. However, Steptoe became upset with the way the Gunnison trial was being conducted and considered the possibility of accepting the governorship. In a letter to an unidentified general—possibly his commanding officer or General Franklin Pierce, as he often referred to him—Steptoe wrote:

> Your enclosing my appointment as governor of the territory was received a few days ago. It is not possible for me today to choose the proper course for me to pursue but I will endeavor to accept or decline by the next mail. In all events, I propose to take my command over to San Francisco and it has resumed its march today. I have much to write to you about and I will try to give you an insight into Mormon affairs. Judge Kinney authorized me to say that if I shall decline the office he will accept it should it be offered to him.

In another letter, dated 26 March 1855, Steptoe suggested that a government force be established in the southern part of the territory to assume at once entire control of the Indians. Until recently the Indians had been "taught to believe that the Americans were feeble in comparison with the Mormons and learned from me for the first time what position the latter held in our great national family." By the time of his departure, he would probably have refused to sign a petition similar to the one he had earlier supported requesting that Young be retained as governor and superintendent of Indian Affairs.

When it became apparent that Steptoe would not serve as governor, Judge Kinney offered his services, as Steptoe said he would. But President Pierce chose not to take advantage of Kinney's offer, and when none of his personal candidates would accept the position, Pierce tabled the decision. According to the act that created the territory, Young would remain governor since no one else had been appointed.

Meanwhile, Bernhisel was busy trying to explain some of Young's less temperate statements. The *Baltimore Daily Sun* quoted the Utah governor as saying that he would remain in office "until the Lord Almighty says Brigham, you need not be governor any longer." Bernhisel sent a clipping of this article to Young, gently scolding him for such remarks and urging him to tell reporters and printers not to publish such statements as they were intended for the Saints only. Bernhisel said that such statements can "frequently be twisted or tortured so as to rebound to your injury or the injury of the entire church." He continued:

> I have to meet all of these things here face to face and explain, palliate, contradict, deny, as the case may be and though the battle may be fought ever so successfully and victory perch on our banner, yet they leave a deep black stain behind. If they, that is the rumors, did not prevent us as already intimated from obtaining appropriations and other favors there is no one in our quiet and peaceful valley who would care less what a lout or lost and ruined world thought or said of us than your humble servant.

In reply, Young elaborated his philosophy of life, that God rules the affairs of men. He wrote, "Let small men or large men, officers of state, emperors, kings, or beggars say or do what they please, it is all the same to the Almighty. The king upon his throne, the president in his chair, the judges upon the bench and the beggar in the street are all overruled in their actions by the Almighty God of heaven and earth. Who can successfully fight against him?" Young then responded directly to the issue of the *Baltimore Daily Sun* article:

> President Pierce and all hell could not remove me from office. I will tell you what I did say and what I now say. The Lord reigns and rules in the armies of heaven and he does his pleasure among the inhabitants of the earth. He sets up a kingdom here and pulls down another there at his pleasure. He walks in the midst of people and they know it not. He makes

kings, presidents, and governors at his pleasure. Hence, I conclude that I shall be governor of Utah territory just as long as he wants me to be and for that time neither the president nor the United States nor any other power can prevent it. Then brethren and sisters do not be worried about my being dismissed from office but when the president appoints another man to be governor of Utah territory you may acknowledge that the Lord had done it for we should acknowledge his hand in all things. All people are in the hands of the Almighty and he governs and controls them though they cannot perceive neither do they acknowledge his hand-iwork. He exalts the president to be head of the nation and places kings upon their thrones. There is not a man that escapes his cognizance and he brings forth his purposes in the latter day.[2]

Whether or not Young intended his remarks to be belligerent, they increased the disposition in Washington to ridicule Young and his followers. For example, Connecticut senator Truman Smith pointed out how difficult it would be to welcome Young as a fellow congressman and assist his forty wives to seats in the chambers. Later, during the campaign of 1856, parades preceding the election some-times featured Young as an object of disdain. Edward Tullidge, a nineteenth-century Mormon historian, exaggerated only a little when he wrote that "in every campaign [parade] . . . Brigham Young with six wives, most fashionably dressed, hooped skirts and all, each with a little Brigham in her arms, occupied one wagon drawn by oxen."

Before debate over the Kansas-Nebraska bill concluded, the Mor-mon question was raised again with the proposal to extend the fed-eral land system to the new territories, New Mexico and Utah, sub-ject to such modifications as their peculiarities required. One modification suggested that the act should not benefit any person

---

[2] Young expressed this philosophy many times, especially when things were not going the way he hoped. Still, it is difficult to reconcile this fatalism with many of the activities Young otherwise pursued—as when he lashed out at people who did not do the things he wanted or expected. A case in point is Young's letter to Bernhisel when it became apparent that he would not be re-appointed governor:

Tell Mr. Franklin Pierce that the people of the territory have a way—it may be a very peculiar way but an honest one of sending their infernal, dirty, sneaking, rotten-hearted, pot-house politicians out of the territory and if he should come himself it would be all the same. Talk about democracy or republicanism, how did our fathers of 1776 do when the government of England sent judges upon the country. Were they right in doing as they did? And shall we submit to their cussed tyranny and not resist? No, by the means of our defeated fathers who bled for liberty, no. Tell Mr. Pierce this, that we ask no odds of him nor the factious blood-stained rabble which seems to him such a high and mighty honor to preside over. When we have a president of the people and not of a party, I shall feel that a representation has taken place in our country.

having more than one wife. While some questioned the constitutionality of such an act, Hyrum Waldridge, a New York Democrat, made a reply which would be echoed by reform-minded congressmen for decades: "I do not propose to say whether it is constitutional or not, I am viewing this as a great moral question." Although Young had asserted in a celebrated 1859 interview with Horace Greeley that slavery was a divinely sanctioned institution, both census reports for 1850 and 1860 found only forty to fifty slaves in the region. Polygamy, not slavery, would become a moral issue for Utah.

In the 1856 presidential contest, the Mormon question was a convenient red herring. The Democratic platform, adopted on 2 June, endorsed the Kansas-Nebraska Act's "non-interference by Congress with slavery in state and territory." About two weeks later the Republican party, meeting in Philadelphia, nominated John C. Fremont and William L. Dayton. One of the platform's planks, which was greeted with tremendous applause, read: "Resolved that the constitution confers upon Congress sovereign powers over the territories of the United States for their government and that in the exercise of this power it is both the right and the imperative duty of Congress to prohibit in the territories those twin relics of barbarism, polygamy and slavery."

One of the most violent denunciations of polygamy came in the summer months of 1856 when John U. Pettit of Indiana denounced popular sovereignty "which admits the patriarchal institution of slavery into Utah and makes it the political twin of that other patriarchal institution, Governor Young's multiplicity of wives. It brings together there for the first time in Christian lands, the Turkish slave bazaar and the Turkish harem and bids them live in love together under the sanction of our laws."

Stephen Douglas maintained in 1857 that nine-tenths of Utahns were aliens by birth and did not have any allegiance to the United States, that they were bound by horrid oaths and terrible penalties to recognize and maintain the authority of Brigham Young, and that the government of which Young was head was more powerful than the United States in civil and religious affairs. It was also reported that the Mormons were forming alliances with Indians in Utah and adjoining territories, were encouraging the Indians to be hostile, and were organizing bands of followers under the name of "Danites" or "destroying angels." Douglas concluded:

> Let us have these facts in an official shape before the president and Congress, and the country will soon learn that in the performance of the

high and solemn duty devolving upon the executive, and Congress, there will be no vacillating or hesitating policy. Should such a state of things actually exist as we are led to infer from the reports and such information comes in an official shape, the knife must be applied to this pestiferous disgusting cancer which is gnawing into the very vitals of the body politic. It must be cut out by the roots and seared over by the red hot iron of stern and unflinching law.

Such publicity in Washington forced U.S. president James Buchanan, Pierce's successor, to replace Young as governor.

While both Democrats and Republicans were condemning polygamy, confrontations took place in Utah between federal officials and church leaders that led to further negative reports in Washington. President Buchanan became convinced that the Mormons were in a state of rebellion and that a sizable portion of the United States Army should accompany the new, non-Mormon governor to control any opposition.

One of the first federal appointees to become involved in controversy was David H. Burr, newly appointed surveyor general of the territory. Many Mormons looked upon Burr's survey as a potential threat, knowing that title to the lands they had occupied was tenuous in the absence of Mexican grant, Indian treaty, or congressional enactment. Some tried to impede the surveyor's work, and Burr reported to superiors that he had been threatened with violence and that Mormons were encouraging Indians to resist the surveying parties. By the spring of 1857, Burr gave up his work in Utah, claiming that he had been denounced from the pulpit and that his life was in danger. He asserted that his associates had been beaten and threatened with death. Mormon leaders denied Burr's claims and accused Burr of conspiracy to defraud the public.

The organization of the Brigham Young Express and Carrying Company (see chap. 8), was another development leading to confrontations and damaging reports. This large scale enterprise was designed to aid immigration to Utah, to improve mail service, and to facilitate the movement of passengers and freight between the Missouri River and Salt Lake City.

The plan involved establishing way stations and supply depots approximately fifty miles apart from Omaha to Salt Lake City. Each station would be supported by a mile-square village equipped with mills, shops and storehouses, and other necessities. In order to finance the mammoth project, Young felt it was necessary to obtain the government mail contract, which at that time was held by W. M. F. Magraw. Magraw's service was unsatisfactory, and his contract had been cancelled in October 1856, giving the Mormons an opportunity to bid on the new contract. Believing that the church would not be given the contract, Young used Hiram Kimball as a front to bid for the award. The prospect of using the BYX Co.'s facilities to carry the mail made it possible for Kimball to underbid all others; he was awarded a four-year contract for monthly mail service between Independence, Missouri, and Salt Lake City on 9 October 1856.

This contract allowed Young to proceed with his colonizing plan, and soon Mormon "work" missionaries were called to build the villages. By April 1857, three companies of 100 men each had been dispatched east with necessary equipment and supplies to build the needed way stations. Unfortunately for the Mormons, several of these villages were to be built on Indian lands, and they had not sought or received approval for such establishments. Thus Thomas S. Twiss, Indian agent on the upper Platte, criticized the plan and called for government action. In one letter, addressed to the U.S. Commissioner of Indian Affairs, J. W. Denver, Twiss reported:

> In a communication addressed to the Indian office dated April last, I called attention of the department to the settlements being made within the boundaries of this agency by the Mormon church clearly in violation of the law, although the pretext or pretense under which these settlements are made is under the cover of a contract of the Mormon church to carry the mail from Independence Missouri to Salt lake City. On the 25th of May, a large Mormon colony took possession of the valley of Deer Creek 100 miles west of Fort Laramie and drove away a band of Sioux whom I had settled there in April and whom I had induced to plant corn. I left the Indian band on the 23rd of May to attend to matters connected with the Cheyenne band in the lower part of the agency. I have information from a reliable source that these Mormons were about 300 in number and have plowed and planted 200 acres of prairie and are building houses sufficient for the accommodation of 500 persons and have a large herd of cattle, horses and mules. I am persuaded that the Mormon church intends by this plan, thus partially developed, to monopolize all the trade with the Indians and whites within [and] passing through the Indian territory. I respectfully and earnestly call the attention of the department to the invasion and enter my protest against its occupation of Indian country in force and the forced ejection of the Indians from the place where I had settled them. I am powerless to control this matter for the Mormons obey no law enacted by Congress. I would respectfully request the president . . . to issue such order as in his wisdom and judgment may seem best to correct the evil complained of.

In response to Twiss's objection, Hiram Kimball learned that his contract had been cancelled, ostensibly for failure to deliver the mail before a set deadline. The letter describing the expiration time did not arrive until after the time had expired, and it seems likely that officials in Washington were aware of this and used it as an excuse to cancel the contract.

Another complaint regarding the Mormon handling of Indian affairs came from Garland Hurt, the Indian agent who came to the territory in 1855. An educated gentleman from Kentucky, Hurt established amiable relations with the Mormons at first. He helped to create three Indian farms with Brigham Young's approval. However, news of the approach of a U.S. Army contingent to seat the new governor caused the Mormons to become wary of "Gentiles in their midst," and by mid-August, when Bishop Aaron Johnson reported that the Indians on the Spanish Fork farm had become hostile to the church and sympathetic to the Americans, Hurt was treated with suspect.

There is some confusion as to the events that caused Hurt to leave the territory, but he claimed that on 27 September 1857 he was warned by Indian friends that a large body of Mormon Dragoons was only a mile away threatening him with arrest or bodily harm. He was able to elude them and, with a large body of Indians, made his way to South Pass where he sought the protection of the army. While wintering near Fort Bridger, he wrote a letter to the newly appointed governor, describing his ordeal and adding a list of Mormon atrocities and anti-American attitudes.

At the time the BYX Co. was engaged in its colonizing program, the federally appointed judges in Utah were engaged in quite a different program. Chief Justice Kinney, who pretended to be friendly to the Mormons, sent a number of angry dispatches to the government. He condemned Utah's probate courts and spoke of his fear of personal violence at the hands of Mormon assassins. In the critical months before Buchanan's decision to send troops to the territory, Kinney informed U.S. attorney general Jeremiah Black that the Mormons were "inimical to the Government of the United States and to all its officers who are not of their particular faith."

Territorial associate justice George P. Stiles had been a prominent Mormon in Nauvoo but had recently been excommunicated from the church. He had antagonized some Mormons by trying to limit the Mormon court system. A number of Mormon lawyers, led by James Ferguson, challenged his authority and intimidated him in his court. He appealed to Young for protection, but the governor claimed he could not enforce U.S. laws.

A short time later, some rowdies invaded Stiles's office, seized some of his books and records, and made a bonfire of them in a nearby outhouse. Fortunately, the district court records were not among those burned, but this incident gave credence to the report that the Mormons were in a state of rebellion, having seized and destroyed the territorial supreme court records and intimidated a federal judge. Stiles went to Washington to confirm many of the accusations made by other Mormon opponents.

Although both Kinney and Stiles were responsible for some anti-Mormon feelings in the east, it remained for their fellow judge, Associate Justice W. W. Drummond, to prompt Buchanan to send an army to Utah. Ironically, Drummond's character and record were such that his accusations should have had little influence, but apparently the authorities in Washington were unaware of his immorality and incompetency. When Drummond added his condemnations to the others and recommended that a non-Mormon be appointed governor and be supported "with sufficient military aid," Buchanan was ready to act.

Drummond had brought a courtesan with him to Salt Lake City and passed her off as his wife. As reported in the *Deseret News*, he had deserted his wife and family in Illinois. Yet Drummond took it upon himself to lecture the Mormons on the evils of polygamy. By the spring of 1857, he went to Carson Valley, ostensibly to hold court for Judge Stiles, but continued on his way to San Francisco, where he created a sensation with his newspaper accounts of developments in Utah. On arriving in New Orleans, he sent a letter of resignation to Attorney General Black, dated 30 March 1857. His reasons for resigning were:

(1) That Brigham Young is the head of the "Mormon church"; and, as such head, the "Mormons" look to him, and to him alone, for the law by which they are to be governed; therefore no law of Congress is by them considered binding in any matter;

(2) That he [Drummond] knew that a secret, oathbound organization existed among all the male members of the church to resist the laws of the country, and to acknowledge no law save the law of the priesthood, which came to the people through Brigham Young.

(3) That there were a number of men "set apart by special order of the church, to take both the lives and property of any person who may question the authority of the church." The judge also alleges—"That the records, papers, etc. of the supreme court have been destroyed by order

230

of the church, with the direct knowledge and approbation of Governor B. Young, and the federal officers grossly insulted for presuming to raise a single question about the 'treasonable act.'

(4) "That the federal officers of the territory are constantly insulted, harassed, and annoyed by the Mormons, and for these insults there is no redress.

(5) "That the federal officers are daily compelled to hear the form of the American government traduced, the chief executives of the nation, both living and dead, slandered and abused from the masses as well as from all the leading members of the church."

(6) The judge also charged discrimination in the administration of the laws as against "Mormon" and Gentile; that Captain John W. Gunnison and his party were murdered by Indians; but "under the orders, advice and direction of the Mormons"; that the "Mormons" poisoned Judge Leonidas Shaver, Drummond's predecessor; that Almon W. Babbitt, secretary of the territory had been killed on the plains by a band of "Mormon" marauders, who were "sent from Salt Lake City for that purpose, and that only," under direct orders of the presidency of the Church of Latter-day Saints, and that Babbitt was not killed by Indians as reported from Utah.

Drummond further explained to the attorney general that he was making his resignation public because the Democratic party was in power "and therefore, is the party that should now be held responsible for the treasonable and disgraceful state of affairs" existing in Utah territory. Admitting that he had "accomplished little good while there," he expressed his belief that "if there was a man put in office as governor of that territory, who is not a member of the church (i.e. Mormon), and he be supported with a sufficient military aid, much good would result from such a course." "But," he continued, "as the territory is now governed . . . it is noonday madness and folly to attempt to administer the law in that territory. The officers are insulted, harassed, and murdered for doing their duty, and not recognizing Brigham Young as the only lawgiver and lawmaker on earth."

President Buchanan, barely in office two months, decided to follow Drummond's advice to appoint a non-Mormon governor for Utah and support him with sufficient military force. A combination of politics, prejudice, greed, fanaticism, persecution psychology, deliberate lying, great distances, and a lack of communication all contributed to the tragic military maneuver historians would later label "Buchanan's Blunder."

14.
The Utah
War

U.S. president James Buchanan, who took office in March 1857, was convinced by May that the Mormons were in rebellion against the federal government. Without properly investigating the situation, Buchanan appointed a new governor to replace Brigham Young and ordered units of the U.S. Army to accompany the appointee. The resulting military expedition was a fiasco for the Buchanan administration and brought suffering to the soldiers, territorial officials, and Mormons called into active duty in the territorial militia (called the Nauvoo Legion) to guard mountain passes against this invasion.[1] Although no lives were directly lost, the threat of the approaching army was the primary cause of the tragic Mountain Meadows Massacre. Economic costs for transporting and maintaining the U.S. Army, plus expenditures by the Mormons in raising a defense force and abandoning Salt Lake City and northern colonies, were enormous. Clearly, sending the army was a costly mistake, and the responsibility must be shared by government and Mormon officials alike.

The idea of providing military support for territorial officials in Utah did not begin with Buchanan. Feelings against the Mormons flowed strongly in Washington, D.C., during the winter of 1851–52 when the so-called "runaway" officials began making their reports.

---

[1] The freighting company of Russell, Majors, and Waddell, which carried the supplies for the 2,500-man federal army, suffered severe economic losses at the hands of Mormon raiders.

When territorial secretary Harris was subsequently offered Young's position, he asked for an armed escort but was refused. Colonel Steptoe led a 175-man military contingent to Utah in 1854 and was so disturbed with the Mormon influence on the Indians that he recommended establishing a force "somewhere in the south in order that the government may assume the entire control of these Indians."[2] Still no one chose such a drastic response to the Mormon problem until territorial associate justice W. W. Drummond's 1856 letter to Buchanan, asserting that the only solution was to appoint a non-Mormon governor, accompanied by a posse comitatus to support his authority in the midst of a disloyal and rebellious people.

Surprisingly, when Buchanan delivered his inaugural address on 4 March 1857 he made no reference to Utah. Apparently he was unaware of Utah's challenge to the authority of the federal government. But by the end of April he was convinced of the need for a new Utah governor supported by federal troops. He issued a military order dated 28 May 1857 ordering the gathering of a body of troops at Fort Leavenworth to march to Utah. Buchanan and his cabinet did not expect the Mormons to resist such a military force. In fact, many eastern leaders, including the president and his cabinet, were laboring under the false impression that the Mormons would welcome the soldiers as saviors to redeem them from a living hell. According to such thinking, polygamy had cracked the unity of the Mormon people and, as one editor suggested, "will cause a stampede among the women and be a blow to the Mormon church and crush it to atoms." Secretary of State Lewis Cass instructed the new governor to offer federal protection to all Utahns who wished it. Washington apparently believed that a large portion of the population would wish nothing more than to escape from the cruelties of Mormondom.

Once the decision to send troops had been made, two problems confronted Buchanan. One was to find a competent governor who would accept the challenge, who was capable, tactful, courageous, and willing to travel 2,000 miles from Washington to govern a community composed of people who had treated federal officers contemptuously in the past. In addition, Washington officials also needed to find new federal judges and a superintendent of Indian Affairs, since the incumbents had resigned or run away from Utah out of

FELT MANY 'MORMONS' WOULD RUN TO ARMY ARMS

---

[2] As early as March 1856, Young's counselor Jedediah Grant commented that the Mormons were tired "of this eternal threatening with the armies of the United States."

fear. Not until the second week of June did the government find a suitable candidate in Alfred Cumming, a native of Georgia.

Cumming had been mayor of Augusta and during the epidemic of yellow fever that raged the year of his election (1849) had been an effective administrator. He had served with General Zachary Taylor's army in Mexico and later at the Jefferson Barracks in Missouri. He had been appointed superintendent of Indian Affairs on the upper Missouri and was serving in this capacity when he accepted the appointment as governor of the Territory of Utah. Historian Norman F. Furniss has suggested that Cumming's initial acceptance was probably conditional, for he journeyed to Fort Leavenworth, Kansas, presumably to inspect the preparations for the campaign before agreeing to take the position. Secretary of State Cass did not send Cumming his commission until 13 July.

The second task was to bring together an effective army to make the long trek across the prairies and mountains to Utah. Such an assignment required an effective leader. The initial appointee was General W. S. Harney who oversaw the military in the Kansas uprising, but it was decided to keep him in Kansas. This led to the belated appointment of General Albert Sidney Johnston, a highly regarded officer from the South, who was forced to travel west hurriedly to try to catch up with his troops.

The new governor received his instructions from the secretary of state, whose attitude was essentially peaceful and said that he foresaw no opposition from the Mormons. Still Cumming was authorized to employ a civil posse to enforce obedience, and if that action should fail he could call on the army.

The new governor's orders were somewhat confused regarding polygamy. Although they advised Cumming to observe the constitutional guarantee of freedom of worship, their wording indicated the administration's attitude toward the Mormons. "The government," Cass wrote, "did not intend to interfere with any peculiar opinions of the inhabitants however deplorable in themselves or revolting to the public sentiment of the country." In plain words, Cumming was instructed to be considerate of the Mormons' religious opinions and feelings and to use the army only as a last resort. On the other hand, the secretary of war, John B. Floyd, suggested that "prudence" required General Johnston to "anticipate resistance—general, organized and formidable—and that you should shape your movements as if resistance were certain."

235

Despite this advice, the army sent an advance contingent to Salt Lake City under the command of Captain Stewart Van Vliet to procure food for the winter, apparently anticipating a friendly reception. Secretary Floyd had been advised in late May that it was already too late to send troops west. But the secretary, intent on carrying out Buchanan's instructions, ordered the advance contingents to leave Fort Leavenworth immediately and continued to encourage the other units to leave the post as soon as possible. Thus, the military began moving in a disjointed fashion without effective leadership and with difficulties of geography and supply confronting them.

The slow-moving, ox-drawn supply wagons had been sent ahead in several different segments, and by mid-summer their vehicles, plus huge herds of animals—horses, mules, and cattle—and contingents of the U.S. Army were moving toward Fort Laramie. The trek was no secret to the Mormons. One of the first to learn of the troop movement was Mormon businessman Abraham O. Smoot, in Kansas City at the time. When Smoot delivered the Utah mail to the postmaster at Independence, Smoot was told that they had received instructions from Washington to withhold mail to Salt Lake City for the present because "the unsettled state of things in Salt Lake rendered the mails unsafe." Smoot, realizing that the BYX Co. was effectively out of business, proceeded to disband its stations and move its stock and property westward. About 120 miles east of Fort Laramie, his party met Porter Rockwell on his way east with more mail. Rockwell returned with the men to Fort Laramie on 17 July. Here they decided that someone should return to Utah as quickly as possible and convey the news, while the rest should bring the BYX property west. Smoot, Judson Stoddard, and Rockwell were chosen. They hitched their best animals to a light spring wagon on the evening of 18 July and left for the 413-mile journey to Salt Lake City. They arrived on the evening of 23 July, having made the journey in five days plus a few hours, only to find that Young and other dignitaries were in Big Cottonwood Canyon near Silver Lake celebrating the tenth anniversary of the arrival of the Saints in the Salt Lake Valley.

Thus the setting for the announcement that Utah was being invaded by a military force was dramatic. Young had invited some 2,500 people to join him for a three- or four-day anniversary celebration. People had begun wending their way to the mouth of Big Cottonwood Canyon on 22 July, and the next morning Young led a long line of carriages and wagons into the canyon. Before noon the cavalcade had reached the campground at Silver Lake some 8,000 feet above sea level. Early in the afternoon the company camped,

236

and soon all were busy with the arrangements for the celebration the following day. A local lumbering company had provided three lumber-floored boweries for afternoon concerts and evening dances. Captain Ballo's band, the Nauvoo Brass Band, and bands from Springville, Ogden, and Salt Lake City played throughout the day. Several units of the Nauvoo Legion lent a military touch to the celebration. The American flag had been unfurled on two of the highest peaks near the camp and on the tops of two of the tallest trees.

On 24 July the celebration began with the early firing of a cannon, followed by a number of speeches and patriotic songs. At about noon Smoot, Stoddard, and Rockwell, accompanied by Judge Elias Smith, rode into camp with news of "war." They delivered their message quietly to Young and his counselors, and the afternoon's merriment went on as usual. About sunset the camp assembled for prayers and Daniel H. Wells made a few remarks about the news from the east, gave instructions about leaving the area the following day, and concluded with prayer.

Remarkably, the people did not panic. Their leaders had already emphasized that "the Lord of hosts is with us," "we are in the right and in God's hands," and "all will be well." As early as 28 June the *Deseret News* had reported debates in the East as to whether there was any "necessity of sending troops and officers to establish peace in Utah." And on 5 July, Young, speaking in the tabernacle, had commented "in regards to troops coming here as has been rumored, should 1,500 or 2,000 come what will we see? You will see that they will ask us to make their soldiers behave themselves until they can get out of this place, which they will do as soon as possible. They are not coming here to fight us, though if they were to, I should pray that the Lord would bring those here that mobbed us in days gone by and just let us look at them. But no, the priests, senators and politicians wish to have innocent soldiers sent here to fight us."

After considering the best means of resistance, Young recommended a scorched earth policy:

> This people are free; they are not in bondage to any Government on God's footstool. We have transgressed no law, neither do we intend so to do; but as for any nation coming to destroy this people, God Almighty being my helper, it shall not be! . . . I am not going to permit troops here for the protection of the priests and the rabble in their efforts to drive us from the land we possess. The Lord does not want us to be driven, for He has said, "If you will assert your rights, and keep my commandments, you shall never again be brought into bondage by your enemies." . . . They say that the coming of their army is legal; and I say that it is not;

they who say it are morally rotten. Come on with your thousands of illegally-ordered troops, and I promise you, in the name of Israel's God, that they shall melt away as the snow before a July sun. . . . I have told you that if this people will live their religion all will be well; and I have told you that if there is any man or woman who is not willing to destroy everything of their property that would be of use to an enemy if left, I would advise them to leave the Territory. And I again say so to-day; for when the time comes to burn and lay waste our improvements, if any man undertakes to shield his he will be treated as a traitor; for "judgment will be laid to the line, and righteousness to the plummet." . . . Before I will again suffer as I have in times gone by there shall not one building, nor one foot of lumber, nor a fence, nor a tree, nor a particle of grass or hay, that will burn, be left in reach of our enemies. I am sworn if driven to extremity, to utterly lay waste this land in the name of Israel's God, and our enemies shall find it as barren as when we came here.

YOUNG & KIMBALL ARE MAD

The following day, Young's counselor Heber C. Kimball delivered a characteristically fiery speech: "Send 2500 troops here, our brethren, to make a desolation of this people. God almighty helping me I will fight until there is not a drop of blood in my veins. Good God I have enough wives to whip the United States for they will whip themselves." Two weeks later, Kimball, backed by Young, added that he would no longer serve the United States as a citizen.

COME HOME & DEFEND YOUR FAMILIES

In view of the invasion of our territory by the United States Troops, our mission is to call all the Elders home from the States and Europe that they may take care of their families, and from hence forth Israel will take care of themselves, while the world goes to the Devil. A great exertion will be made to get every family possible out of the States, as should they remain, and difficulties exist between us and the government it would be very unsafe for Saints to remain in the States. . . . The States evidently have commenced a war with us, and are determined to put an end to us or our religion, neither of which they can do, as they have commenced a job they never can accomplish, we may expect a mighty howling from the regions below. The Gentiles can never again put their yoke on Israel, and some funny times will be seen before they will acknowledge our Independence. One thing is certain, they cannot exterminate the Saints, neither can they make them forsake their religion.

Because of their millennial beliefs, Mormons interpreted the United States' aggression as the beginning of the federal government's collapse.[3] Military and political action against God's people would

---

[3] Believing that the Second Coming was near, Brigham Young prayed daily that the Lord would hasten his work. Heber Kimball was quick to predict that neither the

be the catalyst that would start the United States on the road to destruction. Wilford Woodruff wrote in his journal in December 1857:

> I have always believed that the United States in a national capacity and under the form of law seeks to destroy the Church and Kingdom of God from off the earth. They are turning the last key to send the nation asunder and they will be broken as a potter's vessel and cast down as a nation to rise no more forever. But whenever the rulers of any nation trample their own constitution and laws underfoot and oppress and destroy the weak because they have the power and the people love to have it so, they sow the seeds to their own disillusion and they will reap their own destruction.

Kimball asserted that the United States could not hope to win any battles against the Saints, for the Mormons would subdue any evil military force and would dictate the terms of peace to the fallen political state.[4] "With us," Young said, on 9 August, "it is the Kingdom of God or nothing. And we will maintain it or die in trying, though we shall not die in trying." Kimball promised the Saints that "this is the Kingdom of God and when they fight us they fight God, and Jesus Christ and the Holy Ghost and all the prophets. Set your heart at rest, then you need not be troubled or frightened at all. For as the Lord liveth and we live we will come out victorious." John L. Butler, in his diary, expressed a similar sentiment, writing, "And there they were, poor ignorant souls didn't know that they had come to fight the Lord's anointed and were fighting against God himself. They little knew the power they were fighting against."

Young and other church leaders decided to resist the approaching army and in effect to defy the U.S. government. Rather than capitulate, they would raze the larger cities and abandon the territory. Publicly they based their hope on the fact that they were the Lord's anointed and that God would take care of them, but as a precaution Young also sent representatives east to try to settle the matter peaceably.

Young risked the accomplishments of ten years' hard work and sacrifice on the assumption that the military invasion was designed to destroy the church. He attempted to justify the Saints' resistance on what historian Norman Furniss termed a "legalistic quibble." The act creating Utah territory provided "that the executive power and

Latter-day Saints nor the Kingdom of God would ever be obliterated. But "nations that raise the weapons of war against this people shall perish by those weapons."

[4] Such optimism led Kimball to speculate that "Brother Brigham Young will become President of the United States."

authority in and over said territory of Utah shall be vested in a governor who shall hold his office for four years and until his successor shall be appointed and qualified unless sooner removed by the President of the United States," and that "the Governor and Secretary to be appointed as a force that shall, before they act as such respectably taken oath or affirmation before the District Judge or some Justice of the Peace in the limits of said territory, duly authorized to administer oaths and affirmations by the laws now enforced therein or before the Chief Justice."

Young had been appointed governor in 1850, and when Steptoe decided not to accept his appointment to replace Young in 1854-55, Young was left in office, although he had not been appointed for another term and could be replaced at the pleasure of the president of the United States at any time. Thus, acting as the chief territorial executive, Young forbade all armed forces from entering Utah and ordered the territorial militia to be in readiness to repel any invaders. He also declared martial law throughout the territory on 5 August:

> We are invaded by a hostile force who are evidently assailing us to accomplish our overthrow and destruction. . . . Our opponents have availed themselves of prejudice existing against us because of our religious faith, to send out a formidable host to accomplish our destruction. We have had no privilege, no opportunity of defending ourselves from the false, foul, and unjust aspersions against us before the nation. The Government has not condescended to cause an investigating committee or other person to be sent to inquire into and ascertain the truth, as is customary in such cases. . . .
>
> The issue which has been thus forced upon us compels us to resort to the great first law of self preservation and stand in our own defense, a right guaranteed unto us by the genius of the institutions of our country, and upon which the Government is based. Our duty to ourselves, to our families, requires us not to tamely submit to be driven and slain, without an attempt to preserve ourselves. Our duty to our country, our holy religion, our God, to freedom and liberty, requires that we should not quietly stand still and see those fetters forging around, which are calculated to enslave and bring us in subjection to an unlawful military despotism. . . . This is, therefore,
>
> 1st:—To forbid, in the name of the People of the United States in the Territory of Utah, all armed forces, of every description, from coming into this Territory, under any pretence whatever.
>
> 2nd—That all the forces in said Territory hold themselves in readiness to march, at a moment's notice, to repel any and all such threatened invasion.

RESIN FOR A TERM OF MARSHAL LAW

240

> (3d:)—Martial law is hereby declared to exist in this Territory, . . . and no person shall be allowed to pass or repass into, or through, or from this Territory, without a permit from the proper officer.[5]

Since no announcement of the coming of the army had been sent, Young chose to regard them as an armed mob. Young had also not yet been formally notified that he was being replaced as governor. Declaring martial law, he used whatever technicalities of law he could find to justify trying to prevent the army from entering the territory. When the army finally occupied the Fort Bridger area of Green River County, Cumming expected to take his oath of office from one of the justices there. But Green River County had been disorganized by the Utah legislature and attached to Great Salt Lake County for election, revenue, and judicial purposes. This reorganization was intended to insure that Cumming could not establish a government at Green River and occurred only a few days prior to Cumming's attempt to establish his position within the territory of Utah.[6]

Norman Furniss's study of Mormon speeches and writings during this period suggests that the church did not pursue a single policy in the critical months of late 1857 and early 1858. Its strategy appeared to pass through two phases. The first course, followed from July to early October 1857, seems to have been one of determined resistance to Buchanan's expedition. When Daniel H. Wells sent out orders to district commanders of the Nauvoo Legion on 1 August, he warned, "In such times when anarchy takes place of orderly government, and mobocratic tyranny usurps the power to rule, the Mormons are left to their inalienable right to defend themselves." In early September, Young wrote to the Saints in Honolulu that the people of Utah would resist aggression "by making an appeal to God, and our own right of arms," and later in the month Samuel W. Richards repeated the same sentiments to Thomas L. Kane. As if preparing for a long war, the church recalled its missionaries from abroad,

---

[5] A similar proclamation was also issued on 15 September.

[6] While criticizing Young's "legalistic quibbling" for resisting the U.S. army, Norman Furniss respected Young's fear of undisciplined troops. Describing them as men "drawn from" less-stable elements of society "who were persuaded to enlist in the unpopular army" because of desperate poverty, Furniss asserted that many were "exceedingly stupid" and "so depraved that they would sell their last article of clothing for liquor." Many officers were so prejudiced that they voiced their desire to destroy Mormonism by executing their leaders and despoiling their followers. In addition, Mormon leaders had good reason to fear the impact on their community of the hundreds of teamsters, wagon-masters, camp followers, and other civilians accompanying the army.

closed its outposts in California and Carson Valley, and made other arrangements of a military nature.

Despite this bold talk, however, Mormon leaders had no desire to plunge their people into a struggle with the United States. Their resistance was finally confined to the burning of grass and supply wagons, the stampeding of stock, and other acts designed to slow the advance of the army. Behind this policy lay their belief that if war could be avoided until the winter, the church and government might settle the differences between them peacefully. But if the Nauvoo Legion and the weather both should fail to halt the army at the Salt Lake Valley, Mormon leaders initially planned to fight behind the territory's natural fortifications, first in Echo Canyon and then in other strongholds.

HOPED FOR WINTER & PEACE

For a number of years Young had convinced himself that there were many regions in the mountains where his people could hide, retreats capable of concealing the entire church. In mid-September he expressed this belief to Colonel William H. Dame, militia commander in southern Utah, as follows: "In case U.S. government should send an overpowering force we intend to desolate the territory, conceal our families, stock, and all other effects in the fastness of the mountains, where they will be safe while the men waylaying our enemies attack them from ambush and stampede their animals." Still Mormon leaders did not at first doubt that all would be well. Although at times they cautioned their people to prepare to evacuate and destroy their property, they also believed that such extreme measures would not be required. "Our enemies are in the pit," the church historian wrote, "and there is fair prospect of their being destroyed without our shedding their blood."

OUR HOPES OUR PREPERATION

The Mormon strategy entered another phase in November 1857 when the mood of the hierarchy began to shift from assurance to concern for the future. Even though the army's tardy departure from Leavenworth, the arrival of winter, and the raids on the army's supply trains had combined to create the situation the Mormons had desired and an early engagement with the troops had been avoided, U.S. adjutant general James Ferguson reported from Fort Bridger in January that the Mormons were "baffled, crippled and dispirited." "Without firing of a single gun on our part," Ferguson continued, "they were most effectively defeated in all their large bravado epilogued in a cold seat around the ashes of Fort Bridger's supply."

PHASE TWO CONCERN

The Saints had cause for depression. News of the government's activities was far from encouraging. Instead of reexamining its policy now that the expedition had become winter-bound at Fort Bridger,

242

the administration, by January, was preparing to reinforce the army and launch an attack from California on Utah's indefensible western border. Although a few eastern newspapers had become critical of the government, no significant Gentile demand for negotiation with the Mormons emerged. Despite the euphoria of the previous summer, Mormons now faced the reality of how unprepared they were for any encounter with an organized army. Supplies of clothing were low, production of powder inadequate, and the territorial arsenal dilapidated. Young, Wells, Kimball, and their associates were soon forced to admit the folly of resisting the expedition either in open battle or by a "scorched earth" campaign.

[margin note: NO GENTILE SUPPORT]

[margin note: REALIZE HOW POORLY PREPARED]

Part of the problem was financial. The Mormons were unable to raise the necessary money to finance a war. But their lack of arms and ammunition was even more critical. Ferguson's report claimed that at least a third of potential soldiers were unarmed and many more badly equipped. No gun powder had been manufactured, only a small amount of lead had been mined. Should the army come in force, the Mormons would not be able to resist them. The stationing of troops in Echo Canyon and the building of fortifications had evidently kept the army from attempting entry through the narrow canyon, but a careful look at the terrain would convince military personnel that the fortress was not impregnable. The valley was open, and a few mountain cannons would have overcome Mormon resistance.

[margin note: NO ARMS]

In a formal council on 18 March attended by the First Presidency, eight apostles, and some of the military, Young advised the Saints to go into the desert and let the people of the United States destroy themselves. Three days later, in a special conference at the tabernacle, Young told his audience "if we were to open the ball upon them by slaying the United States soldiery just so sure they would be fired up with anger to lavishly spend their means to compass our destruction. Thousands and millions, if necessary, would furnish the means if the government was not able." Retreat into the uninhabited areas nearby was the only alternative left to the Saints.

[margin note: RETREAT TO DESERET ONLY POSSIBILITY]

As the weather grew milder during March, the fear of a sudden attack from Fort Bridger increased, and additional militia men were called up. By 9 April more than 600 troops were in Echo Canyon and other strategic points east. But the Mormon War passed from aimless marches to negotiation.

The key person here was Colonel Thomas L. Kane, who had befriended the Mormons during their trek west. Young had called upon Kane for assistance the previous year, asking him to urge the appointment of Mormons to the vacant territorial positions. Kane, a Philadelphian, now received permission from President Buchanan to act as an independent negotiator in the Utah standoff. Buchanan wrote to Kane, "As you have been impelled by your own sense of duty to visit Utah and having informed me that nothing can divert you from this purpose, it affords me pleasure to commend you to the favorable regard of all the officers of the United States whom you might meet in the course of your travels." Apparently wishing to apprise himself of the Mormons' plans before meeting with the civil and military officers at Camp Scott, Kane went by sea to southern California via Panama and hurried to Salt Lake City by way of San Bernardino under the pseudonym of "Dr. Osborne." By early March he had reached the territory and entered into secret conferences with members of the hierarchy. The situation seemed so serious that Kane believed their best hope was for a truce which would give them time to evacuate the territory. He wrote to his father, "The day may be and probably is passed to make peace, but not to save our poor fellows."

[margin note: COL CAME TO TALK]

On the evening of 12 March, Kane reached Camp Scott, Wyoming, near Fort Bridger, too exhausted to dismount from his horse or even to speak. After a lengthy sleep he was ready to persuade civil and military officers that there was no need to attack the Mormons. Admittedly his task was difficult. Camp Scott was a military post, commanded by a humorless individual who wished everyone to observe protocol. Kane had to persuade General Johnston, shocked by the Saints' apparent treason and irritated at his own embarrassing position, to forego exterminating Young's followers. Kane faced still other problems of diplomacy. Governor Cumming was jealous of his prerogatives and inordinately concerned about the status of his reputation in the East. Already fretting over his subordinate position in the camp as a civil officer whose powers were negligible in a military garrison, Cumming was a difficult man for sensitive discussions.

[margin note: KANE GOES TO FT BRIDGE BY PURP FOR MORMONS]

Kane spoke first with Johnston, not Cumming, and unfortunately offended Johnston in several ways. Thereafter the military commander refused to communicate with Kane personally. All communications between them were written, even though only a few hundred yards separated the two. *[margin note: FUNNY]*

Kane was more successful in dealing with Cumming. The governor accepted the administration's position that negotiation should precede military force and decided to visit Utah before the army marched. Cumming informed Johnston on 3 April of his intention to set out for Salt Lake City within two days. Cumming's letters to his wife show that he left Camp Scott with little intention to negotiate. Rather, he planned simply to assert the authority of the federal government and carry out the specific instructions given him in Washington.

But the situation was changing in Washington. Captain Van Vliet, of General Johnston's advance company, had returned to Washington to appraise President Buchanan personally of the situation in the territory. He was accompanied to Buchanan's office by territorial representative John Bernhisel. Public pressure and more accurate information induced Buchanan to issue a proclamation on 6 April 1858, offering to forgive the inhabitants of the territory for the alleged acts of disloyalty provided they became law-abiding citizens.

Two special commissioners, L. W. Powell and Ben McCulloch, were sent to Utah. Although they were "not authorized to enter into any treaty or engagement with the Mormons," they brought assurances to the Mormons that the movement of the army to Utah had nothing to do with religion. If the presidential appointees were accepted and the Mormons complied with official laws and acts, there would no longer be any reason to retain the army in the territory except to keep the Indians in check and secure the passage of immigrants to California. The commissioners were instructed to communicate freely and to act in concert with Johnston and Cumming and to avail themselves of the services of Kane. "To restore peace in this matter is the single purpose of your commission," they were told and were given permission to use "your discretion and wisdom in any communication that you may have with the Mormon people."

The commissioners held a full and free conference with Johnston and Cumming. Cumming, who had recently returned from Salt Lake City, stated that the local militia had been disbanded except for a few troops under his direction, but the commissioners refused to accept this. In fact, their communication from Camp Scott on 1 June reflected a complete reliance on the army, distrust of the Mormons, and little appreciation of Cumming. Anticipating troop movements, the Mormons had virtually abandoned Salt Lake City and colonies north of Utah Valley just prior to Cumming's visit. The commissioners saw this as a first step to fighting or as a device to escape contact with military and civil authorities. The government representatives correctly hypothesized that "the great difficulty we will have to encounter in the execution of our commission will be to cause them to submit quietly to the control of the army in Salt Lake Valley."

McCulloch and Powell next entered the valley for a first-hand look at the situation. They suffered personal discomforts with the rest of those who camped in the heart of the city, where they had the alternative of boarding at the Globe Hotel or continuing their camp life. Cumming was an exception who lived with his wife in the Staines Mansion, later known as the Devereaux House. Cumming, who had been respectfully received and afforded every facility in the conduct of his office, proclaimed that the new federal civil regime was fully recognized. This satisfied one of the three basic demands made of the Mormons by the president—obedience to the Constitution and laws. The second required the Mormons to accept the presidential pardon and pledge themselves to become good citizens. Since they believed that they were already good citizens and were not guilty of any offense, they quibbled about this requirement but finally agreed to it.

The largest problem was the disposition of the army. Mormon resistance had made the army a symbol of federal authority, and thus the troops had to be permitted to enter the valley and establish a military base. The commissioners gained General Johnston's promise that he would not move his troops from Camp Scott until they had negotiated with Mormon leaders. However, the embittered general began to move the troops toward Utah on 4 June, prior to the agreed time. This action angered both Mormon leaders and the peace commissioners, but the Mormons finally bowed to the inevitable and agreed to permit the army to enter their stronghold if they would promise to establish their base a considerable distance from any Mormon city.

On 14 June, Cumming issued a proclamation in which he pronounced that "peace is restored to our territory. The full and free pardon had been accepted." "Fellow citizens," he said, "I offer you my congratulations for the peaceful and honorable adjustment of recent difficulties, the resumption of normal order was desired. Those citizens who have left their homes I invite to return as soon as they can do so with propriety and convenience."

Meanwhile, the army, which had left Camp Scott on 13 June, was approaching the Mormon capital. Crossing Muddy Creek at the Bear River, the men tramped down Echo Canyon and on 26 June entered the valley. Before the column reached Salt Lake City, General Johnston issued orders to his regimental commanders preventing anyone from leaving ranks on the march. At the same time he instructed quartermasters and commissary officers to keep their herds

246

from trespassing on private property. Having taken these precautions, Johnston sent his forces through the city. From his hiding place, Robert T. Burton saw the first men arrive at 10:00 a.m. and watched until the rear guard had passed through the empty streets at 5:30 p.m. The church historian noted that the army marched in strict order and discipline and that one soldier, Philip Saint George Cook, removed his cap as he rode through the city out of respect for the Mormon Battalion, which he had commanded more than a decade ago. One particularly memorable moment occurred when a soldier rode up to the band master, perhaps as they were passing Brigham Young's house, and whispered a request, "One-Eyed Rily," an obscene ballad popular at the time.

[margin note: MARCHING THRU CITY]

In order to prevent his men from disturbing the semi-deserted city, Johnston ordered the column to cross the Little Jordan River west of the settlement and had a guard posted on the bridge to prevent any soldier's return. He was nevertheless aware that this could serve only as a temporary camp since the forage along the modest stream could not support his animals for more than a few weeks. He also knew that the Mormons, assembled in a congested throng near Provo, might soon return home.

The strategy of abandoning the city had been submitted to the church members at a special conference on Sunday, 21 March 1858. Young explained that the approaching crisis required the removal of all women, children, and grain before laying the city and country to waste. A company of 500 families, comprised of those who had never previously been driven from their homes, was given the honor of leading the hegira. Quickly thereafter, the highway reaching southward was dotted with migrating groups, livestock, and what possessions could be carried. Empty wagons from southern communities proceeded in the opposite direction to assist the teamless from the northern settlements.

When word arrived on 8 April that Kane had persuaded Cumming to come to Salt Lake City and assume the duties of his office unattended by the army or military escort, the tension was relieved but the move south continued unabated. Though many of his group did not recognize the significance of the move and delayed their departure, Brigham Young threatened punishment for those who did not comply with his order.

Young had labored under the false impression that there were huge oases in the southwestern deserts, even though David Evans had uncovered no such places during a thorough search in the mid 1850s. Two parties under George W. Bean and William H. Dame, containing more than 100 men, scoured the desolate reaches west of Parowan for non–existent sanctuaries. Although Bean left 45 men to establish a farm in one place, neither detachment found valleys capable of supporting 500,000 people or even a fraction of that number. The failure of these missions did not prevent the exodus, for when the men finally returned, Bean in April and Dame in June, the great move south was already under way.

The Mormons' decision to leave their homes was not irrevocable but was contingent upon the action of Johnston's soldiers. The strategy allowed a few sturdy men to remain in each village and town. In Provo, the church would wait to discover the army's disposition, and if by word or deed the troops should reveal fanatical hatred of the Mormons, the demolition of all buildings would be ordered. Yet Young hoped that such desperate measures would not be necessary, for he did not order the immediate destruction of Mormon homes and had the foundation of the temple concealed rather than razed.

Having once decided to leave their homes, the Mormons set about the task with characteristic vigor: church officials packed their records for removal to Provo, the *Deseret News* press was sent to Fillmore, and grain in the tithing house was distributed among the villages in the southern part of the territory. On 1 April, while Cumming was making his way across the snowy Wasatch Mountains, Brigham Young, George A. Smith, Heber Kimball, and Daniel Wells left Salt Lake City for Provo, their possessions piled high in fifteen wagons. Others, still boarding up the windows of their homes, would follow close behind. Plagued by a scarcity of forage and by rains and, at times, snow, with their women and children unprotected in open carts, the Saints stoically pressed on.

Some historians have set the number involved in this move at 30,000. One enthusiastic diarist returning from a mission to Hawaii said that the flight from Nauvoo looked like a small rivulet by the side of a mighty river compared to the 75,000 men, women, and children now in one continuous line of travel. Cumming recognized that the Mormon evacuation threatened his own goals of removing all obstructions to peace before the army should resume its march into the Salt Lake Valley. If the Saints continued to abandon their homes he could not maintain that the situation in the territory was serene. He could not even be governor if there was no one to govern. Cumming's appeals to Young to halt the exodus were unsuccessful when the latter expressed his intention to stay away himself as long as his church was threatened by the army. In desperation

Cumming visited Provo and the Saints' other temporary homes, hoping to bring the people back by a direct appeal. When he arrived at the campground on the Provo River bottoms (called Shanghai by some), Cumming was pained by the scenes of great trial and suffering. On the public square the church had erected buildings for Young and other members of the hierarchy, but the majority of the Saints were forced to construct whatever cover they could on the treeless expanse. Families with wagons used them as rudimentary houses, others less fortunate made tents out of cloth, built boards or log huts, and fabricated shelters out of willow branches and twigs. Some could only burrow holes into the ground. In this fashion, several thousand Mormons lived in squalor for two months, awaiting instructions to march or to return home.[7]

Once settled on the Provo bottoms a number of Saints became discontented and talked of going back. Yet in spite of the discomfort and occasional grumbling, Cumming received little attention when he urged the Mormons to retrace their steps. Although Young never disclosed his reasons for ordering his followers home, his motivation was clear. Initially he had commanded the Saints to leave their northern settlements lest the army attack in angry remembrance of past frustrations. Once he learned that Johnston's soldiers were under rigid discipline, the major reason for the move vanished. His people, plagued by bad water, flies, dirt, and lack of food, could not remain forever in their makeshift huts. One trusted Mormon in fact had informed Young on 1 July of his plan to return to Ogden as soon as possible. Young knew that others would follow and undoubtedly wished to announce the official end of the exodus before his people abandoned Provo of their own accord. In addition, Gentile sympathy seemed to have been won. Although Eastern editors continued to condemn the Saints' religious beliefs and practices, they praised their heroism.

Whatever the outcome, the church was now forced to send its people back to their homes and crops. Thus the Saints, plodding on foot or bouncing in wagons, finally encountered General Johnston's

---

[7] Mormons have since insisted that despite the misery, sacrifice, and even loss of life accompanying the exodus, the people yielded cheerfully to their church's wishes. Some, though, were less cheerful than others. Many left their homes, not in reply to Brigham Young's mandate but because of social pressure. When, in September 1857, Young had spoken of possible flight from Utah, he warned that if anyone attempted to protect his property, he would be "sheared down." Having decided that the interests of the church did indeed demand flight or at least a semblance of it, Young carried out his warning.

army. Unsure of the proper route to Cedar Valley, the army had marched back and forth between the Wasatch and Oquirrh Ranges until they became entangled with the almost endless line of returning Mormons. The soldiers looked with scorn upon the ragged poverty of the people, and the latter made little effort to conceal their resentment of this new persecution, but neither made a threatening gesture. *INTERESTING PICTURE*

Although the Utah War was settled peaceably, several unfortunate consequences followed. One indirect but tragic result was the massacre of 120 immigrants on 7-11 September 1857 at Mountain Meadows, thirty-five miles southwest of Cedar City. About the same time that word was received in the small southern Utah settlements of the approaching U.S. Army, the Fancher Train, a party of California-bound immigrants composed of families from Arkansas and a group of horsemen who called themselves the "Missouri Wildcats," made their way through central Utah following the southern route to California. Unwise actions by party members, including failure to keep their animals under control and the expression of anti-Mormon sentiments, antagonized the Saints, who had been stirred to a war hysteria by the fiery preaching of Apostle George A. Smith and others. At Cedar City, local citizens, who had been ordered to husband their supplies, refused to sell food to the Fancher train. The angry immigrants expressed hope that the invading army would punish the Mormons and threatened to raise another military force when they arrived in California. Leaving Cedar City, they travelled to Mountain Meadows where they stopped to rest their livestock before the long journey across the Nevada-California desert.

Attracted by the herds of fat cattle and apparently encouraged by some Mormons, a band of Indians had followed the train and decided to attack the immigrants at their encampment. The attack failed, and the Indians turned to their friends and allies, the Mormons. A meeting was held in Cedar City under the leadership of stake president Isaac C. Haight, and proposals were made to wipe out the immigrants before they could get to California and carry out their threats. Calmer heads prevailed, and a rider was sent to Salt Lake City to obtain Brigham Young's advice. His written instructions to let the immigrants pass were received on 12 September, one day too late.

Local leaders decided they could not wait for Young's advice; it would be too dangerous to let the Fancher party spread word in California that the Mormons were aiding the Indians in attacking immigrant trains. John D. Lee, the Mormon in charge of Indian Affairs

(margin, handwritten, vertical) MOUNTAIN MEADOW MASSACRE

in southern Utah, became involved. Under a flag of truce, Lee convinced the immigrants to lay down their arms. Then Mormon militia men, acting under military orders, killed the disarmed immigrant men. The Indians were permitted to kill the women and older children, apparently because the Mormons were concerned about the "shedding of innocent blood." Seventeen small children were spared and ultimately, with government help, returned to relatives in Arkansas.

Federal attempts to apprehend and punish the participants failed as the tight-knit Mormon society closed ranks and protected its members. Lee was apprehended almost twenty years after the massacre and, following two trials, was executed by a firing squad at the scene of the crime. Other leaders such as Isaac Haight experienced such community disapproval that he was disfellowshipped and spent much of his life hiding from federal officials. However, William H. Dame, another local Mormon leader, was able to convince Mormons and non-Mormon federal officials of his innocence and continued to serve in important church positions. This tragic massacre increased the Mormon reputation of fanaticism and made relationships with federal officials even more difficult.

Although the army established Camp Floyd a considerable distance from principal settlements, Salt Lake City soon felt the impact of army personnel and camp followers. Saloons and houses of prostitution became common, and drunken brawls on the streets were routine. Army personnel were usually controlled by their officers, but many were discharged at Camp Floyd and became a threat to local communities. Church historian B. H. Roberts devoted the chapter "A Chapter of Horrors" in his *Comprehensive History of the Church* to describe such problems. While his view is one-sided, there can be no doubt that the puritanism that had characterized the Mormon communities changed substantially as a result of the military presence, their suppliers, and camp followers.

A more serious result of the invasion was the antagonistic attitude and actions of some of the newly installed territorial officials. Cumming made an honest effort at conciliation on the basis of Buchanan's pardon, but the new federal judges, especially Delany R. Eckles, Charles E. Sinclair, and John Cradelbaugh, attempted to punish the Mormons for treason and polygamy, as well as for the Mountain Meadows Massacre. Cradelbaugh intimidated the people of Provo, where his court convened, with the presence of a detachment of 100 soldiers to guard prisoners. Such actions set the tone for

251

difficulties and misunderstandings that continued until after the abandonment of polygamy and the issuance of the Manifesto in 1890.[8]

Although the Utah expedition brought some economic prosperity to the Mormons, this could hardly compensate for the negative influences in the sheltered Mormon settlements. General Johnston's army was an unfortunate episode that could have been avoided. Leaders on both sides share the blame equally.

---

[8] Further adding to Mormon-Gentile differences was the publication of the *Valley Tan*, an anti-Mormon newspaper owned by territorial secretary John Hartnett and edited by Kirk Anderson. Anderson, formerly of the *Missouri Republican*, arrived in Salt Lake City in September 1858 and produced his first issue early in November. Bitterly anti-Mormon, his newspaper circulated primarily in Camp Floyd and survived only eighteen months.

15.
New Colonization
—North and South

The settlement of the Utah War made possible a new program of Mormon colonization. By 1869 approximately 150 new Utah communities existed, about one-third of which were established north of Salt Lake City, mainly in the Bear River and Bear Lake regions. In the southern area of the territory church leaders established a cotton mission along the Virgin and Muddy rivers and a trading outpost on the Colorado. In 1864, the peak year for colonization, thirty new communities were established. The coming of the transcontinental railroad made migration to Utah easier, but immigration was declining, and colonization almost ceased during the late 1860s and was not vigorously resumed until the 1870s.

Members of Parley P. Pratt's southern exploring party had camped at the juncture of the Santa Clara and Virgin rivers on 1 January 1850, but not until the 1851 General Conference was a colony officially proposed for the region. John D. Lee was chosen to lead a settlement there to "raise grapes, cotton, figs, raisins, and other semi-tropical plants." But his group stopped short of the Dixie region and established Harmony in the spring of 1852.

More than a year later, during the October 1853 General Conference, a group of twenty-three missionaries was called to the Indians in southern Utah. With Rufus C. Allen as leader, they arrived at Lee's settlement in May 1854, where they remained until they built their own fort three miles to the north. Meanwhile, contact had been made with the Indians in the region, and in December, Allen instructed Jacob Hamblin, Thales Haskill, Ira Hatch, and others to establish a permanent settlement near present-day Santa Clara and to bring their families with them. They were to learn the native language and to teach the Indians civilization and Christianity. A quart of cotton seed, the gift of Nancy Anderson, a convert from Tennessee, was planted and produced cotton plants and pods "beyond belief." Samples were sent to Brigham Young, who began organizing a cotton mission to colonize the area in earnest. The missionaries at Santa Clara and their families continued to raise cotton successfully, and Zadoch K. Judd constructed the first crude cotton gin in the territory.

In April 1857, twenty-eight families and a number of young men under the direction of Robert T. Covington were called to settle on the Washington Flat east of present-day St. George to experiment further with cotton. Most of the settlers were from the southern states and had high hopes. Unfortunately, the nature of the land crushed their spirits. Barren flats stretched to black lava formations or red sandstone, and, on the lower levels, white alkaline ridges encrusted the surface. The salty residue killed most of the plants that came up. After an unsuccessful attempt, church leaders decided to call fifteen men to establish an experimental farm on the Tonnequint Flat at the confluence of the Virgin and Santa Clara rivers. Naming their settlement Heberville, in honor of Heber C. Kimball, they succeeded in building a dam and planting vegetables and fruit trees as well as cotton plants. They returned in the fall of 1858 with about 575 pounds of cotton lint with seed and 160 gallons of molasses.

By 1860, eight small communities in Washington County were producing a variety of crops. Brigham Young's visit to the area in May 1861 further convinced him of the possibilities of the region. The church's October conference was devoted to promoting immigration, but when Young called for volunteers, only one man raised his hand. Evidently the majority of Young's listeners were satisfied with their situations in the Salt Lake Valley. Undaunted, Young directed Apostle George A. Smith to select a company of 200 people, whose names were read from the stand the following Sunday, 13 October. In addition, fifty families were recruited from Utah County by Apostle John Taylor, and another fifty were recruited from Sanpete County by Orson Hyde. Others were recruited from such areas as Davis, Weber, Tooele, Juab, Millard, and Beaver counties. In all, 309 families were called in 1861 to settle in what became known as Utah's Dixie.[1]

---

[1] Some years later, George A. Smith reported that less than 200 of these first 300

These volunteers were joined by approximately thirty families of Swiss converts, most of whom had been transported to Utah in 1861 in church-owned teams and wagons and fed and housed along the way in tithing houses.[2] Upon arriving in Dixie, the Swiss were given the Big Bend land at what is now Santa Clara and were instructed to raise grapes and fruits to supply the cotton producers.

The majority of these Swiss immigrants had been farmers and were accustomed to hard work. Many, like the Hafen family, came from the canton of Thurgau and had raised grapes from which they made wine. In the old country women who were skilled in spinning and weaving had made their own clothing from homegrown flax, hemp, and cotton. These pioneers came to Utah, not to gain wealth, as they were comfortably established in their homeland, but with a desire to sacrifice all for the gospel. When Daniel Bonelli read their names at the October conference to settle in the southern part of the region, they responded willingly. Bonelli had been appointed their leader, and after the call they formed a company. Brigham Young advised those men and women who had not yet married to "yoke" themselves with companions before leaving Salt Lake City. Several were subsequently married in the Endowment House.

The Swiss had been assigned to raise cotton, make wine, and grow fruit. Dixie pioneers were also instructed to grow figs, grapes for raisins, olives for oil, indigo and madder for dyes, sugar cane for molasses, and tobacco. Ever attuned to the practical side of life, Brigham Young asked publicly on 7 April 1861, "How much do you

---

families fulfilled their mission to the south, but this cannot be substantiated. Certainly not all accepted the call willingly. One colonist, Robert Gardner, said that there were "several yarns about Utah's Dixie. One was—the sheep done pretty well, but they wore their noses off reaching down between the rocks to get the grass." Charles L. Walker wrote, "This is the hardest trial I ever had, and had it not been for the Gospel and those placed over us, I should never had moved a foot to go on such a trip." Perhaps a more typical reaction was that of Elijah Averett. After a hard day in the fields, he returned home only to discover he had been called to Dixie. He dropped into a chair and exclaimed, "I'll be damned if I'll go." But after a few minutes, he stood up, stretched, and said, "Well, if we're going to Dixie we'd better start to get ready." "The news was very unexpected to me," wrote John Pulsipher, "for I had a good home and was well satisfied and had plenty to do." Finally, Goudy Hogan explained: "I have learned that it was profitable to accept all calls made of me by the authorities of the church."

[2] This Swiss company was also noted for its musical talent. George Staheli, who had served as a bugler in the Swiss army, organized a brass band and a choir in his new Santa Clara home. Gottlieb Hirschi and his wife Maryann both had beautiful voices. All along the way during the journey south, the Swiss company furnished entertainment with their singing and music, a much-needed diversion from the monotony of the tedious travel.

suppose goes annually from the territory and has been for ten or twelve years past in gold and silver to supply the people with tobacco? I will say $60,000. . . . Tobacco can be raised here as well as it can be raised in any other place. . . . I recommend for some man to go to and make a business out of raising tobacco and stop sending money out of the territory for that article.''

In promoting the cotton mission, Brigham Young instructed Apostle Orson Hyde to ''send good and judicious men, having reference in your selection to the necessities of a new colony and including a sufficient number of mechanics, such as coopers, blacksmiths, carpenters, masons, plasterers, joiners, etc. if you have them and that you can spare without robbing your settlements.''[3] Apostles Orson Pratt and Erastus Snow, the same two men who were the first to ride into the Great Salt Lake Valley some fifteen years earlier, were chosen as leaders of this company of three hundred families moving to the southern part of the region. Also called as leaders were Horace Eldridge, Jacob Gates, and Henry Harriman of the Council of the Seventy.

By 1 November, the company was ready to leave. A scouting party had gone earlier under the direction of George A. Smith and Erastus Snow to look for suitable places for settlement. The first colonists entered the Virgin River valley on 1 December 1861, with the rest of the company arriving two days later. Orson Pratt and others had dropped out of the larger group to settle in the upper parts of the valley. The Swiss company, under Daniel Bonelli, had already moved on to the Santa Clara region, stopping at the point where the Dixie College campus is now located. The rest of the colonists established a temporary camp while they surveyed what would become St. George. William Carter plowed a ditch using the same plow which had marked the first furrow in the valley of the Great Salt Lake. On either side of this ditch, the wagons were arranged facing each other, and toilet facilities were set up according to patterns the Saints had

---

[3] James Bleak, historian for the Cotton mission, dutifully listed the name of every man, his age, his rank in the priesthood, his previous home, and, for those who reported it, his occupation. Bleak's list included 31 farmers, 1 horticulturist, 2 gardeners, 2 vinedressers, 1 vintner, 2 with molasses mills, 2 dambuilders, 14 blacksmiths, 2 wheelwrights, 1 machinist, 1 millbuilder, 2 millwrights, 3 millers, 10 coopers, 1 adobe maker, 5 masons, 1 plasterer, 1 painter, 3 carpenters, 1 turner, 1 joiner, 1 shinglemaker, 3 cabinetmakers, 1 chairmaker, 1 mineralogist, 2 miners, 2 wool carders, 1 weaver, 1 tailor, 1 hatter, 1 brushmaker, 1 manufacturer, 1 tanner, 5 shoemakers, 4 musicians, 1 fiddler, 3 school teachers, 4 clerks, 1 lawyer, 1 printer, 2 surveyors, 2 daguerreans, 1 butcher, 1 baker, 1 castor oil maker, 1 tobacco maker, 1 drum major, and 1 sailor.

adopted as they crossed the plains: "Gents to the right, ladies to the left." A large tent owned by Asa Calkins was pitched as a central meeting place where community activities could be carried on until the people could move to a townsite.

While the surveyors, under the direction of Israel Ivins, laid out the valley in neat squares, other men scouted the mountains for timber, located deposits of lime, or laid out roads. By Christmas, the prospects seemed bright, but then the rain came, beginning on Christmas Day and continuing for almost three weeks straight. The rains raised the streams of the Virgin and Clara creeks beyond their bounds and carried away some of the best bottom land—the small Swiss settlement was completely under water and the people fled into the hills. The Virgin, usually a narrow stream, was in many places a quarter of a mile wide. The settlers spent most of their first winter trying to build a canal but finally had to abandon the project because the river washed it away as fast as they completed it.

The flood changed conditions for everyone. The cotton farm at Tonnequint with its small orchard of fruit trees, garden, and corn land was destroyed and replaced with miles of mud and debris. Harmony was similarly reduced to a pile of mud. Farms at Pocketville were carried away in great slices. The Swiss colony at Santa Clara clung to the barren hillside. Jacob Hamblin and others of the settlement lost everything—the fort, the orchards, the molasses mill, and a small burr flour mill. This experience would be repeated many times by settlers living along the Virgin and Santa Clara rivers.

The rains stopped in late February. The city survey had proceeded far enough to permit people to move to their lots and begin building their homes. These rains, though undoubtedly greatly depressing for the Saints, brought with them an advantage that the settlers recognized as soon as the brief winter gave way to spring. In Utah's Dixie, the normal rainfall is between 6 to 8 inches annually, and in seasons when precipitation is below average, the country suffers from a dearth of vegetation. But when rain falls abundantly, the whole region blossoms.

Although heavy rains still plagued the campers, Erastus Snow suggested, on 9 January 1862, about six weeks before the people had even moved their wagons and tents onto their town lots, that they erect a stone building for educational and social purposes. He proposed that they complete the structure before any other building in the valley. The idea was at once approved by the enthusiastic citizens, and a subscription list was made with contributions pledged in various amounts ranging from $5 to $50 each and totalling $2,074 from 120 people, not one of whom yet had a dwelling. Easton Kelsey, Joseph Birch, and Jacob Gates were named to the building committee. At another public meeting on 12 January the committee presented plans for a house measuring 40 by 21 feet to be built of rock at an estimated cost of between $3,000 and $5,000.

A conference was held the following 22 March, at which time the community was divided into four wards with a bishop over each. After the meeting they adjourned from the bowery, a temporary meeting place, to the site which had been selected for the St. George Hall and laid the cornerstones. The St. George Hall was in use as early as 1865, unplastered and without a ceiling. It could seat only a hundred people, so the usual meetings and conferences were still held in the bowery until a tabernacle was completed. Ultimately, the St. George Hall was acquired by Edwin Woolley, Jr., Robert Lund, and Thomas Judd for business offices.

The mission had been established to raise cotton, and settlers finally planted their crop beginning on 1 June 1862. The first year's yield was 100,000 pounds of seed cotton. Some of this was made into clothing, some sold in Salt Lake City for grain and other supplies, and some was sent to the Missouri River. The bulk could not be disposed of because they lacked a factory. Some of the cotton was spun in Parowan by a small mill set up by Ebenezer Hanks at Brigham Young's request. Powered by water, the carding and drawing frames were attended by one man, the roving and throstle frames by three girls and an Indian boy. Other settlements made arrangements for machinery to process the cotton on a local basis. John R. Young, who had been appointed to settle at Santa Clara, was called by the Santa Clara bishop in the spring of 1862 to drive an ox team to Omaha to get cotton gins and spinning jennies. Leaving his family in a tent, he drove his team to Omaha and returned with the machinery late in the fall of 1862.

Cotton, which was freighted east by Salt Lake jobbers and the growers themselves, was made into clothing on shares. Brigham Young encouraged this arrangement. By exporting one load of cotton to the East, he said, a man can make cloth enough to clothe his family for many years. Within eighteen months after the cotton missionaries had settled Washington County, about 74,000 pounds of cotton were being freighted east by independent haulers and church teams. The cotton was sold for approximately one dollar a pound. Some was traded for machinery needed to manufacture the cotton. Several dozen bales were also sold in California.

After 1862, the number of acres devoted to cotton began to decline. Acute shortages of food and feed as well as sickness and backbreaking labor affected all of the settlers. Poor soil, unruly rivers, distance from the source of supply and market, and the dreary landscape were enough to try the faith of the staunchest. Church leaders understood these difficulties and responded by remitting tithing, by granting credits at church institutions, by calling additional missionaries to strengthen the settlements, and by arranging for expanded facilities for manufacture. An added encouragement was the increase in the price of cotton in the east and therefore in Utah. Production in 1863 consisted of 56,094 pounds of ginned cotton, priced at approximately 50 cents a pound. Production for 1864 was reportedly larger and valued at up to $1.25 per pound in Utah. The rising price led to a larger planting in 1864 and the introduction of several small carding and spinning machines.

Despite the fact that cotton and other desirables were produced, the colony was not on a sure economic footing. The mission would not succeed until a major factory for producing quality cotton goods was constructed. Clearly the missionaries themselves would never be able to erect such a factory and purchase the necessary machinery with their own savings. Life was too precarious to venture such a large investment without outside assistance.

The disadvantages of specialization in cotton production became evident as early as 1864. That year in General Conference, Erastus Snow asserted that half of the thousand residents of St. George would have to leave unless something was done to relieve the mission. Conference attendees unanimously passed a resolution to assist the cotton mission, and more than one hundred of the wealthier church members in northern Utah were designated "to furnish the needful and substantial requisites to enable the laboring and willing poor" of the cotton mission "to accomplish the work designed by the priesthood and inspiration that sent them there." As a result, many thousands of dollars in cash, merchandise, implements, and equipment were furnished to the southern settlers. However, grasshoppers and worms destroyed most of the crops in Dixie in 1865, and additional assistance was soon needed.

The cotton missionaries had been encouraged to put all of their energy into cotton production, but they had no real way to dispose of their product. Gradually they began to raise less cotton and more grain so that they would have enough to eat. William S. Godbe offered to buy the cotton and take it back east to exchange for goods. At

259

this time, cotton was bringing about a dollar a pound, but Brigham Young encouraged the Saints to hold on to their cotton. He believed it would become more valuable. By 1864 Young had acquired machinery for a factory. A cotton factory was established in Washington, but by this time the Saints were discouraged and had planted only 300 acres of cotton. Explaining this, one local correspondent wrote, "It just doesn't bring any price to justify the raising. The people are poor and some are quite discouraged." However, Young was still determined. He had set out on what he thought was a realistic goal of complete self-sufficiency with respect to cotton, and he regarded the difficulties as obstacles that could be overcome with faith, energy, and persistence. Far from being deterred, he called an additional group of 163 men from northern Utah in 1867 and instructed them to marry and take wives with them. Additional cotton missionaries were called in 1868.

In a further attempt to buttress the cotton mission, church leaders tried three other programs to make it more successful. According to one scheme, St. George was to be the center of a trading area. A port or warehouse would be established on the Colorado River. Goods and immigrants would be brought up the Colorado, then freighted through the Muddy River and Virgin River areas to St. George and on to various colonies in Utah. Additional missionaries would be called to settle the Muddy River area, raise cotton, and support and encourage the cotton missionaries in the Virgin River area. The third plan was a make-work project of sorts. A tabernacle would be built in St. George with funds from other areas of the church and would provide employment to the missionaries who had become discouraged with cotton.

The first of these projects was assigned to Anson Call. Leaving Salt Lake City on 15 November 1864 to explore the area, he enlisted the aid of Jacob Hamblin and others. In mid-November, they went by way of Santa Clara across the Beaver Dam Mountains and along the Virgin River to the Muddy, where they found a site that might support 200 to 300 families. Then they went south to the Virgin River again. On 2 December, Call selected a site for a warehouse some fifteen miles upriver from present-day Boulder Dam. In the meantime, the Deseret Mercantile Association had been formed to raise funds for the project. Call reported that they could establish a warehouse for $20,000 to $30,000. The leaders of the association sent men and supplies and began constructing the warehouse on 13 January 1865. Barges made their way up the Colorado River to Call's Landing, but the steamers failed.

260

Shortly after the beginning of the project, three non-Mormons arrived and claimed possession of Call's Landing, saying they had an earlier claim to the area. It was decided to abandon the project. Work had stopped by July 1865, although the promotion of river traffic continued, mostly for the non-Mormon merchants in Salt Lake City, mining interests, and California merchants. Not until 8 October 1866 did a steamer finally arrive at Call's Landing, this one carrying over a hundred tons of goods. Brigham Young had known that the Pacific Railroad was under construction and that the Colorado River would not be profitable as a highway for goods after completion of the railroad. Thus he chose a difficult assignment for Call and his fellow workers to establish temporary work and to encourage the settlers.

The Muddy River settlements, which were originally part of Call's Landing, became projects in and of themselves. Young had called Thomas S. Smith of Farmington, Utah, to lead these colonies. Smith arrived at his destination on 8 January 1864, about the same time that Call was beginning work on his warehouse. Smith's group began clearing the land and laying out a town site. Within a short time, others joined Smith and soon the company numbered forty-five families. They named their new town St. Thomas in honor of Smith. The new town had 85 one-acre lots. The same number of 2.5-acre lots were surveyed for vineyards. Farm lots contained 5 acres each.

The Muddy River Valley had some advantages. The soil, when free from mineral, was good. The winters were seldom cold, and settlers could work outdoors without discomfort. Meadow land existed for harvesting grass hay. The river was easily controlled, thus eliminating the danger of floods. But there were disadvantages. Rainfall was almost negligible. Communication with communities on the upper Virgin and the northern parts of Utah territory and with California was difficult. Between the Muddy and California lay the hot, treacherous Mohave Desert. The road to St. George was a nightmare. To follow the Virgin with its numerous crossings and its shifting quicksand beds, especially in seasons of high water and flood, was dangerous. The road from the Mormon Well on Beaver Dam Wash to the Muddy was a long stretch of sandy waste with no water. Timber was scarce, and all the lumber used on the Muddy had to be hauled 130 miles over almost impossible roads. The Muddy also had extensive tule swamps and mosquitoes. But despite these handicaps, the Muddy pioneers were determined, not only founding St. Thomas but looking for a site for another town. By this time, 900 acres of good farming land had been surveyed and 600 acres given out to the settlers.[4]

In spite of its name, the Muddy was clear and posed no silt problems, unlike the Virgin. There was little trouble in getting the water on the land. In West Point no ditchwater at first seemed necessary. Simply by cutting through the heavy sod of the river banks settlers were able to let the waters flood out to the land. The Muddy pioneers profited by the experience of the Virgin settlers because they planted three-fourths of their crops in wheat and corn with only 50 acres out of 400 in cotton. Sensing that their survival depended upon their own efforts, they took no chance on trading cotton for grain. They learned too that for wheat to do well it must be planted in the fall so that it would reach maturity before the dry hot weather. By planting at the right time and using what irrigation they could, they were able to get wheat crops ranging from 20 to 75 bushels an acre. Such yields were surpassed nowhere else in the south.

However, success in agriculture did not make up for the hot summers, the malaria and flux, and the flies. By 1867, many colonists had abandoned the mission. When church leaders from St. George came down into the area, they found a discouraged group. They decided to hold a meeting, but as James Bleak recorded, "It seemed rather hard to get enough spirit in the people to have a meeting at all. Officers and people were apathetic." In order to strengthen the southern settlements, particularly the Muddy Mission, church authorities called 158 more men to go south. Most were expected to settle on the Muddy. But at the May 1868 conference in St. George, Bishop Alma H. Bennett reported that of those called only twenty-five or thirty could be found on the Muddy River. Some had not come, and few of those who came remained. Those who had left had not even experienced the rigors of the Muddy summer. What they saw was evidently frightening enough to send them away.[5]

---

[4] In June 1865, another town was established, called St. Joseph, after Joseph Warren Foote. Joseph Simons established a small settlement called Simonsville and had a grist mill for grinding wheat, corn, and salt. He also had a cotton gin which ginned the first cotton grown on the Muddy. Farther up the valley to the northwest was West Point, now Moapa, settled about 1868. Between St. Thomas and St. Joseph lay Overton, founded in 1869, eventually the most important of the Muddy settlements.

[5] In addition, the Indians were becoming hostile. They were constantly stealing cattle; not infrequently they drove them into water and quicksand, for the settlers usually gave the dead livestock to the Indians. Early in 1868 the Indians became threatening when an attempt was made to colonize the upper Muddy. They appeared in the vicinity of the proposed new settlements and demanded that they be paid for the land. The interpreter tried to convince them it would be to their advantage to

But these and other obstacles might have been surmounted if another difficulty had not developed. In 1870, colonists learned that they were not in Utah but in Nevada. In 1866, the U.S. Congress took one full degree of territorial boundary from western Utah and Arizona and added it to Nevada. Thus the towns on the Muddy and those west and northwest of St. George were placed in Nevada. This in itself was not serious, except that the Nevada tax was about five times as high as the amount charged in Utah and had to be paid in gold. The people on the Muddy confronted three alternatives: convince Congress to restore the old boundaries, get a new county created which did not require payment in gold, or leave. In December, Brigham Young, George A. Smith, and Erastus Snow wrote to the leader of the Muddy colonies that they had fulfilled their duty and should now feel at liberty to leave. The colonists voted 123 to 5 to leave. Some settlers made their way back to the north, but most took the advice of Erastus Snow and resettled in the south. About 200 eventually made their way to Long Valley and became the founders of the Orderville and Mt. Carmel communities.

The third project, the building of a tabernacle in St. George, was an encouragement to the cotton missionaries. Year after year all church tithing south of Cedar City was appropriated to build this edifice. Construction commenced in 1867 and was completed eight years later at a cost of approximately $110,000 in labor, materials, and supplies. It was a public works project and as such supported or assisted many missionaries. This was followed by another public works project, the St. George Temple, which was completed in 1877.

Although called a cotton mission, the actual instructions to the missionaries were to raise a variety of semi-tropical crops, including fruit, tobacco, and grapes. The growing of grapes and the wine industry became an important aspect of these colonies. Grapes thrived in most areas on the Virgin River basin. The Swiss settlers in Santa Clara had raised grapes in Switzerland. Dixie could produce more grapes than the people could consume or barter up north. The natural response was to make the surplus into wine, which the settlers began to do with Brigham Young's approval. Young did not object to its moderate use, for wine was served at many social functions

CROPS GROWN

---

have Mormon friends settle near them, but the Indians refused to be mollified. By June 1869, Indians were not only stealing the pioneers' stock but also their wheat. In their desperate situation, the Mormon colonists threatened severe punishment, including death, for those caught stealing. Punishment was actually meted out to some of the Indians. In addition, there was an acute shortage of clothing and a need for farm implements.

with local church officials attending. Young encouraged the use of Dixie wine for the sacrament and recommended that surplus wine be sold to non-Mormons. He condemned drunkenness with characteristic vigor at a conference held in St. George in May 1869, saying that the drunkard and the man who sold him the wine should both be excommunicated. Nevertheless, wine became an important product in St. George in the latter part of the 1860s.

John C. Naegle, an immigrant from southern Germany skilled at winemaking, was called to go to Toquerville to teach the people the correct method of making wine. He and Ulrich Breiner (Bryner) were granted a license by the county in 1867 to operate a distillery. Naegle established a huge wine cellar beneath his rock house in Toquerville. Many of towns of the cotton mission produced wine, the soil between Virgin City and Santa Clara being particularly well adapted for viticulture, and wine became one of the most common articles of trade. It was paid in large quantities as tithing, and not a few gallons went to the irrigation companies in payment of water assessments. Large amounts went to the northern settlements and to the mines in Pioche, Panaca, and Silver Reef.

One man who had high hopes for Dixie's wine industry was Joseph E. Johnson, who editorialized his support in the pages of the *Utah Pomologist*, a newspaper devoted to horticulture and gardening. But Johnson laid his finger squarely on the principal drawback of the local wine industry when he warned, "If we are judged by the quality of wines we have heretofore sent to market, our climate and capacity for producing the choicest fruit will be harshly dealt with, for with our total ignorance in manufacturing wine the most delicious fruit may have been changed into an unsavory beverage." The tithing office at St. George eventually quit taking wine as tithing and abandoned its own wine presses in an effort to discourage its manufacture. Winemaking, as it was carried out, was not lucrative, and this, coupled with moral pressures, ended the industry in Dixie.

By the end of the 1860s, the cotton mission was in serious difficulty, the Muddy missionaries were ready to leave, the Colorado River program had been abandoned, and the people of St. George were struggling to exist on the basis of building projects and make-work projects. Alkali soil, alternating flood and drought, grasshopper and cricket infestation, Indian troubles, backbreaking toil under a broiling sun—these and other calamities caused the less hardy to pull up stakes and try their luck elsewhere. Those who remained frequently had cause to doubt the wisdom of their call. The one specialty that was a continuing success in southern Utah was the production of the

264

grain sorghum molasses. Dixie molasses was a staple export with a ready market in Utah, Nevada, and even in Idaho and Montana. Through the years molasses was the chief means by which the farmers of southern Utah acquired breadstuffs and paid their tithing and taxes. A gallon of molasses for a bushel of wheat was the basis on which cotton missionaries eventually attained equality with their more fortunate brethren to the north. Towards the end of the 1860s, alfalfa (or lucerne) was introduced and proved to be another crop which helped the St. George settlers to succeed where the Muddy River colonists had failed. By 1870, the Dixie settlers had determined what their land would produce—grains, sorghum cane, alfalfa, vegetables, and fruits, including grapes, figs, and pomegranates. Such products helped to balance the pioneer diet as well as supply items for trade. Cotton would mature reasonably well and the cotton factory was established. Gradually, a feeling of permanence spread through the cotton mission in the Virgin River area.

While the church was trying to establish colonies in the Virgin, Muddy, and Colorado River areas, a major effort was also being made to establish colonies in the northern part of the region. Brigham Young had directed most colonization toward the south and southwest because of the severe northern winters. But he remembered that the mountain men had recommended Cache Valley. The 1847 exploring party spoke glowingly of the possibilities there. Within an area of twenty miles, they had found twelve streams. Captain Howard Stansbury had also given a favorable report of the region. In 1855, Young, on behalf of the church, received a grant from the territorial legislature to control the Cache Valley as herd ground. But those caring for the 3,000 head of cattle and horses in the valley in 1855–56 experienced one of the severest winters on record. Of the 2,000 head of church cattle, only 420 survived. So questions remained about the feasibility of settling there.

A colony had been established in 1856 at present-day Wellsville. With the approach of the federal army, the colonists left, storing 1,500 bushels of wheat. This grain had disappeared by the time they returned. After the Utah War, migration into the Great Basin increased and Brigham Young turned his attention again to Cache Valley, especially since Peter Maughan had proved grain could be grown there. Maughan, who had made a temporary home near Willard, returned with his family to Cache Valley in 1859. Soon there were thirty families there, and Maughan's Fort, now Wellsville, became a rendezvous for the settlers who began to move into the valley. In addition to Maughan's Fort, Providence, Mendon, and Logan were settled in the spring of 1859, Richmond in the summer, and Smithfield that fall.

In June 1859 several companies converged on a site on the Logan River to found the city of Logan. They were joined by a smaller group that found a satisfactory field, plowed the land, and planted three acres of wheat on 10 June. Other settlers soon joined them. They obtained logs from Green Canyon and constructed cabins in two rows facing each other along present-day Center Street. By the close of 1859, Logan had assumed the most important position in Cache Valley.

By the end of 1859, Cache Valley contained six small settlements, totalling about 150 families. Peter Maughan wrote to the *Deseret News* extolling the beauty of the valley, and Brigham Young added that no other valley in the territory was equal to this. To those in the drier and more crowded towns around Salt Lake and to immigrants from populous Europe, these descriptions must have evoked a land of promise. Mormon converts from Switzerland who came to Cache Valley in 1859 were attracted by the area's resemblance to their native country and wrote home urging their countrymen to come.

The rush to Cache Valley followed in miniature the pattern set on other American frontiers. The influx of new settlers strengthened the towns already founded and led to the establishment of Hyrum, Millville, and Paradise in the south and Hyde Park and Franklin in the north. In early 1860 almost one hundred new pioneers came to join the small group huddled near Brower's Spring, which came to be known as Richmond. The 1860 census found 2,605 persons living in the valley, including 1,600 native-born Americans, about half of whom had been born in the Utah territory. Residents had come from a number of states and foreign countries, including 450 from England, 149 from Scotland, 100 from Denmark, 97 from Wales, 29 from Ireland, 22 from the Isle of Man, 19 from Switzerland, and smaller numbers from other European countries. Of those who identified their occupations, 328 were farmers, 144 laborers, 28 servants, 11 farm laborers, 5 shoemakers, 3 tanners, 3 carpenters, 2 blacksmiths, 2 millers, 2 millwrights, a machinist, a butcher, a plasterer, a chairmaker, a distiller, a herder, a cooper, and a cabinet maker. The men outnumbered the women 1,312 to 1,293.

The census of Cache Valley settlers did not count the Indians, who were numerous and became a serious problem to the early colonists. Cache Valley had been the home of a sizable band of Northwestern Shoshone, and they came to resent the invasion of their area

CACHE VALLEY BOOM

by the whites. The basic reason for the natives' dissatisfaction, as one Indian agent expressed it, was the Indians' naked and starving condition. As the valleys filled up with the aggressive and hardworking Mormon families and as the game in the mountains disappeared, the Shoshone had no place to turn. The superintendent of Indian Affairs insisted that 1,500 Northwestern Shoshone must either starve or steal and recommended a reservation in Cache Valley as the only location remaining where they could raise grain without resorting to artesian wells for irrigation. The Office of Indian Affairs failed to respond, and soon the suggestion became academic as other Mormon families poured into the valley. By late 1860 Mormons had appropriated nearly all the arable land.

In May 1860 it was reported to Brigham Young that the Indians were hostile, having stolen $1,500 worth of horses over the past several months. To counter the Indian raids, the inhabitants established a military company, which expanded to become a valley-wide military attachment of armed minutemen. That July an Indian was captured for stealing horses and was shot while trying to escape. In the conflict that followed two other Indians and two whites lost their lives. A few days later 1,500 Indians appeared at the end of the valley and demanded food. Their request brought 1,300 pounds of flour from the Saints in Logan. Indian superintendent James Doty reported in 1862 that "the Indians in great numbers are starving and are in a destitute condition. If they are placed where they can have stock and give attention to raising them, I am confident they will cease to be beggars and deprivators. At present they are not satisfied with what I have done for them." 1862 INDIAN PROBLEM

The stage was set for confrontation between the whites and the Indians as miners and immigrants tended to attack the Indians without provocation. Most Utah residents were convinced that the Indians along Bear River in Cache Valley were eager for a fight—an attitude that was strengthened when federal troops killed four Indian hostages because stolen horses had not been delivered to their white owners. A legal motive for a military expedition against the Cache Valley Indian bands came when a group of miners from Grasshopper Diggings in Montana was attacked and some of them killed. The chief justice of Utah territory issued a warrant for the arrests of chiefs Bearhunter, Sandpitch, and Sagwich. Colonel Patrick E. Connor, an Indian-hater, was more than ready to respond and marched his troops by night from Camp Douglas in Salt Lake City. He wanted to insure that news of the army movement would not frighten the Indians into departing and deprive his soldiers of the opportunity for action. But the Shoshone did not intend to leave; they prepared firing positions along Battle Creek, near its confluence with the Bear River in the northern part of Cache Valley. In the early morning of 29 January 1863, they waited as the troops crossed the ice-choked river.

Almost all of the Indians were killed—as many as 300, including almost 90 women and children. In addition, the troops destroyed 70 teepees, captured 175 horses, and gathered over 1,000 bushels of grain. More troubles followed, but on 30 July 1863, some six months later, nine chiefs affixed their mark to a document which dictated that $2,000 worth of goods be distributed among the Indians in exchange for telegraph lines, overland stage routes, stage stations, and railroads through Indian territory.[6]

Settlers from the older Cache Valley communities continued to found new ones on the west side of the valley. Apostle Ezra T. Benson called Israel J. Clark to lead a small band of people, mostly from Logan, to found Clarkston; twelve of these families spent the winter of 1864-65 in the area. That spring, more people came from Mendon and other nearby towns, as well as from Salt Lake City, to strengthen the region. Marriner W. Merrill led a company to explore Oxford, and a small group located there in the fall of 1864, but not until 1867 did the settlers feel safe to move into their city lots. Clifton, Weston, and Dayton were all established by 1867, and soon other towns such as Newton, Trenton, and Amalga were established.[7] The larger Cache Valley settlements, especially Logan, became the base from which the Bear Lake colonies were settled.

The man chosen to colonize the Bear Lake region was Apostle Charles C. Rich. Having returned from San Bernardino and a mission to Europe, Rich was invited to Salt Lake City from his home in Centerville in the late summer of 1863. He and Brigham Young travelled to Cache Valley for church meetings and while there discussed the need to explore Bear Lake as a potential site for settlements. A year earlier, Congress had passed the Homestead Act which offered 160 acres for a small filing fee and evidence of improvements over a five-year period. Young's plan was to settle as many new areas for

---

[6] Difficulties continued until well after the 1860s. But the real power of the Northwest Shoshone was broken at the Battle of the Bear River. This defeat made possible the expansion of more settlements in Cache Valley after January 1863.

[7] One of the most important areas to be settled was Preston. But Preston was not colonized until the 1870s. This was also true of Whitney, Mapleton, Glendale, Mink Creek, Treasureton, and Windor—all in Cache Valley. The land in these areas was less attractive, and settlement took place more slowly.

the increasing number of colonists could be arranged while at the same time keeping non-Mormons at a distance. Patrick Connor, whose defeat of the Indians in the Cache Valley area in January 1863 made possible the expansion of colonization, represented a threat to such planning. He had decided to invite a large Gentile population into the region, primarily through mining opportunities, to dilute the Mormon influence. Knowing of this unoccupied valley northeast of Cache Valley, Young and Rich thought it was time for the Mormons to possess it.

On 23 August 1863, the First Presidency met with members of the Twelve and other church authorities at the home of Ezra T. Benson in Logan. Their purpose was to consider sending a company of men to the Bear Lake Valley that fall. When Young asked Rich's feelings, Rich said he did not feel much like volunteering but was willing to do whatever his president said. After announcing that the Twelve could now do more good at home than abroad and that they should sustain themselves as much as possible without the help of tithing funds, Young said,

> Now what I am about to say to you, will do well to keep to ourselves. We have it in our minds to settle Bear River Lake Valley. I, for one, would like to have a settlement there. As yet I have said nothing to anyone except to Brother Benson. Now if you will keep this matter to yourselves nobody will know anything about it, but otherwise it will be telegraphed to old Abe Lincoln by some of these Army officers and then it will be made a reservation immediately to prevent us from getting it.[8]

By 15 September 1863, Rich had organized a small company of thirty-two men and had left Franklin. Several days later they traversed a beautiful valley of rich, black soil and camped by a trout-rich stream. The company prepared to explore the valley for the families coming to spend the winter.[9]

Within a few days, Rich sent a detailed geographic report to Young. He had decided to move the main camp south to the present

---

[8] Rich must have wondered what kind of a friend he had in Benson, who had told Young that Rich wanted to lead in the settlement. What Rich had said was that he had been home from his European mission only a year and would rather not pull up stakes and move his entire family. In any case, Young seemed convinced that Rich was the man to lead the colony.

[9] Thomas Sleight and twelve others were following closely behind Rich's group. Sleight recorded in his journal that it was difficult getting through the canyon, but part of the problem was that they were taking time to build a road and construct fords for those that followed. When Sleight's group arrived in the valley snow had already fallen.

site of Paris (originally Perris), Idaho. He described the valley as 60 to 70 miles in length and 10 to 15 miles wide and estimated the large lake to be 30 miles long and 8 miles wide. He noted that the water was clear, tasted sweet, and was said to abound with fish of the finest quality. Because of the abundance of water and timber on the west side, Rich believed the settlement should center there. This site had plenty of good land, a large stream, and seemed to be devoid of close stands of timber. In all, Rich's report was optimistic and encouraging.

Throughout the remainder of September, the families moved into the valley along Rich's original route, now called Immigration Canyon. By 6 October, Rich was back in Salt Lake City to report on the Bear Lake venture in General Conference. Shortly after the conference concluded, Rich persuaded two of his San Bernardino missionaries, Richard Hopkins, who had been stake clerk, and Jefferson Hunt, to go to Bear Lake with him. Thomas Miller, Lorin Farr, Joseph Rich, and George Hill, an interpreter of Indian languages, also made the trip.

The weather was good, and the thirty families who had remained in the valley were in good spirits. In fact, two children were born while Rich was on his second visit to the valley. Rich had contacted Washakie of the Northern Shoshone and Tighe, a Bannock chief, telling them of the plan to colonize the valley and requesting their cooperation. The Indians responded favorably on the condition that the Mormons leave the southern end of the valley open as a camping ground for the Indians. They also expected that the Indians would receive food when they visited the area. Rich left the valley in December and spent the remainder of the winter with his families in Davis County but made preparations for a mammoth migration to the Bear Lake region in the spring.

In March, Rich's family began moving to Bear Lake, but the journey was difficult. That May, Brigham Young and a company of 112 others visited the new settlements; they too had difficulty getting through Immigration Canyon. Wilford Woodruff recorded that after they had reached the summit they entered a mudhole six miles long. They reached Paris completely exhausted from the ordeal. Young named Montpelier, Bennington, and Ovid after towns in his native state Vermont. Rich was honored by the naming of Richland County, later shortened to Rich, and the town of St. Charles. The settlers originally thought the valley was in Utah. They later discovered that the southern part was in Utah, but the part they had settled was in Idaho.

Nevertheless, by the end of 1864 nearly 700 settlers had joined the colony.[10]

The winter of 1864-65 was unusually severe. In January, Rich found that the 1,100 inhabitants suffered shortages of wheat, flour, potatoes, and other grains. Some members of the community finally decided to discuss their future with Rich. They arranged for the meeting without announcing what they wanted, but Rich guessed: They had decided to leave the valley. One of their greatest complaints was isolation. They also questioned whether the place was economically viable. Although he later admitted that the region had ten months of winter and two of summer, Rich was committed to the settlement. He replied, "There have been many hardships, I admit, and these we have shared together, but if you want to go somewhere else, that is your right and I do not want to deprive you of it. If you have a mind to leave here, my blessings go with you. But I must stay here, even if I stay alone. President Young called me here and I will remain until he releases me and gives me leave to go." A few families did move to warmer climates, but most decided to remain with their leader.[11]

By October 1866, Rich was beginning to feel the effects of strenuous living. Nevertheless, he continued to lead the community for several years afterwards. In June 1869, Young called David P. Kimball to preside over the newly formed stake in Bear Lake. Later, he called William Budge of Providence, Utah, to move to Bear Lake and become the presiding bishop. By 1869, the Mormon colonies were

---

[10] By 1864, Rich had entered the valley by three routes: north from Franklin over Immigration Canyon; through Ogden Canyon and Huntsville; and by way of Bear River, nearly eighty miles longer than the Immigration Canyon pass. Rich decided to build a road by way of Huntsville in Ogden, primarily because this route was entirely in Utah territory whereas the other routes went either into Wyoming or Idaho.

[11] The Indians also posed a problem. Although Rich had made agreements with the Northern Shoshone and the Bannocks, some settlers in the spring of 1865 broke his pledge and settled in Round Valley at the south end of the lake. Learning this, Washakie destroyed the settlers' crops and fences. Later that year, Rich tried to negotiate with the Shoshone chief to get permission to farm in Round Valley. Ultimately, they received permission, but as the whites occupied more and more Indian land, trouble ensued. Continual surveillance of the Indians became a fact of life. Eventually Rich was able to persuade the chiefs to come to a conference at Fish Haven, where he convinced them that white men were coming no matter what they did and proposed a feast if the Indians would agree to be peaceful. Afterwards, Washakie surveyed the land from the foothills west of Fish Haven and bestowed it on Rich. With sadness he asked Rich to consult the government in Washington to see where the Shoshone should go. Two years later, in 1868, the Wind River Reservation was set aside for their use.

well established, but trouble lay on the horizon.[12] For these outer settlements were in Idaho territory, and the political climate in Idaho was becoming unfriendly toward the Mormons.

---

[12] Mormons had also settled in Malad, Idaho, which became an important trading center. When Idaho became a territory in March 1863, one of the first acts of the legislature was to create Oneida County with a county seat at Soda Springs. Malad was included in this county (as were the Bear Lake settlements later). But by 1866 the people of Malad had lobbied successfully to have the county seat moved from Soda Springs. Many of the Soda Springs settlers were Morrisites, who had been driven out of Utah and were reluctant to turn county records over to the Mormons at Malad. Several members of the Reorganized Church of Jesus Christ of Latter Day Saints also lived in Soda Springs. The struggle between these three communities did not resolve itself until after the 1860s.

16.
Economic
and Religious
Developments, 1858-67

CAMP FLOYD

NON-MORMONS

During the decade following the Utah War, the church continued to grow. The establishment of Camp Floyd in 1858 brought prosperity to the settlements as colonists traded with 4,000 federal troops and 3,000 non-Mormon suppliers, employees, and camp followers. Mormons bartered consumer goods, and several hundred local residents found employment at the camp. Church-supported organizations profited from the sale to the troops of lumber and other supplies. Residents also profited from the sale of surplus army property, especially when the post was abandoned in 1861. A year later, troops from California ordered to Utah to protect the Overland mail established a new post, Camp Douglas, on the hills east of Salt Lake City. The pioneers once again had a source of trade and commerce for their goods and personal labor.

During the same period, the organization of the Pony Express and the completion of the Overland telegraph brought employment and a market for other services and goods. The development of mining in surrounding states and territories also brought opportunity, which increased when mineral wealth was found in the mountains surrounding the Salt Lake Valley. Taking advantage of growing economic opportunities, freighting companies brought thousands of tons of goods into the valley during the mid-1860s.

MINING DEVELOPMENT

Such opportunities allowed church leaders to revise their immigration system. They discontinued handcarts and substituted a system of wagon trains. Wagons could make the round trip from Salt Lake to Missouri in one season, hauling east supplies for immigrants and surplus goods for sale and returning with immigrants and needed machinery. Prosperity enabled the Saints to build important buildings, especially in Salt Lake City, and to provide employment for an increasing number of immigrants. The Salt Lake Theater was completed in 1862, and the Salt Lake Tabernacle was in use by 1867. Work continued on the Salt Lake Temple, but it would not be completed until the mid-1890s.

Minor organizational or doctrinal changes also occurred in the church during this period. A dispute between Apostle Orson Pratt and Brigham Young revealed some theological differences, as well as the difficulty in resolving those differences, especially when the prophet claimed revelation that seemed disharmonious with scripture or with the teachings of church founder Joseph Smith. The decade also produced two Mormon dissident groups, the Morrisites and the Godbeites (discussed in subsequent chapters).

Initially, Mormon colonists considered Johnston's Army the enemy and their suppliers, employees, and camp followers, who settled in Douby Town, or Frog Town (now Fairfield), an undesirable element forced on them and their communities. But they were also desperately poor. Although church leaders originally opposed selling anything to the outsiders, they soon recognized the economic advantage and encouraged the people to get the best price possible for their goods and services. Individual villagers were able to supply the troops with buttermilk, pies, vegetables, butter, eggs, dried fish, dried fruit, and "valley tan" whiskey. They received in exchange cash, clothing, tea and coffee, and valuable equipment. They were also able to sell large quantities of hay, straw, grain, meat, as well as lumber. In fact, the church-supported Big Cottonwood Lumber Company was said to have netted as much as $200,000 in building Camp Floyd. Mormon workers also gained employment by manufacturing adobe bricks, assisting in the construction of the quarters, and performing other specialized services.

Periodic auctions of condemned food, surplus animals, and equipment offered bargains. One of the largest sales disposed of 3,500 large freight wagons for $10 each, many of which cost $150-$175 in the Midwest. Then, in 1861, when the Civil War required that the troops return to the East, Camp Floyd, now named Camp Crittenden, was abandoned, occasioning probably the largest government surplus property sale yet. In one large auction, on 16 July 1861, the army sold approximately $4 million worth of property for an estimated $100,000 cash. About two-fifths was purchased in the name

DOCTRINE CHANGES

CAMP FLOYD CLOSING

of Brigham Young for $40,000. The Walker Brothers and other Mormon colonists made huge profits from these purchases.

One of the most spectacular and least understood developments of the period was the famous Pony Express organized in 1860 by the Russell, Majors, and Waddell Freighting Company. The Pony Express was a propaganda move to demonstrate the feasibility of an all-year mail route through the central part of the country and to obtain a franchise for the mail contract. After establishing approximately 300 stations between Missouri and California, and hiring some eighty riders, the Pony Express began its career on 3 April 1860, expecting to carry the mail to California in ten days. During one winter and two summers, 308 relays were made each way, more than 34,000 pieces of mail being carried. The Pony Express route came through Fort Bridger and over much of the Mormon Trail through the Salt Lake Valley, through Lehi and Tooele County to the Nevada border. It required stations, supplies, station masters, and Pony Express riders, as well as fine horses, which the Mormons were ready to provide. Tragically for Russell, Majors, and Waddell, the experiment was a financial disaster and caused them to lose an estimated $500,000. The Pony Express was discontinued after an eighteen-month career when the Overland telegraph was completed.

Construction of the Western Union Telegraph System was partly contracted to Mormons. Salt Lake City became a junction between the Pacific Telegraph Company from the east and the Western Overland Telegraph Company on the west. Both divisions gave contracts to Brigham Young and through him to other Mormons to help support the construction of approximately 500 miles of line. Church records indicate that at the completion of the line in October 1861, Young received $11,000 in gold for his participation. "I did not touch that gold with my fingers or until it was all paid in," he wrote. "Then I put it in a vessel of water, cleansed it and said what words I wished over it and then I delivered every dime of it for tithing." The telegraph lines meeting in Salt Lake City in October 1861 became the first of three transcontinental, communication-transportation systems with their meeting points in the Utah territory—the other two being the transcontinental railroad in 1869 and the transcontinental telephone system which was completed in Wendover, Nevada, in 1914.

The Saints eventually tried to construct their own telegraph system in the Great Basin to unite the territory and to avoid such tragedies as the Mountain Meadows Massacre. In a sermon in the Salt Lake Tabernacle on 9 February 1862, Young announced that he wanted "a company raised to stretch wire through our settlements in this territory that information may be communicated to all parts with lightning speed." Telegraphic instruments were ordered and arrived in September 1862. A telegraphy school was immediately established, enrolling some fifty young men. A few months later a church line was run from the Council House to Young's office.

However, after this promising start, the program was delayed because of the Civil War, which made it impossible for church leaders to acquire the necessary batteries, insulators, wire, sending and receiving sets, and other equipment. Toward the end of the war, in March 1865, the *Deseret News* questioned why nothing more had been done on the project and suggested that it was now appropriate to complete a line from Logan to St. George. Bishops of the communities along the route were subsequently requested to hold meetings and sound out the feelings of their people. If reactions were favorable, they should send their reports to Young, indicating how many poles each ward would put up and how much money it would furnish. If the reports were universally favorable, church leaders hoped to put up a line during the fall of 1865. After the April conference, a special meeting was held in which it was agreed to start the project.

At this time church leaders decided to extend the line to St. Charles on Bear Lake in the north rather than Logan. Young tried to generate support for the project as he visited various settlements. All during the winter of 1866–67 communities reported that they were cutting poles and surveying lines to complete such a project.

Telegraphy school resumed in Brigham Young's family schoolhouse. John C. Clowes, the operator in the Salt Lake Office of the Western Union Telegraph Company and a Mormon convert, was the instructor. The school contained some thirty pupils from throughout the territory. Most were between twelve and eighteen years of age and were called in much the same way thousands of elders had been called on proselyting missions. Although they were first instructed not to expect compensation, all operators appear to have later received a token wage from local tithing offices, city revenues, or public subscription.[1]

---

[1] For example, Estelle Parks who operated a Sanpete County Office in 1868, received in addition to her board fifty bushels of wheat delivered to her father in Nephi for six months' service. The operator at Beaver was paid with voluntary donations from the local church congregation. When the Moroni office was established, the people were told that they were to satisfy the needs of the telegraph operators. At a church meeting in June 1867, the congregation voted to pay the operator $50 a month in produce or stock, to be raised by assessment or taxes levied by the bishop

The poles for the line were set by the fall of 1866, and the 500 miles of wire and necessary supply of insulators and chemicals arrived on 14 October 1866. By 1 December, the line from Salt Lake to Ogden was complete and Young sent a message greeting the northern Saints and expressing satisfaction with the completion of this part of the line. Telegraphic communication between Logan and St. George opened on 15 January 1867, and the rest of the line was operating within thirty days. In almost every case, work was donated. The bishop of each ward usually called men and boys on labor missions to set the poles and string the lines. These temporary missionaries served without pay except for tithing credit. The line was extended north from Logan to Franklin, Idaho, by December 1869 and on to Paris, Idaho, in 1871. In the Salt Lake area, connection was made with Tooele and Grantsville.[2]

The church-owned Deseret Telegraph Company was incorporated to give direction to the operation of the line. The history of the Deseret Telegraph Company shows that it was never intended to serve as a revenue producer. In fact, the company often operated in the red during its thirty-three-year history from 1867 to 1900. Before the coming of the transcontinental railroad and the subsequent mining boom, receipts were nominal. In 1868, for example, the gross receipts from tolls amounted to only $8,462. By 1873, however, this increased to $75,000. Competition from Western Union, the exhausting of mining deposits, and Mormon business stagnation provoked by the Edmunds Act would cause receipts to drop to $14,000 by 1885. The Deseret Telegraph Line never really made a profit, although some branch lines to the mining settlements helped to subsidize the operation. All losses seem to have been made up out of church tithing funds.

---

and approved by the entire group. Among the early telegraph missionaries was Anthon H. Lund, later a member of the First Presidency, who operated the Mount Pleasant office when it opened on 28 December 1866.

[2] During Utah's mining boom in the early 1870s, lines would be stretched to all important mining districts—from Salt Lake City to Alta and Bingham, from Echo to Coalville, from Payson to the Tintic District, from Beaver to the Star District and Frisco, from St. George to Pioche and Bullionville and other mining areas in southeastern Nevada. Lines were also built in the 1870s to several outlying agriculture settlements—from Toquerville to Kanab and Rockville, Utah, and to Windsor Castle, Arizona (Pipe Springs), the first telegraph line in Arizona. Lines also extended from Moroni to Gunnison and on up the Sevier to Monroe and from Brigham City to Corinne. In some cases the line also extended to newly constructed railway lines. In 1871, 600 miles of telegraph line were in operation and supplies had been ordered to extend the lines within three months 400 miles further in different directions. By 1880 there were 955 miles of lines and 68 offices.

Although a failure from a financial point of view, the Deseret telegraph system was indispensable to the effective administration of the Mormon church's expanding temporal and spiritual affairs. Following completion of the line, Brigham Young could direct the church from St. George, where he spent most of the remaining winters of his life. Lengthy religious messages from Young were sent after midnight when the wires were clear. The Deseret Telegraph saved many lives during the latter half of the Black Hawk Indian War, when the movements of the Indians in the central and southern part of the territory were relayed from settlement to settlement.[3] The line was also reportedly used by Mormons to keep polygamists throughout the settlements informed of the movements of the federal deputies during the anti-polygamy raids following passage of the Edmunds Act in 1882. Ultimately, the line was confiscated by the U.S. government in 1888, then later returned and finally sold to Western Union in 1900.

The completion of the transcontinental telegraph caused the end of the Pony Express. Ben Holladay assumed control of the central Overland California and Pikes Peak Express Company and renamed it the Holladay Overland Mail and Express Company. From 1864 to 1866, this company reigned virtually supreme between the Missouri River and Salt Lake City. This huge concern purchased much of its feed and hired many of its teamsters and other employees in Utah. Hyrum Rumfield, Salt Lake agent for the company, reported that during an eleven-month period from 1861 to 1862 the company purchased approximately "several hundred thousand dollars" worth of supplies in Salt Lake City which they "paid for in glittering gold." Brigham Young, as church president, contracted with the company in 1862 to furnish 50,000 bushels of oats and barley at one dollar in gold per bushel, plus $1.25 for hauling each 100 pounds 100 miles from Salt Lake City. The company began raising its own feed in 1865. In a similar manner the church would furnish men, supplies, and transportation to parties surveying for the transcontinental railroad in 1864.

---

[3] In fact, the outbreak of Indian hostilities seems to have been one of the factors prompting church officials to revive the project in 1865. George Q. Cannon, one of the Twelve Apostles, admitted later that the Deseret Telegraph was necessary "in consequence of Indian troubles." In fact, the first news of General Custer's defeat by the Sioux on the Little Big Horn reached the world through the agency of the Deseret Telegraph. A horseman rode all the way from the army command post at Fort Hall to Franklin, Idaho, in 1876, and the Mormon operator relayed the news of Custer's last stand to federal authorities and newsmen in the east.

Another windfall bringing economic prosperity to the church in the 1860s came with the California volunteers, a military unit sent into Utah in 1862 to guard the Overland Telegraph and Overland Mail from Indians and Confederate troops and to keep a watch on the Mormons. Led by Colonel (later General) Patrick E. Connor, the California volunteers comprised between 750 and 1,500 troops. Refusing to settle at Camp Floyd, Connor insisted on establishing a new post on the bluffs overlooking Salt Lake City, which he named Camp Douglas (later Fort Douglas). Connor, who was hostile toward the Mormons, required that all persons furnishing supplies to the troops repeat their allegiance to the Union. To Brigham Young and most Mormons this was an insult. However, when the short harvest and unprecedented demand during 1863–64 forced the soldiers to ration their grain, Young directed tithing offices to supply limited quantities of grain to them at the rate of $3.00 per bushel. The soldiers were allowed to purchase approximately five tons of flour per week as well as beef and vegetables, but at what Connor regarded as "enormous and unreasonable prices."

The mining boom from the Rockies to the Sierra also opened a large cash market for Mormon produce. Attracted by generous prices offered at the mining camps for flour, salt, dried fruits, and butter, merchants and traders scoured the country for products, especially in the Utah territory. After the Pike's Peak discoveries, more than a hundred large wagons of Utah flour, grain, and other farm produce were freighted to Colorado. Reportedly, more than 10,000 sacks of Utah flour were shipped out in September 1860 alone. Perhaps equal amounts were shipped from Utah to Colorado in 1861 and 1862. Utah exported even more to Idaho and Montana in 1863 and in the succeeding year to Nevada.

The church did not encourage this trade. Leaders feared a depleted food supply and in general objected to a trading economy. But the trade took place nevertheless, and the church's chief function was to organize the farmers in such a way as to assure them of high prices for their produce. Leading farmers and mechanics were invited to a price convention after General Conferences in April and October of each year to establish prices. In assuming chairmanship of their conventions, Young stated "that he appeared as the representative of God in this convention as much as yesterday at conference." The prices agreed upon were approximately double those of the pre-mining period: wheat at $5 per bushel, corn at $4, and flour at $12 per hundred. The list of commodities and services included all grains, meats, dairy products, many vegetables, dried fruit, hay, and freighting. There is no doubt that these conventions increased the bargaining power of Mormons and made it possible for them to furnish their families with comforts that would have otherwise been beyond their reach. Prices were high, some even by modern standards, but buyers in the mining areas did not complain. When freight trains were delayed, prices for flour in the camps could reach as high as a dollar a pound.

All these windfalls bolstered and cushioned the Mormon economy in the 1860s. They supplied cash and capital equipment for manufacturing and agricultural improvements, but they did not lead Mormons to abandon self-sufficiency as a goal.[4]

The occupation of Utah by federal troops during the "Utah War" seemed to intensify the Mormon imperative to gather. No immigration took place in 1858, but as tension eased in 1859 immigration resumed on a large scale. But initially the resources of the Perpetual Emigrating Fund Company (PEF) were so exhausted that those who could not procure teams were advised to cross the plains by handcart. Only one company, consisting of 235 souls with sixty handcarts and six wagons, made such a trek in 1859. Total immigration was much more in 1860, but only two companies of 349 persons came by handcart. The handcart was clearly not popular, although mule trains were sent from Salt Lake Valley to meet each of the companies as they reached Fort Laramie.

Before the end of 1860, church leaders had decided to abandon handcarts in favor of dispatching companies of teams from Utah to bring back immigrants and merchandise. This seemed a natural step, although some questioned whether a yoke of oxen could travel so far in one season. The Perpetual Emigrating Fund, which had inherited most of the animals and properties of the Brigham Young Express and Carrying Company, benefitted from sales to the army and to Russell, Majors, and Waddell in 1858 and 1860. The rush of miners to Colorado drove prices higher and higher, but the outbreak of the Civil War threatened commercial relations between the East and Far West. So Mormons were once again driven to do their own importing and exporting. Mormon teams were to carry provisions for immigrants as well as exports to outfitting centers in Missouri and return to Utah with immigrants and their supplies, manufactured goods, machinery, staple imports, and other items for church and private

---

[4]Considering the obstacles presented by nature, Mormon production did well to keep up with the increases in population. Through immigration and natural increase the population rose from less than 40,000 in 1858 to more than 80,000 in 1869.

use. By transporting their own flour, beans, and bacon to supply the immigrants on these "down and back trips," Mormons reserved their cash to buy machinery and other items for their self-sufficiency campaign.

Merchants and church agents had experimented with round trip freighting between Salt Lake City and the Missouri Valley in 1859. This experiment proved that oxen could make the 2,200 mile round trip in approximately six months if they were properly cared for. Several companies then used the down-and-back scheme in 1860. One of these was led by Joseph W. Young, Brigham's nephew, who captained a thirty-wagon company which left Utah in the spring of 1860 and returned the same fall with new machinery and merchandise. On his return, Young was invited to deliver a sermon on "the science of ox teamology" before the 1860 General Conference. His proposals were favorably received and preparations were made immediately to try out the scheme on a large scale in 1861.

The procedure to be followed was outlined by the First Presidency: "We are rich in cattle, but do not abound in money either at home or abroad, and we desire to so plan and operate as to use our small amount of money and large number of cattle in the best possible manner for accomplishing the best good." First, the number of men, teams, equipment and provisions needed to transport immigrants and machine would be determined. Needs would be apportioned to each ward and settlement on a pro-rata basis. On a specified date in April all the requested men, teams, and supplies were to be in Salt Lake City ready for the trip east. In Salt Lake City they would be inspected and loaded under the direction of the Presiding Bishop and organized into companies of approximately fifty each. The captain of each company would be given complete authority to "see the train through."

Each wagon was to be pulled by four yoke of oxen or its equivalent in mules to carry a thousand pounds of flour. The teams would also take loose oxen, thus providing a market for Utah oxen and keeping within the church $10,000 and $30,000 per year which had previously been paid in the Missouri Valley for cattle and wagons. Other Utah products which could be sold in the Midwest could also be carried. An extra man on horseback was required for each group of four wagons to look after the cattle and hunt for game. The teams were expected to reach the Missouri River in July and return with ten to twenty immigrants per wagon. Some of the wagons would return with church freight, and each community was free to send additional persons and facilities for freighting machinery and other

ROUND TRIP FREIGHTING

imported merchandise.[5] In case the teams sent from Utah were insufficient to transport all the immigrants and freight, the Perpetual Emigrating Fund was prepared to augment the returning caravan by purchasing necessary facilities.[6]

During the six years that church trains were organized, approximately 2,000 wagons, employing some 2,500 men and 17,500 oxen, were sent east for immigrants. As a result, more than 20,000 European immigrants were assisted to Utah; 16,000 came by church train and 229 were listed as PEF immigrants. Approximately 726 purchased their own teams, and the remainder came in independent companies. These figures do not include immigrants from the United States. Total expenditures by the church for this immigration varied from $300,000 to $500,000 annually, for a total of about $2.4 million for the entire period.

Meeting the quota of men and supplies required cooperation within each settlement. In 1862, the stakes of Parowan, Beaver, and St. George, which comprised the southern Utah mission, were asked to send 57 wagons, with three yoke of good cattle each, and provisions for the teamsters' six-month journey and for the immigrants they would bring back. They were also to furnish 57 teamsters and 14 mounted men. On receipt of this call the officers of the southern mission issued calls to each ward and settlement. The town of Harmony, for example, with less than a hundred people, was asked to furnish three outfits of wagons, four yoke of cattle, and a thousand pounds of flour for each wagon. These outfits were raised in one day. The individual contributions were all in kind and ranged from Susan Hill's mat, pillow, night cap, plate, spoon, cups, needles, and thread to John D. Lee's Chicago wagon cover, pair of pants, pair of shoes, three overshirts, flour, bacon, molasses, rifle, and ammunition, to the amount of $122.50. Three young men volunteered as teamsters, and in Sunday meeting they were formally blessed and

---

[5] Church trains often freighted machinery. The 1862 train, for example, purchased and transported 25 carding machines, 100 cotton gins, spinning jennies, a number of nail-making machines, several saws, and many boxes of mill fixings. The 1863 eastbound trains also carried Utah-raised cotton, which was exchanged in St. Louis for cotton cloth.

[6] The individuals who were called or who volunteered to take part in these expeditions were regarded as missionaries, but they were credited on tithing books with the value of service rendered. Those who loaned teams and who contributed flour and other produce were also given tithing credit. In 1864, the amount credited for these services in one valley was: mounted guard, $300; mule wagon and teamster, $250; two yoke of oxen, wagon, $140; a yoke of oxen, $60; a wagon, $50; and a saddle, $5. Often unmarried men would volunteer, hoping to find prospective brides among the incoming immigrants.

set apart. Benjamin J. Redd requested a dance before leaving, which was granted. These men had to travel almost 500 miles to Salt Lake City before even beginning the journey east.

The church trains represented a voluntary, cooperative investment in people, that is, immigrants. They also made possible the importation of needed machinery and merchandise, facilitated the sale of an unknown quantity of surplus cattle and cotton, and made it possible for the PEF to make large purchases of cattle and wagons during the 1860s. This phase of immigration ended with the completion of the transcontinental railroad in 1869.

As immigrants poured into Salt Lake Valley in the 1860s, most were assigned to various local wards for wintering and then were employed on church public works. In addition to foundries, machine shops, and carpentry and paint shops, the public works operated factories which supplied the territory with paper, nails, buttons, wooden buckets, carding machines, and milling machinery. The public works department occasionally constructed roads, bridges, dams, and canals. The largest projects undertaken by church public works in the 1860s were the Salt Lake Theater, the Salt Lake Tabernacle, and continued work on the Salt Lake Temple.

The Salt Lake Theater was constructed in 1861–62 and represented a community investment of some $100,000. With a seating capacity of 3,000 persons, the theater reportedly duplicated, both inside and outside, the famous Drury Lane Theater of London. The auditorium had a parquet, a dress circle, and three balconies. Samuel Bowles, who visited in 1865, wrote, "The building is itself a rare triumph of art and enterprise. No eastern city of 100,000 inhabitants, and remember Salt Lake City has less than 20,000, possesses so fine a theatrical structure. It ranks alike in capacity and elegance of structure and finish along with the opera houses and academies of Boston, New York, Philadelphia, Chicago, and Cincinnati."

The construction of this building utilized nails made by the public works factory out of the iron left behind by Johnston's Army in 1861.[7] The construction also provided labor for scores of European architects, artists, masons, and carpenters. In August 1861, for example, 16 stonemasons, 8 stonecutters, 16 diggers, 3 millwrights, and 15 carpenters were at work on the building. After the roof timbers were placed, some three dozen carpenters were put to work on

---

[7] "Judged from the present period," quipped a contemporary, "one would almost be led to believe that Johnston's Army was sent to Utah to assist the Saints in their recreational activities."

283

the interior. Most of these laborers were paid with tithing orders and in some cases with written promises of future theater tickets. One person recalled that Brigham Young specifically wanted sailors to work on the new buildings because they were used to working at high levels.[8] A sixteen-foot water wheel, formerly used at the sugar works, was placed at a branch on City Creek near the building. Connected with a drive shaft and gearing, the wheel elevated the rock and massive timber used in the construction.

Because the theater was a church enterprise until Mormon artists leased it from the church in 1873, performers were often called as missionaries. One young lady was "requisitioned" with the following: "Dear Brother and Sister Colebrook, Would you allow your daughter Nelly to act upon the stage; It would please me very much. Your brother, Brigham Young." During these years admission was commonly paid by receipt for delivery of a quantity of produce, poultry, or livestock at the General Tithing Office, and performers were also paid from tithing. The Salt Lake Theater was the first important theater west of the Mississippi throughout the remainder of the nineteenth century. During its heyday, the best actors and actresses in the nation performed on its stage.

The Salt Lake Tabernacle, an immense elliptical turtleback auditorium 250 feet long, 150 feet wide, and 80 feet in height, which can seat 8,000–10,000 people, was constructed from 1863 to 1870 and dedicated in 1875. The most interesting feature of the building is the self-supporting wooden roof with its lattice arches held together with wooden pins. The rounded dome was made of rawhide tied together with leather thongs. Its construction required more than 1.5 million feet of lumber. Architects boasted that it was the largest hall in the world unsupported by columns. Especially notable were its acoustical properties, particularly after the completion of the gallery in 1870. Previously, pine branches had to be hung from the ceiling to break the reverberations of sound against the walls.

Exclusive of the organ, which was made of native materials, the building cost some $300,000. About 150 men worked at any one time for approximately two years to complete the exterior. Much of the labor was done by immigrants, particularly in 1867, a poor year financially for most new settlers. One new immigrant who found work

[8]One of these sailors was George Jarvis, a one-eyed Englishman who obtained food and clothing for his family of six in this way during the crucial winter of 1861–62. By spring, Jarvis had earned enough credit to obtain "a steady yoke of oxen" and took his family to St. George. There he helped build the St. George Tabernacle and later the St. George Temple.

284

on the building reported that despite the general slump he could earn in two days enough to last him a whole week and enough in fourteen days to provide for the whole winter. Typical wages, or credits, were $2, $3, $3.50 per day, depending on the work performed.

The third important building under construction during the 1860s was the Salt Lake Temple, begun in 1853 but not completed until 1893. The foundation was initially of sandstone but was torn up when a large granite quarry was located in Little Cottonwood Canyon, twenty miles southeast of the city. Except during the Utah War, several hundred tithing artisans worked steadily on the structure. Other workers brought lumber from a sawmill in Big Cottonwood Canyon. About fifty teams from the various wards in Salt Lake Valley hauled rock from the quarry to the temple site, where stonecutters dressed the large stones. Three or four yoke of oxen were required for each load, which consisted of one huge block and two smaller blocks. Larger granite blocks weighed as much as five tons; blocks weighing three tons were common. Cattle yards to take care of three hundred head of cattle were constructed near the Little Cottonwood quarry. Hay was furnished by the public works, and each ward was asked to furnish grain for the animals. The drivers lodged near the corral in tents. With luck, teams could go from Salt Lake City to the quarry and return with a load to the temple site in two days.

In general, church leaders tried to restrict the use of tithing funds to the purchase of imported machinery and supplies and, after the construction of a railroad to the quarry in 1873, to pay for the freight. Construction of the railway made it possible for whole trainloads of granite blocks to be rolled onto the temple grounds every few days as needed. Threatened famine from grasshoppers and other natural crises interrupted the work repeatedly, and it was also suspended in 1868–69 during the construction of the transcontinental railroad.

Although the Utah War temporarily reduced the number of missionaries, missionary work continued to function, especially in Great Britain. Louis A. Bertrand, a native of France living in Salt Lake City, tried to take the gospel to France. He arrived in March 1861, applied for permission to preach, but was prohibited. As a result the French Mission remained closed for many years. The church encountered more success in the Scandinavian Mission led from 1857 to 1860 by Hector C. Haight and then Carl Winterbourg. Proselyting continued in South Africa, where William Fotheringham and other missionaries arrived in 1861. Missionary work also continued in Australia, New Zealand, and Tasmania, but little progress was made. In general, these

285

were difficult years for missionary work, both in Europe and elsewhere.[9]

Concurrently, the Reorganized Church of Jesus Christ of Latter
Day Saints (RLDS), headed by Joseph Smith III, the oldest living son
of Joseph Smith, was founded and began a missionary effort to the
Mormons in Salt Lake City. RLDS missionaries enjoyed little success
in Utah but were nonetheless able to convince a few Mormons to
join them. Many RLDS converts subsequently gathered around Malad,
Idaho, which became a center of the RLDS church in the West. RLDS
missionaries also encountered some success in San Bernardino, California, where almost half of the Mormon settlers had refused to leave
when they were recalled by Brigham Young in 1857.

A final development during the 1860s was a doctrinal dispute
between Apostle Orson Pratt and Brigham Young concerning the
nature of God. These two men, who had been colleagues since the
organization of the Quorum of the Twelve Apostles in 1835, had different temperaments and saw some things differently. Pratt was an
intellectual, whereas Young, with little formal education, was a pragmatist who spoke in concrete terms and was not hampered by an
appeal to scriptures. He was much more concerned with inspiration
and the words of the living prophets than Pratt. Pratt rejected Young's
Adam-God teaching as irrational, not in harmony with the scriptures,
and not in accordance with Joseph Smith's teachings, whereas Young
criticized Pratt's emphasis on the characteristics of godliness, such
as divine omniscience. Young believed that God continued to progress
in knowledge; Pratt did not. In January 1860, Young called the Twelve
Apostles together to consider Pratt's doctrines.

Initially, Pratt refused to recant, but after a series of interviews
and meetings throughout the next several months he relented. However, tensions surfaced again five years later, in 1865, because Pratt
had published the reminiscences of Joseph Smith's mother in 1853,

---

[9] Walter Gibson attempted to take over the church in Hawaii after missionaries
were recalled. At that time, church records listed approximately 4,000 members, in
name at least, who were struggling to survive in the absence of the missionaries.
Gibson organized the new members, assumed the presidency of the Hawaiian Mission, and resolved to purchase all the government lands on the island of Lanai. Not
having the necessary means, he proceeded to organize a church independent of the
church in Utah. He created a quorum of twelve apostles, high priests, seventies, and
bishops, and sold these offices to the natives. Even women received from his hand
the honor of priestess. He sent missionaries to other islands and gathered more natives
to Lanai. Eventually, however, Gibson was excommunicated, and Utah apostle Joseph
F. Smith assumed charge of church affairs. Gibson went on to become an important
man in Hawaiian history, becoming prime minister and helping to develop the idea
of Hawaii for Hawaiians.

which Young felt contained serious error. After the First Presidency issued an official proclamation denouncing Pratt's doctrinal speculations and his edition of the Smith history, Pratt wrote to Young on 1 July 1868:

> I have greatly sinned against you . . . Hereafter, through the grace of God assisting me, I am determined to be one with you, and never be found opposing anything that comes through the legitimate order of the Priesthood, knowing that it is perfectly right for me to humbly submit, in all matter of doctrine and principle, my judgment to those whose right it is by divine appointment, to receive revelations and guide the Church.

Although neither Pratt nor Young altered his views significantly, open disagreement between them subsided. Ironically, some of Pratt's speculations, particularly his rejection of the Adam-God theory and his views on God's omniscience, have since come to dominate contemporary Mormon theology, whereas several of Young's theories have been repudiated by twentieth-century church leaders.

YOUNG	ORSON PRATT
LITTLE EDUCATION	ALOT OF EDUCTION
PRAGMATIST	INTELLECTUAL
ADAM—GOD - PRO	ANTI-ADAM GOD
GOD. PROGRESS IN KNOWLEDGE	GOD DIDN'T PROGRESS— HAS IT ALL
FELT SERIOUS ERROR——→	PRINTED J.S. HISTORY

287

17.
The Civil
War Years

Abraham Lincoln's election as U.S. president in November 1860 was the culminating event leading to secession and the Civil War. Although Lincoln was moderate on slavery and generous toward the South, he represented a party with a membership located almost entirely in the north. Unfortunately, the new president did not take office until 4 March 1861, and in the meantime the nation drifted without strong leadership.

The Mormons were interested in and concerned about the success of the Republican party. As early as 19 November 1860, Brigham Young commented on Lincoln's election and quipped that some Democrats were moving to Utah, where they believed their property would be safer. A month later, on 20 December, the same day that South Carolina seceded from the Union, Young revealed his attitude in a letter to William H. Hooper, Utah's representative in Congress. He wrote, "While the waves of commotion are breaking near the whole country, Utah in her rocky fortress is biding her time to step in and rescue the constitution and aid all lovers of freedom in sustaining such laws as will secure justice and rights to all irrespective of creed or party."

South Carolina's action, once it became known in Utah, was seen as fulfillment of a 25 December 1832 prophecy by Joseph Smith, which read, in part: "Behold the southern states shall be divided against the northern states and the southern states will call on other nations even the nation of Great Britain as it is called and they shall also call upon other nations in order to defend themselves against other nations and then war shall be poured out upon all nations."[1] Mormons also expected that this war would lead to the destruction of all nations and to the Second Coming. Although the Civil War did not break out until 9 April 1861, the addresses in the annual church General Conference during the first week in April were concerned with secession. Young said,

> The whole government is gone; it is as weak as water. I heard Joseph Smith say nearly thirty years ago they shall have mobbings to their hearts content if they do not redress the wrongs of the Latter-day Saints. Mobs will not decrease but increase until the whole government becomes a mob, and eventually it will be state against state, city against city, and neighborhood against neighborhood; Methodist against Methodist and so on, and those who will not take up the sword against their neighbors must flee to Zion.

Heber C. Kimball affirmed, "We shall never secede from the Constitution of the United States. . . . The South will secede from the North and the North will secede from us and God will make his people free as fast as we are able to bear it. They send their poor, miserable creatures here to rule us. But the day is not far distant when we will be ruled by the men whom God almighty appoints."

A few months later, John Taylor, speaking at a 4th of July celebration, set the tone of Mormon attitudes toward the conflict:

> We have been banished from the pale of what is termed civilization and forced to make a home in the desert place. Shall we join the North to fight against the South? No. Shall we join the South against the North? As emphatically, No. Why? They have both, as before shown, brought it upon themselves, and we have had no hand in the matter. Whigs, Democrats, Americans, and Republicans have all in turn endeavored to stain their hands in innocent blood and whatever others may do we cannot conscientiously help to wear down the fabric we are sworn to uphold. We know no South, no North, no East, no West; we abide strictly and positively by the constitution and cannot by the intrigues or sophism of either party be cajoled into any other attitude.

---

[1] This prophecy, not published until 1851, was made when South Carolina, dissatisfied with the tariff bill passed by Congress, announced that it would nullify the act. President Andrew Jackson responded by threatening "to hang every man in South Carolina" to enforce the law. However, both South Carolina and Jackson backed down and solved the problem by compromise. Recalling the prophecy in 1843, Smith said, "I prophesied in the name of the Lord God that the commencement of the difficulties which will cause much bloodshed previous to the coming of the Son of Man, will be in South Carolina. It may probably arise through the slave question."

Mormon leaders consistently expressed their feelings that the war had been brought on by the wickedness of the United States, which had rejected Mormonism and permitted the death of the prophet of God and his servants. Because no effort had been made to punish the guilty or to prevent recurrences, the Mormons saw no reason to wonder at secession and dismemberment of such a union. Although the waste of lives was lamentable, a war between the states would avenge the death of Joseph Smith.

The Saints seemed especially gratified that Jackson County was a war zone and that Missouri would suffer the penalty of its cruelties to the Mormons. Besides avenging the blood of the innocent, the Lord would also prepare the way before his coming, which Mormons believed would occur in Jackson County, Missouri. In a letter to Amasa Lyman, William Clayton wrote that such a spirit seemed to operate on Brigham Young's mind: "All Latter-day Saints will not stay here [in Utah] forever. He [Young] talks much and frequently about Jackson County, Missouri."[2]

An interesting summary of the church's teachings in regard to the Civil War and the federal government was written by territorial governor Stephen S. Harding, who arrived in Utah on 7 July 1862. After only six weeks, he wrote a letter to his superiors in Washington, D.C., describing the preaching he had heard in the Tabernacle and elsewhere:

A . . . most important inquiry about these people is this—are they loyal to the government of the United States? I am compelled to answer in the negative and will state some of my reasons which determine my judgment.

In the first place Brigham Young and other preachers are constantly inculcating in the minds of the crowded audiences who sit beneath their teachings every Sabbath that the United States is of no consequence, that it lies in ruins, and that the prophecy of Joseph Smith is being fulfilled to the letter. According to the prophecy, the United States as a nation is to be destroyed. That the Gentiles, as they call all persons outside of their church, will continue to fight with each other until they perish and then the Saints are to step in and quietly enjoy the possession of the land and also what is left of the ruined cities and desolated places. And that Zion is to be built up, not only in the valleys and the mountains but the great center of their power and glory is to be in Missouri where

---

[2] Young was so enthused about returning to Missouri that he prophesied in 1862 that the Saints would go back to Jackson County within the next seven years and proposed in 1863 that missionaries be sent there.

the Saints under the lead of their prophet were expelled many years ago.

Harding mentioned that the Mormons seemed to delight in the fact that the Indians would also be able to benefit after the Gentiles had been cut off.

Harding reported that he had sat in the bowery Sabbath after Sabbath, listening to such declarations, and had seen the Saints wink and chuckle when news of a disaster reached them. "In all the meetings that I have attended," he wrote, "not one word, not one prayer, has been uttered or offered up for the saving of our cause and for the restoration of peace, but on the contrary the God of the Saints has been implored to bring swift destruction on all nations, peoples, and institutions that stand in the way of the triumph of this people." Just two weeks earlier, Harding had heard Heber C. Kimball claim that he was a prophet of the living God and say, "The government of the United States is dead, thank God, dead. It is not worth the head of a pin." Kimball reportedly continued that the worst had not yet happened, that those Gentiles left after the war would be destroyed by pestilence, famine and earthquake, "to which infernal sentiment," Harding wrote, "the crowded benches around me sent up a hearty Amen."

According to Harding, Brigham Young himself taught followers that the governments of the earth were false and should be overthrown, that God had only delegated to the priesthood the right to set up a government. God would appoint a ruler, and all persons who otherwise pretended to have authority to govern were usurpers. Young was said to have asserted that although the Constitution of the United States was a revelation, it had fulfilled its purpose—the formation of a government so that the Mormon church could be organized. According to Young, slavery had nothing to do with the present disturbances, which were in consequence of the persecution the Saints had suffered at the hands of the American people.

Despite such attitudes, Mormon leaders remained loyal to the federal government, perhaps because of the presence of U.S. troops. Upon completion of the telegraph in October 1861, Young sent the first message over the line to J. H. Wade, president of the Pacific Telegraph Company in Cleveland, Ohio, offering congratulations and stating that "Utah has not seceded but is firm for the Constitution and laws of our once happy country." And when the acting governor, Frank Fuller, requested Lieutenant General Daniel H. Wells,

292

commander of Utah's territorial militia, to supply a force of twenty mounted men for thirty days to protect the Overland Trail, the volunteers were on their way the very next day under the command of Robert T. Burton. Young made their task easier when he said, "This I promise you as a servant of the Lord that not one of you shall fall by the hand of an enemy."

The Mormon troops reached Independence Rock twenty days after leaving home. Here they joined Colonel William O. Collins, the acting divisional commander of the Upper Missouri and Platte River districts of the federal forces and became a part of the regular army of the United States. Captain Lot Smith and his company, which had previously hindered the progress of Johnston's Army, were now assigned duty near the Pioneer Crossing of the North Platte River to protect mail and telegraph lines from Fort Bridger to the Sierra Nevada mountains. On 24 June, Smith wrote to Brigham Young from Independence Rock:

> I had an interview with Brigadier General [James] Craig who has just arrived by stage at this point. He expressed himself as much pleased with our promptness in responding to the call of the Federal government and the exertions we have made in overcoming speedily the obstacles on the road to reach this point and spoke well of our people generally. He stated that he had telegraphed President Lincoln to this effect and intended writing him in greater length by mail. . . . He also remarked that the Utah Cavalry were the most efficient troops he had in the service and he proposed to recommend that our service be extended an additional 90 days.

However, this assignment did not materialize because another contingent of the U.S. Army under Colonel Patrick E. Connor arrived from the west to take the place of the Mormon troops.

With the outbreak of the war, Connor enlisted in the Union Army and was appointed colonel of the third California Volunteer Infantry and ordered to Utah to protect the Overland Mail Route. Connor hurried to Salt Lake City on 9 September 1862, where he met with Governor Harding and other federal officials. His 14 September report to the commanding general in San Francisco was extremely critical of Mormon society:

> It would be impossible for me to describe what I saw and heard in Salt Lake. So as to make you realize the enormity of Mormonism suffice it that I found them a community of traitors, murderers, fanatics, and whores. The people publicly rejoice at the reverse to our arms and thank

God that the American government is gone as they term it, while their prophet and bishops preach treason from the pulpit. Federal officers are entirely powerless and talk in whispers for fear of being overheard by Brigham's spies. Brigham Young rules with despotic sway and death by assassination is the penalty of disobedience to his command.

He also discussed the location of the fort:

I found another location which I like better than Fort Crittenden for various reasons. It commands the city and a thousand troops would be more efficient than three thousand on the other side of the Jordan. If the general decides that I shall locate there I intend to quietly entrench my position and then say to the Saints of Utah: "enough of your treason." But if it was intended that I shall merely protect the Overland Mail and permit Mormons to act and utter treason than I had as well locate at Crittenden. The federal officials desire and beg that I locate near the city. The governor especially is very urgent in the matter.

Connor succeeded in convincing General Crum that he should establish his troops on the high bench overlooking Salt Lake City where he could have a commanding position, with guns aimed directly at the home of Brigham Young, if he wished. Because rumors had reached Connor that his troops might meet with resistance, he entered the valley with a war-like demonstration. Stopping only to pay military respects to Governor Harding, Connor located his troops on the hillside overlooking the Mormon capital, which he named Camp Douglas. Brigham Young's reaction was decidedly bitter:

We have done everything that has been required us. Can there be anything reasonable and constitutional be asked that we would not perform? No. But if the government of the United States should now ask for a battalion of men to fight in the present battlefields of the nation while there is a camp of soldiers from abroad located within the corporate limits of this city I would not ask one man to go. I would see them in hell first.

Young saw no need to send the California volunteers to Utah, especially under such a prejudiced leader as Connor. But leaders in Washington could only look at the record, which included Mormon expressions of disloyalty, resistance to the army in 1857-58, unwillingness to furnish troops to the Civil War, and constant preaching of millennial disasters. Washington found it difficult to trust such people to guard the Overland Mail and agreed that the Mormons needed to be guarded. Thus Connor and his troops were established at Camp

Douglas with one eye on the Overland Mail and the other on the Mormons.[3]

The following year, on 9 July 1864, under the pretext that Mormons were depreciating the national currency in favor of the gold standard, Connor appointed Captain Charles Hempstead as Provost Marshal of Salt Lake City. Connor detailed a company of the second California calvary as provost guards and, as if waging war, quartered them on South Temple street across from the entrance to the Tabernacle. Mormons deeply resented this action and referred to it as an outrage upon the feelings of the citizens and petitioned the governor for the removal of the offending unit. Connor reported to superiors that he was simply preparing to resist any attack and that the Mormons, knowing the city was now at the mercy of his guns, were quieting down already although continuing military drills.

ARMY ACROSS ST FROM TAB.

Brigham Young was in Provo when the provost guard was established in downtown Salt Lake City. Rumor spread rapidly that it was an attempt to arrest him by military force. He left for Salt Lake City the next day, escorted by a mounted guard of 200 men. This guard swelled to 500 upon reaching Salt Lake City. Later 5,000 men assembled for any required defensive action. Major General Irving McDowell, the department commander in San Francisco, reminded Connor that his assignment was to guard the mail route not to solve territorial problems and ordered the provost guard removed from the city. He warned Connor against risking war with the Mormons, since such a development would weaken troop strength.

The provost guard incident marked the climax of Mormon-Gentile hostility during the Civil War. Successive northern victories pointed to the defeat of the secessionist cause. Mormon attitudes toward the war were changing. Leaders no longer applauded the war and even seemed to question the idea that it was God's punishment. They began to recognize that the Millennium was not imminent and that the government was not going to collapse. They still predicted the ultimate fulfillment of prophecies, but, as Wilford Woodruff admitted, ''The end is not yet.''

---

[3] In 1863 an early morning salute would be fired at Fort Douglas on receipt of information that Connor had been promoted to the rank of brigadier general because of his victory over the Northern Shoshone. Believing that danger threatened, the Mormons would sound an alarm—perhaps an attempt was being made to seize Brigham Young. A thousand or more Mormon minute men would quickly assemble to protect the city. Such would be the extent of the distrust and lack of communication between the fort and the city over the next decade.

In October 1863 General Conference, Brigham Young estimated that "perhaps one million men had gone to the silent grave in this useless war in a little over two years." Young's use of the term "useless" seems to connote a different attitude than what he had earlier expressed. John Taylor added, "We hear statement after statement, testimony after testimony of raping, murders, burning, desolation, bloodshed, starvation and so on until the recital has become sickening to hear." By 1864 Young even lamented the conditions in Jackson County:

> We inquired by friends who come here in the immigration how it is back there when they came. They said you can ride all day in some places but recently inhabited and not see any inhabitants, any plowing, sowing, any planting. He may ride through the large districts of the country and see one vast desolation. A gentleman said here that one hundred families were burned alive in their own houses in the county of Jackson, Missouri. Whether this is true or not it is not for me to say, but the thought of it is painful.

Such sentiments reflect the humanity of the Mormon leaders in face of the reality of an overwhelming national tragedy.

Though unrelated to the Civil War, the Morrisite Affair, which led to more bitterness and misunderstanding between the Mormons and federal officials, occurred during this period, as well. Several hundred church members, who rejected Brigham Young's leadership, chose to follow Joseph Morris,[4] who announced that God had called him to be the prophet, seer, and revelator for the Mormon church. According to Morris, Brigham Young should attend only to the temporal affairs of the kingdom. Young refused to dignify Morris's proposal for a dual presidency and apparently regarded Morris as demented.

By 1859, Morris had claimed a second revelation which gave him the full keys of the kingdom. Other revelations followed in 1860 and later. These experiences led Morris to believe that the Mormon church was in a state of apostasy. Morris specifically identified Young's counselor, George A. Smith, as one of Lucifer's fallen angels who

---

[4] Joseph Morris joined Mormonism in England in 1847 at the age of twenty-three. Arriving in the United States, he stayed at St. Louis for two years, then served for a time as president of the Mormon branch in Pittsburgh before coming to Salt Lake in 1853. Three unsuccessful marriages by 1857 embittered him against local leaders and the frenzy of the Mormon Reformation gave him the opportunity to denounce the evils he saw around him.

was "rushing the church headlong to destruction." Morris blamed Smith for the Mountain Meadow Massacre, among other things.

Morris announced that he was the seventh angel spoken of by John the Revelator, sent by Jesus Christ to preside over the church and prepare for the Second Coming. Working as a farm laborer in the little community of Slaterville, near Ogden, in 1860, Morris converted his employer, who bore witness that the spirit had told him Morris was a prophet of God.[5] Others were converted. By the fall of 1860, thirty-one Mormons had been excommunicated for following the self-proclaimed prophet. Forced to leave Slaterville, Morris happened to meet John Cook of South Weber, who invited him to his home. When Cook's brother, Richard Cook, bishop of South Weber (also known as Kingston Fort), converted, church officials dispatched apostles John Taylor and Wilford Woodruff to investigate the situation.

The two apostles, accompanied by the Ogden stake presidency, convened a meeting in a little adobe schoolhouse on 11 February 1861. In a dramatic confrontation, Cook asserted his belief in Morris's prophetic calling and Morris announced that he was the seventh angel and held the keys of the kingdom and that all would soon acknowledge his authority. Taylor and Woodruff asked all who believed in Morris to make it known. Morris and Cook, as well as the nine men and seven women who responded, were promptly excommunicated.

Undaunted, Morris announced the organization of the "Church of Jesus Christ of Saints of the Most High" on 6 April 1861. Richard Cook was named first counselor and John Banks,[6] formerly assistant presiding bishop of the Mormon church, was second counselor. A quorum of twelve apostles was also chosen. Within a week, the new church claimed fifty-three members, which grew to 200 during the first three months. A little over a year later, Morris's following had increased to almost one thousand, only about one-half of which were baptized.

The principal attraction of Morris's teachings was his declaration of the imminence of the Millennium. Asserting that Christ would

---

[5] It was rumored that some church members in Slaterville were experimenting with spiritualism and were open to new religious experiences.

[6] John Banks had been a person of considerable promise and importance in the Mormon church. One of the first converts to Mormonism in England, he was an intelligent, gifted speaker. He was sustained as assistant presiding bishop in 1851 but released in 1853 to fill a two-year mission to Ohio. Angered when he was not re-appointed to the presiding bishopric after his mission, he attacked Brigham Young physically and was excommunicated for unchristianlike conduct. He was rebaptized a few days later but was excommunicated again a year later on 23 December 1859 and then became involved in the Morrisite movement.

297

soon return, Morris promised followers that they would own all of the property now held by the Mormons. On 30 December 1862, Morris announced a revelation calling on his followers to comply with the Law of Consecration immediately, promising that Christ's coming would follow such compliance. Most of the members complied, but some soon became dissatisfied and tried to reclaim their property. These dissident members were imprisoned within Kingston Fort, the Morrisite stronghold. When word reached territorial authorities that people were being held against their will, a writ of habeas corpus was obtained from territorial chief justice John F. Kinney and taken to Kingston Fort by Deputy U.S. Marshal Judson Stoddard. Morrisite leaders refused to recognize this writ and a similar one issued three weeks later. Kinney then requested that the territorial militia be activated as a posse comitatus to secure release of the prisoners.

Fearing armed resistance, a posse of 500 men led by Deputy Marshal Robert T. Burton surrounded the Morrisite fortress on 13 June. By this time the posse had increased to approximately one thousand men armed with a variety of weapons, including a small cannon. Morris refused to surrender and instead assured followers that Christ was testing their faith and would stop their enemies at the right time. The posse fired a warning cannon shot which accidentally fell into the assembled congregation, killing two women and shattering the lower jaw of a third. This led to armed resistance and a three-day seige. When it became clear that Christ would not rescue the beleaguered Morrisites, they hoisted a flag of surrender and permitted Burton and a contingent of soldiers to enter the fort. Apparently Morris refused to surrender to Burton's custody and gun-play ensued, leaving Morris and two women dead and John Banks mortally wounded. Ninety-nine men were taken prisoner and marched to Salt Lake City. Months later seven were convicted of second-degree murder in conjunction with the deaths of two posse members, and sixty-seven others were fined $100 each.

Governor Harding, believing that the affair was based on Mormon anger, pardoned all of the Morrisites and requested Connor to protect them. Most of the Morrisites chose to leave Utah and relocate near Soda Springs, Idaho, where Connor helped them settle.

For non-Mormons the Morrisite Affair was another sign that the Mormons were not ready for self-government. If they could not tolerate defection from their own fold, they could not be trusted to administer justice to all citizens regardless of their faith. C. LeRoy Anderson, a historian of the Morrisite movement, has asserted that if the Saints had "shown more compassion and tolerance for those they considered duped, misguided and even weak-minded, they would have demonstrated in a most convincing way that they were dedicated, not only to even-handed justice, but to mercy as well."

Loyal church members must have wondered what type of people could be led from the fold by such a man as Morris. Was millennialism so important in the conversion process in the early church? And was Brigham Young's practical approach so concerned with material things that church members longed for spiritual experiences? Almost half of the baptized Morrisites bore Scandinavian names. Perhaps language difficulties and the tendency of the English-speaking Saints to belittle the Scandinavians was a factor. Then, too, the call to abandon their homes and farms as Johnston's Army approached in the summer of 1858 had exacerbated their poverty and left many of the members dissatisfied with church leadership. This incident was a serious loss for the church, considering that 1,000 members renounced Brigham Young's leadership and only 40,000 Mormons lived within the region.

Although the Morrisite Affair was disconcerting and annoying, Mormon leaders thought that the Civil War provided an ideal opportunity to gain admission into the Union. Utah territorial delegate William Hooper reminded Congress that Utah was showing its loyalty by trying to get into the Union while others were trying to get out, "notwithstanding our grievances which are far greater than any of those of the seceding states." Writing to LDS official George Q. Cannon, Hooper said, "I consider we can redress our grievances better in the Union than out of it. At least we'll give our worthy Uncle an opportunity of grafting us into his family. And if he doesn't want us we must carve out our own future."

On 6 January 1862, the people of Salt Lake City met in a mass meeting to choose delegates for a constitutional convention. They passed resolutions pointing out past difficulties due to strangers who were not interested in making a home in the territory. These men were not acquainted with the tastes and requirements of the Mormon people and often were disposed to sin, thus producing serious abuses and sanctioning crimes by letting the guilty go unpunished.

After a two-day recess, the convention reconvened on 22 January, at which time a constitution for the State of Deseret was unanimously adopted. This instrument of government was essentially the same as the proposed constitution of 1856 with only slight amendments. On the following day the delegates nominated Brigham Young as governor, Heber C. Kimball as lieutenant governor, and John M.

Bernhisel as representative to Congress. A general election held on 3 March ratified these nominations and designated William H. Hooper and George Q. Cannon to be U.S. senators. The constitution, with a memorial seeking statehood, was presented to Congress on 9 June. It remained in the Committee on Territories until 22 December when committee members decided not to pursue the territory's petition.

The failure to secure admission did not dissolve the State of Deseret as far as the Mormons were concerned. It functioned as a ghost government behind the territorial administration, not only during the war period but for several years afterward. When asked why the unofficial legislative sessions were held, Brigham Young explained that it was "in order that the machinery of government would be ready to function when Congress should recognize the state organization. Privately, the men have thus thought of themselves as the council of the Kingdom of God ready to assume greater political responsibility when the heavenly king might see fit to use them." Once again the idea of the Millennium and its imminence played an important role in the life of the Mormon people.

Notwithstanding their need for more states and the assertion by church leaders that they loved the Constitution and were loyal to the Union, Congress was in no mood to admit them. Justin Morrill of Vermont had introduced an anti-bigamy law in the House of Representatives in the spring of 1860. Morrill's bill was passed by the House and received by the Senate but was left untouched when the 36th Congress adjourned just before the Civil War in March 1861. When the 37th Congress convened, and the southern states were not represented, the Republicans had a clear majority. On 8 April 1862, Morrill again introduced his bill to punish and prevent the practice of polygamy. The bill annulled the Utah Legislative Act of 1851, which incorporated the Mormon church and gave it the right to regulate marriage. Morrill's bill also provided that no religious body in the territories should hold real estate of value in excess of $50,000. The Morrill Bill passed the Senate by a vote of 37 to 2, and Abraham Lincoln signed it into law on 8 July 1862.

Governor Harding had arrived in Utah on 7 July 1862, one day before Lincoln signed the anti-bigamy law. He promised to represent Lincoln's policy of pouring oil on troubled waters by delivering a brilliant 24th of July speech. He commended the Mormons for their achievements and promised cooperation and non-interference with the right of conscience in religious worship. He praised the transformation of the desert as a miracle of labor, stating that "wonderful

300

progress had been made by a wonderful people." His address radiated a spirit of appreciation and kindliness.

Harding at this point seemed relatively unaware of the gossip, rumors, accusations, and bitterness that pervaded the Utah atmosphere, although he must have known of the unpopularity of earlier territorial officials. But the Morrisite tragedy would influence Harding profoundly. Although it climaxed a month before his arrival, he was confronted with its aftermath. Connor, with his California volunteers, came to Utah on 9 September 1862 and influenced the governor's attitude toward the Mormons.

By the time Harding delivered his message to the territorial legislature in December, he was sharply critical of the institutions and practices of the Utahns. Legislators listened with indignation and refused to publish the speech. Most offensive was the governor's reference to the practice of polygamy. Anomalies in the moral world, he pointed out, cannot long endure side by side. Either the laws and opinions of the general community must become subordinate to Mormon customs and opinions or the Mormons must yield to general customs. "The conflict is irrepressible," he concluded. He advised conformity with the act of Congress concerning the practice of polygamy, despite prevailing local opinion that the statute was unconstitutional. Furthermore he questioned the loyalty of the people to the national government and otherwise found fault with the conduct of local officials.

In letters written to his superiors in Washington, on 30 August and on 3 September, Harding criticized Mormon institutions and attitudes and questioned the wisdom of giving statehood to Utah in view of the attitudes of the people and their leaders towards the federal government. Harding's letters probably had a good deal to do with the fact that Congress refused to consider statehood for the State of Deseret when they voted in December.

On 3 February 1863, Harding sent a long communication to secretary of state William H. Seward, denouncing the Mormons and joining with judges Charles B. Waite and Thomas J. Drake in a covert attempt to have Congress deprive Utah's citizens of local judiciary and military powers. The Mormons, upon learning of these political schemes, held a mass meeting on 3 March to condemn the action and adopt resolutions asking for the resignation of the offending federal officials. When the officials refused to resign, the Mormons sent a petition to Lincoln asking him to remove Harding and associate justices Waite and Drake and to appoint other officials in their place. A counter petition circulated at Fort Douglas, which supported the retention of Harding and the judges, also reached Lincoln. But in harmony with his policy of keeping peace with the Mormons, Lincoln removed Harding. To placate the Gentiles, he also removed Judge Kinney and Secretary Fuller, who were reported to be too friendly to the Saints. Tension mounted when rumors spread that Connor's forces planned to arrest Brigham Young on charges of polygamy and take him to the states for trial. The local militia was armed against such a move. Armed guards were stationed around Young's home, and signals were adopted by which armed men could be quickly assembled. In response to one such signal, a thousand men appeared within half an hour and another thousand soon thereafter.

Harding left the territory on 11 June. In his successor, James Duane Doty, Lincoln found a man to represent his policy in relation to the Mormons. Doty had been serving as Indian superintendent of the territory and had won the respect of Gentiles and Mormons alike. Impatient with narrow partisanship, he had sought to bring opposing forces together. His experience and temperament qualified him well for that difficult task.

While serving as superintendent of Indian Affairs, Doty had pleaded for more government help for the Indians in Utah, but Washington officials, more concerned with the Civil War than Indian needs, failed to send supplies. Instead they encouraged him to negotiate treaties to end hostilities. He was aided in these negotiations by the vigorous action of Connor's troops against the Shoshone in the Battle of Bear River in January 1863. In what is often described as a massacre, the soldiers killed at least 224 Indians (according to the official report) and perhaps as many as 300, including almost 90 women and children. In retaliation, Indians attacked Mormon colonies in Cache Valley. But by July, Doty was able to negotiate a treaty with the Eastern Shoshone at Fort Bridger and the Northwestern Shoshone at Box Elder. Two other treaties were negotiated by Doty's successor, I. H. Irish: one with the Western Shoshone in Ruby Valley, Nevada, the other with the Shoshone-Goshute in Tooele Valley. Both treaties asked for safe passage for military forces and the right to establish military posts, wagon roads, and mail, telegraph and railroad routes as well as the right to build and maintain ferries on streams in the area. In return, the government promised to hold the reservation lands in perpetuity and provide regular cash grants for a specific number of years. Unfortunately for the Indians, ratification of the treaties by the U.S. Senate usually took several years and were sometimes refused, leaving the tribes without lands or government benefits.

A case in point was the treaty with the Utes negotiated by I. H. Irish and signed at Spanish Fork in June 1865 in the presence of Brigham Young. The Utes agreed to move to the newly created Uintah Reservation and to give up all lands outside of the reservation in return for which government negotiators promised $25,000 a year for the next ten years; $20,000 a year for the following twenty years; and $15,000 a year for the ensuing thirty years. The agents also agreed to sell the established Indian farms and to provide schools for the reservation. The Utes moved to the reservation, but when the treaty was rejected by the U.S. Senate four years later, they were left without their land and apparently without legal claim against the government.[7]

Despite the Mormon belief that the Indians were Israelites with an important millennial role to play, and notwithstanding efforts to educate Indians to the ways of civilization and to convert them to Mormonism, the gap between Mormon needs and the Indian view of life was too great to bridge in the pioneer period. By 1869 the Indians were reduced in numbers and property and either resettled on undesirable reservation lands or existed in small groups on the outskirts of Mormon communities, living off the charity of Mormon colonists.

Governor Doty helped to negotiate the treaties but died before they were violated and nullified. He lived long enough, however, to help bring the antagonistic factions in Utah together in a tenuous unity during the last months of the Civil War.

Using the re-election of Lincoln as a common cause for celebration, Doty was able to bring Mormons and Gentiles together in a mile-long parade with participants from both the Nauvoo Legion (or territorial militia) and the California volunteers. Later, at a banquet given by the city council to the officers of Camp Douglas, Salt Lake mayor Abraham Smoot toasted the health of President Lincoln and the success of the Union armies. Captain Charles Hempstead

---

[7] Such treatment encouraged a minor Ute leader named Black Hawk to retaliate against the Mormons who had settled in their territory. Beginning with about 30 raiders in 1865, Black Hawk's followers rose to around 300 by the winter of 1866-67, and their raids kept the people of central and southern Utah on alert for three years. During this time approximately 25 settlements were abandoned. By the time peace negotiations had been settled in the summer of 1868, an estimated 80 Indians and 75 whites had lost their lives as a result of the conflict. The cost in economic terms was approximately $1.5 million, which the Mormons essentially bore since no government funds were received for the costs of the military nor for losses sustained as a result of government policies.

303

responded to the health of the mayor and city officials. At the conclusion of the festivities, the citizens of Salt Lake City witnessed a promising spectacle as the Nauvoo Legion escorted the California volunteers back to Camp Douglas. This portended a better future, and even Connor was led to propose during the parade that the *Union Vedette*, an anti-Mormon newspaper he had established at Camp Douglas, had served its purpose and should be discontinued. A little over a month later, when Lincoln was assassinated, Mormons and Gentiles met together in the Tabernacle to hear the virtues and accomplishments of the man who had preserved the Union through four years of civil strife. The Tabernacle was more than crowded, the scene impressive and solemn, and all present shared the deep sorrow of the occasion.

Two months later Governor Doty died and was mourned by the citizens of Utah. Schuyler Colfax, speaker of the U.S. House of Representatives, estimated that Doty was a most "judicious executive and the best this territory ever had, who performed his delicate and responsible duties with firmness and yet with discretion." This statement may have belittled Brigham Young's service, but most would no doubt agree that Doty had done an excellent job. Unfortunately, this brief period of friendliness was only the calm before the storm, for attitudes and events were developing both inside and outside the church that would threaten the continued growth of the Mormon kingdom and lead to defensive measures that would separate Mormons from the rest of the country to a greater degree than ever before.

18.
The Kingdom Threatened

The Mormon kingdom survived the Saints' first precarious years in the Great Basin and, later, the invasion by the U.S. Army in 1857-58. But during the years following the Civil War, four new developments threatened to disrupt Mormon programs in the Rocky Mountains. For political and economic reasons, the expanding mining industry challenged the unity and dominance of the church, while the transcontinental railroad threatened isolation and home industry.

In addition, a radical Republican Congress, having rid the nation of one the "twin relics of barbarism," slavery, now seemed determined to rid the country of polygamy. Pursuing this objective, Congress attempted to pass laws to end church political control. Mormon responses to these developments led to serious internal dissension. A group of Mormon intellectuals and businessmen challenged the concept of a temporal kingdom of God and advocated that the church confine itself to spiritual affairs. Labeled the "New Movement" or "Godbeites," this groundswell failed to attract large numbers of followers but served as a foreshadowing of future attitudes and developments.

[handwritten margin note: GODBEITE PRECURSORS TO FUTURE EVENTS]

The church could have acquired wealth through mining. Mormon leaders were in a position to capitalize on discoveries in the gold fields of California, but instead the church encouraged members in California to leave the fields and gather to the Great Basin (see chap. 3). Later, church leaders learned of the mineral wealth in the mountains that surrounded the Salt Lake Valley.

305

As early as 1848, Thomas and Sanford Bingham, who grazed livestock in Bingham Canyon, had found outcroppings of ore which they believed contained precious metals. This discovery occurred at a time when Brigham Young and other leaders were trying to discourage people from going to the California gold fields. Not surprisingly, Young discouraged the Bingham brothers from mining and asked them to keep the discovery a secret. This policy was temporarily effective, and Mormons did not engage in mining of precious metals until the mid-1860s.

Still Young did not oppose mining as such. He recognized the need for metals and minerals such as coal, iron, salt, lead, and sulphur, all of which were sought after and used during the 1850s and 1860s. However, Utah mining moved into a new phase on the afternoon of 17 September 1863 when a group of Mormon boys, dragging logs in Bingham Canyon, on the west side of the Salt Lake Valley, uncovered argentiferous galena, or silver. This group included George and Alex Ogilvie, John Egbert, and Henry Beckstead. The canyon was being used by George Ogilvie, Bishop Archibald Gardner, and units of the California Volunteers as a grazing area. Ogilvie identified the ore and took a sample of it to Colonel Patrick Connor who had it assayed. Connor had been interested in mining in California and encouraged Ogilvie to locate the mine and to join him in organizing a company which became known as the Jordan Silver Mining Company. On the same day, a party of men and women under the leadership of Captain Arthur Heitz, who were enjoying a picnic and grouse hunt in the canyon, conducted a further search. One member of the party, the wife of camp surgeon Robert K. Reed, located a second vein contiguous to the Jordan claim. A second notice was made, this one crediting Mrs. Reed with the discoverer's share. A third claim, the Vedette, was also filed on 18 September 1863.

Following the discovery and the staking of claims, the parties, some fifty-two persons in all, went to the Jordan Ward meeting house near Bishop Gardner's mill on the Jordan River and organized the West Mountain Quartz Mining District. Following California practice, laws for the government of the district were drawn up and approved. The boundaries of the district were defined to embrace the entire Oquirrh Mountain range. Although Mormon pioneers had previously located veins and organized mining parties, the area encompassing Bingham Canyon became the first recorded mining claim in the territory and the first mining district to be formally organized and recorded.

SILVER DISCOVERED

Connor immediately recognized that the existence of this mineral wealth might solve what he called "the Mormon Problem." Within a month after these discoveries, he wrote to his superior in San Francisco,

> Having reason to believe that the territory is full of mineral wealth, I have instructed commanders of posts and detachments to permit the men of their commands to prospect the country in the vicinity of their respective posts whenever such course would not interfere with their military duties, and to furnish every proper facility for the discovery and opening of mines of gold, silver, and other minerals. The results so far have exceeded my most sanguine expectations.

Connor's solution was to encourage a gold or silver rush to Utah, bringing thousands of non-Mormons and thus balancing the population in the territory and lessening the church's influence, especially in politics.[1] With Connor's encouragement, troops swarmed over the Bingham Canyon and adjoining areas. The Vedette claim was followed by the Galena, the Empire, the Kingston, the Julia Dean, and the Silver Hill claims. Other volunteers organized the Wasatch Mountain Mining District to include all the Wasatch Mountains from Weber Canyon to Provo. This was accomplished within two months after the initial discovery in Bingham Canyon.

Brigham Young's reaction to these developments came less than three weeks after the initial discovery in a sermon delivered during General Conference:

> Who feeds and clothes and defrays the expenses of hundreds of men who are engaged in patrolling the mountains and canyons all around us in search of gold? Who finds supplies for those who are sent here to protect the two great interests, the mail and telegraph lines across the continent, while they are employed ranging over these mountains in search of gold? And who has paid for the multitude of picks and shovels and spades and other mining tools that they have brought with them? Were they really sent here to protect the mail and the telegraph lines or to discover, if possible, rich diggings in our immediate vicinity, with a view to flood the country with just such a population as they desire to destroy,

---

[1] To publicize the Utah discoveries, Connor founded a daily newspaper called the *Union Vedette* in November 1863. In the first issue, he warned the Mormons that miners and prospectors would be provided with the fullest protection from the military in his district. "The mountains in their hidden mineral wealth," Connor wrote, "did not belong to the Mormons but were the sole property of the nation whose beneficent policy had ever been to extend the broadest privileges to her citizens and with open hand invite all to seek, prospect, and possess the wonderful riches of her widespread domain."

if possible, the identity of Mormon communities and every truth and virtue that remains?

Connor even dispatched troops as far as Raft River in southern Idaho to search for mineral outcroppings. Some were sent to southeastern Nevada, others to the Uintah Basin. He instructed them to look especially for placer mines. The soldiers discovered numerous bodies of ore throughout the territory. Even loose placer gold was discovered in Bingham in 1864. The following spring, gravel washing was initiated, and late the same year extensive load mining was conducted with profit. The value of gold production in the territory rose from virtually nothing in 1860 to $55,000 in 1865, $165,000 in 1868, and $300,000 in 1870. By the end of 1871, about $1 million in gold had been recovered from the Bingham Canyon gravels.

The search for silver was conducted in a similar way. Outcroppings and veins of silver-bearing ore were found in several locations. Rather than being abundantly located in a free condition, however, silver was found mixed with several other metals (usually lead, copper, and zinc) in either oxide or sulphide ores. Oxide and carbonate ores were located close to the surface, and the rock was already partially broken down due to oxidation. Sulphide ores, on the other hand, were located below the water table, in sulphur-bearing solutions. The mining of silver required a complementary process of milling and smelting in order to recover the metal.

The first significant find of silver lead ore was made by the volunteers in East Canyon, Tooele County. There had been legends that Treasure Hill was sacred to the Indians, who gathered there each year to hold council and to obtain metal for bullets. Attracted by these stories, volunteers located an outcropping of lead ore which became known as the Hidden Treasure Mine. Other finds were discovered in Little Cottonwood Canyon in the summer of 1864 and afterwards. Another group of volunteers, the Second Cavalry, established a camp on the western slope of the Oquirrh Range called Camp Relief and surveyed the town of Stockton, named after Connor's hometown in California. Prospecting success came quickly. In April 1864 the Rush Valley deposits were discovered by men of Company L. Early assays proved to be rich in silver, and the Rush Valley Mining District was organized on 11 June 1864. The new district embraced the western slope of the Oquirrh Range, the West Mountain District the eastern slope.

By the fall of 1865 over 500 mining claims were located in the Rush Valley District. Most of these were within two miles of Stockton, which by 1866 had forty families and 400 inhabitants. So promising were the finds that Connor invested an estimated $80,000 of his own funds in the claim and persuaded friends to advance additional sums. One result of these efforts was the erection of the Pioneer Smelting Works at Stockton in 1864. A reverberatory furnace was completed a short time later. Several other trial furnaces were built, and $100,000 worth of machinery was purchased by the Knickerbocker and Argenta Mining and Smelting Company of New York to separate gold and silver from lead.

But Connor and his Californians, whose experiences had been limited to mining and milling gold ores, found the art of smelting the Stockton ores beyond them. Moreover, charcoal was scarce and transportation rates were high. After a year they suspended their work, but their experiments proved that the ores could be reduced and smelted profitably with improved technology. All of these activities— prospecting, mining, and furnace building—were, according to Connor, executed "with great energy, my officers and men have prospected the country and succeeded in discovering rich gold- and silver-bearing rock. It is now a settled fact that the mines of Utah are equal to any west of the Missouri River and awaits only the advent of capital to develop them."

The end of the Civil War led to the disbanding of the volunteers, and army-sponsored mining in Utah ceased. The troops sought to preserve their rights by amending district bylaws to permit each locator to hold his claim indefinitely provided a specified minimum amount of work be done. This action effectively prevented the development of the Rush Valley District for some years. With the departure of the volunteers, little mining or smelting occurred in the territory until the completion of the railroad in 1869.[2]

Connor and his associates tended to ascribe their failures to Mormon opposition. President Young advised Mormon farmers and craftsmen to remain on their farms and in their shops and not aid the miners. Young thought that Connor's efforts were doomed anyway and that there was no advantage in putting time and energy into a failing enterprise. Connor himself remained in the army until April 1866, then returned to Stockton, Utah, to resume his mining and smelting ventures, intending to make Stockton a great mining center.

[2] Prior to that time, transportation was inadequate; superior opportunities existed in neighboring territories. Those trying to separate the lead and silver ores were too inexperienced to succeed.

WHY? (handwritten, left margin)

WHAT RAILRO, MEAT (handwritten, left margin)

The coming of the transcontinental railroad insured Utah's future as a mining state. Ironically, Mormons had colonized a region rich in metallic wealth yet were determined not to take control of that resource. Connor's plan to bring into Utah huge numbers of Gentiles did not materialize. Miners never threatened the Mormon advantage in the Utah territory. Nevertheless, many of those who subsequently became wealthy as a result of Utah mines would exert during the 1880s and 1890s a strong political, social, and cultural influence on the territory and state, and profitable mining would no doubt encourage Gentiles to immigrate. The railroad would thus end Mormon isolation, further threatening the church's goal of self-sufficiency. Nevertheless, Young wanted to aid Mormon immigration and to facilitate trade, and he thus helped to build the railroad. But he also tried to ensure that his people would not be overwhelmed by its coming.

When the territorial legislature was organized in 1852, one of the first measures to be considered was a memorial to the U.S. Congress petitioning that it take under advisement a bill promoting a transcontinental railroad. Several years later a mass meeting generated another petition to Congress asking that a route be approved to pass through Salt Lake City. The Mormon petition obviously had no effect on the congressional decision. The Saints were viewed as one more special interest group trying to further their own ends.

Young's association with the Union Pacific Railroad began shortly after that company was organized. When the company began selling stock to finance construction, Young became one of the initial subscribers, purchasing five shares valued at $1,000 each. Several years later in 1865, he was appointed to the board of directors.

Union Pacific officials began to survey their proposed route in 1863, and by 1864 engineers had reached the Utah territory. Division engineer Samuel B. Reed called on Young for men and supplies to assist in the survey work, which Young agreed to furnish. Reed visited Young on several occasions as work progressed, once speculating that construction through the Rocky Mountains would cost less per mile than the road built across Iowa.[3] Young's assistance with the survey netted him $4,692, which he applied to his stock subscription. Reed reported his favorable impressions of Young and his followers to associates in the East.

---

[3] Despite such enthusiasm, bringing the road through northern Utah was to involve greater sacrifice in time and money than any other section on the Union Pacific line.

In 1865, further survey work was undertaken to determine the feasibility of several alternate routes through Utah, and the Union Pacific again availed itself of Young's services. In mid-1865 the Union Pacific began laying track west of Omaha, and by early 1868 tracks were into present-day Wyoming. Company officials were certain they would reach Salt Lake City before winter. Thomas C. Durrant, vice-president of the Union Pacific, wrote to Young about the availability of men to work on the road. Young reported that men could be obtained for $1.00 to $2.25 per day, plus room and board. Several weeks later, Reed telegraphed Young to ask about obtaining oats, barley, and flour from Utah communities. Young replied that these commodities were available but that prices were high because of the demand for such items at the gold mines. After another inquiry, Young again contacted Reed to inform him that flour would be available in July.

The following month Thomas Durrant telegraphed Young asking if he would take a Union Pacific Railroad contract to grade the roadbed from the head of Echo Canyon to the Great Salt Lake. He made it clear that Young and his followers were to be given the first option for all work done near their communities if terms could be reached and called on Young to name his price.[4] Durrant required that the work be completed before winter. If his labor force permitted, Young was also requested to send a number of hands to Green River. Young did not favor sending church members so far away, preferring that they work under their own contractors, but was happy with this opportunity to add to the wealth of Zion and so made hands available.

Young asked Union Pacific officials to calculate the fairest rates for all parties and proposed to accept their estimate plus 10 percent. He asked that his contract extend west from the mouth of Echo Canyon to the southern shore of the Great Salt Lake via Salt Lake City if the southern route were chosen. If the alternate northern route were chosen, he required that he have the contract from Echo to the northern shore of the Great Salt Lake and as far west as the Union Pacific might extend itself. This was satisfactory with Union Pacific representatives Samuel B. Reed and Silas C. Moore, and a contract was drawn up and signed on 21 May 1868.

---

[4] The work was to be priced per cubic yard, according to the materials used in grading—dirt, shale, rock. Tunnel work was to be priced in the same manner according to the type of material encountered.

Still uncertain of the size of the labor force needed to meet his obligations, and not wanting to bring in Gentiles, Young immediately made preparations to augment the domestic force with new immigrants. He wrote to church representative Franklin D. Richards about the difficulties that might arise in Utah if a large number of laborers were suddenly taken out of the domestic farming and manufacturing labor pool and proposed that Richards get immigrants to the terminus of the railroad by mid-July. Young suggested that they could travel more quickly by steamer than by sailing vessel, marking a new turn in Mormon immigration. These immigrants were to be met at the end of the line by wagon trains from Utah to transport them to the valley. The Union Pacific had agreed to transport laborers, tools, and supplies to the western end of the line, so Young not only eased his financial situation by bringing in immigrants at a reduced rate but provided the necessary hands to increase his labor force, as well.

Although Young signed the contract with the Union Pacific he did not supervise the work personally but turned the project over to his sons, Joseph A., Brigham Jr., and John W., who found subcontractors to handle the masonry and grading jobs required on the road. The subcontractors were Mormon bishops or other Mormons, about a hundred in all, whose contracts ranged in length from a few hundred yards to several miles. The largest single contract was let to Joseph A. Young and Bishop John Sharp. These two men, who had organized the firm of Sharp & Young, contracted for the tunneling and rock work no one else was willing to assume. Sharp ultimately became the real leader in the promotion of railroad activities in Utah and was labeled "the railroad bishop." His major problem was that he could not find enough men for the work. With the contract period one half over and most contractors behind in their jobs, every available man had been hired. Although additional men in Utah communities could have worked on the line, Joseph Young specified that Sharp not endanger the food supply by allowing too many to leave their farms to work on the railroad.

Sharp had 1,400 men employed in Weber Canyon by mid-December 1868. Even after winter set in, the work continued, and by mid-January 1869, the group had advanced into Echo Canyon. By this time Union Pacific officials, feeling that the Mormon employees could not complete the tunnels on time, asked if the Mormons would withdraw their men in favor of railroad employees. Young agreed, but within a month Reed decided that the railroad employees were making less progress than the Mormons under Sharp and Young and asked the Mormons to resume work on the tunnels. A

312

temporary track was laid around the tunnels until they could be completed. By this means, Young's contract for the road was essentially completed by 1 March 1869. Sharp continued to work in Weber Canyon, completing the last tunnel in mid-April.

All that remained was the uniting of the Union Pacific and Central Pacific lines. Congress decided that this should take place at Promontory Summit north of the Great Salt Lake, some fifty miles west of Ogden. This was to become the official dividing point between the two lines. Festivities took place on 10 May 1869, and the last rail was laid at 11:45 a.m. A distance of 1,882 miles between San Francisco and Omaha had been spanned, linking the nation from east to west.[5]

Mormon leaders had been concerned that the railroad might bypass Salt Lake City. Two possible routes were considered: a southern route through Weber Canyon, south to Salt Lake City, then skirting the southern end of the Great Salt Lake, west across the Nevada desert; or a northern route from Weber Canyon to Ogden, then north to Promontory and the northern end of the Great Salt Lake to Humboldt Wells, Nevada, leaving Salt Lake City completely off the main line. Church officials lobbied for the southern route. Mass meetings were held, petitions were circulated, Congress was memorialized, and church writers and politicians were pressed into service. Despite these efforts, Union Pacific officials decided on the northern route because it was shorter and better supplied with timber and water.[6]

The Central Pacific, which had decided on the northern route, kept this information from the Mormons in order to secure their assistance in speeding up the construction of their line. Young urged more

---

[5] In spite of the national celebrations, Brigham Young did not attend festivities at either Promontory or Salt Lake City. The celebration conflicted with his annual trip to the southern part of the territory, and faced with a choice, Young chose the latter. Sharp was appointed to act as Young's personal representative at the driving of the last spike.

[6] General Dodge, of Union Pacific, wrote of the reaction of Mormon officials to this decision as follows:

It was our desire and the demand of all the Mormons that we should build through Salt Lake City, but we bent all our energies to find a feasible line passing through the city and around the south end of the Great Salt Lake and across the desert to Humboldt Wells, the controlling point in the line. We found the line so superior on the north of the lake that we had to adopt the route with a view of building a branch to Salt Lake City. But Brigham Young would not have this and appealed over my head to the board of directors who referred the question to the government directors who finally sustained me. Then Brigham Young gave his allegiance to the Central Pacific, hoping to bring them around the south end of the lake and force us to connect with them there. He went even so far as to deliver in the Tabernacle a great sermon denouncing me and stating the road could not be built nor run without the aid of the Mormons.

and more of his followers to take contracts for the grading of the Central Pacific line, in part, to impede the progress of the Union Pacific road west from Weber Canyon. He hoped to force UP officials to connect with Salt Lake City.

Union Pacific also chose to bypass a promising business center because of time constraints. UP officials were anxious to finish their road and to lay as much track as possible before the Central Pacific arrived. A branch line to Salt Lake City would be simple to construct. Young finally relented.

While laborers and bosses were being recruited to work on the Union Pacific contract, Leland Stanford, representing the Central Pacific, had also approached Young. He hoped the church would assume responsibility for constructing the Central Pacific road from Humboldt Wells, Nevada, to Ogden, Utah—a distance of about 200 miles. This contract was signed in the fall of 1868 in the names of Apostle Ezra T. Benson, Lorin Farr, and Chauncey W. West. Benson was the ecclesiastical leader in Cache Valley, and Farr and West were prominent church figures in Weber County. The contract was for approximately $4 million. Young's letters during the summer and fall of 1868 reflect great satisfaction at this favorable turn of events.[7]

Although the motive was profit, the actual hiring of workers was handled much the same as other church projects: workers either volunteered or were called, and each was expected to consult his bishop before leaving. The usual arrangement was for a ward or group of wards to form a company resembling the colonizing companies of previous years with a church-appointed president to look after their interests. These companies were almost invariably constrained by church standards: no swearing, no work on Sunday, no drinking, and each man was to pay a faithful tithe. In some cases, the profits on the contracts would go toward the building of a meetinghouse or some other religious purpose. Various ward companies vied with one another in the speed and excellence of their work.

---

[7] One excerpt also suggests the paternalistic view which Young took of church and community projects:

> Work on my railroad tracks are progressing rapidly. Several jobs are already completed, and nearly all of the light work would have been done 'ere [before] this had the work been staked out in time. The western company, that is Central Pacific, are wishing me to contract to grade 200 miles for them which I expect to begin as soon as the stakes are driven. These contracts give us many advantages besides furnishing money for labor to those whom the grasshoppers have left but little . . .

A major controversy developed about whether Ogden or Corinne should be the main junction of the railroads. Anticipating the problem some five months before completion of the line, Young met with property owners in the western part of Ogden and conditionally proposed to buy their property for a railroad town and depot. Church members sold him the land at less than market value, and Young in turn offered the land to Union Pacific and Central Pacific officials free of charge on the condition they locate their depot and shops there. The amazed railroad officials, who had not counted on this boon, agreed to recommend the junction of the two roads be located at Ogden rather than Corinne. Within ten years, the budding Gentile capital of Corinne was virtually a ghost town, and Ogden became the main railroad center.

Mormons had difficulty collecting on their contracts. By August 1869, the Central Pacific still owed a million dollars, and the Union Pacific even more. Central Pacific agreed to pay within the month all but $200,000 of its indebtedness, but the Union Pacific failed to make a similar concession, causing a near-panic in Salt Lake City. Laborers were destitute, and contractors were heavily in debt to the merchants and other creditors. Worry over his financial status was listed as a direct cause of the death of Apostle Ezra T. Benson. Church officials were faced with the dual task of pressing railroads to keep faith with the Mormons and of quieting their followers with assurances that everything would be done to resolve the debts.

In an attempt to obtain satisfaction from the Union Pacific, Young sent John Sharp to Boston to confer with UP officials. After an interview with Vice-President Thomas Durrant and others, Sharp wrote, "They had no flattering news for me as far as money is concerned in the settlement." They did offer him various construction materials, including iron from the surpluses on hand at Echo and elsewhere, which could be used in building the Utah Central Railroad the church was planning to construct from Ogden to Salt Lake City. By September 1869, Sharp was able to telegraph Young that the railroad was settling the indebtedness with $600,000 worth of iron and rolling stock to be forwarded as soon as possible and another $200,000 to be paid later, presumably in cash.[8]

---

[8] Young did not receive the profits on the venture some have claimed. Orson F. Whitney, a Mormon historian and church leader, uncritically repeated the assertion that Young realized a profit of about $800,000 on the Union Pacific contract alone. This would have been almost 40 percent of the gross contract receipts. Actually 10 percent of the first $1 million paid by the Union Pacific, or $100,000, is more realistic, and out of this would have come the cost of the contractor. After Young's death

The railroad unquestionably opened a new era for the church and territory. Mormon leaders went ahead with the Utah Central Railroad connecting Salt Lake with the Union Pacific, and before many years they extended the railroad beyond Salt Lake. The Utah Northern Railroad was built from Ogden to Brigham City and Logan, intentionally bypassing Corinne, and from Cache Valley to Idaho Falls and Dillon, Montana, where it could tap the trade of the mining regions around Butte and Helena. The railroad enabled Mormon immigrants to come to the Salt Lake Valley more easily and less expensively and to freight in needed supplies. Despite these benefits, the prospect of increased mining activity, the loss of isolation, and the threat to home industry led church leaders to institute programs to diminish the impact of the railroad.

Mormon leaders instituted three programs to counteract the negative effects of mining and the railroad on the Mormon kingdom. The first, a cooperative program of buying, transporting, and selling merchandise, had been anticipated earlier. The Farm Price Convention called in 1864 has been discussed in conjunction with selling goods to the California volunteers. This convention was superseded in 1865 by collective buying and marketing. Church leaders had repeatedly warned members and Gentile merchants that profiteering would prove their undoing and hinted, in the words of Heber C. Kimball, that unless merchants reduced prices, "we shall turn merchants ourselves." In August 1865, Young said,

> Why not appoint in every ward in the territory a good businessman who is filled with integrity and truth to make contact for the people of the ward and let the convention prices be the rule or not sell. Why not draw money for our grain and spend it ourselves instead of allowing those who have no interest with us to handle it for us and pocket fortunes which we shall enjoy and lay out in redeeming the earth and building up the kingdom of God in all the world. We can do this if we will.

Later, during the October conference, Young wished "the brethren in all of our settlements to buy the goods they must have and freight them with their own teams. And then let every one of the Latter-day Saints, male and female decree in their own hearts that they will buy of nobody else but their own faithful brethren who will do good

---

in 1877, the clerks and administrators going over his accounts found the profits on the railroad contract to have been about $88,000. In settling Young's estate, administrators accepted the church's proof that the contract was a church project rather than a private arrangement and placed the $88,000 to the church's credit rather than to Young's heirs.

with the money they thus obtain." This became the fundamental program of the cooperative system that developed, that the Mormons would organize themselves to do their own buying and transporting and that they would not trade with Gentiles.

While trade with Gentile merchants never completely ceased, the non-Mormon merchants were classified as either friendly or as enemies. The *Deseret News* declared in July 1866,

> We have two classes of merchants in this community. Distinctions that we venture to say cannot be found anywhere else for it is presumable that in no other community could a class of traders be found who would professedly and practically be open about [being] enemies of the people among whom they reside and from whom they draw their wealth, actively endeavoring to injure them before the nation and the world and striving to bring evil upon them. There is such a class here who have no interest in common with the people here, who hate the Mormons and are not slow to declare it. There is another class whose interest are critically and avowedly identified with the interests of the community.

Young added in December 1866 that he wanted the Saints to "build up the Kingdom of God unitedly and let our open and secret enemies alone. Let the saints spend their money with those merchants who pay their taxes and seek to build up this place and develop the country. Let our enemies alone. What? All outsiders? Not by any means. I trade with outsiders all of the time."

When twenty-three leading Gentile merchants either from fear or cunning made a public offer to sell out to the Mormons and withdraw from the territory, Young's reply was prompt and direct:

> Your withdrawal from the territory is not a matter about which we feel any anxiety. So far as we are concerned you are at liberty to stay or go as you please. In business we have not been exclusive in our dealings or confined our patronage to those of our own faith. But every man who has dealt fairly and honestly and confined his attention to legitimate business whatever his creed has found friendship in us.

As Congress began to pass acts designed to injure Mormon financial stability, a wave of indignation followed, and Young changed his tone, saying that he wished "our friends to lift their voices against the vile wretches who are seeking to destroy our innocent and industrious people. Sustain those who sustain the Kingdom and fight those who fight against it. Cease to sustain them."

The first step in the direction of church-sponsored cooperative merchandising was taken in September 1868 when Young recommended that Mormons not trade another "cent with a man who does

not pay his tithing and help gather the poor and pray in his family."
He suggested that those who traded with outsiders be excommunicated. Cooperative merchandising was to substitute for trading with
"enemies." Church officials proposed to the October 1868 General
Conference "that we sustain ourselves and those who sustain us."
The motion was "approved unanimously," and the groundwork for
organizing cooperative merchandising was laid out.

The success of the cooperative movement hinged on the formation of a successful parent store, or cooperative wholesale establishment. A number of meetings were held in Salt Lake City about forming such an institution in October 1868, and a tentative organization
was completed on the 16th. Young was elected president, and other
positions were filled with local church and business leaders. "The
purpose of the new institution," Young said, "is to bring goods here
and sell them as low as they can possibly be sold and let the profit be
divided among the people at large." The constitution and bylaws of
the association were approved on 24 October 1868 and provided
that the organization be called Zion's Cooperative Mercantile Institution, or ZCMI, with an authorized capitalization of $3 million con-
sisting of 30,000 shares valued at $100 each. On 1 December 1870,
the association was incorporated for a term of twenty-five years.

Under the cooperative plan, each ward was to have a branch of
ZCMI, which could buy from the parent store. Also, Mormon merchants were expected to give up their own establishments and trade
their inventory for capital stock in the new company. Young threatened to set up a church-backed wholesale establishment in Provo in
order to get some of the Mormon merchants to cooperate.

Three of the largest Salt Lake City firms, William Jennings,
Eldredge and Clawson, and Sadler and Teasdale, offered to serve as
the central wholesale establishments for Zion's Cooperative. Henry
W. Lawrence, a prominent merchant, said he could not understand
how people were going to benefit from the change since it would
merely concentrate the trade into a few stores and the rest would be
empty and the men out of business. Lawrence thought that either
the parent store should go into retailing (as it eventually did) or that
retailers should retain their inventories for the convenience of the
customers. Young replied that the region needed big department
stores to which people could come and get their goods cheaply, and
that there were too many people in the retailing business. Two-thirds
of them ought to find other work, such as preaching, Young asserted.

ZCMI finally opened for business in the Eagle Emporium, formerly the site of William Jennings's store, a block south of church

headquarters. It handled dry goods, clothing, hats, caps, boots, shoes, and similar goods. Another store was opened in the old Constitution Building where Eldredge and Clawson had been established. Six weeks after the opening of ZCMI, seventy-eight cooperative stores were in operation and plans were well advanced for many others. By the end of the 1860s, all wards or settlements had at least one such store; Salt Lake City had seventeen. At least 115 such cooperatives were founded during the decade after 1869.[9]

The cooperative movement expanded to include such organizations as the Deseret Tanning and Manufacturing Association and the Deseret Agriculture and Manufacturing Society and to encompass such enterprises as woolen mills, herds of sheep, and lumber mills. There were cooperative iron works, cooperative banks, and cooperative textile factories, including the Washington cotton factories and the Provo woolen mills. Many other activities began to function on a cooperative basis under the direction of the local church leadership. However, the retailing and industrial cooperatives, which formed an important part of this system in 1869, did not flourish as did ZCMI. With local cooperatives, periodic depression in trade brought about failures; with others, liberal credit policies with individual customers were decisive. Poor and discontinuous management, particularly during periods of harassment by federal authorities, caused difficulties.

Besides organizing merchants and cooperative industries, church leaders decided to organize members to resist the anticipated evil effects of the mining and railroad intrusions. Men were organized into local units called the School of the Prophets, and women into the rejuvenated women's Relief Society, an organization founded in Nauvoo but largely inactive thereafter. Young convened the first School of the Prophets, named after a similar organization Joseph Smith had established during the 1830s in Ohio, in Salt Lake City in December 1867. Under Young, the school functioned as an extension of the Council of Fifty (which continued to play an important role in shaping Mormon economic and political policy). The central, or Salt Lake City, school was composed of over 900 leading men and

---
[9] In general, ZCMI and its member cooperatives were agents of the church in accomplishing desired social and economic objectives above and beyond those connected with producing, importing, and marketing the merchandise at reasonable prices. However, this movement was in direct opposition to the laissez-faire philosophy dominating the nation and became the object of considerable ridicule, although the Brigham City Cooperative flourished so well during the depression of 1873 that it gained some national recognition and favorable comment.

319

was parent to branch schools in the principal settlements. Approximately 5,000 priesthood members belonged to the branch schools.

These were not schools in the usual sense—the organization was more of a forum or town meeting of leading priesthood holders in which theology, church government, and church and community problems were discussed and appropriate action taken. The First Presidency and other general authorities directed these meetings and instructed local leaders. The School of the Prophets sometimes resembled an economic planning conference. Members discussed economic problems posed by the coming of the railroad and adopted measures to accomplish their objectives. Admission was by card only, and sessions were closed to the public.

The school attempted to prevent or minimize the influx of new migrants and businesses, which might threaten the morality of the community or undermine its basic economic structure and function. School members voted to minimize the influx of railroad workers by constructing the railroad themselves. The group thought it better for the Saints to work for nothing, if necessary, than let outsiders come in.

The school wanted to further minimize the influx of undesirable outsiders by deflating reports of Utah's mineral wealth. When mining expanded, requiring additional workers, Mormon laborers were urged to do the work rather than make it necessary for the mining industry to import outside labor into the territory. The school supported the Utah manufacturing company which was organized to manufacture wagons, carriages, and agricultural machinery, and endorsed a furniture manufacturing enterprise, an association to further the development of the silk industry, the $300,000 Provo Woolen Mills, and a number of minor projects, including a wooden bucket factory and ink and match factories.

School members criticized Mormon suppliers and buyers who refused to patronize local Mormon enterprises. Consistent trading with competing eastern firms made a member persona non grata and endangered his fellowship in the church. Investment in cooperative enterprises, though risky, was urged on all Mormon capitalists. Young, as trustee-in-trust, also invested part of the common fund of the community in the manufacturing cooperatives. The School of the Prophets actively tried to solve the land problem since no land office had been established in Utah and the title to the land was problematic. The school also participated in drives to raise cash for the Perpetual Emigrating Fund. Members pledged to observe the Word of Wisdom. (The 1867 Word of Wisdom campaign was the first major step in eventually making abstinence from tea, coffee, tobacco, and alcohol as much a test of faith as colonizing or missionary work.)

At the same time the School of the Prophets was instilling dedication and solidarity in the men, the women's Relief Society was being rejuvenated in each ward and settlement. Eliza R. Snow, plural wife of both Joseph Smith and Brigham Young, was appointed by the First Presidency to take charge of the womens' movement. Snow had been secretary of the first female Relief Society in Nauvoo, Illinois, and Young now asked her to organize the sisters to meet the challenge posed by the coming of the railroad.

The Relief Society was organized to visit the sick, helpless, and needy, and, under the bishop, to collect the means necessary to assist them. They were also to begin clothing themselves in the work of their own hands. In fact, all women of the territory were expected to minimize purchases from stores and find employment in their own homes, to diminish female extravagance and thereby relieve hard-pressed husbands to devote a larger share of their time and money to building the kingdom. In this same context, Young personally organized the young women of the church into a cooperative retrenchment association and called on them to avoid following current fashions and purchasing unnecessary items. This organization ultimately led to the Young Ladies' Mutual Improvement Association, which would become prominent in the following century.

The Relief Society was also to help with the cooperative general stores. Sisters were advised to take stock in the stores, patronize them exclusively, and prepare to set up retail outlets for their own handiwork. In many cases the Relief Society took over the management of cooperative stores originally established under the priesthood and operated their own establishments, as well. They also promoted the home industry movement, including a local silk industry. However, much of the promotion of silk came after the 1860s.

A number of Mormon merchants and intellectuals, attuned to the laissez-faire currents of the post-Civil War era, reacted negatively to Young's new programs. Privately, they viewed Young as a fanatical, ignorant despot who employed a subservient priesthood for unworthy purposes. These men believed that church policy was intentionally building a wall between Mormons and Gentiles and that the church was unduly concerned with material rather than spiritual matters. They were upset with Young's opposition to the mining industry, as well.

The two key players were E. L. T. Harrison and William Godbe. Harrison, an architect by profession but a literary man by avocation, was the intellectual leader of the movement. Converted in England by the logic of Apostle Orson Pratt, Harrison had worked in responsible assignments in England, heading the church bookstore, working in the church's business office in London, contributing to the *Latter-day Saints' Millennial Star*, and serving as church immigration agent in Liverpool and president of the London Missionary Conference. He was regarded as genial and pleasant, was witty, light-hearted, friendly, and faithful in his duties during the early days. However, in Utah he became critical of church policies and teachings, especially the idea of a temporal kingdom, and began publishing a journal called *Peep O'Day,* which offered mild criticisms of the Mormon program but which discontinued in December 1864.

About this time Harrison became involved in a working partnership with Eli Kelsey, William H. Shearman, and most importantly William S. Godbe. Godbe and Harrison seemed to complement each other. While Harrison may have been the intellectual stimulus of the movement, Godbe provided the balance, weight, and activity. The two shared much in common; both were British converts, had profound religious experiences in their youths, were intellectual and sophisticated, and possessed literary talent. Godbe was a successful merchant and by the late 1860s was one of the ten most wealthy men in the territory. He had served as city councilman, as president of one of the local Seventies quorums, and as a bishop's counselor in the Thirteenth Ward. He was a friend and protege of Brigham Young and possessed social position, talent, and influence. Edward Tullidge, another associate, and Shearman were both British converts and also had literary abilities. All three men had served in the British mission and held positions in the presidency of the London Conference.

Kelsey also became an important member of the group. Kelsey, an American, was older than the others, who were in their thirties. He had known Joseph Smith, came to Utah early, and had been the first mayor of Tooele. All of these men were active in their priesthood quorums and held important positions in their communities. Godbe and Shearman, along with Thomas Stenhouse, a later Godbeite dissenter, had helped found the *Juvenile Instructor*, which became the voice of the Mormon Sunday schools.

These five men were talented, well educated, literate, and attuned to the intellectual currents of their age. By the time the church began its cooperative economy movement these men had already become

322

disenchanted with many of the fundamentals of Mormonism.[10] Having left orthodox Mormonism, they were searching for another source of faith, which they believed they found in nineteenth-century spiritualism—communication with the dead through a medium.

In January 1868, they organized the *Utah Magazine*, with Godbe as publisher and Harrison as editor. Godbe and Harrison were in New York on business in October 1868 when the church announced in General Conference that it would organize a commercial cooperative. Apparently, Godbe was aware that this was coming and that he would be expected to join. While in the East, both men discussed their feelings about the church. During their three-week stay in New York, they apparently participated in spiritual seances, probably with the renowned medium Charles Foster. They came to believe that Mormonism was a preparation for something higher. Joseph Smith had been an imperfect spiritual medium, Brigham Young far less. Young had performed his mission by shepherding the Saints west where they might be molded to a new heavenly purpose. Godbe and Harrison decided that their magazine should advocate evangelical spiritualism grafted onto Mormon roots. Mormonism would provide the system—the priesthood—to vitalize the world with a new spiritualism. The higher truths were secured only by seeking the most worthy spirits, usually through the use of mediums or seers. Biblical figures, deceased Mormons, celebrated intellects of the past could thus return and convey religious and philosophical truth. The key lay in a purified priesthood which would unite the mortal and immortal worlds and provide spiritualism for the first time with a system capable of self regulation and proselytizing.

Returning from New York in mid-November 1868, Harrison and Godbe secretly organized active opposition to church rule. Their intimates included Kelsey, Tullidge, and Shearman, as well as T. B. H. Stenhouse, editor of the pro-Mormon *Salt Lake Telegram*; Fanny Stenhouse, his wife; John Tullidge, musician brother of Edward Tullidge; Fred Perris, a surveyor and engineer; Joseph Silver, a labor

---

[10] Tullidge claimed that he had for many years doubted virtually everything about Mormonism save the mission of its founder. Kelsey said that he had long since discarded the dogma that God had ever chosen one individual, family, race, or sect to hold the oracles or keys to salvation to the exclusion of the rest of the human family. Shearman had become alienated from local church authorities and barely escaped excommunication because of his opposition to the doctrine which the Godbeites described as blind obedience to the priesthood.

leader and writer; George Watt, a church recorder and former secretary to Brigham Young; and Henry Lawrence, partner in the
Kimball-Lawrence company, a leading Salt Lake City firm.

The *Utah Magazine* began to attack the church's wage policies
and finally in October came out with an important article titled "The
True Development of the Territory." This article argued that Utah,
given its questionable agricultural endowment, could achieve
increased prosperity by developing its mineral resources. Within four
years Brigham Young was advocating similar logic. However, in 1869,
the article seemed subversive, and the authors and publishers were
called before the School of the Prophets only hours after the appearance of the article. All seven men were disfellowshipped from the
school pending an explanation of their conduct. Church leaders called
on Orson Pratt, whom the Godbeites most admired, as well as Wilford
Woodruff and George Q. Cannon to council the Godbeite leaders.
Harrison and Godbe refused to compromise. As a result, Young
announced that Harrison and Godbe would be tried for their membership and called upon members of the School of the Prophets to
refrain from reading the *Utah Magazine*.

Ultimately, most of the Godbeites were, at their own request,
excommunicated. They then organized their own Church of Zion,
which met for a time in the old Thirteenth Wardhouse but failed to
attract many adherents—probably no more than 200. One of their
most important converts was Amasa Lyman, a longtime apostle who
had been relieved from his church calling in 1867 for false doctrine.
He sympathized with the Godbeite movement and was especially
attracted to spiritualism. Some of his daughters were also involved
in the spiritualist movement. Acting as a medium between 1870 and
1873, Lyman travelled from town to town holding seances. When
Orson Hyde and Frank B. Richards called on him to inform him of
his excommunication in 1870, he said, "Well, my dear brethren, you
are now simply, as it were, at the foot of the mountain whereas I
have been where you are now but unlike you I have gone to the
summit of the mountain. And traversed this plateau and gone far
beyond making the heights of another mountain far beyond and
removed from this one."[11]

[11] Part of the appeal of spiritualism to Mormons was that it allowed them to see
Mormonism as the first phase of a greater movement. Such teachings and actions by
a leading apostle and other leaders must have been discouraging to traditional church
members, but the overall impact of the Godbeite movement seems to have been
slight. Ironically, several of the economic principles advocated by the Godbeites would
be adopted by the church within the next few years.

While the church was dealing with both internal and external threats, a reforming congress in Washington, D.C., was busily engaged in passing legislature to rid the nation of polygamy. Slavery had been outlawed by the Thirteenth Amendment (passed in 1865), which Southern states were required to adopt to regain admission into the Union. The 1867 Reformation Acts allowed blacks to vote and to become members of state legislatures.

Among the measures considered to eliminate polygamy was the Wade Bill proposed by Senator Benjamin Wade of Ohio in 1866. This bill would have placed the Nauvoo Legion, which still functioned in Salt Lake City as a territorial militia, under control of the federal governor, prohibited church officials from solemnizing marriages, given authority to the U.S. marshal to select all jurors, given authority to the governor to appoint county judges, taxed all real and personal property of the church in excess of $20,000, and required the trustee-in-trust to make a full report under oath each year to the governor of all financial operations, including property acquired and disposed of, bank deposits, and investments. This bill failed to pass, but most of its features would be incorporated in the bill presented by Senator Abram H. Cragin of New Hampshire from 1867-69. The Cragun Bill also proposed to abolish trial by jury in cases arising under the anti-bigamy act of 1862. However, the Cragin Bill was withdrawn in favor of the Cullom Bill.

The Cullom Bill, proposed by Representative Shelby M. Cullom of Illinois, 1869-70, would have placed in the hands of the U.S. marshal and the U.S. attorney all responsibility for selecting jurors, confined polygamy cases to the exclusive jurisdiction of the federal judges, deprived plural wives of immunity as witnesses in cases involving their husbands, and declared cohabitation a misdemeanor. This bill also authorized the president to send a portion of the U.S. Army to Utah and to raise 25,000 militia in the territory in order to enforce the law. The property of all Mormons leaving the territory to evade prosecution was to be confiscated and used under Gentile jurisdiction for the benefit of Mormon families. This bill passed the House but failed in the Senate. Another bill was also proposed in 1869 by Congressman James Ashley of Ohio. The Ashley Bill provided for the dismembering of Utah by transferring large portions of the region to Nevada, Wyoming, and Colorado. This bill also failed to pass.

Such bills demonstrated what little sympathy existed for the Mormons in the nation's capital. The bills passed by the House were defeated in the Senate, often with the vote of Southern senators who,

325

oppressed by the federal government, were sympathetic to the Mormon plea for self-determination. However, even the southerners did not condone plural marriage.

By the end of the 1860s, the Mormon concept of the Kingdom of God was being threatened on virtually all fronts. External challenges, such as mining, the railroad, and federal legislation, and internal threats, such as the Godbeite movement, left the church in a precarious position as leaders began contemplating the coming decades.

19.
The Establishment
of Zion
in Retrospect

Colonization and confrontation—the two themes announced in the introduction of this history—are even more central in retrospect since the colonizing process involved confrontation with arid land, great distances, native inhabitants, "Gentiles," and officials and policies of the federal government. Most historians of Western America have pronounced the Mormon colonization of the Great Basin a success and have recognized Brigham Young as one of the great colonizers in American history. Indeed, Allen Nevins called him "the most commanding single figure of the American West," and Herbert E. Bolton wrote, "Without his dauntless spirit, his genius for organization, his flair for practical affairs, and his dominating personality, he could not have held his people together, attracted new thousands of converts from Europe, inspired them with the courage necessary to undergo the hardships of pioneer life, and provided the economic basis necessary to sustain them in a most difficult and remote frontier."

Much of Young's success came from his hard-headed practicality, his determination to achieve economic independence, and his conviction that he was engaged in the work of the Lord and that God rules in human affairs. He never doubted the church would succeed. Individuals might falter and fail, enemies might attempt to destroy the kingdom, but God had decreed its ultimate triumph. In a letter to Orson Hyde, dated 28 July 1850, Young stated the basic philosophy which gave him courage and confidence despite overwhelming odds:

We feel no fear. We are in the hands of our Heavenly Father, the God of Abraham and Joseph, who guided us to this land, who fed the poor Saints on the Plains with quails, who gave his people strength to labour without bread, who sent the gulls of the deep as Saviors to preserve (by devouring the crickets) the golden wheat for bread for his people, and who has preserved his Saints from the wrath of their enemies, delivering them from a bondage more cruel than that inflicted upon Israel in Egypt. He is our Father and our Protector. We live in his Light, are guided by his Wisdom, protected by his Shadow, upheld by his Strength.

Elizabeth Wood Kane, wife of Thomas L. Kane, personally observed Young's actions over a period of two months while accompanying Young's party on a trip from Lehi to St. George in 1872. Her report helps to explain his powerful influence in the daily lives of church members.

I strolled out on the platform afterwards, to find President Young preparing for our journey—as he did every morning afterwards—by a personal inspection of the condition of every wheel, axle, horse, and mule, and suit of harness belonging to the party. He was peering like a well-intentioned wizard into every nook and cranny, pointing out a defect here and there with his odd, six-sided staff engraved with the hieroglyphs of many measures; more useful though less romantic, then a Runic wand. . . . I was amused at his odd appearance; but as he turned to address me, he removed a hideous pair of green goggles, and his keen, blue-gray eyes met mine with their characteristic look of shrewd and cunning insight. I felt no further inclination to laugh. His photographs, accurate enough in other respects, altogether fail to give the expression of his eyes.

At Parowan, near the end of the journey, she wrote:

When we reached the end of a day's journey, after taking off our outer garments and washing off the dust, it was the custom of our party to assemble before the fire in the sitting room, and the leading "brothers and sisters" of the settlement would come in to pay their respects. . . . They talked to Brigham Young about every conceivable matter, from the fluxing of an ore to the advantages of a Navajo bit, and expected him to remember every child in every cotter's family. And he really seemed to do so, and to be at home, and be rightfully deemed infallible on every subject. I think he must make fewer mistakes than most popes, from his being in such constant intercourse with his people. I noticed that he never seemed uninterested, but gave an unforced attention to the person addressing him, which suggested a mind free from care. I used to fancy that he wasted a great deal of power in this way; but I soon saw that he was accumulating it.

328

Surely this helps to explain the apparent paradox that was Brigham Young, for although he criticized, scolded, and threatened his followers, he also stayed close to them, remembered their names, listened to their problems, and from his own experience, his powers of observation, and his reservoir of common sense, gave them counsel and advice. And because he was so confident of himself and sincere in his devotion to the kingdom, they took the scoldings and threats as part of the package and followed him as their divinely inspired leader even if it meant taking another wife, moving to an uninhabited wilderness, or simply staying home and trying to live with the difficulties of everyday life in pioneer Utah.

Although Young was responsible for much of the success of Mormon colonizing efforts, he was aided by hundreds of lesser known leaders, some with abilities rivaling his own. Supported by strong counselors and a Quorum of Twelve Apostles, Young was able to call upon hundreds of men to serve as bishops. These local leaders carried the actual burden of colonizing the communities. They, in turn, were supported by the thousands of men and women who were converted to the church and who were willing to accept calls to "establish and build up Zion" in difficult and remote places. Every one of the 250 communities established during the Saints' first twenty years in the Rocky Mountains had its roster of heroes and heroines who lived lives of incredible hardship, sustained only by their faith and the fellowship of the other committed Mormons in their settlements. As twentieth-century LDS apostle John A. Widtsoe has written:

> Such achievements were not accomplished without failures and costly mistakes. Brigham did not learn to be a colonizer overnight. Much of the early colonization was done in a rather haphazard manner as compared with the later colonization programs in Utah's Dixie and the communities established in Cache and Bear Lake Valleys. . . .
>
> Despite such failures, the remarkable achievement of establishing 250 communities in a desert land and building up a self-sustaining economy in two decades cannot be gainsaid. The Mormon pioneers not only survived, but developed large scale irrigation techniques. They also built substantial homes and public buildings, established educational programs, and promoted activities in cultural arts as well as community recreation. It was a remarkable achievement which laid the foundation for the Mormon influence in western America, and to a lesser extent in the nation and many parts of the world.

Although they succeeded in confronting the physical challenges posed by the land, the pioneers' confrontation with the Indians, the

329

"Gentiles," and the federal government was less successful and left many unsolved problems by the end of the 1860s. Of these three, the Indian problem was the most nearly solved, but the solution was not one the settlers could be proud of. Although Mormon leaders advocated a policy of fairness in dealing with the Indians and tried to teach them civilization and the Mormon gospel, they were unsuccessful in winning many to their program. The Saints needed the land occupied by the Indians and did not have the time or patience to work cooperatively with the native inhabitants.

During their first three years in the Great Basin, the Mormons asserted the right to occupy Indian lands without compensation, advocated extermination of noncooperative tribes, and recommended removal of the Indians to some other area. Young's famous 1851 statement that "it is cheaper to feed the Indians than to fight them" came only after considerable fighting had taken place. Such an attitude revealed Young's pragmatism, although he also felt a religious obligation to reclaim them from their "fallen" condition and to make them self-sufficient neighbors. To achieve this goal he instituted Indian farms, called on his people to settle near them to teach them the art of husbandry, and sent missionaries among them to teach them Mormonism. He also took vigorous action to end the Indian slave trade and encouraged his people to adopt Indian children as a means of helping them. These programs failed to help the majority of native inhabitants, and church leaders were soon entangled in the Walker and Black Hawk wars and were working with federal officials in reservation programs. Despite the Mormon leaders' goodwill toward the Indians, the gap between the two cultures was too great, and the time allowed for accommodation too short for successful cooperation.

Unfortunately for the Indians, they also became victims of the struggle between the Mormons and the federal government. Washington officials, fearful that Mormons were using government funds to enhance their own goals, refused to give the Indians the help that both Mormon and non-Mormon agents recommended. By 1869 the Indians were reduced in numbers and property and were either settled on undesirable reservation lands or in small groups on the outskirts of Mormon communities, living off the charity of people who occupied their lands.

The result of the confrontation with non-Mormon "Gentiles," including official representatives of the federal government, was that the Mormon became more withdrawn and distrustful of outsiders.

Sizable numbers of Gentiles had come to the territory, at times comprising 10 to 15 percent of the population: miners after gold in California, settlers and traders along the Oregon and California trails, appointees of the federal government with dependents, Johnston's Army with its civilian hangers-on, the California volunteers at Camp Douglas during the Civil War years, transcontinental railroad builders, union organizers of miners, and ministers shepherding the Gentile flocks and reclaiming "misguided Mormons."

Many of these people were only temporary residents and moved on without becoming seriously involved with the Mormons. Some admired the Mormon accomplishments and spoke highly of their character. But beginning with the "run-away officials" of 1851, Gentiles in the region resented Mormon attitudes and practices and sent a steady stream of critical reports, both official and unofficial, to the East. Mormon leaders responded defensively, and, at times, their rhetoric sounded threatening. They succeeded in polarizing the population, pitting the "outsider" minority against the Mormon majority. This antagonism reached serious proportions by the late 1860s. Anticipating the completion of the transcontinental railroad, church leaders in 1868 instituted their "defensive economy," which called on church members to trade only with fellow Saints and thus threatened the prosperity of the Gentile merchants. The Godbeite movement organized a number of prominent Mormons in criticizing the "defensive economy" and calling on the church leaders to end their opposition to the federal government and their exclusive attitudes towards the non-Mormons. Some of the Godbeites joined with non-Mormons to form a political party to oppose church domination of politics and published a newspaper to champion their cause.

At the same time, a reform-minded Congress was attempting to force the Mormons to abandon their theocratic government and the practice of plural marriage. There were even threats of sending another U.S. Army to force Mormon compliance with U.S. laws. The 1860s closed with the church well established as far as colonization was concerned but seriously threatened by confrontation with non-Mormons in Washington, D.C.

Frederick Jackson Turner has asserted that the frontier environment had a profound impact on westward moving Americans, causing them to forsake their former ways and making them more democratic, self-reliant, and individualistic. But the Mormons, confronting the frontier, seemed to become more theocratic and group oriented. Group loyalty became a prized trait, and willingness to sacrifice personal comforts and desires to build the kingdom admired attitudes.

331

In addition to their common faith, most Saints had the shared experience of crossing the Great Plains and participating in a colonizing venture they believed would prepare them for the Second Coming. The result was a unique class of Americans, with conflicting loyalties, attitudes, and practices that made them suspect by fellow Americans. Dominated by religious leaders who believed that every aspect of life, including political and economic matters, should be in harmony with theocratic principles of the Kingdom of God and who defended the practice of polygamy, the Latter-day Saints almost invited criticism and persecutions.

Despite the difficulties of the environment and the opposition of outsiders, the Mormon pioneers built a solid establishment during the first two decades that was able to survive and grow into the successful church and culture so prominent a part of the American West today.

Brigham Young (1801–77), second president of the LDS church, oversaw the colonization of some 250 settlements throughout the American West during the mid-nineteenth century.

Heber C. Kimball (1801–68) was first counselor to Brigham Young in the LDS first presidency from 1848 until his death.

Jedediah M. Grant (1816–56), sustained as second counselor to Brigham Young in 1854, was a fiery orator whose calls to repentance inaugurated the Mormon Reformation.

*Daniel H. Wells (1814–91)
served as commander of
the Utah territorial militia
until his appointment in
1857 as successor to
Jedediah M. Grant in the
LDS first presidency.*

*George A. Smith (1817–75)
was a territorial legislator,
official LDS church
historian, and successor to
Heber C. Kimball in 1868
as first counselor to
Brigham Young.*

*Orson Hyde (1805–78),
president of the LDS
quorum of twelve apostles,
helped to colonize both
northern and southern Utah.*

*Parley P. Pratt (1807–57),
an LDS apostle and
territorial colonizer and
legislator, was killed in
Arkanas by the husband of
one his plural wives.*

Orson Pratt (1811–81), an LDS apostle, was an intellectual apologist and pamphleteer who publicly disagreed with Brigham Young on doctrinal subjects.

John Taylor (1808–87), third president of the LDS church, was an articulate defender of Mormon doctrine.

Wilford Woodruff (1807–98), fourth president of the LDS church, kept voluminous diaries chronicling many important events in early Utah history.

Amasa Lyman (1813–77), an LDS apostle, helped to direct the San Bernardino and gold missions, and later affiliated with the Godbeite movement for which he was excommunicated.

*Ezra T. Benson (1811–69),
an LDS apostle, presided
over church settlements in
Cache Valley until his death.*

*Charles C. Rich (1809–83),
an LDS apostle, directed the
San Bernardino and gold
missions and later helped to
settle the Bear Lake Valley
region in northern Utah.*

Erastus Snow (1818–88), an LDS apostle, helped to colonize the church's southern settlements in Utah's Dixie.

John Smith (1781–1854), an uncle of Mormon church founder Joseph Smith, was presiding LDS patriarch and the first president of the Salt Lake Stake.

The earliest known photograph of the First Presidency and Quorum of the Twelve Apostles (ca. 1868). They are, front row, left to right: George A. Smith, Brigham Young, and Daniel H. Wells; back row, left to right: Orson Hyde, Orson Pratt, John Taylor, Wilford Woodruff, Ezra T. Benson, Charles C. Rich, Lorenzo Snow, Erastus Snow, Franklin D. Richards, George Q. Cannon, Brigham Young, Jr., and Joseph F. Smith.

The old Salt Lake Tabernacle, left, and thatch-roofed bowery, right (ca. 1855).

Temple Square looking south down Main Street (ca. 1853). To the right is the Salt Lake Tabernacle; to the left, the foundation of the Salt Lake Temple.

The Salt Lake Tithing Office and Deseret Store (also known as the Bishops' Storehouse) on the corner of Main and South Temple streets (ca. 1858) where faithful Mormons donated one-tenth of their goods.

The Salt Lake Endowment House, located on Temple Square and separated from the Salt Lake Tabernacle by a high fence, was built of adobe in 1855 and used for the next thirty-four years to solemnize temple marriages prior to the completion of the Salt Lake Temple.

The south wing of the Utah State House at Fillmore, Millard County, Utah, as it looks today, where the territorial legislature met in 1855–56. The building was never completed and the legislature moved the state capital to Salt Lake City in 1856.

William Jenning's Eagle Emporium, early home of the wholesale headquarters of ZCMI (ca. 1885), on the southwest corner of South Temple and Main streets, was the hub of the communal retail network which evolved into the ZCMI department store chain.

Samuel Brannan (1819–89) was a colorful and ambitious entrepreneur who tried to convince Brigham Young to locate in northern California. Moving to California himself, he made a fortune, mostly in land speculation.

John D. Lee (1812–77) southern Utah colonizer and Indian agent, played an important role in the tragic Mountain Meadows Massacre of 1857. Excommunicated from the LDS church, he was later tried by civil courts and executed.

Chief Washakie (1804?–1900), for sixty years chief of the Shoshone Indians in the Wyoming-Utah-Idaho area, was a friend of Brigham Young, Jim Bridger, and General Albert Johnston.

Chief Kanosh was one of several Indian leaders with whom the Mormons interacted during their early years in the Great Basin.

Harriett Decker Young,
wife of Lorenzo Dow Young,
was one of three women in
the original 1847 party of
Utah pioneers.

Eliza R. Snow (1804–87), a
plural wife of both Joseph
Smith and Brigham Young,
was a prolific writer who
served as president of the
Female Relief Society from
1867 until her death.

John M. Bernhisel (1799–1881), Utah's territorial representative to Congress during the 1850s, was a skilled diplomat in defending Mormon rights, especially after the public announcement of plural marriage.

Almon W. Babbitt (1813–56), Utah's first territorial secretary and treasurer, was killed by Indians while returning from a trip to the nation's capital.

Perry E. Brocchus, a Utah territorial associate justice, opposed plural marriage, wrote a report to superiors in Washington, D.C., critical of the Mormons, and later left the territory with other "runaway officials" because of "Mormon persecution."

Thomas L. Kane (1822–83), a friend of Brigham Young, helped to negotiate an end to the Utah War.

*James Buchanan
(1791–1868), fifteenth
president of the United
States, decided to send
federal troops under
Albert S. Johnston to
subdue the "rebellious"
Mormons in 1857–58.*

*Albert Sidney Johnston
(1803–62), commander of
the 1857 expedition against
the Mormons, remained in
Utah until the Civil War
when he joined the
Confederate Army.*

The Bugle Corps of Johnston's Army practicing at Camp Floyd (later Fort Crittenden) in Rush Valley, southwest of Salt Lake City (ca. 1859).

A view of the commanding general's quarters, looking west, at Camp Floyd (ca. 1859).

The Utah territorial militia protected the settlers from attack—especially during the Utah War.

John F. Kinney (1816–1902) served as Utah territorial chief justice from 1854 to 1857 and from 1860 to 1863, when he became Utah's delegate to Congress.

Alfred Cumming (1802–1873) replaced Brigham Young as territorial governor and served from 1857 to 1861.

Colonel Patrick Edward Connor (1820–91) organized the California Volunteers and helped to establish Camp Douglas east of Salt Lake City.

Camp Douglas (later Fort Douglas) housed the California Volunteers of the U.S. Army during the Civil War.

*James Duane Doty
(1799–1865) was appointed
superintendent of Indian
Affairs for Utah in 1861 and
territorial governor in 1863
until his death.*

*William S. Godbe
(1833–1902), a successful
Salt Lake City businessman,
protested Brigham Young's
temporal policies, was
excommunicated in 1867,
and later organized the
Church of Zion.*

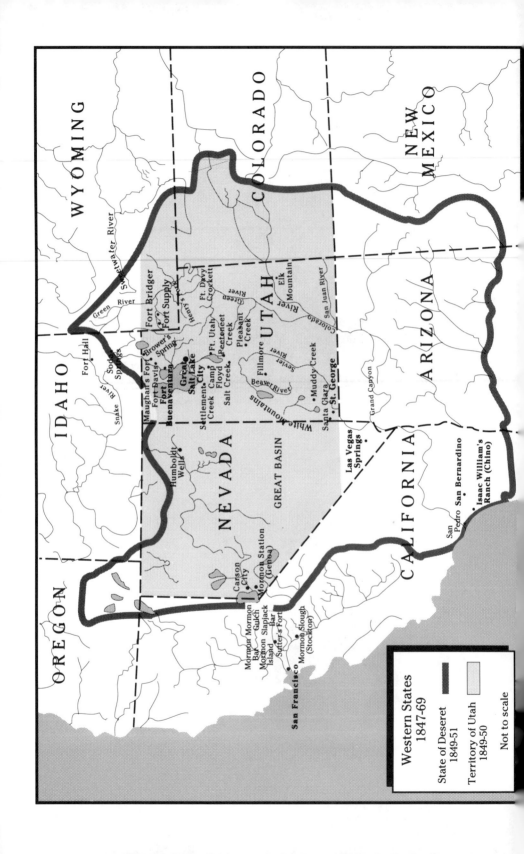

Western States
1847-69

State of Deseret
1849-51

Territory of Utah
1849-50

Not to scale

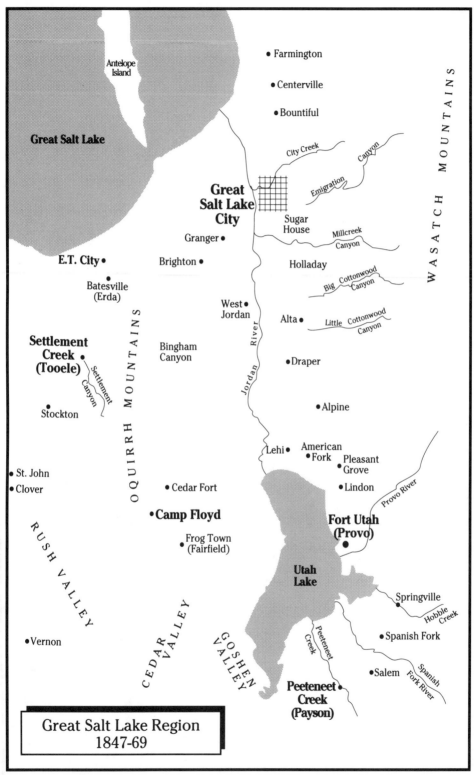

Great Salt Lake

Antelope
Island

Farmington
Centerville
Bountiful

Great
Salt Lake
City

City Creek

Emigration   Canyon

Granger

Sugar
House

Millcreek
Canyon

E.T. City

Brighton

Holladay

Big Cottonwood
Canyon

Batesville
(Erda)

West
Jordan

Alta

Little Cottonwood
Canyon

Settlement
Creek
(Tooele)

Bingham
Canyon

Draper

Settlement
Canyon

Jordan River

Alpine

Stockton

St. John
Clover

Lehi

American
Fork

Pleasant
Grove

Cedar Fort

Lindon

Provo River

Camp Floyd

Frog Town
(Fairfield)

Fort Utah
(Provo)

Utah
Lake

Springville

Hobble Creek

Vernon

Spanish Fork

Peeteneet Creek

Salem

Spanish Fork River

Peeteneet
Creek
(Payson)

OQUIRRH MOUNTAINS

WASATCH MOUNTAINS

RUSH VALLEY

CEDAR VALLEY

GOSHEN VALLEY

Great Salt Lake Region
1847-69

Not to scale

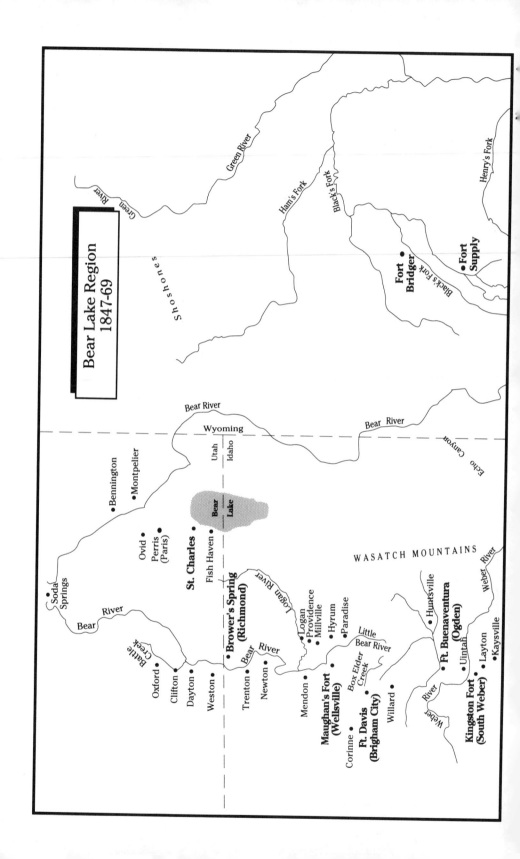

Bear Lake Region
1847-69

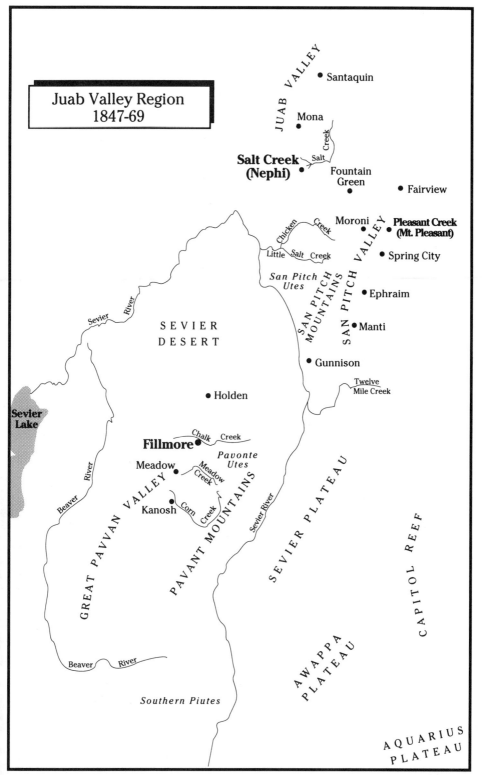

Juab Valley Region
1847-69

JUAB VALLEY

• Santaquin

• Mona

Salt Creek
(Nephi) •
Salt Creek

• Fountain
Green

• Fairview

Chicken Creek

• Moroni

Pleasant Creek
(Mt. Pleasant) •

Little Salt Creek

• Spring City

San Pitch
Utes

SAN PITCH MOUNTAINS

SAN PITCH VALLEY

• Ephraim

• Manti

SEVIER
DESERT

Sevier River

• Gunnison

Twelve
Mile Creek

• Holden

Sevier
Lake

River

Beaver River

Chalk Creek

Fillmore •

Pavonte
Utes

Meadow •

Meadow Creek

Kanosh •

Corn Creek

PAVANT MOUNTAINS

GREAT PAVVAN VALLEY

Sevier River

SEVIER PLATEAU

CAPITOL REEF

Beaver River

Southern Piutes

AWAPPA PLATEAU

AQUARIUS PLATEAU

Not to scale

St. George & Las Vegas Areas
1847-69

Not to scale

Sevier River

LITTLE SALT LAKE VALLEY
(PAROWAN VALLEY)

Paragonah
Parowan

Panguitch Lake

Center Creek

Orderville
Mt. Carmel

Muddy Creek

Coal Creek
Muddy Creek (Cedar City)

THE KOLOB PLATEAU

ESCALANTE DESERT

Fort Harmony

Ash Creek

Toquerville

Virgin River

Mountain Meadow

Washington Flat
St. George
Tonnequint Flat

Santa Clara
Santa Clara River

Heberville
Virgin River

BEAVER DAM MOUNTAINS

Virgin River

VIRGIN MOUNTAINS

St. Thomas

Muddy River

Colorado River

MUDDY MOUNTAINS

Call's Landing

Las Vegas Springs

Bibliography

Unless otherwise noted, all unpublished manuscripts are housed in the archives of the Historical Department, Church of Jesus Christ of Latter-day Saints, Salt Lake City, Utah.

"Acts of the Twelve Apostles, 1849–1870." Unpub. ms.

———— Allen, James B. "Ecclesiastical Influence on Local Government in the Territory of Utah." *Arizona and the West* 8 (Spring 1966): 35–48.

————, and Glen M. Leonard. *The Story of the Latter-day Saints.* Salt Lake City: Deseret Book, 1976.

Anderson, Nels. *Desert Saints: The Mormon Frontier in Utah.* Chicago: University of Chicago Press, 1942.

Arrington, Leonard J. "The Deseret Telegraph—A Church-Owned Public Utility." *Journal of Economic History* 11 (Spring 1951): 117–39.

————. "Taming the Turbulent Sevier: A Story of Mormon Desert Conquest." *Western Humanities Review* 5 (Autumn 1951): 393–406.

————. "Iron Manufacturing in Southern Utah in the Early 1880's: The Iron Manufacturing Company of Utah." *Bulletin of the Business Historical Society* 25 (Sept. 1951): 149–68.

————. "The Settlement of Brigham Young's Estate, 1877–1879." *Pacific Historical Review* 21 (Feb. 1952): 1–20.

————. "The Provo Woolen Mills: Utah's First Large Manufacturing Establishment." *Utah Historical Quarterly* 21 (April 1953): 97–116.

————. "Objectives of Mormon Economic Policy." *Western Humanities Review* 10 (Spring 1956): 180–85.

————. "Planning an Iron Industry for Utah, 1851–1858." *Huntington Library Quarterly* 21 (May 1958): 237–60.

————. *Great Basin Kingdom: An Economic History of the Latter-day Saints, 1830–1900*. Cambridge: Harvard University Press, 1958.

————. "Religion and Economics in Mormon History." *Brigham Young University Studies* 3 (Spring/Summer 1961): 15–33.

————. *From Wilderness to Empire: The Role of Utah in Western Economic History*. Salt Lake City: University of Utah, Institute of American Studies, 1961.

————. *The Changing Economic Structure of the Mountain West, 1850–1950*. Logan, UT: Utah State University Press, 1963.

————. "The Mormons and the Indians, A Review and Evaluation." *The Record* (Friends of the Library, Washington State University, Pullman) 31 (1970): 5–29.

————. *Charles C. Rich: Mormon General and Western Frontiersman*. Provo, UT: Brigham Young University Press, 1974.

————, Feramorz Y. Fox, and Dean L. May. *Building the City of God: Community and Cooperation Among the Mormons*. Salt Lake City: Deseret Book, 1976.

————, and Ronald K. Esplin. "Building a Commonwealth: The Secular Leadership of Brigham Young." *Utah Historical Quarterly* 45 (Summer 1977): 216–32.

————, and Davis Bitton. *The Mormon Experience: A History of the Latter-day Saints*. New York: Alfred A. Knopf, 1979.

Bancroft, Hubert Howe. *History of Utah, 1540–1886*. 1889; reprint ed., Salt Lake City: Bookcraft, 1964.

Barrett, Gwynn W. "Dr. John M. Bernhisel: Mormon Elder in Congress." *Utah Historical Quarterly* 36 (Spring 1968): 143–67.

Barrett, Ivan J. "History of the Cotton Mission and Cotton Culture in Utah." M.A. thesis, Brigham Young University, 1947.

Baumgarten, James N. "The Role and Function of the Seventies in L.D.S. Church History." M.A. thesis, Brigham Young University, 1960.

Bean, George Washington. *Autobiography of George Washington Bean, a Utah Pioneer of 1847, and his Family Records*. Flora D. B. Horne, comp. Salt Lake City: Utah Printing Co., 1945.

Beecher, Dale F. *The Office of Bishop: An Example of Organizational Development in the Church*. Task Papers in LDS History, No. 21. Salt Lake City: Historical Department, Church of Jesus Christ of Latter-day Saints, 1978.

Bergera, Gary James. "The Orson Pratt-Brigham Young Controversies: Conflict Within the Quorums, 1853 to 1868." *Dialogue: A Journal of Mormon Thought* 13 (Summer 1980): 7–49.

Bigler, Henry. Diary.

Boyle, Henry G. Journal. Special Collections, Harold B. Lee Library, Brigham Young University, Provo, Utah.

Brooks, Juanita. *The Mountain Meadows Massacre*. 1950; new ed., Norman: University of Oklahoma Press, 1962.

————, ed. *On the Mormon Frontier: The Diary of Hosea Stout, 1844–1861*. 2 vols. Salt Lake City: University of Utah Press/ Utah State Historical Society, 1964.

————. *John Doyle Lee: Zealot, Pioneer Builder, Scapegoat*. Glendale, CA: Arthur H. Clark, 1972.

Brown, James. *Life of a Pioneer, Being the Autobiography of James Brown*. Salt Lake City: George Q. Cannon & Sons, 1900.

Brown, Thomas D. *Journal of the Southern [Utah] Indian Mission: Diary of Thomas D. Brown*. Juanita Brooks, ed. Logan, UT: Utah State University Press, 1972.

Buerger, David John. "The Adam-God Doctrine." *Dialogue: A Journal of Mormon Thought* 15 (Spring 1982): 14–58.

Bullock, Thomas. Journal and papers. Unpub. mss.

Burton, Richard F. *The City of the Saints and Across the Rocky Mountains to California*. Fawn M. Brodie, ed. New York: Alfred A. Knopf, 1963.

Campbell, Bruce L., and Eugene E. Campbell. "Early Cultural and Intellectual Development." In Poll et al. 1978, 295–316.

————. "Pioneer Society." In Poll et al. 1978, 275–294.

Campbell, Eugene E. "A History of the Church of Jesus Christ of Latter-day Saints in California, 1846–1946." Ph.D. diss., University of Southern California, 1952.

————. "Authority Conflicts in the Mormon Battalion." *Brigham Young University Studies* 8 (Winter 1968): 127–42.

————. "Brigham Young's Outer Cordon: A Reappraisal." *Utah Historical Quarterly* 41 (Summer 1973): 220–53.

————. "Early Colonizing Patterns." In Poll et al. 1978, 133–152.

————. "Governmental Beginnings." In Poll et al. 1978, 153–174.

————. "The Mormon Migrations to Utah." In Poll et al. 1978, 113–132.

Cannon, George Q. "Twenty Years Ago. A Sketch." *Juvenile Instructor* 4 (1869): *passim*.

Christian, Lewis Clark. "A Study of the Mormon Westward Migration Between February, 1846, and July, 1847, with Emphasis On and Evaluation of the Factors that Led to the Mormons' Choice of Salt Lake Valley as the Site of Their Initial Colony." Ph.D. diss., Brigham Young University, 1976.

Clark, James R. "The Kingdom of God, the Council of Fifty, and the State of Deseret." *Utah Historical Quarterly* 26 (April 1958): 130–48.

Clayton, William. *William Clayton's Journal*. Salt Lake City: Clayton Family Association, 1921.

Coates, Lawrence G. "Mormons and Social Change Among the Shoshoni, 1853–1900." *Idaho Yesterdays* 15 (Winter 1972): 2–11.

Cowley, Matthias. *Wilford Woodruff*. Salt Lake City: The Deseret News Press, 1909.

Creer, Leland H. *The Founding of an Empire: The Exploration and Colonization of Utah, 1776–1856*. Salt Lake City: Bookcraft, 1947.

————. "The Evolution of Government in Early Utah." *Utah Historical Quarterly* 27 (January 1958): 23–42.

Daughters of Utah Pioneers. *History of Tooele County.* Salt Lake City: Daughters of Utah Pioneers, 1961.

Dibble, Charles E. "The Mormon Mission to the Shoshoni Indians." *Utah Humanities Review* 1 (January, April, July 1947): 53–73, 166–77, 279–93.

Draper, Richard D. "Babylon in Zion: The LDS Concept of Zion as a Cause for Mormon-Gentile Conflict, 1846–1857." M.A. thesis, Arizona State University, 1974.

Egan, Howard. *Pioneering the West, 1846 to 1878.* Richmond, UT: Howard R. Egan Estate, 1917.

Ellsworth, S. George. *Utah's Heritage.* Santa Barbara, CA: Peregrine Smith, 1972.

Furniss, Norman F. *The Mormon Conflict, 1850–1859.* New Haven: Yale University Press, 1960.

Gates, Susa Young. "From Impulsive Girl to Patient Wife: Lucy Bigelow Young." *Utah Historical Quarterly* 45 (Summer 1977): 270–88.

Gowans, Fred R., and Eugene E. Campbell. *Fort Bridger: Island in the Wilderness.* Provo, UT: Brigham Young University Press, 1975.

————. *Fort Supply: Brigham Young's Green River Experiment.* Provo, UT: Brigham Young University Press, 1976.

Hafen, LeRoy R. "Handcarts to Utah, 1856–1860." *Utah Historical Quarterly* 24 (October 1956): 309–17.

————, and Ann W. Hafen, eds. *The Utah Expedition, 1857–58: A Documentary Account.* Glendale, CA: Arthur H. Clarke, 1958.

————. *Handcarts to Zion: The Story of a Unique Western Migration, 1856–1860.* Glendale, CA: Arthur H. Clark, 1960.

Hansen, Klaus J. *Quest for Empire: The Political Kingdom of God and the Council of Fifty in Mormon History.* East Lansing: Michigan State University Press, 1967.

Hartley, William. "Mormons, Crickets, and Gulls: A New Look at an Old Story." *Utah Historical Quarterly* 38 (Summer 1970): 224–39.

Hefner, Loretta Lea. "The Apostasy of Amasa Mason Lyman." M.A. thesis, University of Utah, 1977.

Hilton, Lynn M., ed. *The Story of Salt Lake Stake of the Church of Jesus Christ of Latter-day Saints; 125 Year History, 1847–1972.* Salt Lake City: Salt Lake Stake, 1972.

Historians' Office Journal and Letterpress Books. Unpub. mss.

Holbrook, Joseph. Diary; typescript. Copy in author's possession.

Hubbard, George U. "Abraham Lincoln as Seen by the Mormons." *Utah Historical Quarterly* 31 (Spring 1963): 91–108.

Hunter, Milton R. *Brigham Young the Colonizer.* 3rd ed. Independence, MO: Zion's Printing and Publishing Co., 1945.

Hyde, John, Jr. *Mormonism: Its Leaders and Designs.* New York: W. P. Fetridge & Co., 1857.

Irving, Gordon. "The Law of Adoption: One Phase of the Development of the Mormon Concept of Salvation, 1830–1900." *Brigham Young University Studies* 14 (Spring 1974): 291–314.

Ivins, Stanley S. "Notes on Mormon Polygamy." *Western Humanities Review* 10 (Summer 1956): 229–39.

Jackson, Donald, and Mary Lee Spence, eds. *The Expeditions of John Charles Fremont.* 2 vols. Urbana: University of Illinois Press, 1970–73.

Jackson, Richard H. "Righteousness and Environmental Change: The Mormons and the Environment." *Essays on the American West, 1973–74.* Provo, UT: Charles Redd Center, 1975, pp. 21–42.

————. "The Mormon Village: Genesis and Antecedents of the City of Zion Plan." *Brigham Young University Studies* 17 (Winter 1977): 223–40.

————, ed. *The Mormon Role in the Settlement of the West.* Provo, UT: Brigham Young University Press, 1978.

Jenson, Andrew. *Latter-day Saint Biographical Encyclopedia.* 4 vols. Salt Lake City: Andrew Jenson History Company, 1901–36.

Jessee, Dean C., ed. *Letters of Brigham Young to His Sons.* Salt Lake City: Deseret Book, 1974.

Journal History of The Church of Jesus Christ of Latter-day Saints. Unpublished daily history of the Mormon church.

Journal of Discourses. 26 vols. London and Liverpool: Latter-day Saints' Book Depot, 1855–86.

Koritz, Alvin Charles. "The Development of Municipal Government in the Territory of Utah." M.A. thesis, Brigham Young University, 1972.

Larson, Andrew Karl. *"I Was Called to Dixie": The Virgin River Basin: Unique Experiences in Mormon Pioneering.* Salt Lake City: Deseret News Press, 1961.

Larson, Gustive O. *Prelude to the Kingdom: A Mormon Desert Conquest, a Chapter in American Cooperative Experience.* Francestown, NH: Marshall Jones Co., 1947.

————. "The Mormon Reformation." *Utah Historical Quarterly* 26 (Jan. 1958): 45–63.

————. *Outline History of Utah and the Mormons.* Salt Lake City: Deseret Book, 1958.

————. "Utah and the Civil War." *Utah Historical Quarterly* 33 (Winter 1965): 55–77.

————. "Government, Politics, and Conflict." In Poll et al. 1978, 243–256.

————. "The Mormon Gathering." In Poll et al. 1978, 175–192.

Lee, John D. Journals. Special Collections, Harold B. Lee Library, Brigham Young University, Provo, Utah, and Historical Department, Church of Jesus Christ of Latter-day Saints, Salt Lake City, Utah.

————. *A Mormon Chronicle: The Diaries of John D. Lee, 1848–1876.* 2 vols. Robert Glass Cleland and Juanita Brooks, eds. San Marino, CA: Huntington Library, 1955.

Lobb, Ann Vest, and Jill Mulvay Derr. "Women in Early Utah." In Poll et al. 1978, 337–356.

337

Lyon, T. Edgar. "Nauvoo and the Council of the Twelve." F. Mark McKiernan et al., eds., *The Restoration Movement: Essays in Mormon History* (Lawrence, KS: Coronado Press, 1973), pp. 167–206.

————, and Glen M. Leonard. "The Churches in the Territory." In Poll et al. 1978, 317–336.

Markham, Stephen. "Report." In Neff 1945.

May, Dean L. "Economic Beginnings." In Poll et al. 1978, 193–216.

————. "Towards a Dependent Commonwealth." In Poll et al. 1978, 217–242.

Melville, J. Keith. *Highlights in Mormon Political History*. Provo, UT: Brigham Young University Press, 1967.

Miscellaneous Minutes Collection. Brigham Young Papers.

Morgan, Dale L. *A History of Ogden*. Ogden, UT: Ogden City Commission, 1940.

————. "The State of Deseret." *Utah Historical Quarterly* 8 (April, July, October 1940): 65–239.

————. *The Great Salt Lake*. 1947; reprint ed., Albuquerque: University of New Mexico Press, 1973.

Neff, Andrew L. *History of Utah, 1847–1869*. Edited by Leland H. Creer. Salt Lake City: Deseret News Press, 1940.

Nelson, Lowry. *The Mormon Village: A Pattern and Technique of Land Settlement*. Salt Lake City: University of Utah, 1952.

Nibley, Preston. *Exodus to Greatness: The Story of the Mormon Migration*. Salt Lake City: Deseret News Press, 1947.

O'Neil, Floyd, and Stanford J. Layton. "Of Pride and Politics: Brigham Young as Indian Superintendent." *Utah Historical Quarterly* 46 (Summer 1978): 236–50.

Orme, Michael. "The Causes of the Mormon Reformation of 1856–57." *Tangents III*, Spring 1975, 15–43.

Page, Albert R. "Orson Hyde and the Carson Valley Mission, 1855–1857." M.A. thesis, Brigham Young University, 1970.

Palmer, Grant H. "The Godbeite Movement: A Dissent Against Temporal Control." M.A. thesis, Brigham Young University, 1968.

Papanikolas, Helen, ed. *The Peoples of Utah*. Salt Lake City: Utah State Historical Society, 1976.

Patrick, John R. "The School of the Prophets: Its Development and Influence in Utah Territory." M.A. thesis, Brigham Young University, 1970.

Peterson, Charles S. "The Hopis and the Mormons, 1858–1873." *Utah Historical Quarterly* 39 (Spring 1971): 179–94.

————. "Jacob Hamblin, Apostle to the Lamanites, and the Indian Mission." *Journal of Mormon History* 2 (1975): 21–34.

————. *Utah: A Bicentennial History*. New York: W. W. Norton, 1977.

Peterson, Paul H. "An Historical Analysis of the Word of Wisdom." M.A. thesis, Brigham Young University, 1972.

————. "The Mormon Reformation." Ph.D. diss., Brigham Young University, 1981.

Poll, Richard D. "The Mormon Question Enters National Politics, 1850–1856." *Utah Historical Quarterly* 25 (April 1957): 117–31.

――――――, Thomas G. Alexander, Eugene E. Campbell, David E. Miller, eds. *Utah's History*. Provo, UT: Brigham Young University Press, 1978.

Pratt, Orson. "Interesting Items Concerning the Journeying of the Latter-Day Saints from the City of Nauvoo, until Their Location in the Valley of the Great Salt Lake. (Extracted from the Private Journal of Orson Pratt.)" *Latter-day Saints' Millennial Star* 11–12 (1849–50): *passim*.

――――――. Papers. Unpub. mss.

Pratt, Parley P. Papers. Archives, Historical Department, Church of Jesus Christ of Latter-day Saints, Salt Lake City, Utah, and Special Collections, Harold B. Lee Library, Brigham Young University, Provo, Utah.

President's Office Journal.

Pulsipher, John. Journal.

Quinn, D. Michael. "Organizational Development and Social Origins of the Mormon Hierarchy, 1832–1932: A Prosopographical Study." M.A. thesis, University of Utah, 1973.

――――――. "The Evolution of the Presiding Quorums of the LDS Church." *Journal of Mormon History* 1 (1974): 21–38.

――――――. "The Mormon Hierarchy, 1832–1932: An American Elite." Ph.D. Diss., Yale University, 1976.

――――――. "The Mormon Succession Crisis of 1844." *Brigham Young University Studies* 16 (Winter 1976): 187–233.

――――――. "The Practice of Rebaptism at Nauvoo." *Brigham Young University Studies* 18 (Winter 1978): 226–32.

Reinwand, Louis G. "An Interpretive Study of Mormon Millennialism During the Nineteenth Century with Emphasis on Millennial Developments in Utah." M.A. thesis, Brigham Young University, 1971.

Remy, Jules, and Julius Brenchley. *A Journey to Great-Salt-Lake City*. 2 vols. 1861; reprint, New York: AMS Press, 1971.

Rich, Charles C. Papers.

Rich, Russell R. "History of the Latter-day Saint Settlement of the Bear Lake Valley, 1863–1900." M.A. thesis, Brigham Young University, 1948.

――――――. *Ensign to the Nations: A History of the Church from 1846 to the Present*. Provo, UT: Brigham Young University Press, 1972.

Ricks, Joel E. *Forms and Methods of Early Mormon Settlement in Utah and Surrounding Region, 1847 to 1877*. Logan, UT: Utah State University Press, 1964.

Roberts, B. H. *A Comprehensive History of The Church of Jesus Christ of Latter-day Saints, Century 1*. 6 vols. Salt Lake City: Church of Jesus Christ of Latter-day Saints, 1930.

Rogers, Samuel. Journal. Special Collections, Harold B. Lee Library, Brigham Young University, Provo, Utah.

Salt Lake City Stake. High Council Minutes.

Schindler, Harold. *Orrin Porter Rockwell: Man of God, Son of Thunder*. Salt Lake City: University of Utah Press, 1966.

Searle, Howard C. "The Mormon Reformation of 1856–1857." M.A. thesis, Brigham Young University, 1956.

Sessions, Gene A. *Mormon Thunder: A Documentary History of Jedediah Morgan Grant*. Urbana: University of Illinois Press, 1982.

Smith, Joseph Fielding. *Essentials in Church History*. 26th ed. Salt Lake City: Deseret Book, 1973.

Steele, John. "Extracts from the Journal of John Steele." *Utah Historical Quarterly* 6 (Jan. 1933): 2–28.

Stegner, Wallace. *The Gathering of Zion: The Story of the Mormon Trail*. New York: McGraw-Hill, 1964.

Taylor, John. Journal. B. H. Roberts Papers.

Taylor, P. A. M. "Early Mormon Loyalty and the Leadership of Brigham Young." *Utah Historical Quarterly* 30 (Spring 1962): 102–32.

———, and Leonard J. Arrington. "Religion and Planning in the Far West: The First Generation of Mormons in Utah." *Economic History Review* 11 (Aug. 1958): 71–86.

Taylor, Samuel W. *The Kingdom or Nothing: The Life of John Taylor, Militant Mormon*. New York: Macmillan, 1976.

Tullidge, Edward W. *The History of Salt Lake City and Its Founders*. Salt Lake City: E. W. Tullidge, 1886.

Tyler, Daniel. *A Concise History of the Mormon Battalion in the Mexican War, 1846–47*. Salt Lake City: Juvenile Instructor Press, 1881.

Tyler, S. Lyman. "The Indians in Utah Territory." In Poll et al. 1978, 357–370.

Walker, Ronald W. "The Commencement of the Godbeite Protest: Another View." *Utah Historical Quarterly* 42 (Summer 1974): 217–44.

Watson, Eldon J., ed. *Manuscript History of Brigham Young, 1846– 1847*. Salt Lake City: Eldon J. Watson, 1971.

West, Ray B. *Kingdom of the Saints: The Story of Brigham Young and the Mormons*. New York: Viking Press, 1957.

Whitney, Orson F. *History of Utah*. 4 vols. Salt Lake City: George Q. Cannon & Sons, 1892–1904.

Wood, Joseph S. "The Mormon Settlement in San Bernardino, 1851–57." Ph.D. diss., University of Utah, 1967.

Woodruff, Wilford. Journal. Also in Scott G. Kenney, ed., *Wilford Woodruff's Journals*, 9 vols. Midvale, Utah: Signature Books, 1983–85.

Young, Brigham. Office journal and papers.

———, et al. "Manuscript History of Brigham Young."

Young, Kimball. *Isn't One Wife Enough?* New York: Henry Holt, 1954.

Young, Levi Edgar. *The Founding of Utah*. New York: Charles Scribner's Sons, 1923.

Young, Lorenzo Dow. "Journal." *Utah Historical Quarterly* 14 (1946): 133–70. (Entries from April 1846 to September 1847 are by his wife Harriet.)

Yurtinus, John. "A Ram in the Thicket: The Mormon Battalion in the Mexican War." Ph.D. diss., Brigham Young University, 1975.

Index

About the Author

Eugene E. Campbell was a professor of history at Brigham Young University until his retirement in 1980. He is the co-author of *Fort Bridger: Island in the Wilderness, Fort Supply: Brigham Young's Green River Experiment,* and *The Life and Thought of Hugh B. Brown.* His articles on Western American and Mormon history won awards from the Utah State Historical Society and the Mormon History Association. Dr. Campbell helped found the Mormon History Association and also served as a consultant to the National Endowment of the Humanities. He completed work on *Establishing Zion: The Mormon Church in the American West, 1847–1869* shortly before his death in April 1986.